Children Exposed to Marital Violence

Children Exposed to Marital Violence

Theory, Research, and Applied Issues

Edited by

George W. Holden
Robert Geffner
Ernest N. Jouriles

American Psychological Association
Washington, DC

Published by
American Psychological Association
750 First Street, NE
Washington, DC 20002

Copies may be ordered from
APA Order Department
P.O. Box 92984
Washington, DC 20090-2984

In the UK and Europe, copies may be ordered from
American Psychological Association
3 Henrietta Street
Covent Garden, London
WC2E 8LU England

Typeset in Minion by EPS Group Inc., Easton, MD

Cover designer: Minker Design, Bethesda, MD
Printer: Braun-Brumfield, Inc., Ann Arbor, MI
Technical/production editor: Ida Audeh

Library of Congress Cataloging-in-Publication Data
Children exposed to marital violence : theory, research, and applied issues / edited by
  George W. Holden, Robert A. Geffner, and Ernest N. Jouriles.—1st ed.
      p.   cm.—(APA science volumes)
    Based on the First International Conference on Children Exposed to Family
  Violence, held June 6–8, 1996 in Austin, Tex.
    Includes bibliographical references and index.
    ISBN 1-55798-472-7
    1. Children and violence—Congresses.   2. Children of abused wives—
  Congresses.   3. Family violence—Psychological aspects—Congresses.   4. Social
  work with children—Congresses.
  I. Holden, George W.   II. Geffner, Robert.   III. Jouriles, Ernest N.
  IV. International Conference on Children Exposed to Family Violence
  (1st : 1996 : Austin, Tex.)   V. Series
  HQ784.V55C445   1998
  362.82'923—dc21
                                                                          97-45616
                                                                          CIP

British Library Cataloguing-in-Publication Data
A CIP record is available from the British Library

Printed in the United States of America
First edition

APA Science Volumes

Attribution and Social Interaction: The Legacy of Edward E. Jones

Best Methods for the Analysis of Change: Recent Advances, Unanswered Questions, Future Directions

Cardiovascular Reactivity to Psychological Stress and Disease

The Challenge in Mathematics and Science Education: Psychology's Response

Changing Employment Relations: Behavioral and Social Perspectives

Children Exposed to Marital Violence: Theory, Research, and Applied Issues

Cognition: Conceptual and Methodological Issues

Cognitive Bases of Musical Communication

Conceptualization and Measurement of Organism–Environment Interaction

Converging Operations in the Study of Visual Selective Attention

Creative Thought: An Investigation of Conceptual Structures and Processes

Developmental Psychoacoustics

Diversity in Work Teams: Research Paradigms for a Changing Workplace

Emotion and Culture: Empirical Studies of Mutual Influence

Emotion, Disclosure, and Health

Evolving Explanations of Development: Ecological Approaches to Organism–Environment Systems

Examining Lives in Context: Perspectives on the Ecology of Human Development

Hostility, Coping, and Health

Measuring Patient Changes in Mood, Anxiety, and Personality Disorders: Toward a Core Battery

Organ Donation and Transplantation: Psychological and Behavioral Factors

The Perception of Structure

Perspectives on Socially Shared Cognition

Psychological Testing of Hispanics

Psychology of Women's Health: Progress and Challenges in Research and Application

Researching Community Psychology: Issues of Theory and Methods

Sleep and Cognition

Sleep Onset: Normal and Abnormal Processes

Stereotype Accuracy: Toward Appreciating Group Differences

Stereotyped Movements: Brain and Behavior Relationships

Studying Lives Through Time: Personality and Development

The Suggestibility of Children's Recollections: Implications for Eyewitness Testimony

Taste, Experience, and Feeding: Development and Learning

Temperament: Individual Differences at the Interface of Biology and Behavior

Through the Looking Glass: Issues of Psychological Well-Being in Captive Nonhuman Primates

Uniting Psychology and Biology: Integrative Perspectives on Human Development

Viewing Psychology as a Whole: The Integrative Science of William N. Dember

APA expects to publish volumes on the following conference topics:

Computational Modeling of Behavior Processes in Organizations

Dissonance Theory 40 Years Later: A Revival With Revisions and Controversies

Experimental Psychopathology and Pathogenesis of Schizophrenia

Global Prospects for Education: Development, Culture, and Schooling

Intelligence on the Rise: Secular Changes in IQ and Related Measures

Marital and Family Therapy Outcome and Process Research

Models of Gender and Gender Differences: Then and Now

Occasion Setting: Theory and Data

Psychosocial Interventions for Cancer

As part of its continuing and expanding commitment to enhance the dissemination of scientific psychological knowledge, the Science Directorate of the APA established a Scientific Conferences Program. A series of volumes resulting from these conferences is produced jointly by the Science Directorate and the Office of Communications. A call for proposals is issued twice annually by the Scientific Directorate, which, collaboratively with the APA Board of Scientific Affairs, evaluates the proposals and selects several conferences for funding. This important effort has resulted in an exceptional series of meetings and scholarly volumes, each of which has contributed to the dissemination of research and dialogue in these topical areas.

The APA Science Directorate's conferences funding program has supported 47 conferences since its inception in 1988. To date, 36 volumes resulting from conferences have been published.

WILLIAM C. HOWELL, PhD
Executive Director

VIRGINIA E. HOLT
Assistant Executive Director

Contents

Contributors   **xi**

Preface   **xiii**

1   Introduction: The Development of Research Into
Another Consequence of Family Violence   1
George W. Holden

Part One: Theoretical and Conceptual Issues

2   The Impact of Woman Abuse on Children's Social
Development: Research and Theoretical Perspectives   21
Sandra A. Graham-Bermann

3   Children Exposed to Marital Conflict and Violence:
Conceptual and Theoretical Directions   55
E. Mark Cummings

4   Children as Invisible Victims of Domestic and
Community Violence   95
Joy D. Osofsky

Part Two: Research

5   Using Multiple Informants to Understand Domestic
Violence and Its Effects   121
*Kathleen J. Sternberg, Michael E. Lamb,
and Samia Dawud-Noursi*

6   Correlates of Adjustment in Children at Risk   157
Timothy E. Moore and Debra J. Pepler

7   Heterogeneity in Adjustment Among Children of
Battered Women   185
Honore M. Hughes and Douglas A. Luke

8   Descartes's Error and Posttraumatic Stress Disorder: Cognition and Emotion in Children Who Are Exposed to Parental Violence   223
    B. B. Robbie Rossman

9   The Emotional, Cognitive, and Coping Responses of Preadolescent Children to Different Dimensions of Marital Conflict   257
    Mark A. Laumakis, Gayla Margolin, and Richard S. John

10 Parenting Behaviors and Beliefs of Battered Women   289
    George W. Holden, Joshua D. Stein, Kathy L. Ritchie, Susan D. Harris, and Ernest N. Jouriles

Part Three: Applied Issues

11 Breaking the Cycle of Violence: Helping Families Departing From Battered Women's Shelters   337
    Ernest N. Jouriles, Renee McDonald, Nanette Stephens, William Norwood, Laura Collazos Spiller, and Holly Shinn Ware

12 Child Custody Disputes and Domestic Violence: Critical Issues for Mental Health, Social Service, and Legal Professionals   371
    Peter G. Jaffe and Robert Geffner

13 Appraisal and Outlook   409
    George W. Holden, Robert Geffner, and Ernest N. Jouriles

Name Index   423
Subject Index   437
About the Editors   449

Contributors

E. Mark Cummings, Department of Psychology, University of Notre Dame

Samia Dawud-Noursi, Section on Social and Emotional Development, National Institute of Child Health and Human Development

Robert Geffner, Family Violence and Sexual Assault Institute, Tyler, Texas

Sandra A. Graham-Bermann, Department of Psychology, University of Michigan, Ann Arbor

Susan D. Harris, Department of Psychology, University of Northern Arizona

George W. Holden, Institute of Human Development and Family Studies and Department of Psychology, University of Texas at Austin

Honore M. Hughes, Department of Psychology, St. Louis University

Peter G. Jaffe, London Family Court Clinic, London, Ontario, Canada

Richard S. John, Department of Psychology, University of Southern California

Ernest N. Jouriles, Department of Psychology, University of Houston

Michael E. Lamb, Section on Social and Emotional Development, National Institute of Child Health and Human Development

Mark A. Laumakis, Department of Psychology, University of Southern California

Douglas A. Luke, School of Public Health, Saint Louis University

Gayla Margolin, Department of Psychology, University of Southern California

Renee McDonald, Department of Psychology, University of Houston

Timothy E. Moore, Psychology Department and LaMarsh Research Centre on Violence and Conflict Resolution, York University, Toronto, Ontario, Canada

William Norwood, Department of Psychology, University of Houston

Joy D. Osofsky, Division of Child Psychiatry, Louisiana State University Medical Center

Debra J. Pepler, Psychology Department and LaMarsh Research Centre on Violence and Conflict Resolution, York University, Toronto, Ontario, Canada

Kathy L. Ritchie, Department of Psychology, Indiana University at South Bend

B. B. Robbie Rossman, Department of Psychology, University of Denver

Laura Collazos Spiller, Department of Psychology, University of Houston

Joshua D. Stein, Department of Psychology, University of Texas at Austin

Nanette Stephens, Department of Psychology, University of Houston

Kathleen J. Sternberg, Section on Social and Emotional Development, National Institute of Child Health and Human Development

Holly Shinn Ware, Department of Psychology, University of Houston

Preface

This volume is intended to provide readers with the most recent work by leading researchers concerning the problem of children exposed to marital violence. As such, the volume serves multiple functions: It provides a current review of the theory and research, an analysis of how and why children react to marital violence the way they do, a guide for future research, and a discussion of several of the implications for social policy and intervention. More generally, we hope that this book will help raise the level of awareness about a significant and widespread social problem.

Given those multiple purposes, this book should appeal to a diverse audience. Those who study or are interested in the problem of family violence will find this volume a useful resource for learning about the most recent investigations into this relatively new area of family violence research. A range of research-related topics are raised. Chapters address a variety of theoretical perspectives, methodological issues, and independent and dependent variables that are thought to be related to children's exposure to marital violence. Because the focus of this book is on the fundamental question of how one feature of the environment influences children's development, this volume should appeal to those who study developmental, clinical, and educational psychology, as well as social work, sociology, and nursing.

In addition to those more basic research topics, chapters also address several practical applications concerning law enforcement, intervention, and child custody considerations. Consequently, individuals who come into contact or work with or on behalf of children exposed to marital violence will benefit from the book. In particular, child protection or mental health workers, law enforcement officials, school counselors, and those in the legal professions will better understand the issues and implications associated with exposure to marital violence.

The impetus for this book came from a conference held in Austin, Texas, from June 6 to 8, 1996. That meeting, entitled First International Conference on Children Exposed to Family Violence, was organized by the Institute of Human Development and Family Studies at the University of Texas at Austin and the Family Violence & Sexual Assault Institute in Tyler, Texas. More than 350 people attended. Participants were researchers from several areas within psychology and from disciplines such as psychiatry, sociology, social work, and nursing. Although the conference focused on research, it was attended also by professionals who work on a daily basis with these children, deal with them in legal domains (attorneys and law enforcement officers), or serve as their advocates. If place of residence is used as an index of inclusion, participants included residents of 44 states and three countries.

That conference was actually not the first one to be held on children of battered women. In 1992, a conference convened in Minneapolis, Minnesota, but was focused on the more limited topic of intervention issues associated with children of battered women (see Peled, Jaffe, & Edleson, 1995). In contrast, the Austin conference addressed a wider range of topics. Although some attention was devoted to children's intervention programs, the primary focus was on better understanding the variability in children's responses to marital violence. The meeting was widely regarded as a great success: It provided a forum for exchanging ideas, developing contacts, and promoting quality research in the area. Although the conference served as a forum for researchers and workers in this area, it was only a beginning. Because participant response was so enthusiastic, the Second International Conference was held (in London, Ontario, Canada) in June 1997. A third conference is being planned for late 1998.

The conference, and in turn, this book, would not have occurred without the generous financial support provided by the American Psychological Association (APA), The RGK Foundation, and The Hogg Foundation. Several graduate and many undergraduate students from the University of Texas at Austin devoted a considerable amount of time to help run the conference. The graduate students deserving special recognition were Pam Miller, Rachel Hannah, and Jai Shim, who worked diligently in organizing and directing a large number of volunteers. The staff from the Family Violence & Sexual Assault Institute, and especially Mary Sals-Lewis (the former executive director) and Kristell Hines, were instrumental in taking care of many of the conference-related logistics and organization. We also thank Virginia Holt and Cheri Lane from the APA Science Directorate and Joy Chau, Peggy Schlegel, and especially Judy Nemes at APA Books for their encouragement, guidance, and assistance in bringing both the conference and this book to fruition. To all those organizations and individuals we are most grateful.

REFERENCE

Peled, E., Jaffe, P. G., & Edleson, J. L. (Eds.). (1995). *Ending the cycle of violence: Community responses to children of battered women.* Thousand Oaks, CA: Sage.

1

Introduction: The Development of Research Into Another Consequence of Family Violence

George W. Holden

It is an unfortunate truth that violence is endemic to most societies. According to the United Nations, no less than 47 violent ethnic or political conflicts took place around the world in 1993. Over a 10-year period, such conflicts have resulted in an estimated 1.5 million deaths to children, 4 million serious injuries, and 10 million children traumatized (Benjamin, 1994). Across the United States, violence is rampant in many communities. For example, in one survey taken in an inner city, as many as one-third of the children had witnessed a shooting (Dyson, 1990). Furthermore, it is increasingly being realized that homes are not safe havens for children. Not only are children the recipients of physical abuse, but they also are victimized by the violence that occurs between their parents, the topic of this volume.

Children in maritally violent homes have been called the "forgotten," "unacknowledged," "hidden," "unintended," and "silent" victims. When these children are compared with other victims of family violence and maltreatment, such as battered women or children who have been physically or sexually abused, these labels are indeed accurate. The children exposed to marital violence have received insufficient attention for far too long.

By any estimate, a sizable population of troubled children has been largely overlooked. The figure most commonly cited comes from Bonnie Carlson (1984), whose projections are based on inferences made from the First National Family Survey data (Straus, Gelles, & Steinmetz, 1980). She estimated that at least 3.3 million children between the ages of 3 and 17 years are exposed to family violence in the United States each year. However, she acknowledged that her estimate probably underestimated the extent of the problem because it did not include divorced mothers (who may have left an abusive partner) or children younger than age 3. A more recent projection from the Second National Family Violence Survey has revised that number upward. Murray Straus (1991) estimated that each year, 10 million children are exposed to marital violence.

In fact, even more children may be exposed to marital violence than either of those estimates indicate. For example, in an inner-city sample of more than 300 mothers, Spaccarelli, Sandler, and Roosa (1994) found that 30% of mothers of 10- to 12-year-old children reported that they had been physically assaulted by their husbands or partners. Louise Silvern and her colleagues (1995) asked college students to report on whether they had experienced violence between their parents. Silvern et al. found that 37% of the 550 undergraduates reported being exposed to some form of parental partner abuse, most commonly throwing an object at a partner, pushing, shoving, or slapping. Extrapolating to the general population in the United States of 48 million children who live in two-parent homes, this would mean that about 17.8 million children may be exposed to marital violence. Even this rate may represent an underestimate, given that college students typically come from economically advantaged homes and that, in the Silvern et al. sample, the divorce rate was lower than in the general population. As this study highlights, the prevalence of children exposed to marital violence remains an open question, and much more research into the incidence and prevalence of this national crisis is needed.

Although there is ample evidence that women have been abused by their husbands and partners through the ages (e.g., Pleck, 1987), researchers, clinicians, and policy makers have been slow in recognizing the problems of children exposed to family violence. In fact, the first published articles on such children only appeared in 1975—almost 15 years after Kempe and his colleagues "discovered" physical child abuse (Kempe, Silverman, Steele, Droegemueller, & Silver, 1962). That year, a British physician (Levine, 1975) and a British social worker (Moore, 1975) each independently published reports describing samples of children who had been exposed to marital violence. Those descriptive reports began to identify problems in these children such as aggressive behavior, anxiety disorders, insomnia, and truancy.

Despite those two early alarming reports, fully 5 years elapsed before the third study was published. Thereafter empirical studies began to appear occasionally in the scientific journals. However, the first study containing a matched comparison group was not published until 1981. In that study, Alan Rosenbaum and K. Daniel O'Leary (1981) compared boys from maritally violent homes, nonviolent but maritally discordant homes, and nonviolent and maritally satisfactory homes. It is ironic that in their pioneering study, Rosenbaum and O'Leary were unable to detect a significant relation between growing up in a violent home and an increased rate of behaviorial or emotional problems.

To assess the depth of the literature on children exposed to marital violence, I conducted a review of empirical published articles. Journals were scanned, electronic bibliographies were consulted, and references from known articles were perused. That process resulted in the identification of 56 articles published between 1975 and 1995. The number of publications per year is shown in Figure 1. Several observations can be made about this figure. First, the positive aspect depicted by the figure is that the number of publications is slowly increasing. Although the slope is not steep, clearly more attention has been devoted to this population of children in recent years. A less encouraging observation is that the total number of articles on these children published in peer-reviewed journals amounts to only 56 articles. Given the magnitude of this problem, there is a clear shortage of information about how these children are affected. Such a small number of studies also attests to the fact that research in this area is still in its infancy.

The 56 journal articles are supplemented by a few review articles

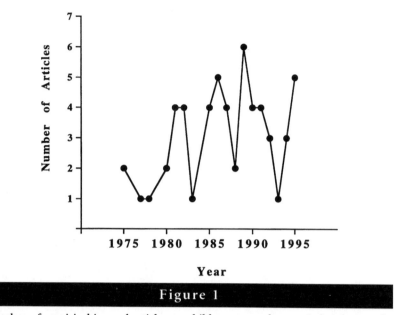

Figure 1

Number of empirical journal articles on children exposed to marital violence published between 1975 and 1995.

(e.g., Fantuzzo & Lindquist, 1989), several chapters, and at least three books that focus on the children of battered women. In 1990, Peter Jaffe, David Wolfe, and Susan Wilson published *Children of Battered Women*, an important book that reviewed the research available on the children and presented many of the key issues concerning these children. Only two other books focus on these children: an edited volume by Einat Peled, Peter Jaffe, and Jeffrey Edleson (1995) that addresses intervention issues with these children, and a book by Einat Peled and Diane Davis (1995) on group treatment of these children. Within those books and articles there has been some disagreement over what to call children who reside in maritally violent families. Some terminological issues related to the topic are discussed next.

ISSUES OF TERMINOLOGY

Most often, children from violent homes have been labeled "witnesses" to or "observers" of marital violence. However, these children may more accurately and inclusively be described as being "exposed" to violence. First, children may not have actually watched their parents assault each other but instead overheard the incident, seen the results (e.g., bruises), or experienced its aftermath when interacting with their parents. Second, the term *exposed* avoids the potential confusion with children who actually testify as "witnesses" in court proceedings, as Geffner and Pagelow (1990) pointed out.

The data are somewhat inconsistent concerning the type of exposure children receive. In one study, two-thirds of the battered women reported that their children were aware of most of the marital arguments (e.g., Holden & Ritchie, 1991). Similarly, Hilton (1992) found that most of the mothers interviewed acknowledged that their children had observed marital violence or its aftermath. Other studies found lower rates of reported exposure. In one study, for example (O'Keefe, 1994), battered mothers reported that 46% of their children had observed husband-to-wife aggression and 12% had seen wife-to-husband aggression. Given the limited research on this question, it is difficult to evaluate the accuracy of these reports. Abused women may deny, minimize, underreport, or just not be aware of the degree of their children's exposure to the violence. When multiple informants (i.e., parents and children) are asked about levels of exposure, agreement often is limited (e.g., O'Brien, John, Margolin, & Erel, 1994).

A second, more controversial terminology issue concerns what to call the violence that occurs between the man and woman. After considering the alternatives, we reluctantly settled on *marital violence*. *Domestic violence* was another option, but it includes other forms of maltreatment such as child abuse or elder abuse. *Partner violence* fails to capture the notion that the parent–child relation is of fundamental concern here. However, we realize that in some cases of what we label marital violence, the adults were not legally married. Perhaps a more accurate term would be *wife abuse* or *woman abuse*, because men are the perpetrators of marital violence in the vast majority of cases (Kurz, 1993). Yet women are not passive bystanders to the violence directed toward them. Some mothers also engage in marital aggression for defensive, retaliatory, strategic, or initiating purposes (see Straus, 1993).

Rather than attempting to prejudge or impose limits on the nature of the violence, we opted to use the more inclusive term *marital violence.*

EFFECTS OF EXPOSURE

The corpus of empirical literature clearly establishes that children who live in maritally violent homes are at risk for a wide variety of problems. Associating marital violence with children's emotional and behavioral problems has been the primary question in most of the research published to date. In studies that are sometimes referred to as "first generation" research on the topic, numerous investigators have successfully linked children's exposure to family violence with a range of behavior and adjustment problems.

Prototypical studies have collected data from mothers and children who were temporarily residing in a battered women's shelter. To document the nature of the problems, investigators have commonly given mothers behavior checklists to fill out. Although several different indices of behavior problems have been used, the Child Behavior Checklist (CBCL) by Thomas Achenbach (Achenbach & Edelbrock, 1981) has been the instrument of choice for most researchers. And for good reason: It can be used with children aged 2–16 years (in its different forms), it covers a wide range of behavioral problems, it assesses social competence, it is easy to fill out for mothers (using a 3-point scale), there are comparable forms for parents and teachers (or shelter staff), and it has very good psychometric properties and normative information. The checklist has an overall score of behavior problems as well as two major subscale scores for externalizing (e.g., noncompliance, aggression, cruelty to animals, destructiveness) and internalizing problems (e.g., withdrawal, depression, fears, anxiety). A brief overview of the findings concerning the types of behavior problems these children experience follows.

Behavioral and Adjustment Problems

Using the CBCL and other instruments has been useful for identifying a variety of behavioral and adjustment problems experienced by children reared in maritally violent homes. Many of these children show a wide range of externalizing and internalizing problems, such as non-compliance, aggression, anxiety, and depression (e.g., Holden & Ritchie, 1991; Jouriles & Norwood, 1995; McCloskey, Figueredo, & Koss, 1995). There is also evidence for long-term effects of childhood exposure to marital violence, including depression, low self-esteem, and various trauma-related symptoms (Silvern et al., 1995). The extent of the problems is such that in any one sample, a sizable percentage of children have problems at a level that warrants clinical intervention. Many investigators have replicated the finding that these children are at high risk for experiencing behavior problems at the clinical level. Depending on the study, anywhere from 25% to 75% of these children may have problems that are considered severe enough to warrant clinical intervention (McDonald & Jouriles, 1991). The median percentage of children reaching the clinical level of behavior problems is about 40% in these studies—significantly higher than the rates for comparison groups (10%).

In addition to internalizing and externalizing problems, a wide array of mental health problems has been identified. A list of these problems, based on a summary by Barnett, Miller-Perrin, and Perrin (1997), is provided in Exhibit 1. Although the problems assessed by the CBCL have been replicated in many studies, other behavioral problems should be considered tentative and in need of replication. The exhibit indicates that the negative consequences from exposure to marital violence are not limited to compromised mental health functioning. There is at least preliminary evidence for a range of other behavioral, health, school, and social interaction problems that these children commonly experience. Interestingly, many of the same problems (e.g., anxiety, depression, fears, hostility, somatization) also appear in adults who are victims of violent crimes (Norris & Kaniasty, 1994).

Characteristics of Children

Although there is no typical pattern of problems manifested by children exposed to marital violence, the particular problem or problems exhibited may be governed to some degree by the children's age and gender.

7

Exhibit 1

Children's Problems Associated With Exposure to Marital Conflict

Attention deficit disorder
Externalizing Problems
    Aggression
    Alcohol and/or drug use
    Anger
    Conduct disorder
    Cruelty to animals
    Destructiveness
    Noncompliance
    Oppositional
Internalizing Problems
    Anxiety
    Depression
    Excessive clinging
    Fears
    Low self-esteem
    Passivity, withdrawal
    Sadness
    Self-blame
    Shyness
    Suicidality
Posttraumatic stress disorder symptoms (anxiety, flashbacks, hyperalertness, guilt, nightmares, numbing of affect, sleep disturbances)
Separation Anxiety
Social Behavior–Competence Problems
    Beliefs in violence in relationships
    Deficits in social skills
    Low empathy
    Poor problem-solving skills

Exhibit continues

Exhibit 1 (Continued)

School Problems
    Academic performance
    Poor conduct
    Truancy
Other
    Intergenerational transmission of violence
    Obsessive–compulsive
    Somatic problems (headaches, enuresis, insomnia, ulcers)
    Temperamentally difficult

Note. From *Family Violence Across the Lifespan* (pp. 141–142) by O. W. Barnett, C. L. Miller-Perrin, and R. D. Perrin, 1997, Thousand Oaks, CA: Sage. Copyright 1997 by Sage. Adapted by permission.

With regard to age, younger children are more likely to exhibit somatic complaints and experience greater distress than older children who may take on one or more specific externalizing or internalizing problems (Jaffe et al., 1990).

More studies have addressed the issue of how a child's gender affects his or her reaction to the violence. Given that fathers typically perpetrate violence and mothers are the victims, it is commonly thought that boys may react differently than girls. To date, the data on gender of child effects have been inconsistent. Some studies have found that girls are more negatively affected than boys (e.g., Spaccarelli et al., 1994), but other studies only find that difference on internalizing problems (Christopoulos et al., 1987; Holden & Ritchie, 1991). In contrast, some studies have found that boys have more externalizing problems (Jouriles & Norwood, 1995; Wolfe, Jaffe, Wilson, & Zak, 1985), and still other investigators report no gender differences (e.g., O'Keefe, 1994). Part of the problem may be caused by the relatively small sample sizes that are common in this difficult research area. Nevertheless, whether (and if so, how) children's gender interacts with exposure to marital violence remains to be determined.

Other Key Variables

One or more studies have identified or proposed several variables that may moderate or mediate the effects of marital violence on the children, such as (a) the nature of the violence (e.g., severity and chronicity); (b) ethnicity; (c) the level of stress experienced by the mother; (d) the quality of mothering; (e) whether the child was also the recipient of verbal or physical abuse; and (f) child characteristics (self-esteem, personality characteristics) that may buffer the child. Although it is beyond the scope of this introduction to review the evidence for each of those variables, one potential moderator deserves more discussion. It is increasingly being recognized that children who are exposed to marital violence (and who are being traumatized just by living in that environment) are also at increased risk of being victimized in other ways as well. Most commonly, such children are at risk for being physically abused by one or both of their parents. Hughes, Parkinson, and Vargo (1989) have graphically labeled this the *double whammy effect*. Although the research in this area of co-occurrence is limited and beset with methodological problems, studies report an overlap of exposure to marital violence and physical abuse that ranges from 20% to 100%, with a median of 59% (Appel, Angelelli, & Holden, 1997). Presumably some children who both are exposed to marital violence and are physically assaulted themselves are more likely to have problems, but this is not always the case (Sternberg et al., 1993). There is some evidence that children in maritally violent homes are also at increased risk for sexual abuse (McCloskey et al., 1995).

Research Limitations

Despite the findings concerning these children's functioning, significant limitations in the quality of the research in this area must be acknowledged. Methodological limitations include inadequate or inconsistent definitions of marital abuse, inadequate assessments of the nature of the violence and general family context, too many retrospective and correlation research designs in the absence of longitudinal studies, small samples, samples from battered women's shelters that may not be representative of the more general population of battered women and their children, a lack of comparison groups, use of nonstandard surveys or "clinical impressions," and a reliance on the battered women as a source of the data (see Fantuzzo & Lindquist, 1989). Another equally serious problem is that many studies have been atheoretical, which inhibits development of a coherent understanding of the nature and effects of the violence. Finally, previous research can be faulted for largely failing to investigate or adequately to address two questions. First, few investigators have attempted to address what are the processes or mechanisms by which children are affected by the violence. Second, there have been few efforts to try to link research in this area with its implications for social policy or intervention practices. Evidently, despite the knowledge that has been learned in this area over the past two decades, many more questions remain unanswered.

THIS VOLUME

A relatively high number of children who are exposed to marital violence exhibit emotional, behavioral, or other types of problems. Remarkably, at least some of the children from violent homes seem to survive that experience relatively unscathed—at least in terms of exhibiting few behavior problems. The research literature published to date has not yet arrived at a clear understanding of what features in the environment or what characteristics of the children themselves cause some children to react in particular ways and some children to be resilient.

With that backdrop, some of the unique characteristics of the present volume can be better appreciated. Several chapters in the volume focus exclusively on building a stronger theoretical and conceptual foundation for which to understand how children are affected by marital violence. Other chapters investigate methodological issues or demonstrate how the quality of research in this area can be improved by overcoming some of the common methodological limitations present in many prior investigations. Some of the chapters stand out because they begin to tackle the "why" question. What are the mechanisms or processes by which marital violence results in certain behavioral problems in children? Finally, some of the chapters in the present volume address contemporary problems in our society by applying research results to social policy or intervention issues.

As the title suggests, this book is divided into three sections. Section 1 focuses on theoretical and conceptual issues that have been missing from much of the previous research. Section 2 contains research reports that address methodological issues, the differential outcomes of children exposed to marital violence, and variables that may affect children's outcomes. Chapters in the final section deal with two critical applied issues.

The chapter by Sandra Graham-Bermann integrates several theoretical perspectives in arriving at a conceptual model of key variables that affect child adjustment. She argues that at least two sets of theories are needed to explain how children respond to marital violence. Most generally, theory is needed to understand the child's developmental context. For example, she advocates using an ecological model to recognize how different levels of the environment affect the family. A relationships model is also needed to explain the nature of the child's relations within the family. A second set of theories, most generally the developmental psychopathology model but also trauma and social learning theory, is also needed to explain how violence between parents affects and interferes with the child's development.

The chapter by E. Mark Cummings takes a more narrow theoretical focus. Drawing from the considerable theory and research that has accumulated in the past 15 years or so in the area of marital conflict, he discusses key conceptual and research issues as they relate to violent families. He addresses the need to recognize the family functioning context and how children react to the stress and cope with it. He raises a variety of issues (e.g., child characteristics, the nature and chronicity of the conflict) that need to be taken into account to understand children's outcomes. Then he proposes that many of these issues—and understanding children's reactions to marital violence—can be framed around an "emotional security hypothesis."

The chapter by Joy Osofsky also highlights the need for recognizing the child's context, but she highlights a different context: the one outside the family. She addresses and compares children's exposure to community violence with exposure to marital violence. She draws parallels between the research findings in the two domains and presents important research and social policy recommendations for understanding and eventually reducing the prevalence of these forms of violence.

Section 2 begins with a chapter that focuses on a thorny methodological problem in this area of research: the quality of data derived from one informant. As indicated above, most research in this area has relied on mothers' reports of the violence and of their children's functioning. The problem of mothers as sole informants is the focus of the chapter by Kathleen Sternberg, Michael Lamb, and Samia Dawud-Noursi. Sternberg and her colleagues present data from their multi-informant longitudinal study (including mothers, fathers, teachers, peers, and the children themselves) about the similarities and discrepancies between informants' reports.

The next empirical chapter is by Timothy Moore and Debra Pepler and identifies several types of negative outcomes experienced by children exposed to marital violence. They compare the functioning of children exposed to family violence with three other groups of children (homeless, mother-headed, and two-parent families) on a range of behavioral, emotional, and other outcome variables. Although marital violence does not have uniform effects on children, studies like this that include multiple comparison groups present a clearer picture of the unique effects associated with marital violence.

The chapter by Honore Hughes and Douglas Luke focuses directly on the issue of variability in children's outcome. Specifically, their study was designed to see whether groupings of children could be identified on the basis of differential child outcomes. In the first study of its kind, cluster analysis analytic procedures are used to identify five child outcome typologies. The groups include the expected: children who are depressed and have high levels of general distress. The authors also identified two surprising groups of children who are doing relatively well despite their circumstances.

Robbie Rossman takes a unique approach to investigating the effects of exposure to marital violence. Rather than focus on behavioral problems as the outcome of interest, she examines how emotional reactions to violence may interact with the cognitive functioning of the children. She then tests a model of the interrelations and finds support for the link between exposure to marital violence and impaired processing of information.

The next research chapter, written by Mark Laumakis, Gayla Margolin, and Richard John, addresses a different question from the previous empirical studies. Instead of correlating reports of violence with child outcomes, they focus on dissecting those aspects of exposure to marital violence that may be the most damaging to children. They do this by conducting an experimental study concerning children's affective, cognitive, and coping responses to audiotaped scenarios depicting various aspects of marital conflict (e.g., name calling, physical aggression). By using simulations of conflict, the authors reveal the particular features of the conflict that are associated with particular child outcomes.

In the final chapter in the section, my colleagues and I (Joshua Stein, Kathy Ritchie, Susan Harris, and Ernest Jouriles) confront a different issue. Rather than focusing on children, we examine battered women's parenting beliefs and behavior, something that is commonly assumed to be a key mediator of children's adjustment. Three studies are presented addressing the question of whether maritally abused mothers use aggression with their children and show diminished parenting abilities. Our findings conflict with much of the conventional wisdom about these mothers.

The final section focuses on some of the research implications for social policy and intervention with this population of children. One of the most urgent issues concerns how to intervene with children who have been exposed to marital violence. Ernest Jouriles, Renee McDonald, Nanette Stephens, William Norwood, Laura Spiller, and Holly Ware describe a pioneering program for battered women with young children who are exhibiting aggressive/oppositional behavior. They present some hopeful but preliminary results for the effectiveness of their multicomponent program.

A second major applied issue concerns legal responses to this type of family violence. Many of the children being reared in violent homes eventually wind up in law offices or the courtroom. The chapter by

Peter Jaffe and Robert Geffner raises key and complex issues concerning child custody and visitation access. They propose several types of solutions that would benefit the children, the mothers, and the legal justice system. That chapter is followed by a summary by the editors that is designed to integrate the preceding chapters and to consolidate suggestions for future research directions.

Research over the past 15 years has clearly revealed that children exposed to marital violence may develop a variety of problems. What is less clear is the underlying theoretical reasons for the emergence of the behavior problems, what features of the hostile environment the children are reacting to, what characteristics of the children and parents may mediate or exacerbate behavior problems, why there is such variability in children's outcome, and what needs to be done with these children. The chapters in this volume go a long way in beginning to answer those and related questions.

REFERENCES

Achenbach, T. M., & Edelbrock, C. S. (1981). Behavioral problems and competencies reported by parents of normal and disturbed children aged four through sixteen. *Monographs of the Society for Research in Child Development, 46*(1, Serial No. 188).

Appel, A. E., Angelelli, M. J., & Holden, G. W. (1997). *The co-occurrence of spouse and physical child abuse: A review and appraisal.* Manuscript submitted for publication.

Barnett, O. W., Miller-Perrin, C. L., & Perrin, R. D. (1997). *Family violence across the lifespan.* Thousand Oaks, CA: Sage.

Benjamin, A. (1994). *Children at war.* London: Save the Children.

Carlson, B. E. (1984). Children's observations of interparental violence. In A. R. Roberts (Ed.), *Battered women and their families* (pp. 147–167). New York: Springer.

Christopoulos, C., Cohn, D. A., Shaw, D. S., Joyce, S., Sullivan-Hanson, J., Draft, S. P., & Emery, R. E. (1987). Children of abused women: I. Adjustment at time of shelter residence. *Journal of Marriage and the Family, 49*, 611–619.

Dyson, J. L. (1990). The effect of family violence on children's academic performance and behavior. *Journal of National Medical Association, 82,* 17–22.

Fantuzzo, J., & Lindquist, C. (1989). The effects of observing conjugal violence on children: A review and analysis of research methodology. *Journal of Family Violence, 4,* 77–94.

Geffner, R., & Pagelow, M. D. (1990). Mediation and child custody issues in abusive relationships. *Behavioral Sciences and the Law, 8,* 151–159.

Hilton, N. Z. (1992). Battered women's concerns about their children witnessing wife assault. *Journal of Interpersonal Violence, 7,* 77–86.

Holden, G. W., & Ritchie, K. L. (1991). Linking extreme marital discord, child rearing, and child behavior problems: Evidence from battered women. *Child Development, 62,* 311–327.

Hughes, H. M., Parkinson, D., & Vargo, M. (1989). Witnessing spouse abuse and experiencing physical abuse: A "double whammy?" *Journal of Family Violence, 4,* 197–209.

Jaffe, P., Wolfe, D. A., & Wilson, S. (1990). *Children of battered women.* Newbury Park, CA: Sage.

Jouriles, E. N., & Norwood, W. D. (1995). Physical aggression toward boys and girls in families characterized by the battering of women. *Journal of Family Violence, 9,* 69–78.

Kempe, R. S., Silverman, F. N., Steele, B. F., Droegemueller, W., & Silver, H. K. (1962). The battered child syndrome. *Journal of the American Medical Association, 181,* 107–112.

Kurz, D. (1993). Physical assaults by husbands: A major social problem. In R. J. Gelles & D. R. Loseke (Eds.), *Current controversies on family violence* (pp. 88–103). Newbury Park, CA: Sage.

Levine, M. B. (1975). Interparental violence and its effects on the children: A study of 50 families in general practice. *Medical Science Law, 15,* 172–176.

McCloskey, L. A., Figueredo, A. J., & Koss, M. P. (1995). The effects of systemic family violence on children's mental health. *Child Development, 66,* 1239–1261.

McDonald, R., & Jouriles, E. N. (1991). Marital aggression and child behavior problems: Research findings, mechanisms, and intervention strategies. *Behavior Therapist, 14,* 189–192.

Moore, J. G. (1975). Yo Yo children: A study of 23 violent matrimonial cases. *Child Welfare, 8*, 557–566.

Norris, F. H., & Kaniasty, K. (1994). Psychological distress following criminal victimization in the general population: Cross-sectional, longitudinal, and prospective analyses. *Journal of Consulting and Clinical Psychology, 62*, 111–123.

O'Brien, M., John, R. S., Margolin, G., & Erel, O. (1994). Reliability and diagnostic efficacy of parent's reports regarding children's exposure to marital aggression. *Violence and Victims, 9*, 45–62.

O'Keefe, M. (1994). Adjustment of children from maritally violent homes. *Families in Society, 75*, 403–415.

Peled, E., & Davis, D. (1995). *Groupwork with children of battered women: A practitioner's manual.* Thousand Oaks, CA: Sage.

Peled, E., Jaffe, P. G., & Edleson, J. L. (Eds.). (1995). *Ending the cycle of violence: Community responses to children of battered women.* Thousand Oaks, CA: Sage.

Pleck, E. (1987). *Domestic tyranny.* New York: Oxford University Press.

Rosenbaum, A., & O'Leary, K. D. (1981). Children: The unintended victims of marital violence. *American Journal of Orthopsychiatry, 51*, 692–699.

Silvern, L., Karyl, J., Waelde, L., Hodges, W. F., Starek, J., Heidt, E., & Min, K. (1995). Retrospective reports of parental partner abuse: Relationships to depression, trauma symptoms and self-esteem among college students. *Journal of Family Violence, 10*, 177–202.

Spaccarelli, S., Sandler, I. N., & Roosa, M. (1994). History of spouse violence against mother: Correlated risks and unique effects in child mental health. *Journal of Family Violence, 9*, 79–98.

Sternberg, K. J., Lamb, M. E., Greenbaum, C., Cicchetti, D., Dawud, S., Cortes, R. M., Krispin, O., & Lorey, F. (1993). Effects of domestic violence on children's behavior problems and depression. *Developmental Psychology, 29*, 44–52.

Straus, M. A. (1991, September). *Children as witness to marital violence: A risk factor for life long problems among a nationally representative sample of American men and women.* Paper presented at the Ross Round Table "Children and Violence," Washington, DC.

Straus, M. A. (1993). Physical assaults by wives: A major social problem. In R.

J. Gelles & D. R. Loseke (Eds.), *Current controversies on family violence* (pp. 67–87). Newbury Park, CA: Sage.

Straus, M. A., Gelles, R. J., & Steinmetz, S. K. (1980). *Behind closed doors: Violence in the American family*. Garden City, NY: Doubleday.

Wolfe, D. A., Jaffe, P., Wilson, S. K., & Zak, L. (1985). Children of battered women: The relation of child behavior to family violence and maternal stress. *Journal of Consulting and Clinical Psychology, 53,* 657–665.

PART ONE

Theoretical and Conceptual Issues

The Impact of Woman Abuse on Children's Social Development: Research and Theoretical Perspectives

Sandra A. Graham-Bermann

ESTABLISHING THE CONTEXT

The Problem

What are the parameters of normal social development for children? Pending such knowledge, does the presence of woman abuse impede normal child development? If so, in what ways? These issues are discussed in this chapter. Generally, most theorists who describe normal child development have included the cornerstone of a "good enough" home environment (Winnicott, 1965). Over the years, researchers have agreed that the features most needed in a nurturing home for the child are a supportive family and opportunities to interact with peers and others outside the family (Baumrind, 1993)—what family systems theorists have otherwise discussed as connectedness and permeability of boundaries (Minuchin, 1974). Conversely, families that are abusive and violent to the child are generally considered to be outside of the range of the adequate environment for optimal child development (Scarr, 1992). Less clear is just how much woman abuse interferes with normative child development and in what particular ways it may harm the developing child.

Of course, addressing such issues requires a consistent definition of both exposure to domestic violence and the impact of such violence on the child. On the one hand, any child whose mother has been battered is considered by many researchers as having been exposed to domestic violence. Yet for others, exposure to violence can be defined in terms of dosage, for example, whether the child has observed the violence and the intensity and frequency of such events. Unfortunately, definitions of harm to the child tend to vary from setting to setting and even from study to study, and disciplinary differences often serve to further compound the problem of definition (Giovannoni & Becerra, 1979). For example, in the courtroom the construct of harm is burdened with the need for evidence of damage. Though children may be physically injured when they attempt to intervene in the fights of adults and manifest the bruises of harm, many psychologists would contend that a child who witnesses the abuse of his or her mother has been psychologically abused. To rephrase: For most mental health researchers and workers, the mere exposure to domestic violence is itself a form of child maltreatment (Wolfe & McGee, 1994).

To further complicate the picture, children exposed to domestic violence also are presumed to be at higher risk for being physically and sexually abused themselves than are children in non-woman-abusing families (Jaffe, Wolfe, & Wilson, 1990). Moreover, the rates of sibling violence in these and other families are only now being explored (Graham-Bermann & Cutler, 1994; Graham-Bermann, Cutler, Litzenberger, & Schwartz, 1994; Straus, Gelles, & Steinmetz, 1980). Further defining and parsing the various types of abuse and their relative and distinct impacts on the child is an important but highly formidable task; indeed, in many instances—we do not yet know how many—various forms of violence coexist (e.g., multiply abused, severely distressed, "pan-violent" families).

Conceptual Models

As guides to disentangling these many issues, conceptual models that place the child's exposure to domestic violence in context are helpful. Developmental psychopathology models posit that children in high-risk families may be protected from negative outcomes by the presence of buffering circumstances, such as positive relationships with other adults (Cicchetti & Rizley, 1987). Similarly, developmental psychopathology models favor prospective and longitudinal studies. Longitudinal studies of adult populations indicate that social convoys, or strong social networks that last over time, protect against negative mental health outcomes (Antonucci & Akiyama, 1995). At present, however, little comparable research and sparse evidence are available on how children in woman-abusing families actually cope with the violence and abuse surrounding them. In fact, researchers are just beginning to understand how the events of domestic violence affect children's social worlds, such as their relationships with teachers, friends, and others in their interpersonal social networks (Sternberg et al., 1993).

Nonetheless, research on the resilience of children living in other deleterious family circumstances can provide leads for research on children of domestic violence. To offer two examples, some developmental psychopathology investigators have found that the mother's education and her low level of depression can protect children against some otherwise expected negative outcomes (Garmezy, 1985; Graham-Bermann, Banyard, Coupet, Egler, & Mattis, 1996; Masten & Coatsworth, 1995; Masten, Miliotis, Graham-Bermann, Ramirez, & Neeman, 1993; Sameroff & Seifer, 1990). Similarly, stress in the child's environment may be moderated by a host of protective elements, such as socioeconomic status, parenting style, and peer and sibling relationships (Rutter, 1987; Sameroff, 1995).

Vulnerability factors, such as family violence, are presumed to work throughout development so as to detract from the achievement of successful adaptation and competence (Cicchetti & Lynch, 1995). However, as Rutter (1987) noted, risk factors are not causal in and of themselves but rather indicate more complex processes that can account for psychopathological outcomes in the child. To exemplify, the presence of violence per se may not directly affect adjustment; rather, it may affect the child's relationships with others or damage the child's social expectations, thereby affecting his or her adjustment, and these processes may, in turn, be subject to variation by gender.

The risk and resilience model inherent in developmental psychopathology approaches is important for contextualizing the violent events in the home and for describing the ways in which buffers and challengers can diminish or protect the child's social development. These approaches also build on (indeed, incorporate) Bronfenbrenner's (1979) tripartite ecological schema, which emphasizes that people are affected by many interconnected and nested systems. Bronfenbrenner initially identified at least three system levels arranged from distal to proximal: the macrosystem, the exosystem (nested within the macrosystem), and the microsystem (nested within the exosystem). Under the best of research conditions, the amount of violence or risk contributed by each level of the child's ecosystem might be calculable or at least estimable. This estimate would include interaction effects and feedback effects across the system levels. The reality, of course, is more complex than can be approximated in most research endeavors. Hence, the macrosystem level would include the larger community and social institutions. Risks posed by these social institutions are considered to be distal stressors for the child. Here the amount of television and movie violence, society's tolerance for abusers, and the lack of a strong community response when abuse does occur (e.g., no court sentences for abusers) may all play a part in the extent to which violence in the family affects the child (Eron, Huesmann, & Zilli, 1991; Huesmann, Eron, Loefkowitz, & Walder, 1984). Additional social stressors such as racism, poverty, and poor educational opportunities may further put the child at risk for harm by this form of family violence; studies of poor families have shown that poverty exacerbates negative events for children (McLoyd & Wilson, 1991).

At the exosystem level, the family's connectedness with the immediate neighborhood would include the quality of the neighborhood, such as the availability of local social support and helping agencies and the presence of extended family members. These proximal social contacts may be decisive in moderating the harm to the child. Conversely, the role of community violence is salient as well and may exacerbate the effect of family violence on the child (Aber, 1994).

The microsystem level describes the range of intrafamilial connections and behaviors that can affect the individual child. Of course, the behavior of family members proves to be most salient here, as are the types and frequency of family violence events. Crucial questions here may have to do with whether the child receives any explanation for the violence in the family. Is the child blamed for the violence? Understanding the division of roles within the family also is salient in this regard. Does the child serve as a mediator to family conflict (e.g., as a peacemaker or a distracter from parental disputes)?

However, the child is also part of the family microsystem and so should not be omitted from the equation. He or she is not merely a passive recipient of family influences and inputs but is an active, as well as reactive, agent and participant in family transactions (Sameroff, 1995). The child helps shape events. Thus, his or her responses to the violence may, in part, be a function of temperament, intelligence, or some other "intraindividual" quality that may serve to mediate the child's responses to the violence and hence presage the child's adjustment in the short and long term. Thus, to the family dynamics of violence one must add the "intraindividual" or personal level, which would include (among other phenomena) the child's understandings about violence and beliefs about relationships with other people, about the family, and about his or her developing sense of self. Relevant examples include internalized familial norms, roles, identities, and relationship paradigms. It is with these latter phenomena (i.e., the child's understandings and beliefs about the violence, the family, and the self) that this chapter is most especially concerned.

FRAMING THE ISSUES

In this chapter, I suggest ways in which the abuse of the woman affects the social development of children exposed to such violence in their homes. I attempt to demonstrate that the presence of domestic violence puts children at risk for early problems in social development, that is, in their relationships with people in the home, with parents and siblings, and with those outside the home (e.g., friends and peers). To these ends, I review and critique the evolution of empirical research efforts in the field. This review is followed by a discussion of several theoretical frameworks for construing the results of the research, developing new research directions, and exploring the processes by which the abuse of women affects children's social development. In the course of this discussion, preliminary evidence is presented that suggests that exposure to domestic violence may be related to the development of deleterious relationship paradigms or schemas—those internalized models of behavior that both influence expectations and motivate behavior in the developing child.

I begin with a brief review of results of the "first generation" of research on the children of battered women. These early studies (e.g., Hughes & Barard, 1983; Jaffe et al., 1990; Wolfe, Jaffe, Wilson, & Zak, 1985) document the connection between woman abuse and various types of symptomatology in the child. Such studies, in turn, spawned a "second generation" of research, in which researchers (Graham-Bermann, Levendosky, Porterfield, & Okun, 1996; McCloskey, Figueredo, & Koss, 1995; Sternberg et al., 1993) sought to test models inclusive of the assessment of maternal mental health and several types of violence within the family. These research efforts are briefly reviewed, followed by a discussion of the most recent studies. The latter demonstrate that researchers are just beginning to understand how domestic violence affects the adjustment of very young children and adolescents (Graham-Bermann & Levendosky, 1997; Rossman, Bingham, & Emde, 1996; Wolfe, 1996).

In the course of this overview, three theories are used to help make sense of the research and clinical phenomena observed in children raised in violent families. Specifically, social learning theory, trauma theory, and relationships theory are brought to bear on the relevant issues. For the moment, consider matters from the vantage point of relationships theory. To do so suggests most immediately that children of battered women learn and then internalize distorted images of relationships, family roles, and gender roles. The theory posits that the children then rely on these scripts or paradigms to understand and to interact with others. The family and relationship paradigms serve to motivate expectations of other people and to guide the child's own

scripted behaviors. In this way, the effects of early interpersonal problems in relationships can be traced. Thus, this chapter intends to place
the research on children exposed to domestic violence in the broader
theoretical context, to draw out implications of existing research on
issues of child social development, and to propose theory-based questions for future study.

Studies Linking Battering to Child Adjustment Problems

A substantial body of evidence has consistently demonstrated that approximately 30–40% of all children raised in woman-abusing families
are at higher risk for psychopathology than children raised in nonviolent families (Fantuzzo & Lindquist, 1989). This greater level of risk is
manifested in short-term, medium-term, and longer term vulnerabili-
ties. Specifically, studies have shown that children of battered women
have higher rates of both internalizing and externalizing behavior problems, lower self-esteem, more depression, and greater attentional difficulties in school than children raised in nonviolent families (Davis &
Carlson, 1987; Hughes, 1988; Hughes & Barard, 1983; Jaffe et al., 1990).
Subsequent research has found these children to be at risk for developing delinquent behavior during adolescence (B. Carlson, 1990; Koss
et al., 1994; Wolfe, 1994) or for manifesting violence inside and outside
of the home during adulthood (Sugarman & Hotaling, 1989).

A primary goal of many early studies in this area was to establish
a relationship between woman abuse and the child's problems in adjustment. In some studies these associational results implied that domestic violence led to negative outcomes for the child. However, other
early studies used regression analyses and included domestic violence
and maternal mental health to account for approximately 24–30% of
the variance in the child's adjustment with these variables (Jaffe et al.,
1990).

More recent studies have focused on delineating multiple forms of
violence within the family and on testing models that include either
some risk or some protective factors, and they have focused on outcomes other than just child behavioral symptoms. When Sternberg and
colleagues (1993) assessed the relative impact of child abuse and do-

mestic violence on the child's adjustment, they found that children with both types of abuse fared no worse than children with child abuse alone; however, they also found that children who were exposed to the abuse of their mothers but who were not themselves abused had the same level of symptomatology as those who had been abused and also had experienced the abuse of their mothers. Similarly, others have studied systemic family violence and measured the additive effects of domestic violence and parental abuse of the child on the level of child behavioral problems (McCloskey et al., 1995; O'Keefe, 1994). Recent work also has included the impact of domestic violence on parenting (Holden & Ritchie, 1991; Levendosky & Graham-Bermann, 1996a) and the role of the broader community context (Spiracelli, Sandler, & Roosa, 1994) in accounting for the child's adjustment. These studies have shown that the impact of exposure to domestic violence on the child is moderated by the quality of parenting and by other stressors (e.g., community violence).

One example of an expanded model is shown in Figure 1. In a study of 121 children ages 7 to 12 years, my colleagues and I (Graham-Bermann, Levendosky, Porterfield, & Okun, 1996) tested a similar model of the ways in which the child's relationships with others in the environment provided support or additional stress to the child exposed to domestic violence. Variables included mother's stress and depression; various types of violence to the mother; and both positive and negative social support from a range of people in the child's environment, including teachers, other relatives, mothers, fathers, and friends. The model received support and provided evidence that the presence of negative relationships added direct risk to the child's problems in adjustment and heightened, or moderated, the deleterious impact of the mother's mental health; on the other hand, the presence of positive social support did not contribute to the child's adjustment or assuage the effects of mother's mental health on the child's adjustment. Although this study did a better job of explaining one type of risk to the child's behavioral adjustment (i.e., low social support), it did not do better than previous studies at predicting outcomes for the child. Taken together, these variables accounted for only 27% of the variance in child adjustment.

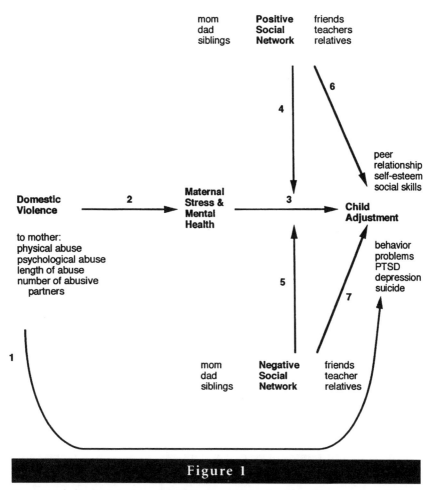

Figure 1

An expanded conceptual model of factors influencing the adjustment of children exposed to domestic violence. PTSD = posttraumatic stress disorder.

Seven Suggestions for Future Research on Children Experiencing Domestic Violence

The problems inherent in the early studies include, among other things, their varying definitions of domestic violence (i.e., some researchers studied only the physical violence to the mother, whereas others assessed whether the child had actually observed the battering or had

29

experienced additional types of family violence). In fact, research in this area has focused almost exclusively on the frequency of physical violence against the mother. There has been little study of the family circumstances within which physical violence against the mother is nested. Thus, there has been little evaluation of the emotional and psychological abuse of mothers by their partners or of the ways in which psychological abuse of the mother affects the socio-emotional development of children in the family. Nonetheless, research on abused women indicates that physical violence perpetrated by the partner is always nested in a web of intimidation, inclusive of threats, insults, psychological abuse, and controlling tactics; indeed, these are regular features of the interaction between the abuser and the mother (Marshall, 1992; Straus, Hamby, Boney-McCoy, & Sugarman, 1995; Tolman, 1989; Walker, 1983). Hence, the context of domestic violence includes both coercive and control tactics that the child observes on a daily basis and that provide the background for the less frequent acts of physical violence (Browne, 1993; Cascardi & O'Leary, 1992; Dutton & Painter, 1993; Herman, 1992b). The following observations may be made:

1. Studies of the emotional abuse of children in families with domestic violence have not been undertaken to date. There have been studies of children who have been direct targets of emotional abuse, and these have linked the emotional abuse to other types of maltreatment in the family (e.g., to child physical abuse and to negative adjustment in children; Garbarino, Guttmann, & Seeley, 1986; Grusec & Walters, 1991; Hart, Germain, & Brassard, 1987; McGee & Wolfe, 1991), but no one has studied the emotional climate of woman-abusing families. There is every reason to expect that the general ambiance of these homes is associated with negative social and emotional outcomes for the child (see Hughes & Graham-Bermann, in press, for a review).

2. Few researchers have studied or controlled for the number of abusive partners the mother has had, the chronicity of her abuse, or the length of the child's exposure to this violence. The inclusion of these variables in future studies will help clarify the definitional

problems of exposure to domestic violence. Studies might also be undertaken of other kinds of abuse that might have occurred in the home (e.g., sexual abuse) and whether girls are more at risk for particular kinds of adjustment problems than boys.

3. Few developmental or prospective studies of woman-abusive families have been done. Because the research literature to date has focused almost exclusively on children in the middle childhood years, at this point there is compelling need to explore the effects of growing up with domestic violence for children of all other ages. Hence, the effects of domestic violence on infants, preschool-age children, and the developing adolescent still demand investigation.

Our understanding is further limited by the paucity of longitudinal studies; available cross-sectional studies exclude both the process and the theory of change. Take the question of gender differences as an example. It is unclear whether girls are more at risk for problems in adjustment than are boys exposed to domestic violence. With a developmental perspective, the question can be reframed. Perhaps girls do better during the violence, when the mother turns to them for help and support prior to the mother leaving the batterer; but then, perhaps girls manifest symptoms later when the mother has adjusted and found new friends or even her next partner and the daughter has lost her critical role. In other words, are there sleeper effects that differ by gender? Long-term, prospective studies are needed to address these questions.

4. It is imperative to follow what happens to the approximately 60% of children who are seemingly not overtly affected by the violence when initially assessed—in other words, those presumably resilient children who are not above the clinical cutoff levels. Do they get worse? If so, under what conditions? Are some children simply never affected by exposure to this violence? If so, what distinguishes these children from others?

5. Broader ways of looking at adjustment outcomes are required. There is a heavy reliance on the Child Behavior Checklist (Achenbach & Edelbrock, 1983) to evaluate adjustment problems in the child. Most often this is completed by the child's mother, who, as

a reporter, is usually depressed and traumatized by the violence. To date, only a few studies have used the child's other caretakers (e.g., fathers, grandmothers, older siblings) or teachers as a source of information about the child, and there are no published studies of the fathers' views of their children. Similarly, studies that have used observation by one or more trained coders unconnected with the family are virtually nonexistent and should be undertaken.

6. The implications of domestic violence for children from different cultures and ethnic groups should be explored. Though some researchers in the area have sampled a significant number of individuals from minority groups, they did not specifically design their studies to examine ethnic differences (Graham-Bermann, 1996a; McCloskey et al., 1995). Doing so is important, because ways of coping with violence and whether community supports are used (including whether to call the police) may be different for various populations, which, in turn, may adversely affect ways in which children cope with domestic violence.

7. It is necessary to go beyond the family to include the additive impact of poverty and neighborhood violence to domestic violence. For example, Garbarino, Kostelny, and Dubrow (1991) studied the role of accumulated stress on children's adjustment and found that community violence contributed to the children's adjustment problems. Studies of resilience in families living in high crime neighborhoods indicate that children whose mothers restrict their access to the neighborhood have better outcomes than children whose mothers do not keep the child inside the home (Dubrow & Garbarino, 1989; Jayaratne, 1993). Nonetheless, in families with domestic violence, this very strategy might serve to further expose the child to risk while simultaneously reducing the child's access to extrafamilial forms of support.

THEORETICAL GROUNDING

Theory-driven work is needed to frame research hypotheses, to understand results, and to test the ways in which violent behavior is passed from one generation to the next. To this end, I review and consider three possible theoretical explanations for the impact of domestic violence on children's social development. These are not mutually exclusive theories. Although they have developed from different traditions, there are conceptual overlaps and even ways of melding them so as to explain more comprehensively the ways in which children are affected by domestic violence.

Social Learning Theory

Explanations

Patterson (1982), Eron (Huesmann et al., 1984), and others have shown that behavior patterns that are overlearned in early childhood interactions with others are automatically used by the child when adapting to new circumstances and situations. The social learning explanation has been used to describe the ways in which children from violent families learn aggression tactics (Patterson, Dishion, & Bank, 1984). Although the focus of domestic violence research has been on the physical violence to the mother, research on battered women would suggest that the behavior of children raised in woman-abusive families reflects the entire complex of behaviors, meanings, intentions, and actions by those whose purpose is subduing and controlling the woman (Hamby, Poindexter, & Gray-Little, 1996; Marshall, 1992; Tolman, 1989). These behaviors are conveyed to the child through direct modeling and reinforcement (Jouriles, Murphy, & O'Leary, 1989; Jouriles & Norwood, 1995).

Thus, in addition to aggression tactics, children may learn to manipulate, to cajole, and to coerce others to have their needs met—in essence, to show the beginnings of antisocial personality. These children may identify with the aggressor (their father or their mother's partner). Other children may learn that the only way to coexist with others is to submit, to blame oneself, or to give up in the face of difficulty. Is it always girls who identify with the mother? Similarly, what about siblings in the same family? Are some children in the same family more affected by exposure to such violence than others? Is it possible to predict which

Table 1

Frequency of Five Kinds of Domestic Violence Directed at the Mother and Differences Between Two Sample Groups

Violence type	Violent families				
	Mother abused ($n = 60$)		Comparison ($n = 61$)		
	M	SD	M	SD	Difference
Control tactics	106.30	88.77	20.49	34.61	6.98**
Physical threats	57.42	65.19	7.06	16.77	5.80**
Sexual coercion	31.85	65.26	7.60	30.88	2.61*
Mild violence	36.19	58.51	1.74	7.30	4.45**
Severe violence	27.07	51.22	2.11	8.30	3.70**

$*p < .05.$ $**p < .001.$

child would be most affected? If so, would the prediction be based on age differences? Family role differences? Sex differences? Similarly, do some children identify with both parents? Under what conditions do these children exhibit their learned behavior? In any case, the social learning theory posits that these lessons are "hard-wired" into the child's behavioral repertoire because they are performed by people the child loves and they are reinforced with violence and trauma.

How might one begin to explore hypotheses derived from such theoretical premises? I offer some possibilities. It is, for instance, possible to document the frequency of psychological maltreatment incidents in woman-abusing families. In one study, the family climate of 60 children whose mothers were abused was compared with that of 61 children raised in comparable but less violent families. The control tactics, physical threats, presence of sexual coercion, and the number of mild and severe violence incidents during the past year were assessed (Graham-Bermann, Levendosky, Porterfield, & Okun, 1996). Table 1 shows the frequencies of each type of domestic assault to the mother and the differences between the two groups. Although each type of violence was present for at least some families in each group, the children in the woman-abusive families were exposed to significantly more control tactics, threats, and acts of coercion and physical violence than were children in the comparison group.

A second study has since shown that children exposed to domestic violence learn power and control tactics in addition to physical aggression and display both behaviors in social interactions with peers outside the home. A multimethod study of 46 preschool-age children demonstrated that the lessons of domestic violence are learned early in life and can be seen in the social interactions and emotional adjustment of 3- to 5-year-old children (Graham-Bermann & Levendosky, 1997). In this study, mothers rated the frequency of emotional and physical abuse during the past year, their own level of mental health, and their child's adjustment. In addition, the free play of each child in a small group setting was evaluated by two independent observers on three separate occasions. The levels of emotional expression and regulation, interaction with peers and caregivers, and the observers' impressions of the child were assessed. Children exposed to parental violence had many more behavioral problems, exhibited significantly more negative affect, responded less appropriately to situations, were more aggressive with peers, and had more ambivalent relationships with caregivers than those from nonviolent families. Their aggression also took the form of bullying and insulting others. Yet, surprisingly, they were just as happy in their play as were the comparison children. Regression analyses showed that emotional abuse of the mother and mother's self-esteem were the most significant predictors of both the child's adjustment and social behavior.

Other studies of preschool-age children who were exposed to domestic violence found them to be less empathic than children not exposed to domestic violence (Hinchey & Gavelek, 1982) and, as expected, to have higher levels of behavior problems than older children from woman-abusing families (Davis & Carlson, 1987).

Future Studies With a Social Learning Perspective

In future studies, the kinds of social behaviors expected to be associated with learning both physical aggression and control tactics should be distinguished depending on the age of the child. Hence, infants might show problems in emotion regulation, from clinging behavior to an inability to inhibit negative affect. Preschoolers might evidence more aggression in the form of temper tantrums, whereas others might exhibit withdrawal or a difficulty in relating to their siblings and peers. In studies of children during middle childhood, those exposed to domestic violence have significantly more problems with aggression, anxiety, and depression (Fantuzzo & Lindquist, 1989). Nonetheless, it is expected that their social development also is impeded by their inadequate repertoire of social skills and by their learned expectations of the behavior and intentions of others. Learned behaviors that may find expression in the preadolescent years could take the form of early antisocial behavior (e.g., stealing) or avoidance of social situations. As demonstrated by studies of dating violence, researchers must examine (a) the problems with intimate relationships experienced by adolescents who as children have seen their mothers physically or psychologically maltreated and (b) the differential impact of exposure to violence on what different children in the family have learned, depending on their age, their identities, and their relationships with one another.

Trauma Theory

Explanations

Studies of social learning theory suggest that children have learned and incorporated the lessons of violence and that, without intervention, they grow up and tend to repeat those lessons or behaviors. On the other hand, trauma theory offers explanations for behaviors not necessarily referenced or predicted by social learning theory. These behaviors include traumatic arousal, avoidance of people or places associated with the violence, and intrusive memories or flashbacks of the traumatic events.

Several factors affect the way the child copes with exposure to a traumatic event, such as the abuse of the mother. These include the child's perception of the danger of the event and his or her estimation of protection from harm either for the self or others (Freud, 1926/

1959). The meaning of the event to the child and the immediate response of caretakers also influence the degree of trauma that the child may experience (Pynoos, Sorenson, & Steinberg, 1993). Too frequently the child is left to construct his or her own meaning or interpretation of violent events. To date, few researchers have inquired about how often children receive information regarding the violence in the family and from whom the information, if given, is received. The import of such questions is highlighted in one study (Graham-Bermann, 1996b) in which more than half of 120 battered women with children ages 7–12 reported that they did not tell their children anything by way of explanation following the worst violent episode of the previous year and that when they did offer an explanation, approximately 10% blamed the child for the violence. What male batterers say to children has yet to be systematically researched, though clinical reports suggest that they are given to denial, minimization, and externalization of blame.

Furthermore, the ways in which children generally react to a trauma should be explored. Children with posttraumatic stress symptoms may show an exaggerated startle response (Ornitz & Pynoos, 1989), dissociation (Putnam, 1985; Putnam, Helmers, & Trickett, 1993), traumatic memories and intrusive play (Davies, 1992; Sugar, 1992; Terr, 1990), and a general vulnerability to stress (Goodwin, 1988; Green, 1983). Pynoos (1994) has detailed the initial traumatic stress exposure, traumatic reminders, and secondary stress that also can affect the child.

How, then, do children react to witnessing the abuse of their mothers? The construct of complex traumatic stress was described by Herman (1992a), who viewed responses to extreme stress along a continuum, rather than as a single disorder (e.g., posttraumatic stress disorder [PTSD]). This also may be appropriate for describing the effects of spouse abuse on children, because children exposed to such violence most often are not reacting to a unitary event and hence may show a variety of symptoms. Children also may be subject to revictimization at any time, as when they view additional assaults or are reminded of them. Studies of television violence show that children are exposed to many images of violent incidents each day—images that can remind the child of a previous battering event (Eron et al., 1991). Over time, many children may learn that they are powerless to do anything to stop domestic violence. Furthermore, woman abuse often escalates and may be worse on one occasion than on the preceding occasion (Herman, 1992a). For the child, a persistent atmosphere of intimidation and threat can repeatedly stimulate posttraumatic play involving family members (Davies, 1992; Terr, 1981). For instance, a child who has observed the father slamming the mother's arm in the car door may perseverate in playing out the same scene every day with a toy car and dollhouse figures.

Children in families of domestic violence may be further damaged and harmed by the lack of available support and abundant negative role and relational models, that is, the available relational models are the very ones children may wish to reject but are often doomed to repeat (Graham-Bermann, 1996a). Moreover, children often do not have even one parent who is able to respond reasonably in ways to inoculate them against the further negative effects of traumatic abuse (Herman, 1992a). Whereas the positive attachment with a parent often mediates distress for children in other stressful circumstances (Martini, Ryan, Nakayama, & Romenofsky, 1990; McFarlane, Policansky, & Irwin, 1987), children in families with domestic violence may not have access to such support. Hence, the child exposed to domestic violence may be vulnerable to the effects of unrelenting distress.

To sum up, the epigenesis of the trauma experienced by children in woman-abusing families is not directly comparable to the trauma induced by single events outside of the family. Posttraumatic stress symptoms of children from woman-abusing families may be recurrent and ongoing, and the violence and abuse are best understood as continuous rather than discreet or unitary traumatizing events (e.g., being in a fire). Furthermore, the traumas associated with domestic violence are unique in that both the mother and the father are involved in the trauma to the child, albeit in different ways and with differing roles (Dutton & Painter, 1993).

Future Studies Assessing Trauma in Children of Abused Women

How can one begin to decipher or disentangle these phenomena? We (Graham-Bermann & Levendosky, in press) designed a study to identify the range of trauma symptoms found in 64 children who were exposed to the physical and emotional maltreatment of their mother by their father or mother's partner during the past year. Unlike most studies of the children of batterers, this sample consisted of families living in the community. Psychological abuse included the frequency of acts of coercion and threats, whereas physical abuse included the frequency of both mild and severe physical violence. Using the criterion of the fourth edition of the *Diagnostic and Statistical Manual of Mental Disorders* (American Psychiatric Association, 1994) for diagnosing PTSD in adults and recommended for diagnosing PTSD in children, we measured 17 posttraumatic symptoms in the child, each experienced directly in conjunction with the violence. In addition, posttraumatic stress symptoms were related to other indices of the individual child's adjustment. Results showed that more than half of the children had the symptoms of intrusive reexperiencing, and 42% experienced traumatic arousal symptoms. Fewer children evidenced avoidance reactions to the violence. However, 13% qualified for a complete diagnosis of PTSD.

Although not all children have traumatic-level responses when exposed to violence, it is readily seen that a child who either has posttraumatic stress symptoms or whose mother has posttraumatic stress symptoms may encounter difficulties in social development. Yet the specific links of trauma and children's social behavior have yet to be made. For example, the child may avoid either specific people in the family or potentially conflictual situations, or the child may experience reminders of traumatic events at inopportune times, such as when playing with others. Traumatic intrusions may interfere with attentional focus and concentration at school and ultimately may influence school achievement. A traumatized mother may be less available to provide bonding, protection, and support to the developing child. Given that more than half of the children in the study just cited showed the symptom of "intrusive reexperiencing," it is clear that, for many children, the devastating effects of domestic violence continue well beyond the time frame of the violent events themselves. Future studies are needed to address these issues.

Relationships Theory Explanations

One of the important tasks of early childhood is the development of secure family relationships, which affect all future social relationships. Several theories of relationships contribute to our understanding of the ways in which family experiences presage the child's relationships with other people throughout life. Both object relations theory and attachment theory are predicated on the idea that an individual develops an internal representational model of relationships on the basis of previous experiences with significant others, that is, primary caregivers and siblings (Bowlby, 1988; Sroufe & Fleeson, 1986; Sullivan, 1953). Internal models can be modified over time through new experiences in significant relationships, yet it is the initial models developed in early childhood from experience with the primary caregivers that generally are believed to have more influence than later experiences. An added and important contribution was made by Laing (Laing & Esterson, 1964), who posited that entire interactional sequences observed or experienced by the child were themselves internalized and remembered. Reiss (1981) has made the same claim. Thus, children are presumed to internalize not just part objects (cf. Klein, 1932/1949) or individual people (e.g., father, mother) but entire interpersonal transactions that are repeated in the family and that also include the child in interaction with others. Such internal representations are not static; they are dynamic enactments of family events. The additional contribution of these interactional viewpoints is the supposition that children carry not only dynamic images of learned behavior but also of learned interactional sequences and patterns, and thus they have portable sets of expectations of themselves and others that are embedded in a web of social circumstances.

Similarly, Janoff-Bulman (1992) and others have hypothesized that family violence damages the development of the child's safe, reliable expectations about other people (Erikson's, 1950, "basic trust"). Some research has shown that child maltreatment can lead to distorted internal representational models of relationships (V. Carlson, Cicchetti, Barnett, & Brunwald, 1989; Crittenden, 1988; see Cicchetti & Carlson, 1989, for a review). The relationships paradigm of children exposed to domestic violence might include the deleterious elements of domination and control in interpersonal interaction and expectations of what it means to be a man or a woman and might be organized around the dynamics of the family roles and interactional scripts that they have observed or experienced.

The effects of domestic violence can be seen in the earliest social relationships where children learn to resolve and to regulate emotions in social interactions with others (Eisenberg et al., 1993). The development of social relationships in children is crucial to long-term adjustment outcomes, including friendship, social skills, academic success, self-esteem, and well-being. During the preschool years (ages 3 to 5), parents, and particularly mothers, are involved in facilitating the development of the child's relationships with others (Hart, Ladd, DeWolf, & Muth, 1991; Profilet & Ladd, 1994). In addition, the quality of the child's relationship with the mother during this critical time period affects his or her ability to develop age-appropriate relationships with others (Kerns & Barth, 1995; Putallaz & Costanzo, 1991).

Three studies that include parenting processes of battered women (Graham-Bermann & Levendosky, 1997; Levendosky & Graham-Bermann, 1996a, 1996b) demonstrate that both parenting stress and parenting strengths affect the child's level of adjustment. Other research has found that high levels of marital satisfaction in families of preschool children are positively related to parenting practices and that low levels are related to more hostile or neglectful parenting practices (Kerig, Cowan, & Cowan, 1993; Turturo, 1994). It is possible, therefore, that young children in families with domestic violence are less likely to form healthy relationships with either their abusive father or their mother and that this may also negatively affect other important relationships in their lives (e.g., with siblings and peers).

What evidence is there for this claim? There is some preliminary evidence that children who grow up in woman-abusive families have different sets of concerns and expectations for themselves and others, relative to children who have not been exposed to such family violence. In one study of the middle childhood years (ages 6 to 12), children of battered women were more worried and concerned about the safety of their mothers and sisters, and more worried about the potential for harm by their father, than were children in comparable but less violent families (Graham-Bermann, 1996a).

Is there any evidence that witnessing domestic violence affects the child's relationships with peers and friends? In fact, there is some suggestive evidence on this count as well. A study by Graham-Bermann, Levendosky, and Lynch (1996) found that children of battered women spent less time with their friends, were less likely to have a best friend, and had lower quality friendships than did children from nonviolent families. Moreover, their worries about family members were generalized to others outside the home: Children of battered women were more worried about the safety of and potential for harm to their friends than children living in nonviolent families (Graham-Bermann, 1996b).

Future Studies of Social Cognitions

The internal relationships model is akin to the schema construct described by social cognitive psychologists (Cantor & Kihlstrom, 1987; Kelly, 1955). Social schemas or constructs are said to help the child organize new experiences and also shape expectations about other people. When it comes to the child's understanding of family functioning and family roles, the developing child builds a construct of the roles of men and women, fathers, mothers, children, and siblings in the family. These constructs, which grow and are amended by experience, develop into paradigms of what the social world is like (Reiss, 1981). When the child is raised in a family with domestic violence, the family roles that develop often include the violence and coercion which the child sees on a regular basis. Given this set of assumptions, one can ask whether children who witness domestic violence have different views of the roles of men and women in the family relative to children from nonviolent families.

One study was undertaken to try to document the ways in which witnessing domestic violence affects children's developing sense of what it means to be a family member. The lessons learned about family roles and gender roles were studied for a group of 7- to 12-year-old children of battered women using an amended version of Orlofsky's (1981) measure of family and gender roles (Graham-Bermann & Levendosky, 1996). For this study the items were presented in the form of a card sort, and the questions were modified for children who were asked to name who was more likely to undertake a particular household task in the present—the mother, the father, or both. They then were asked to describe who would be doing each of these same tasks presuming that they grew up and got married—the mother, the father, or both. This study suggested that current images of fathers' family roles were stronger when there was less abuse within the family. Also, children's images of men's and women's family roles in the future differed by gender. That is, girls had stronger images of themselves as mothers in the future if they were not depressed or plagued by low self-competence (poor self-image) in the present. On the other hand, boys' images of themselves as fathers in the future varied with the current amount of violence in the family. In this way, violence in the family can be seen to influence children's social expectations of appropriate family roles both in the present and in their projections of the future. For example, for boys, violence in the home directly affected the strength of their identification with paternal roles and their expectations of themselves as fathers.

SUMMARY

In this chapter, several ways of viewing the issues pertinent to the impact of domestic violence on children's social development have been introduced. The discussion of theory and research was framed, first by using two similar yet different models of behavior: the developmental psychopathology model and the ecological model. These multilevel descriptions of interactive systems provided backdrop and perspective for the ways in which domestic violence affects and interferes with children's social development. The addition of the individual child's voice —his or her level of understanding and reaction to the violence—were then used to amplify and shape the subsequent discussion.

By using these models one can explain the occurrence of change over time and the importance of crucial periods of development. Contextual responses in ameliorating stress to the child are important. Furthermore, domestic violence trauma and the child's needs at particular times have developmental significance. For example, the impact of violence or trauma that occurs at age 1, at age 5, or at age 13 presumably varies relative to the tasks and concerns of the child at each age; also influential are the child's family as it exists in the child's present, the child's past history, and the attendant elements of protection and risk offered at both the family and community level systems. Hence, witnessing domestic violence can be expected to affect the child's developmental needs in ways that are becoming clearer. Those at risk earlier may not be at risk later given a particular context, such as extent of community violence, number of partners, maternal stress, and exposure to violent media.

The three theories that have been discussed in this chapter have further served to frame the discussion of results of specific studies and as a means for linking the various findings together. Thus, the three theories were used to explain the effect of the violence on the children, the pattern of their present behavior problems, and the impact of current trauma on their future behavior. To recapitulate, when children are traumatized, the development of their social relationships can be impeded by the trauma symptoms they experience. Furthermore, the child may have learned inadequate coping skills or inappropriate emotion regulation strategies, which can lead to frustration and anger. The anger is expressed in social interaction with others and creates interpersonal problems, such as rejection by peers. Moreover, the traumatized child who is not able to cope well may experience trouble concentrating at school and may fall further behind academically.

These theories help explain sleeper effects, or the prospective impact of domestic violence on the child. Given that most of the research in this area is focused on identifying current symptoms and problems in the child, it is important to recognize that many children may have problems later or may not show any negative effects at all. Trauma theory and interpersonal theories help explain these observed differences.

Finally, the use of both theories and models allows speculation on the ways in which children's reactions to the events can be modulated and modified. By identifying protective factors, such as how the events are explained to the child, who is blamed, the quality of maternal mental health, social supports, resources in the broader community context, and so on, one may work to develop clinical and education programs and to take a preventive stance against this form of family violence. Ultimately, action is required on a societal level to eliminate the continued vulnerability of women and children to domestic violence.

REFERENCES

Aber, J. L. (1994). Poverty, violence and child development: Untangling family and community level effects. In C. A. Nelson (Ed.), *Minnesota Symposium on Child Psychology: Vol. 27. Threats to optimal development: Integrating biological, psychological, and social risk factors* (pp. 229–272). Hillsdale, NJ: Erlbaum.

Achenbach, T., & Edelbrock, C. (1983). *Manual for the Child Behavior Checklist and Revised Child Behavior Profile.* Burlington: University of Vermont, Department of Psychiatry.

American Psychiatric Association. (1994). *Diagnostic and statistical manual of mental disorders* (4th. ed.). Washington, DC: American Psychiatric Association.

Antonucci, T. C., & Akiyama, H. (1995). Convoys of social relations: Family and friendship within a life span context. In R. Blieszner & V. H. Bedford (Eds.), *Handbook of aging and the family* (pp. 355–372). Westport, CT: Greenwood Press.

Baumrind, D. (1993). The average expectable environment is not good enough: A response to Scarr. *Child Development, 64,* 1299–1317.

Bowlby, J. (1988). *A secure base: Clinical applications of attachment theory.* London: Routledge.

Bronfenbrenner, U. (1979). *The ecology of human development.* Cambridge, MA: Harvard University Press.

Browne, A. (1993). Violence against women by male partners: Prevalence, outcomes, and policy implications. *American Psychologist, 48,* 1077–1087.

Cantor, N., & Kihlstrom, J. (1987). *Personality and social intelligence.* Engelwood Cliffs, NJ: Prentice-Hall.

Carlson, B. (1990). Adolescent observers of marital violence. *Journal of Family Violence, 5,* 285–299.

Carlson, V., Cicchetti, D., Barnett, D., & Brunwald, K. (1989). Disorganized/disoriented attachment relationships in maltreated infants. *Development and Psychopathology, 25,* 525–531.

Cascardi, M., & O'Leary, K. D. (1992). Depressive symptomatology, self-esteem and self-blame in battered women. *Journal of Family Violence, 7,* 249–259.

Cicchetti, D., & Carlson, V. (1989). *Child maltreatment: Theory and research on the causes and consequences of child abuse and neglect.* Cambridge, England: Cambridge University Press.

Cicchetti, D., & Lynch, M. (1995). Failures in the expectable environment and their impact on individual development: The case of child maltreatment. In D. Cicchetti & D. Cohen (Eds.), *Developmental psychopathology: Vol. 1. Theory and methods* (pp. 32–71). New York: Wiley.

Cicchetti, D., & Rizley, R. (1987). Developmental perspectives on the etiology, intergenerational transmission, and sequelae of child maltreatment. In D. Cicchetti & R. Rizley (Eds.), *New directions for child development: Developmental perspectives on child maltreatment* (pp. 31–55). San Francisco: Jossey-Bass.

Crittenden, P. M. (1988). Distorted patterns of relationship in maltreating families: The role of internal representation models. *Journal of Reproductive and Infant Psychology, 6,* 183–189.

Davies, D. (1992). Intervention with male toddlers who have witnessed parental violence. *Families in Society: The Journal of Contemporary Human Services, 72,* 515–524.

Davis, L., & Carlson, B. (1987). Observation of spouse abuse: What happens to the children? *Journal of Interpersonal Violence, 2,* 278–291.

Dubrow, N. F., & Garbarino, J. (1989). Living in the war zone: Mothers and young children in a public housing project. *Child Welfare, 68,* 3–20.

Dutton, D. G., & Painter, S. L. (1993). The battered woman syndrome: Effects of severity and intermittency of abuse. *American Journal of Orthopsychiatry, 63,* 614–622.

Eisenberg, N., Fabes, R. A., Bernzweig, J., Karbon, M., Poulin, R., & Hanish, L. (1993). The resolution of emotionality and regulation to preschoolers' social skills and sociometric status. *Child Development, 64,* 1418–1438.

Erikson, E. H. (1950). *Childhood and society.* New York: Norton.

Eron, L. D., Huesmann, L. R., & Zilli, A. (1991). The role of parental variables in the learning of aggression. In D. J. Pepler & K. H. Rubin (Eds.), *The development and treatment of child aggression* (pp. 169–188). Hillsdale, NJ: Erlbaum.

Fantuzzo, J. W., & Lindquist, C. U. (1989). The effects of observing conjugal violence on children: A review of research methodology. *Journal of Family Violence, 4,* 77–94.

Freud, S. (1959). Inhibitions, symptoms and anxiety. In J. Strachey (Ed. and Trans.), *The standard edition of the complete works of Sigmund Freud* (Vol. 20, pp. 75–172). London: Hogarth Press. (Original work published 1926)

Garbarino, J., Guttmann, E., & Seeley, J. W. (1986). *The psychologically battered child: Strategies for identification, assessment, and intervention.* San Francisco: Jossey-Bass.

Garbarino, J., Kostelny, K., & Dubrow, N. (1991). What children can tell us about living in danger. *American Psychologist, 46,* 376–382.

Garmezy, N. (1985). Stress resistant children: The search for protective factors. In J. E. Stevenson (Ed.), *Recent research in developmental psychopathology* (pp. 213–233). Oxford, England: Pergammon Press.

Giovannoni, J., & Becerra, R. (1979). *Defining child abuse.* New York: The Free Press.

Goodwin, J. (1988). Post-traumatic symptoms in abused children. *Journal of Traumatic Stress, 1,* 475–488.

Graham-Bermann, S. A. (1996a). Family worries: The assessment of interpersonal anxiety in children from violent and nonviolent families. *Journal of Clinical Child Psychology, 25,* 280–287.

Graham-Bermann, S. A. (1996b). *Worry about friends: The transmission of interpersonal anxiety of children in families with domestic violence.* Manuscript under review.

Graham-Bermann, S. A., Banyard, V., Coupet, S., Egler, L., & Mattis, J. (1996). The interpersonal relationships and adjustment of children in homeless and economically distressed families. *Journal of Clinical Child Psychology, 25,* 250–261.

Graham-Bermann, S. A., Cutler, S. E., Litzenberger, B. W., & Schwartz, W. E.

(1994). Perceived sibling violence and emotional adjustment during childhood and adolescence. *Journal of Family Psychology, 8,* 85–97.

Graham-Bermann, S. A., & Cutler, S. E. (1994). The Brother-Sister Questionnaire (BSQ): Psychometric assessment and ability to predict well functioning and dysfunctional childhood sibling relationships. *Journal of Family Psychology, 8,* 224–238.

Graham-Bermann, S. A., & Levendosky, A. A. (1996, August). *Stereotypes of mothers and fathers in families of domestic violence.* Presented at the 14th biennial meeting of the International Society for the Study of Behavioural Development, Quebec City, Quebec, Canada.

Graham-Bermann, S. A., & Levendosky, A. A. (1997). The social functioning of preschool-age children whose mothers are emotionally and physically abused. *Journal of Emotional Abuse, 1,* 59–84

Graham-Bermann, S. A., & Levendosky, A. A. (in press). Traumatic stress symptoms in children of battered women. *Journal of Interpersonal Violence.*

Graham-Bermann, S. A., Levendosky, A. A., & Lynch, S. (1996). *Relationships with friends and the adjustment of children exposed to domestic violence.* Manuscript under review.

Graham-Bermann, S. A., Levendosky, A. A., Porterfield, K., & Okun, A. (1996). *The impact of woman abuse on children: The role of social relationships and emotional context.* Manuscript under review.

Green, A. H. (1983). Dimensions of psychological trauma in abused children. *Journal of the American Academy of Child and Adolescent Psychiatry, 22,* 231–237.

Grusec, J. E., & Walters, G. C. (1991). Psychological abuse and childrearing belief systems. In R. H. Starr, Jr. & D. A. Wolfe (Eds.), *The effects of child abuse and neglect: Issues and research* (pp. 186–202). New York: Guilford Press.

Hamby, S. L., Poindexter, V. C., & Gray-Little, B. (1996). Four measures of partner violence: Construct similarity and classification differences. *Journal of Marriage and the Family, 58,* 127–139.

Hart, C. H., Germain, R., & Brassard, M. (1987). The challenge: To better understand and combat psychological maltreatment of children and youth. In M. Brassard, R. Germain, & S. Hart (Eds.), *Psychological maltreatment of children and youth* (pp. 3–24). New York: Pergammon Press.

Hart, C. H., Ladd, G. W., DeWolf, M., & Muth, S. M. (1991, April). *Correlates of parental involvement in preschooler's peer relations.* Paper presented at the meeting of the Society for Research in Child Development, Seattle, WA.

Herman, J. L. (1992a). Complex PTSD: A syndrome of survivors of prolonged and repeated trauma. *Journal of Traumatic Stress, 5,* 377–391.

Herman, J. L. (1992b). *Trauma and recovery.* New York: Basic Books.

Hinchey, F. S., & Gavelek, J. R. (1982). Empathic responding in children of battered mothers. *Child Abuse and Neglect, 6,* 395–401.

Holden, G. W., & Ritchie, K. L. (1991). Linking extreme marital discord, child rearing, and child behavior problems: Evidence from battered women. *Child Development, 62,* 311–327.

Huesmann, L. R., Eron, L. D., Loefkowitz, M. M., & Walder, L. O. (1984). Stability of aggression over time and generations. *Developmental Psychology, 20,* 1120–1134.

Hughes, H. (1988). Psychological and behavioral correlates of family violence in child witnesses and victims. *American Journal of Orthopsychiatry, 58,* 77–90.

Hughes, H. M., & Barard, S. J. (1983). Psychological functioning of children in a battered women's shelter: A preliminary investigation. *American Journal of Orthopsychiatry, 53,* 525–531.

Hughes, H. M., & Graham-Bermann, S. A. (in press). Children exposed to the physical and emotional abuse of their mothers: A critical review of studies. *Journal of Emotional Abuse, 1.*

Jaffe, P., Wolfe, D. A., & Wilson, S. (1990). *Children of battered women.* Newbury Park, CA: Sage.

Janoff-Bulman, R. (1992). *Shattered assumptions: Toward a new psychology of trauma.* New York: Free Press.

Jayaratne, T. E. (1993, April). *Neighborhood quality and parental socialization among single, African-American mothers: Child gender differences.* Paper presented at the biennial meeting of the Society for Research in Child Development, New Orleans, LA.

Jouriles, E. N., Murphy, C. M., & O'Leary, K. D. (1989). Interspousal aggression, marital discord, and child problems. *Journal of Abnormal Child Psychology, 57,* 453–455.

Jouriles, E. N., & Norwood, W. D. (1995). Physical aggression toward boys and girls in families characterized by the battering of women. *Journal of Family Psychology, 9,* 69–78.

Kelly, G. A. (1955). *The psychology of personal constructs.* New York: McGraw Hill.

Kerig, P. K., Cowan, P. A., & Cowan, C. P. (1993). Marital quality and gender differences in parent-child interaction. *Developmental Psychology, 29,* 931–939.

Kerns, K. A., & Barth, J. M. (1995). Attachment and play: Convergence across components of parent–child relationships and their relations to peer competence. *Journal of Social and Personal Relationships, 12,* 243–260.

Klein, M. (1949). *The psycho-analysis of children.* London: Hogarth Press. (Original work published 1932)

Koss, M. P., Goodman, L. A., Browne, A., Fitzgerald, L. F., Keita, G. P., & Russo, N. F. (1994). *No safe haven: Male violence against women at home, at work, and in the community.* Washington, DC: American Psychological Association.

Laing, R. D., & Esterson, A. (1964). *Sanity, madness and the family.* London: Tavestock.

Levendosky, A. A., & Graham-Bermann, S. A. (1996a). *The moderating effects of parenting stress on children's adjustment in woman-abusing families.* Manuscript under review.

Levendosky, A. A., & Graham-Bermann, S. A. (1996b). *Parenting in battered women: A developmental psychopathology approach.* Manuscript under review.

Marshall, L. (1992). Development of the severity of violence against women scales. *Journal of Family Violence, 7,* 103–121.

Martini, D. R., Ryan, C., Nakayama, D., & Romenofsky, M. (1990). Psychiatric sequelae after traumatic injury: The Pittsburgh Regatta accident. *Journal of the American Academy of Child and Adolescent Psychiatry, 29,* 70–75.

Masten, A. S., & Coatsworth, J. D. (1995). Competence, resilience and psychopathology. In D. Cicchetti & D. J. Cohen (Eds.), *Developmental psychopathology: Vol. 2. Risk, disorder, and adaptation* (pp. 715–752). New York: Wiley.

Masten, A. S., Miliotis, D. M., Graham-Bermann, S., Ramirez, M., & Neeman,

J. (1993). Children in homeless families: Risks to mental health. *Journal of Consulting and Clinical Psychology, 61,* 335–343.

McCloskey, L. A., Figueredo, A. J., & Koss, M. P. (1995). The effects of systemic family violence on children's mental health. *Child Development, 66,* 1239–1261.

McFarlane, A. C., Policansky, S. K., & Irwin, C. (1987). A longitudinal study of the psychological morbidity in children due to natural disaster. *Psychological Medicine, 17,* 727–738.

McGee, R. A., & Wolfe, D. A. (1991). Psychological maltreatment: Towards an operational definition. *Development and Psychopathology, 3,* 3–18.

McLoyd, V. C., & Wilson, L. (1991). The strain of living poor: Parenting, social support, and child mental health. In A. C. Huston (Ed.), *Children in poverty: Child development and public policy* (pp. 105–135). New York: Cambridge University Press.

Minuchin, S. (1974). *Families and family therapy.* Cambridge, MA: Harvard University Press.

O'Keefe, M. (1994). Linking marital violence, mother–child/father–child aggression, and child behavior problems. *Journal of Family Violence, 9,* 63–78.

Orlofsky, J. L. (1981). Relationship between sex role attitudes and personality traits and the Sex Role Behavior Scale-1: A new measure of masculine and feminine role behaviors and interests. *Journal of Personality and Social Psychology, 40,* 927–940.

Ornitz, E., & Pynoos, R. (1989). Startle modulation in children with posttraumatic stress disorder. *American Journal of Psychiatry, 146,* 866–870.

Patterson, G. R. (1982). *Coercive family processes.* Eugene, OR: Castalia.

Patterson, G. R., Dishion, T. J., & Bank, L. (1984). Family interaction: A process model of deviancy training. *Aggressive Behavior, 10,* 253–267.

Profilet, S. M., & Ladd, G. W. (1994). Do mothers' perceptions and concerns about preschoolers' peer competence predict their peer management strategies? *Social Development, 3,* 205–221.

Putallaz, M., & Costanzo, P. R. (1991, April). *Relation of parental framing of social interaction to children's social competence.* Paper presented at the biennial meeting of the Society for Research in Child Development, Seattle, WA.

Putnam, F. (1985). Dissociation as a response to extreme trauma. In R. P Kluft (Ed.), *Childhood antecedents on multiple personality* (pp. 66–97). Washington, DC: American Psychiatric Press.

Putnam, F. W., Helmers, K., & Trickett, P. K. (1993). Development, reliability, and validity of a child dissociation scale. *Child Abuse and Neglect, 17,* 731–741.

Pynoos, R. S. (1994). Traumatic stress and developmental psychopathology in children and adolescents. In R. S. Pynoos (Ed.), *Posttraumatic stress disorder: A clinical review* (pp. 65–98). Lutherville, MD: Sidran Press.

Pynoos, R., Sorenson, S., & Steinberg, A. (1993). Interpersonal violence and traumatic stress reactions. In L. Goldberger & S. Breznitz (Eds.), *Handbook of stress: Theoretical and clinical aspects* (2nd ed., pp. 550–573). New York: Free Press.

Reiss, D. (1981). *The family's construction of reality.* Cambridge, MA: Harvard University Press.

Rossman, R. B. B., Bingham, R. D., & Emde, R. D. (1996). *Symptomatology and adaptive functioning for children exposed to normative stressors, dog attack, and parental violence.* Manuscript under review.

Rutter, M. (1987). Psychosocial resilience and protective mechanisms. *American Journal of Orthopsychiatry, 57,* 316–331.

Sameroff, A. (1995). General systems theories and developmental psychopathology. In D. Cicchetti & D. Cohen (Eds.), *Developmental psychopathology: Vol. 2. Risk, disorder, and adaptation* (pp. 659–695). New York: Wiley.

Sameroff, A. J., & Seifer, R. (1990). Early contributions to developmental risk. In J. Rolf, A. S. Masten, D. Cicchetti, K. Nuechterlein, & S. Weintraub (Eds.), *Risk and protective factors in the development of psychopathology* (pp. 52–66). New York: Cambridge University Press.

Scarr, S. (1992). Developmental theories for the 90's: Development and individual differences. *Child Development, 64,* 1333–1353.

Spiracelli, S., Sandler, I. N., & Roosa, M. (1994). History of spouse violence against mother: Correlated risks and unique effects in child mental health. *Journal of Family Violence, 9,* 79–98.

Sroufe, L. A., & Fleeson, J. (1986). Attachment and the construction of relationships. In W. W. Hartup & Z. Rubin (Eds.), *Relationships and development* (pp. 36–54). Hillsdale, NJ: Erlbaum.

Sternberg, K. J., Lamb, M. E., Greenbaum, C., Cicchetti, D., Dawud, S., Cortes, R. M., Krispin, O., & Lorey, F. (1993). Effects of domestic violence on children's behavior problems and depression. *Developmental Psychology, 29*, 44–52.

Straus, M., Gelles, R., & Steinmetz, S. (1980). *Behind closed doors: Violence in the American family.* Garden City, NY: Anchor.

Straus, M. A., Hamby, S. L., Boney-McCoy, S., & Sugarman, D. B. (1995, July). *The Partner Relationship Profile: A package of instruments for research and clinical screening.* Presented at the 4th International Family Violence Research Conference, The Family Research Laboratory, Durham, NH.

Sugar, M. (1992). Toddlers' traumatic memories. *Infant Mental Health Journal, 13*, 245–251.

Sugarman, D. B., & Hotaling, G. T. (1989). Violent men in intimate relationships: An analysis of risk markers. *Journal of Applied Social Psychology, 19*, 1034–1048.

Sullivan, H. S. (1953). *The interpersonal theory of psychiatry.* New York: Norton.

Terr, L. C. (1981). Forbidden games: Post-traumatic child's play. *Journal of the American Academy of Child and Adolescent Psychiatry, 20*, 740–759.

Terr, L. C. (1990). *Too scared to cry.* New York: Basic Books.

Tolman, R. (1989). The development of a measure of the psychological maltreatment of women by their male partners. *Violence and Victims, 4*, 159–177.

Turturo, K. A. (1994, August). *An investigation into the relation between marital quality and parenting style.* Presented at the 102nd Annual Convention of the American Psychological Association, Los Angeles, CA.

Walker, L. E. (1983). The battered woman syndrome study. In D. Finkelhor, R. J. Gelles, G. T. Hotaling, & M. A. Straus (Eds.), *The dark side of families: Current family violence research* (pp. 31–49). Beverly Hills, CA: Sage.

Winnicott, D. W. (1965). *The maturational processes and the facilitating environment: Studies in the theory of emotional development.* New York: International Universities Press.

Wolfe, D. A. (1994). *Promoting healthy, nonviolent relationships: A group approach with adolescents for the prevention of woman abuse and interpersonal violence.* London, Canada: University of Western Ontario, Department of Psychology.

Wolfe, D. A. (1996). *Empowering youth to promote non-violence: Issues and solutions.* Newbury Park, CA: Sage.

Wolfe, D. A., Jaffe, P., Wilson, S. K., & Zak, L. (1985). Children of battered women: The relation of child behavior to family violence and maternal stress. *Journal of Consulting and Clinical Psychology, 53,* 657–665.

Wolfe, D. A., & McGee, R. (1994). Dimensions of child maltreatment and their relationship to adolescent adjustment. *Development and Psychopathology, 6,* 165–181.

3

Children Exposed to Marital Conflict and Violence: Conceptual and Theoretical Directions

E. Mark Cummings

Marital discord and violence and children's adjustment problems have long been linked (e.g., Hubbard & Adams, 1936; Towle, 1931). Children from conflictual homes are at risk for both externalizing (e.g., aggression) and internalizing (e.g., anxiety) disorders (Davies & Cummings, 1994; Emery, 1982; Grych & Fincham, 1990; Katz & Gottman, 1993). Marital conflict and violence are also linked with broader family dysfunction (Emery, 1989). For example, marital conflict may mediate the effects of divorce (Amato & Keith, 1991), parental depression (Downey & Coyne, 1990), sexual and physical abuse (Browne & Finkelhor, 1986; Jouriles, Barling, & O'Leary, 1987), and alcoholism (El-Sheikh & Cummings, in press).

Children respond emotionally to adults' disputes. They cry; express anger; freeze; become distressed (e.g., covering their ears with their hands); ask to leave the room; describe discomfort, anxiety, or concern; or report anger, sadness, fear, guilt, shame, or worry. Children may also react physiologically (heart rate, blood pressure, skin conductance, vagal tone), become aggressive, or become involved as third parties, mediating between or comforting angry parents (e.g., E. M. Cummings, 1994; El-Sheikh, Ballard, & Cummings, 1994; Emery, Fincham, & Cummings, 1992; Jouriles, Murphy, & O'Leary, 1989; Katz & Gottman, 1995a).

Marital violence is especially disturbing; it is at a negative extreme of a continuum of marital conflict. From the children's perspective, exposure to marital violence is very distressing, if not emotionally abusing. Although the use of the word *abuse* may be questioned, exposure to marital violence is at the very least a significant source of adversity that contributes to children's risk for the development of psychopathology.

However, the impact of marital violence should not be oversimplified or considered in isolation. Marital conflict is a single element of family functioning, interacting with others in affecting children. Similarly, violence is associated with other behaviors (e.g., throwing things; Jouriles, Norwood, McDonald, Vincent, & Mahoney, 1996) and verbalizations (e.g., threats to leave; Laumakis, Margolin, & John, 1998, this volume) that may exacerbate effects. Moreover, its impact undoubtedly depends on its severity, chronicity, and intensity (Kerig, 1996).

Furthermore, children's response processes (e.g., emotional insecurity, sensitization) are affected by multiple family systems (parent–child, marital, sibling). For example, conduct disorders are increased by problems in the parent–child and marital relationships (Jouriles, Barling, & O'Leary, 1987). Exposure to conflict and violence in one family system affects responses to conflict and violence in other family systems. For example, physical abuse increases children's sensitivity to marital conflicts (E. M. Cummings, Hennessy, Rabideau, & Cicchetti, 1994; Hennessy, Rabideau, Cicchetti, & Cummings, 1994). This chapter begins with a familywide perspective on the implications of marital conflict and violence.

It is useful to order forms of marital discord on a continuum from constructive to destructive. Conflict and violence are expressed in many ways and with widely differing effects and outcomes (E. M. Cummings & Davies, 1994a). Studying only extreme behaviors exaggerates the negative implications of marital conflict and also ignores positive effects of constructive conflict styles on children in better functioning marriages. Whereas violence per se may never be constructive, other conflict styles (e.g., problem solving) are constructive. Some behaviors in conflict situations are beneficial. For example, resolution reduces children's distress (E. M. Cummings, Simpson, & Wilson, 1993; Reiter & El-Sheikh, 1996). As another example, children's concerns are reduced by explanations that parental conflicts do not have long-term or serious negative implications, even when not explicitly resolved (E. M. Cummings & Wilson, in press). In summary, the multiplicity and continuum of forms and levels of marital conflict, aggression, and violence, and their effects on children must be considered. This chapter also considers the effects of specific forms of interadult conflicts on children, including aggression and violence, and evidence for a distinction between constructive and destructive forms of conflict from the children's perspective.

The very complexity of these issues poses significant challenges for research. How does one think about or study the effects of marital conflict on children? What are the significant variables and the likely outcomes? How does one understand how effects of exposure to violence, for example, relate to children's risk for adjustment problems? A variety of useful ways of thinking about these questions have emerged in recent years; they are considered here as a necessary foundation for future, process-oriented study.

Finally, given the knowledge that has accumulated in recent years, theories are needed to organize and make conceptual sense of the data and to point out new directions for study (E. M. Cummings & Davies, 1994a). Recently, evidence has emerged to indicate that children's sensitization to stress caused by exposure to marital conflict and violence may be a key mediating process. Moreover, an emotional security hypothesis (E. M. Cummings & Davies, 1996; Davies & Cummings, 1994) has been proposed as an organizing framework for making theoretical sense of the overall pattern of children's emotional, cognitive, and behavior responses. The chapter ends with a discussion of these theoretical notions regarding the processes mediating child outcomes.

In the following sections, therefore, I examine (a) marital conflict and violence as they pertain to family functioning, (b) conceptualizations relevant to the process-oriented study of marital conflict, (c) marital conflict and violence on a continuum and the distinction between constructive and destructive conflict, and (d) sensitization and emotional insecurity as theoretical constructs for the processes mediating effects of marital conflict and violence on children.

MARITAL CONFLICT AND FAMILY FUNCTIONING

Traditional models of family and child development have focused on parent–child relationships and have paid scant attention to broader family functioning, including marital (or interpartner) relations. For example, family violence and abuse are often considered primarily in terms of the parent's physical abuse of children. However, marital relations, including conflict, are central to children's well-being. Children's exposure to interparental conflict and violence is a significant source of adversity and may contribute to children's risk for psychopathology.

The relation between marital conflict and children's adjustment problems are frequently reported in nonclinical samples but are even more robust in clinical samples (Fincham & Osborne, 1993), particularly when there is marital violence (Jouriles, Bourg, & Farris, 1991; Wolfe, Jaffe, Wilson, & Zak, 1985). The association between interspousal violence and adjustment problems in children is well-established, but until recently it was not widely recognized. Jaffe, Wolfe, and Wilson noted in their 1990 volume, *Children of Battered Women*, that "It was not until the past decade that family discord and spousal violence reached center stage as possible predeterminants of developmental psychopathology" (p. 33).

Comorbidity of Marital Conflict, Adversity, and Abuse Within the Family

Marital conflict and violence, adversity, and abuse can be comorbid conditions (e.g., E. M. Cummings & Davies, 1994a, 1994b; Davies & Cummings, 1994; Grych & Fincham, 1990). For example, marital conflict is associated with increased emotional and financial stress on families, and interparental violence and violence by parents toward children are highly correlated. Marital conflict factors in children's adjustment in homes that are characterized as disturbed for other reasons. Marital conflict is a significant factor in the effects of divorce on children. It may influence children's development long before the divorce occurs (Block, Block, & Gjerde, 1986), and outcomes of divorce in terms of children's adjustment are related to the extent and form of marital conflict (Amato & Keith, 1991). The effects of custody arrangements following divorce also vary significantly as a function of the type and level of marital conflict. Joint custody may not be advisable at all when marital conflict is high or when chronic interparental violence is present, whereas joint custody might be recommended otherwise (Emery, 1994; Johnston & Roseby, 1997). Marital conflict and parental depression also are highly correlated. Recent analyses suggest that marital conflict is a more significant predictor of some forms of adjustment problems than parental depression per se (E. M. Cummings, 1995a; E. M. Cummings & Davies, 1994b, 1996; Downey & Coyne, 1990). Marital conflict and alcoholism are also interrelated. Exposure to interparental conflict and violence are among the most disturbing aspects of parental alcoholism from the children's point of view and may be a predictor of adjustment problems in these children (El-Sheikh & Cummings, in press; West & Prinz, 1987).

In summary, multiple forms of adversity are associated with marital conflict. Models of family adversity, violence, abuse, and child development must incorporate the effects of the marital (or interpartner) system on children's and family's functioning. Including marital factors in the equation is likely to increase the prediction of child outcomes, and, at a conceptual level, to provide a more sophisticated view of the familial causes of child outcomes.

Marital Conflict and the Dysfunction of Other Family Systems

A sole focus on the parent–child system offers a limited and oversimplified view of pathways of influence within the family. Each of the behaviors of parents and children in parent–child interactions is influenced by the quality of the marital relationship and by other family events and relationships outside of the parent–child system (E. M. Cummings & O'Reilly, 1997). Correlations are frequently reported between marital conflict and violence and problems in other family systems (Holden & Ritchie, 1991; Jouriles & Farris, 1992; Jouriles et al., 1991; Katz & Gottman, 1995b). Marital conflict may carry over into parents' interactions with children (Jouriles & Farris, 1992; Mahoney, Boggio, & Jouriles, 1996). Marital conflict is correlated with difficulties in parent–child discipline and child-rearing practices, patterns of coercive family interactions, and negative sibling relationships (E. M. Cummings & Davies, 1994a, 1995). Furthermore, marital conflict fosters the emotional and psychological unavailability and lack of responsiveness of parents, increasing the insecurity of parent–child emotional bonds and the quality of parent–child attachments (Davies & Cummings, 1994). Associations have also been reported between marital conflict and various forms of child abuse. Thus, interspousal aggression and child physical abuse have been linked (e.g., Jouriles et al., 1987). Marital conflict also has been associated with child sexual abuse (e.g., Browne & Finkelhor, 1986).

The evidence thus suggests interrelations between marital conflict, the functioning of other family systems (e.g., family structure; Lindahl & Malik, 1997), and children's risk for the development of psychopathology. After reviewing this evidence, E. M. Cummings and Davies (1994a) concluded that "Children's mental health problems do not develop out of parallel and independent disturbances within the family. Rather, disturbances in each family subsystem affect the other subsystems, and broad problems in family functioning are likely to be associated with negative child outcomes" (p. 106).

On the other hand, positive marital relations and conflict resolution styles may foster positive outcomes in other family systems. Thus, conflict resolution may ameliorate negative emotional reactions to marital conflict and even violence (e.g., E. M. Cummings et al., 1993). Similarly, a healthy parent–child relationship may help children cope with marital conflict. For example, secure parent–child attachments may buffer children from the effects of exposure to marital conflict and violence

(Emery, 1989). Interrelations between family systems are outlined in Figure 1.

Cumulative Impact of Family Stress

Marital (or interpartner) conflict and violence and dysfunction in other family systems may have a cumulative impact on negative emotional and behavioral processes in children. Marital discord is associated with children's emotional and behavioral disregulation, attempts to control or regulate the dysfunctional interactions between the mother and father, and representations of the self and family members' relationships that are more negative and pessimistic about the future (Davies & Cummings, 1994). These response processes in children are similar to those linked with the impact on children of dysfunction in other family systems, such as coercive parent–child relations or insecure parent–child attachment (e.g., E. M. Cummings & Davies, 1994a; Davies & Cummings, 1994). Children's own dispositions (e.g., temperament) also interact with problems in family functioning in influencing the likelihood that children develop dysfunctional coping responses, processes, and styles (Davies & Cummings, 1994). Dysfunctional coping responses, processes, and styles, in turn, are linked with the development of psychopathology. Figure 1 illustrates how multiple family systems may affect common processes in children. In this regard, Patrick Davies and I (E. M. Cummings & Davies, 1994a) surveyed the literature and proposed that multiple forms of "family adversity may affect children's development through their action on common processes and mechanisms. Consequently, . . . joint effects may occur, which could be additive, interactive, or multiplicative" (p. 108).

Learning, negative reinforcement, and modeling may also be factors in the common impact of marital and parent–child systems on children. That is, children may learn behavioral and cognitive styles for coping with everyday events both from observing their parents in interparental situations and from their own interacting with the parents. Beach (1996) reported that maternal attributions of causality, internality, and globality in analogue conflict situations with a "spouse" were significantly correlated with similar attributional styles on similar di-

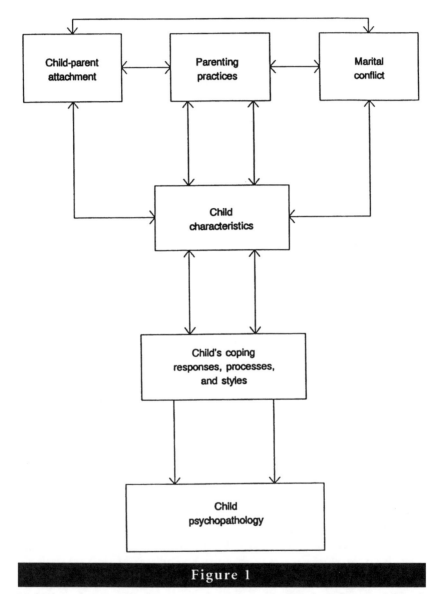

Figure 1

Multiple pathways and processes in the impact of marital conflict on children's coping styles and adjustment. From *Children and Marital Conflict: The Impact of Family Dispute and Resolution* (p. 89) by E. M. Cummings and P. T. Davies, 1994, New York: Guilford Press. Copyright 1994 by Guilford Press. Reprinted by permission.

mensions in their children's responses to analogue conflict situations with a "peer." Statistically significant relations were also found between maternal positive communications and positive reciprocity in analogue conflict situations with a "spouse" and children's similar behaviors with a "peer," suggesting that children may learn constructive lessons about handling conflict situations from constructive parental models for handling conflict.

As another example, children who witness spousal abuse exhibit adjustment problems similar to those of children who are victims of parental violence (Jaffe et al., 1986). Similarly, exposure to one form of violence in the family may affect reactions to others (e.g., Hennessy et al., 1994). With regard to the physical, emotional, and sexual abuse of children, Jaffe et al. (1990) stated that "it is widely acknowledged that . . . different forms of maltreatment also give rise to many of the same developmental adjustment problems, suggesting that very similar psychological processes may be commonly responsible for the children's reactions to trauma" (p. 68). In summary, increasing evidence suggests that (a) marital conflict is a significant source of adversity and risk for adjustment problems for children in families, and (b) marital conflict and other forms of adversity in the family are interrelated. Similarly, positive marital relations and marital satisfaction may support positive functioning in families, fostering children's adaptive development (E. M. Cummings & O'Reilly, 1997). Marital relations serve as a foundation for emotional processes and their regulation within the family and thus have a role in modulating, ameliorating, or exaggerating the risk associated with other family events. Marital relations lay a foundation for consistency, solidarity, and warmth across family subsystems (Lindahl & Malik, 1997). Marital relations may also mediate the quality of sibling relations (Stocker, Stall, & Ahmed, 1997). However, an important caveat is that researchers' understanding of these processes and relationships is at an early stage; it is largely based on global assessments of family events and their interrelations and on correlational analyses. Research is needed on process-oriented methods that can support more conclusive results.

PROCESS-ORIENTED MODELS: TOWARD AN UNDERSTANDING OF PROCESSES MEDIATING CHILD OUTCOMES

Correlations between marital conflict and violence and child adjustment are well-established; their further documentation has reached a point of diminishing returns. The study of family violence and adversity should move to the next stage: the careful differentiation between and among the processes mediating child outcomes. Researchers and clinicians should be increasingly concerned with identifying (a) causal relations, (b) directions of effect, and (c) multiple pathways of effect (E. M. Cummings, 1995b; Fincham & Osborne, 1993; Grych & Fincham, in press-a). To move in this direction, new ways of thinking about the effects of marital conflict and violence on children are needed (E. M. Cummings & Davies, 1994a). In this next section, I examine stress and coping approaches and the developmental psychopathology perspective, in particular, as useful conceptual directions toward thinking about mediating processes.

Stress and Coping Approach

The stress and coping approach offers a useful heuristic for conceptualizing complex social processes at a microsocial level. Lazarus and Folkman (1984), who pioneered this approach, defined *stress* as "a particular relationship between the person and the environment that is appraised by the person as taxing or exceeding his or her resources and endangering his or her well-being" (p. 19). *Coping* is conceptualized as a dynamic process, that is, "the changing thoughts and acts that the individual uses to manage the external and/or internal demands of a specific person–environment transaction that is appraised as stressful" (Folkman, 1991, p. 5).

When coping is viewed from a contextual perspective, emphasis is placed on the specific thoughts and acts that the individual uses to cope with specific contexts, as guided by personal appraisals of situations, especially perceived ability to cope (i.e., coping efficacy). Individual differences also figure prominently, including personal dispositions, family history, age, and gender. Interactions between the individual and specific environmental contexts find expression in multidimensional coping processes and strategies that develop into stable patterns leading over time to either adjustment or maladjustment in functioning (see also Grych & Fincham, 1990; Sroufe & Rutter, 1984).

Furthermore, family adversity does not lead directly to diagnoses of psychopathology in children. The development of psychopathology in family contexts reflects a series of microsocial processes that occur interactively over a period of time, reflecting gradual adaptations by children to family circumstances. Coping patterns that develop in specific social contexts mediate relations between family background and experiences, on the one hand, and child development outcomes, on the other.

Thus, negative outcomes in children develop over time as a result of person–environment interactions that gradually shape how children respond and react to socio-emotional events and interactions. The "product" of marital conflict and violence are specific, maladaptive emotional, social, and cognitive response patterns and dispositions. Adjustment problems in children are most informatively understood in terms of coping processes, as opposed to simply diagnostic classification (E. M. Cummings & El-Sheikh, 1991). Thus, a stress and coping approach to the study of the impact of adverse family conflict and violence on children outlines a way of articulating the active response processes of individual children in specific family contexts that may lead to and underlie diagnostic classifications (see Figure 1).

Inspired by this approach, several years ago we (E. M. Cummings & Cummings, 1988) proposed a process-oriented framework for approaching the study of the impact of marital conflict on children. Our initial model is presented in Figure 2. This model posited that children's family background of experiences, their own personal characteristics, and the context and stimulus characteristics of anger expressions each influenced their stress and coping responses, which could be conceptualized in terms of specific cognitive, emotional, social, or physiological responses or, more broadly, as coping strategies or styles. We further posited that over time, these response patterns would contribute to

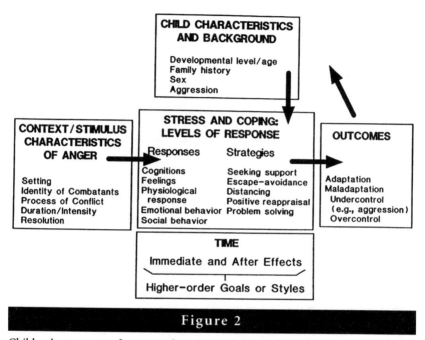

Figure 2

Children's processes of stress and coping with marital conflict. From "A Process-Oriented Approach to Children's Coping With Adults' Angry Behavior," by E. M. Cummings & J. S. Cummings, 1988, *Developmental Review*, 3, p. 299. Copyright 1988 by Academic Press. Reprinted by permission.

adaptive functioning or, alternatively, to maladaptive outcomes reflecting adjustment problems.

This model placed emphasis on studying specific contexts of exposure to marital conflict; individual differences between children in coping responses, including their histories of exposure to marital conflict; and the multidimensional nature of coping processes. This model was followed by a long series of process-oriented empirical investigations that relied primarily on analogue (e.g., E. M. Cummings, 1987) but also field (e.g., E. M. Cummings, Davies, & Simpson, 1994; Grych, Seid, & Fincham, 1992) methods to specify more precisely causal relations at a microsocial level. These new findings are extensively reviewed, and their implications for marital and family functioning considered, in *Children and Marital Conflict* (E. M. Cummings & Davies, 1994a).

Our 1988 framework was followed by Grych and Fincham's (1990) model, which further advanced conceptualizations of the role of children's appraisal processes in coping with marital conflict. Theoretical models have been expanded to consider the impact of marital conflict on children through changes in the family system's functioning, especially parent–child relations (E. M. Cummings & Davies, 1994a). More recently we have presented a theory of the role of children's sense of emotional security in organizing and directing children's coping processes and adjustment in reaction to marital conflict (E. M. Cummings & Davies, 1996; Davies & Cummings, 1994).

The model in Figure 2 thus provides bases for conceptualizing multiple pathways of effect associated with marital conflict from a stress and coping perspective. In addition, this model can be elaborated to incorporate the impact of other forms of child adversity, including but not limited to marital conflict and violence. For example, one can consider the context or stimulus characteristics of family adversity more generally (e.g., divorce and custody, child maltreatment, parental depression, alcoholism), rather than limiting the model to marital anger expression as a family context. Moreover, the conceptualization of family history can be broadened to include histories of adversity in addition to marital conflict. Similarly, children's emotional security is posited to derive from parental behavior toward children (e.g., hostility or abuse, emotional unresponsiveness or neglect) and from marital conflict history. Recent work has moved toward broadening theoretical models of family adversity and further developing conceptualizations of emotional security and other processes that account for the effects of these experiences on children's development (E. M. Cummings & Davies, 1994a, 1996).

A Developmental Psychopathology Perspective

A developmental psychopathology perspective also emphasizes dynamic processes of interaction between multiple intra- and extra-organismic factors, as contrasted with traditional relatively static notions of associations between global characterizations of family backgrounds and child outcomes. The study of process is again assumed to require the examination of multiple domains and responses (e.g., cognitive, emotional, physiological) and also effects that emerge over time. For example, a child exposed to marital violence may even act as a caretaker for the parents and appear to be functioning well. However, these undue burdens on the child may contribute to the development of problems that emerge much later (hence the label *sleeper effects*).

Contextual factors associated with person–environment interactions are assumed to underlie process. Thus, the meaning and interpretation that children ascribe to marital conflict and violence in the broader context of the family may also be at least as significant as the occurrence of particular interparental behaviors. Conceivably, children may evidence little negative outcome if parents are very expressive and emotional during conflicts but usually resolve their disagreements. On the other hand, children may have difficulty adjusting when parents rarely fight openly, but any occurrence of conflict seems to carry serious implications for the future intactness of the family. Certain nonviolent anger expressions may be as distressing to children as violent behaviors. For example, parental threats to leave the family may upset children as much as exposure to physical violence (Laumakis, Margolin, & John, 1998).

Another emphasis is the study of developmental processes underlying both normal development and adjustment problems. It is assumed that a focus only on extremes provides a limited window into mediating processes. With regard to marital conflict, specific types and intensities of conflict elicit very different responses from children, so that a focus on one element of conflict (e.g., overt violence) yields limited information about the effects of conflict and violence on children and a potentially narrow, even misleading, perspective on key mediating processes and developmental sequelae. Thus, the study of harmonious and adverse family contexts are mutually informative and essential to the emergence of understanding of process.

Furthermore, from the standpoint of understanding process, children who do not develop problems growing up in high-risk environments are just as interesting as those who do, but the focus has traditionally been on those children who develop psychopathology. What protective factors, or personal or environmental sources of resiliency, account for children's adaptive outcomes in very adverse circumstances? Conversely, children from low-risk family environments who develop adjustment problems are at least as interesting for the advancement of the understanding of mediating processes as those who develop competently. What stress factors, or personal or environmental sources of vulnerability, explain why some children have difficulty when most do not? Again, the study of the range of family environments around issues of marital conflict and violence is likely to advance understanding (see also Grych & Fincham, in press-b).

Researchers who study stress and adversity have neglected positive processes and events. The developmental psychopathology perspective also calls attention to the significance of these events to understanding development in adverse family circumstances. Studying resiliency, compensatory, and protective factors, in particular, are promising directions for an advanced understanding of the role of positive processes in children's functioning when there is marital conflict or violence. For example, the absence of positive communications may be as significant as the presence of negative conflict behaviors: Beach (1996) reported that children's perceptions of low positive marital communications were significant predictors of children's adjustment problems, independent of conflict behaviors.

Exposure to Violence: Persisting, Not Short-Term, Effects

Acts of hostility and violence between parents may be relatively rare and short-lived, even in discordant marriages. However, the effects of exposure to these events are not short-lived or limited to the time of exposure to these events. On the contrary, children's fundamental notions of the quality and safety of marital and family relations may be profoundly influenced by their (relatively infrequent) exposure to marital conflict and violence. For example, exposure to acts of marital violence may threaten and undermine children's sense of the predictability and warmth within the family, causing children to worry, be chronically aroused, and feel threatened and emotionally distressed. Because these events can have such impact, they may significantly affect children's general patterns of emotional, cognitive, and behavioral functioning, not only to marital conflict, but to a wide range of familial and extrafamilial stressors. Histories of exposure to marital conflict and violence repeatedly have been linked with children's patterns of emotional, behavioral, and cognitive coping with stress in other contexts; these response patterns, in turn, have been linked with children's risk for adjustment problems (E. M. Cummings & Davies, 1994a). Appreciating the potentially wide-ranging impact of children's exposure to acts of interparental conflict and violence is essential to conceptualizing the mediating processes that may be set in motion by such exposures.

Mediating Processes: Gender and Age Differences

Marital conflict and violence have been associated with distress and risk for adjustment problems for children of all ages (E. M. Cummings & Davies, 1994a). However, mediating processes and outcomes may vary significantly by the age and gender of the children. Research has usually been concerned with children up to about 10 years of age, but increasing evidence suggests that older children also are affected. For example, Harold and Conger (1997) reported that marital conflict was associated with adolescent distress, increased risk for internalizing problems, and increased risk for externalizing problems among boys. Moreover, there may be important differences in processes mediating outcomes for boys and girls. Self-blame has been more closely linked with adjustment problems in girls, whereas coping efficacy and perceived threat have been more closely linked with adjustment in boys (E. M. Cummings, Davies, & Simpson, 1994; Kerig, 1997).

Differences between boys and girls in mediating processes may also change with age. For example, several studies have reported that in childhood, boys are more prone to angry reactions and girls to sadness in response to adults' conflict, but that by later childhood and early adolescence boys more often react with sadness whereas girls more frequently react with anger (E. M. Cummings, Ballard, & El-Sheikh, 1991; E. M. Cummings, Ballard, El-Sheikh, & Lake, 1991).

It is also important to distinguish between the conflict behavior of fathers and mothers. Osborne and Fincham (1996) investigated child outcomes and showed that the association between marital conflict and father–child relations provides information over and beyond that provided by only including the path from marital conflict to mother–child relations. Kerig, Cowan, and Cowan (1993) reported that fathers with higher marital satisfaction were more positive and assertive with their first-born daughters, compared to their first-born sons, and their daughters were more compliant with their commands. Another study reported that girls judged their fathers to be more angry than did boys, even though independent observers did not note such differences between fathers of boys and girls (Crockenberg & Forgays, 1996).

The study of processes mediating relations between marital conflict and violence and child outcomes is underway. A related, recurring theme is the need to differentiate between constructive and destructive conflict. What is known about positive and negative forms of marital conflict and their effects on children's functioning? This question is addressed in the next section.

MARITAL CONFLICT ON A CONTINUUM: THE DISTINCTION BETWEEN DESTRUCTIVE AND CONSTRUCTIVE CONFLICT

Studies of the effects on children of relatively negative versus positive forms of marital conflict styles largely have been based on analogue methods (E. M. Cummings & Davies, 1994a). This is a methodological limitation. However, because of the absence of questionnaires (until recently) that adequately discriminated forms of conflict styles and the ethical concerns raised by inducing marital conflicts in front of children, researchers have largely relied on analogue methods (E. M. Cummings, 1995b). Although these methods offer precision and experimental control, support from field methods is needed so that firm generalizations can be made, particularly for some findings. I note below when results of analogue procedures and field instruments have produced converging results.

Conflict Behaviors That Increase Children's Distress

Physical Aggression or Violence

In analogue studies, children reported that they perceived conflicts involving aggression as more negative and described more negative emotional reactions to these conflicts than to conflicts that did not involve aggression (e.g., E. M. Cummings et al., 1989). This finding has also received support from parental reports of children's reactions in the home (E. M. Cummings, Zahn-Waxler, & Radke-Yarrow, 1981). The pattern of results indicates that physical violence is among the most disturbing forms of marital interaction for children, and it is the most clearly linked with their adjustment problems.

However, other forms of aggression are also disturbing for children and are related to children's adjustment problems. Ballard and Cummings (1990) reported that children reacted as negatively to analogue presentations of parental aggression toward objects as to interpartner aggression. In addition, Jouriles et al. (1996) found that other forms of marital aggression (e.g., insulting or swearing at the partner; throwing, smashing, or kicking something; threatening to hit or throw something at the partner) and marital violence were each correlated with children's adjustment problems in a marital therapy sample and a women's shelter sample, respectively. Furthermore, the other forms of marital aggression assessed still related to children's adjustment problems, even after controlling for the frequency of marital violence.

Some types of conflicts may contain messages that children find as disturbing as marital violence. Thus, Laumakis et al. (1998) reported that conflicts involving threats to leave and physical aggression elicited similar, high levels of negative reactions from children. Moreover, such conflicts elicited more negative emotional reactions and predictions of negative outcomes than conflicts with name-calling, negative voice, or positive affect. These results support the notion that children react to the negative implications of marital conflict for marital and family relationships and support the consideration of multiple types and expressions of marital and family conflict and violence in models of the effects of extreme marital discord on children.

Nonverbal Conflict or the Silent Treatment

These forms of conflict expression are not adequately assessed by any of the questionnaire instruments for recording rates of forms of marital conflict in the home. However, children's reactions to analogue presentations of nonverbal conflict or the silent treatment indicate that they are significantly distressed by these behaviors, and, in some studies, reactions are indistinguishable from reactions to verbal conflicts (e.g., E. M. Cummings, Ballard, & El-Sheikh, 1991).

Intense Conflicts and Conflicts About Child-Related Themes

A single analogue study (Grych & Fincham, 1993) supports the intuitively appealing notion that more intense conflicts elicit more negative reactions than less intense conflicts. The notion that conflicts about child-related themes are more distressing than conflicts about other issues also was supported (Grych & Fincham, 1993), although a recent study was inconclusive on this point (Davies, Myers, & Cummings, 1996).

Withdrawal

In addition to overt conflict behavior, the withdrawal of parents from conflict may signal marital distress to children. Katz and Gottman (1997) recently reported that husband withdrawal, indexed by observationally based codes of husband anger and stonewalling, predicted children's increased risk for adjustment problems. Cox, Paley, and Payne (1997) found that marital withdrawal was more predictive of child outcomes than marital conflict. Another recent study reported that mothers' and fathers' avoidance or capitulation were each related to children's behavior problems (Mahoney, Lape, Query, & Wieber, 1997).

Contextual Factors: Parents' Positive Communications and Self-Perceptions

Beach (1996) found that the children of mothers who reported less ability to make themselves feel better emotionally following negative confrontations with a "spouse" in an analogue conflict situation had higher rates of adjustment problems. Furthermore, as noted above, children who reported low maternal positive communication in conflict situations were also more likely to have adjustment problems. Brody, Arias, and Fincham (1996) reported that parental attributional styles about conflict were related to children's attributional styles and risk for adjustment problems.

Conflict Behaviors That Reduce Children's Distress

Mutually Respectful, Emotionally Modulated Conflicts

In one of the few studies to examine children's reactions to actual marital discussions of disagreements in the presence of children in the laboratory, Easterbrooks, Cummings, and Emde (1994) reported that toddlers evidenced little distress in reaction to a conflictual discussion between parents in a sample of parents who almost always expressed conflicts in mutually respectful and emotionally well-modulated tones. On the other hand, parental anger expression, which was relatively uncommon, was associated with negative emotional reactions by children.

Conflict Resolution

A long series of analogue studies has demonstrated that children's distress, and other negative reactions, are dramatically reduced when conflicts are resolved (see E. M. Cummings & Davies, 1994a, and Davies & Cummings, 1994, for extensive reviews). The highly controlled presentation of stimuli leaves little doubt that conflict resolution was responsible for the reduction in negative responding, which has significant theoretical implications regarding the importance of the meaning of conflicts, rather than simply their occurrence, for children's reactions. Moreover, a recent field study that used a new questionnaire to assess conflict resolution reported that marital conflict resolution was more consistently associated with child adjustment (i.e., reduced adjustment problems) than even negative elements of conflict (e.g., frequency, severity; Kerig, 1996).

Furthermore, conflict resolution may sometimes ameliorate the negative impact on children of exposure to marital violence. E. M. Cummings et al. (1993) found ameliorative effects of conflict resolution on children's emotional responses to conflicts that were nonverbal or verbal or that included physical aggression. Similarly, Cheskes and El-

Sheikh (1996) found that conflict resolution ameliorated children's negative emotional reactions for each of these types of conflicts. In this instance children were asked to respond as though the actors were their parents.

However, it should be noted that children were responding to analogue presentations in these two studies. Moreover, the actors' resolutions appeared genuine, and there was no history of prior conflict to compromise the apparent sincerity of the resolutions. As is contended throughout this chapter, children react to the meaning of conflicts for marital and family relations on the basis of their past histories of exposure to conflict and the nature and form of current conflict stimuli. Although the question awaits empirical testing, children's responses to resolution may not be positive if marital violence has occurred chronically in the past within the family, even following supposed resolutions. On the other hand, conflict resolution may be relatively uncommon in high-conflict homes, so that such endings to conflicts might well carry more (rather than less) weight for such children. Consistent with this notion, Hennessy et al. (1994) found that physically abused children from high-conflict homes benefited more, rather than less, from conflict resolution than a comparison group.

However, a distinction should be made between ameliorated marital violence and constructive conflict. The model for disrespect, hostility, and negativity toward a loved one indicated by violent behavior militates against marital violence ever being constructive. Nonetheless, the meaning of marital violence for children may be ameliorated by conflict resolutions or apologies, that is, the perception that the immediate threat and danger to the self, marriage, and family may be reduced. The extent to which children's emotional security is increased is likely to depend on the broader pattern of marital interactions. The severity and chronicity of violence are likely to be critical, that is, constructive messages may be more perceptible when marital aggression is relatively low in intensity (e.g., a single, low-intensity behavior) than when violence is intense, prolonged, and chronic. In summary, the relative impact of marital violence followed by resolution or apologies depends on children's past and current appraisals and emotionality in response to marital conflict and violence; at the same time, however, children (marriages and families) are likely to benefit from any progress toward resolution and positive endings, even in the most negative family contexts.

Unfortunately, current field instruments and methods have only begun to incorporate this dimension into assessments, so that correspondences between the (extensive) support for the beneficial effects of conflict resolution found in a series of varied analogue tests remains to be thoroughly examined by field research. On the other hand, the results are very powerful, and there are no conflicting data. Furthermore, a recent study adapting a method for obtaining parental report of conflict resolution in the home provides support for the notion that marital conflict resolution is linked with children's emotional security and positive adjustment outcomes (Davies & Cummings, in press; see also Myers, 1997).

Progress Toward Resolution and Other Information About Resolution

Analogue studies also indicate that children benefit from any progress toward resolution, that is, distress reactions are reduced even when parents (actors) do not fully resolve conflicts. Furthermore, and somewhat surprisingly, children's distress reactions are reduced greatly even when adults have resolved conflicts behind closed doors, only indicating resolution by changed (to positive) affect after emerging from another room entered in the midst of conflict. Children also benefit from hearing brief explanations that conflicts are resolved (E. M. Cummings, Simpson, & Wilson, 1993) or even that conflicts are not resolved but that parents expect that they will be (E. M. Cummings & Wilson, in press). Furthermore, children are sensitive to the emotional as well as thematic content of conflict resolution (Shifflett-Simpson & Cummings, 1996). That is, children are slightly more distressed by an angry apology than a friendly apology, but any form of apology elicits much less self-reported concern about the parents (actors) and personal distress than continued conflict.

Impact of Conflict Histories: Sensitization

Children's conflict histories in the home also predict their responding to conflicts. The findings support a "sensitization hypothesis," that is, histories of exposure to background anger, marital conflict, and inter-parental violence are predictors of children's greater emotional (e.g., distress), behavioral (e.g., aggression), and social (e.g., mediation in parental disputes) reactions to marital conflict, which, in turn, are linked with their increased risk for adjustment problems.

Sensitization is reported in controlled analogue studies in which children's responses to "marital conflict" are examined (e.g., E. M. Cummings, Vogel, Cummings, & El-Sheikh, 1989; El-Sheikh, 1997). Evidence for sensitization caused by repeated exposure to marital conflict is also found in field studies of children's reactions to actual marital conflicts (E. M. Cummings et al., 1981; E. M. Cummings, Zahn-Waxler, & Radke-Yarrow, 1984), laboratory simulations of conflict (E. M. Cummings, Iannotti, & Zahn-Waxler, 1985), and parental report of marital conflict histories (e.g., Ballard, Cummings, & Larkin, 1993; J. S. Cummings, Pellegrini, Notarius, & Cummings, 1989; Gordis, Margolin, & John, 1997; O'Brien, Margolin, John, & Krueger, 1991; Rogers & Holmbeck, 1997).

Thus, Laumakis et al. (1998) reported that children from high-conflict homes evaluated conflicts more negatively than children from low-conflict homes, with boys exposed to high-conflict marriages more likely to report an intervention response, particularly in response to marital physical aggression. Furthermore, when conflict "histories" are artificially created in the laboratory, results are consistent with the pre-dictions of the sensitization hypothesis (e.g., E. M. Cummings et al., 1985; El-Sheikh & Cummings, 1995; El-Sheikh, Cummings, & Reiter, in press).

These results have important theoretical implications for under-standing the processes that mediate the impact of marital conflict on children's adjustment. In particular, these results suggest that emotional, behavioral, and social dysregulation caused by parental conflicts and evident during exposure to marital conflict mediates the impact of mar-ital conflict and violence on children. It is not difficult to imagine how children's greater proneness to dysregulation in the face of stressful family events might lead to the development of adjustment problems over time (E. M. Cummings & El-Sheikh, 1991). The process of sen-sitization is thus emerging as a key suspect in the search for the processes that mediate children's risk for adjustment problems caused by their exposure to marital conflict and violence.

Other findings worthy of note include the following: (a) There appear to be consistent individual differences in reactions to conflict organized around patterns of emotional responding (E. M. Cummings, 1987); (b) these individual differences appear to be stable over time (E. M. Cummings, 1987; E. M. Cummings et al., 1984); and (c) patterns of family violence (e.g., child physical abuse) are associated with increased sensitization to parental conflicts (e.g., E. M. Cummings, Hennessy, Rabideau, & Cicchetti, 1994). These findings suggest that processes mediating responding to marital conflict are stable; they are related to broader patterns of individual functioning, particularly surrounding emotional regulation; and they also are related to general patterns of conflict and violence in the family. Finally, several recent studies document that exposure to marital conflict affects children both directly because of exposure and indirectly by changing parenting practices (e.g., Harold & Conger, 1997; Harold, Fincham, Osborne, & Conger, 1997; Harrist & Ainslie, in press; Margolin, Christensen, & John, 1996; O'Brien, Bahadur, Gee, Balto, & Erber, 1997).

THEORETICAL MODELS: AN EMOTIONAL SECURITY HYPOTHESIS

Although relations between marital conflict and violence and children's adjustment problems are long established, only recently has progress been made toward a comprehensive theoretical account. Several theoretical models recently have been advanced for these relations (Crockenberg & Forgays, 1996; Davies & Cummings, 1994; Emery, 1989; Feldman & Downey, 1994; Grych & Fincham, 1990; Wilson & Gottman, 1995). These models are complementary and emphasize similar points. Common elements among the models include the following: (a) Children react to the meaning of marital conflicts for the child, family, and marriage, not just the occurrence of conflict; and (b) the meaning is personal and emotional and is related to children's appraisals and emotional reactions to conflict, not just the fact of conflict (see especially Harold et al., 1997).

However, the identification of contextual, emotional, and cognitive factors that mediate outcomes, and even evidence for sensitization, does not constitute a comprehensive theory that explains why and how marital conflict affects children. How do children evaluate meaning? How does this process of emotional and cognitive evaluation make sense in terms of processes known to be important to children from the perspective of developmental theory?

Davies and Cummings (1994) proposed that children evaluate meaning in terms of their assessment of the emotional security implications of marital conflict for themselves and the family. Children have good reasons to be concerned about destructive marital conflict: It is emotionally unpleasant, has negative implications for important family relationships, declines the quality of parenting, can proliferate to include the child, and increases the likelihood of long-term family problems. Emotional security is also related to other processes evident in child development and general family functioning, part of the whole of child and family development, and not a new process unrelated to reactions to other family events. The notion of emotional security is consistent with more general family and child development models, and specifically the literature on parent–child attachment. This construct has a long history in psychiatry, psychoanalytic, and clinical traditions. Based on the data, which suggest the primacy and immediacy of emotionality in reactions to conflict, and a functionalist perspective that posits that emotions serve appraisal and organizing functions, we (E. M. Cummings & Davies, 1996) proposed that an emotional security hypothesis described a key domain of processes mediating relations between marital conflict and violence and children's adjustment. This hypothesis is described in further detail.

Specific Theoretical Definition

Emotional security as a construct appears to have a shared, implicit definition in the literature. However, the concept has rarely been subject to precise definition. To address this gap, Patrick Davies and I have presented an explicit definition of emotional security (E. M. Cummings & Davies, 1996):

Emotional security is a latent construct that can be inferred from the overall organization and meaning of children's emotions, behaviors, thoughts, and physiological responses, and serves as a set goal by which children regulate their own functioning in social contexts, thereby directing social, emotional, cognitive, and physiological reactions. (p. 126)

Thus, whereas recent theory stresses that children react to conflict in terms of their assessment of the meaning of conflict for family functioning and their own well-being, the emotional security hypothesis proposes that the emotional security implications of conflicts are especially important. Building on attachment theory (Sroufe & Waters, 1977), emotional security is seen as a paramount factor in children's regulation of emotional arousal and organization and in their motivation to respond in the face of marital conflict. Emotional security is conceptualized from a contextualistic perspective, emphasizing the interplay between socio-emotional and biological processes. Although emotional security is described as the set goal of regulatory functioning, as noted above, various specific regulatory systems are conceptualized to be subsumed within emotional security as an operating process, that is, emotional regulation, regulation of exposure to family affect, and internal representations of family relations. An important implication for the study of the distinction between constructive versus destructive conflict from the children's perspective is that contexts of marital conflict are evaluated by children in terms of their emotional security implications for the child and the family, and these appraisals, in turn, serve to motivate and regulate children's emotional regulation, regulation of exposure to marital conflict, and internal representations of marital relations. In other words, children do not just react to the occurrence of marital conflict but to whether marital conflict has destructive versus constructive implications for personal and family functioning from the child's point of view.

Theoretical Tenets

The emotional security hypothesis thus specifies a particular meaning against which children appraise the implications of marital and family conflict for themselves and their families, suggests how that meaning is personal, and indicates why children respond emotionally (Davies & Cummings, 1994). In important respects this model builds on and complements the cognitive–contextual model proposed by Grych and Fincham (1990), which stresses how children's cognitive processing and coping behaviors are shaped by the characteristics of marital conflict and contextual factors such as past experience with conflict, gender, expectations, and mood. However, although cognition is acknowledged as important to coping processes, the present model places greater emphasis on emotionality in the very emotion-laden domain of family conflict and, specifically, the significance of emotional security to children's reactions to marital conflict. The key theoretical proposition follows from Davies and Cummings (1994):

> Children's concerns about emotional security play a role in their regulation for emotional arousal and organization and motivation to respond in the face of marital conflict. Over time these response processes have implications for children's long-term adjustment. Emotional security is seen as a product of past experience and primary influence on future responding. (p. 387)

Specific Component Regulatory Systems

The emotional security hypothesis describes the goal of children's functioning in the face of marital conflict. However, various specific regulatory systems are subsumed within emotional security as an operating process (E. M. Cummings & Davies, 1996). These specific components are separate, but also interdependent, in the service of emotional security. The definition of emotional security in terms of these specific systems also articulates specific measurement requirements and avenues toward the precise assessment of emotional security as a mediating process in the face of marital conflict. Each component is assumed to be a function of both current stimuli and past exposures to interparental relations. Specific, multimethod strategies toward the operationalization of these processes have been articulated (e.g., Davies & Cummings, in press).

Emotion Regulation

The emotion regulation component is not the equivalent of emotional security but rather a subset or component. This component consists of children's emotional reactivity and arousal and their capacity to reduce, enhance, and maintain their emotionality in the face of conflict. It can be inferred from subjective report of feelings, overt expression of emotion, and physiological arousal.

Internal Representation of Family Relations

Children's internal representations reflect their appraisals of family events and their active processing of the meaning that events have for their own well-being. This appraisal is a reflection of their sense of emotional security and the implication of events for emotional security. As noted by Grych and Fincham (1990), these internal representations include their primary assessment of the self-relevance and threat of events, and their secondary appraisal of who is responsible, why it is occurring, and whether they have adequate coping skills.

Regulation of Exposure to Family Affect

Children may also attempt to regulate their emotional security by controlling their exposure to marital conflict. The issues with regard to an assessment of emotional security include the repertoire of children's regulatory activities and behaviors (e.g., forms and styles of mediation behaviors), their threshold for onset, and their appropriateness in specific contexts.

Supporting Evidence

For a comprehensive test, a rigorous, multivariate, longitudinal design is required that can effectively test the full construct and distinguish cause-and-effect relations during children's development over time. Although the data marshaled can only be suggestive until the model is tested formally in this way, evidence to support more extensive testing has accumulated. The following summarizes some of the supporting evidence, some of it only suggestive, some of it more cogent:

1. The notion that children evaluate conflict in terms of its emotional

security implications can explain why negative reactions to conflict are so dramatically ameliorated by conflict resolution and why children are so sensitive to any evidence about possible resolution, even when resolutions may be much briefer than conflict episodes. That is, children are concerned about the meaning of conflicts for themselves and their families, not just the occurrence of conflict. Conflict resolution greatly changes the familial implications of otherwise concern-making social situations. Specifically, conflict resolution changes the emotional security implications of conflict.

2. The construct can account for why children evidence sensitization, rather than habituation, when they have histories of exposure to high marital conflict in the home, especially violence. It makes sense that children from such homes would become more activated, because these events are more threatening, realistically, for them. That is, when there is high marital conflict, it is more likely that conflicts proliferate to include the children and that conflicts have more negative short- and long-term implications for the child and family. Even though these children are more distressed, it makes sense for them also to be more likely to try to intervene in conflicts, given the implications (Emery, 1989). In other words, conflicts pose a greater threat to their sense of emotional security.

3. Emotional reactions predict behavioral responses, aggression, self-reported cognitions and feelings, and even heart rate responses (e.g., E. M. Cummings, 1987), whereas other levels of responding thus far have not, which suggests an organizing role of emotionality. In an analogue test, inducing different emotional states systematically predicted differences in multiple types of reactions to interadult conflicts, supporting the basic proposition that emotionality, or the emotional set-point, motivates responding (Davies & Cummings, 1995).

4. The most convincing support is a recent study indicating that multimethod assessments of emotional security mediated relations between qualitative aspects of marital conflict and qualitative differences in child outcomes (Davies & Cummings, in press). In this concurrent test, support was found for a theoretical pathway

whereby negative marital conflict properties led to children's adjustment problems as mediated by reduced emotional security about marital relations. By contrast, greater emotional security mediated a pathway between constructive marital conflict properties (e.g., marital conflict resolution) and reduced adjustment problems. Of the components of emotional security, children's regulation of negative emotionality in reaction to marital conflict was the strongest mediator, but children's representations of the quality of marital relations also mediated relations between marital conflict and child adjustment.

Again, the caveat should be made that this is a new theory and that much of the current support is suggestive, or supports only some propositions, rather than being conclusive. However, after decades of study in the absence of theory, it is important to get on with the business of proposing and improving on theoretical models for the impact of marital conflict and violence on children.

CONCLUSION

The study of relations between marital conflict and violence and child adjustment has made great strides since Emery's (1982) classic formulation of the issues over a decade ago. However, this area of study is at a crossroads, with new methodological and theoretical directions required for future significant advances to occur. This chapter outlines directions for the future study of relations between marital conflict and the family and a theoretical model to guide future research that is consistent with the data in this area and broader traditions in the study of child development and family functioning.

REFERENCES

Amato, P. R., & Keith, B. (1991). Consequences of parental divorce for children's well-being: A meta-analysis. *Psychological Bulletin, 110*, 26–46.

Ballard, M., & Cummings, E. M. (1990). Response to adults' angry behavior in children of alcoholic and non-alcoholic parents. *Journal of Genetic Psychology, 151*, 195–210.

Ballard, M. E., Cummings, E. M., & Larkin, K. (1993). Emotional and cardiovascular responses to adults' angry behavior and challenging tasks in children of hypertensive and normotensive parents. *Child Development, 64*, 500–515.

Beach, B. (1996). *The relation between marital conflict and child adjustment: An examination of parental and child repertoires.* Unpublished manuscript.

Block, J. H., Block, J., & Gjerde, P. J. (1986). The personality of children prior to divorce. *Child Development, 57*, 827–840.

Brody, G. H., Arias, I., & Fincham, F. D. (1996). Linking marital and child attributions to family processes and parent–child relationships. *Journal of Family Psychology, 10*, 408–421.

Browne, A., & Finkelhor, D. (1986). Impact of sexual abuse: A review of the research. *Psychological Bulletin, 99*, 66–77.

Cheskes, J., & El-Sheikh, M. (1996). *Does resolution of interadult conflict ameliorate children's arousal and distress across covert, verbal, and physical disputes?* Manuscript submitted for publication.

Cox, M. J., Paley, B., & Payne, C. C. (1997, April). *Marital and parent–child relationships.* Paper presented at the biennial meeting of the Society for Research in Child Development, Washington, DC.

Crockenberg, S. B., & Forgays, D. (1996). The role of emotion in children's understanding and emotional reactions to marital conflict. *Merrill-Palmer Quarterly, 42*, 22–47.

Cummings, E. M. (1987). Coping with background anger in early childhood. *Child Development, 58*, 976–984.

Cummings, E. M. (1994). Marital conflict and children's functioning. *Social Development, 3*, 16–36.

Cummings, E. M. (1995a). Security, emotionality, and parental depression. *Developmental Psychology, 31*, 425–427.

Cummings, E. M. (1995b). The usefulness of experiments for the study of the family. *Journal of Family Psychology, 9*, 175–185.

Cummings, E. M., Ballard, M., & El-Sheikh, M. (1991). Responses of children and adolescents to interadult anger as a function of gender, age, and mode of expression. *Merrill-Palmer Quarterly, 37*, 543–560.

Cummings, E. M., Ballard, M., El-Sheikh, M., & Lake, M. (1991). Resolution and children's responses to interadult anger. *Developmental Psychology, 27*, 462–470.

Cummings, E. M., & Cummings, J. S. (1988). A process-oriented approach to children's coping with adults' angry behavior. *Developmental Review, 3*, 296–321.

Cummings, E. M., & Davies, P. T. (1994a). *Children and marital conflict: The impact of family dispute and resolution.* New York: Guilford Press.

Cummings, E. M., & Davies, P. T. (1994b). Maternal depression and child development. *Journal of Child Psychology and Psychiatry, 35*, 73–112.

Cummings, E. M., & Davies, P. T. (1995). The impact of parents and their children: An emotional security hypothesis. *Annals of Child Development, 10*, 167–208.

Cummings, E. M., & Davies, P. T. (1996). Emotional security as a regulatory process in normal development and the development of psychopathology. *Development and Psychopathology, 8*, 123–139.

Cummings, E. M., Davies, P., & Simpson, K. (1994). Marital conflict, gender, and children's appraisal and coping efficacy as mediators of child adjustment. *Journal of Family Psychology, 8*, 141–149.

Cummings, E. M., & El-Sheikh, M. (1991). Children's coping with angry environments: A process-oriented approach. In E. M. Cummings, A. Greene, & K. Karraker (Eds.), *Life-span developmental psychology: Perspectives on stress and coping* (pp. 131–150). Hillsdale, NJ: Erlbaum.

Cummings, E. M., Hennessy, K., Rabideau, G., & Cicchetti, D. (1994). Responses of physically abused boys to interadult anger involving their mothers. *Development and Psychopathology, 6*, 31–41.

Cummings, E. M., Iannotti, R., & Zahn-Waxler, C. (1985). The influence of conflict between adults on the emotions and aggression of young children. *Developmental Psychology, 21*, 495–507.

Cummings, E. M., & O'Reilly, A. (1997). Fathers in family context: Effects of marital quality on child adjustment. In M. E. Lamb (Ed.), *The role of the father in child development* (3rd ed., pp. 49–65). New York: Wiley.

Cummings, E. M., Simpson, K., & Wilson, A. (1993). Children's responses to interadult anger as a function of information about resolution. *Developmental Psychology, 29*, 978–985.

Cummings, E. M., Vogel, D., Cummings, J. S., & El-Sheikh, M. (1989). Children's responses to different forms of expression of anger between adults. *Child Development, 60,* 1392–1404.

Cummings, E. M., & Wilson, A. G. (in press). Contexts of marital conflict and children's emotional security: Exploring the distinction between constructive and destructive conflict from the children's perspective. In M. Cox & J. Brooks-Gunn (Eds.), *Formation, functioning, and stability of families.* Mahwah, NJ: Erlbaum.

Cummings, E. M., Zahn-Waxler, C., & Radke-Yarrow, M. (1981). Young children's responses to expressions of anger and affection by others in the family. *Child Development, 52,* 1274–1282.

Cummings, E. M., Zahn-Waxler, C., & Radke-Yarrow, M. (1984). Developmental changes in children's reactions to anger in the home. *Journal of Child Psychology and Psychiatry, 25,* 63–75.

Cummings, J. S., Pellegrini, D., Notarius, C., & Cummings, E. M. (1989). Children's responses to angry adult behavior as a function of marital distress and history of interparent hostility. *Child Development, 60,* 1035–1043.

Davies, P. T., & Cummings, E. M. (1994). Marital conflict and child adjustment: An emotional security hypothesis. *Psychological Bulletin, 116,* 387–411.

Davies, P. T., & Cummings, E. M. (1995). Children's emotions as organizers of their reaction to interadult anger: A functionalist perspective. *Developmental Psychology, 31,* 677–684.

Davies, P. T., & Cummings, E. M. (in press). Exploring children's emotional security as a mediator of the link between marital relations and child adjustment. *Child Development.*

Davies, P. T., Myers, R. L., & Cummings, E. M. (1996). Responses of children and adolescents to marital conflict scenarios as a function of the emotionality of conflict endings. *Merrill-Palmer Quarterly, 42,* 1–21.

Downey, G., & Coyne, J. C. (1990). Children of depressed parents: An integrative review. *Psychological Bulletin, 108,* 50–76.

Easterbrooks, M. A., Cummings, E. M., & Emde, R. N. (1994). Young children's responses to constructive marital disputes. *Journal of Family Psychology, 8,* 160–169.

El-Sheikh, M. (1997). Children's responses to adult–adult and mother–child arguments: The role of parental marital conflict and distress. *Journal of Family Psychology, 11,* 165–175.

El-Sheikh, M., Ballard, M., & Cummings, E. M. (1994). Individual differences in preschoolers' physiological and verbal responses to videotaped angry interactions. *Journal of Abnormal Child Psychology, 22,* 303–320.

El-Sheikh, M., & Cummings, E. M. (1995). Children's responses to angry adult behavior as a function of experimentally manipulated exposure to resolved and unresolved conflict. *Social Development, 4,* 75–91.

El-Sheikh, M., & Cummings, E. M. (in press). Marital conflict, emotional regulation, and the adjustment of children of alcoholics. In K. Barrett (Ed.), *New directions in child development: Emotion and communication.* San Francisco: Jossey-Bass.

El-Sheikh, M., Cummings, E. M., & Goetsch, V. (1989). Coping with adults' angry behavior: Behavioral, physiological, and self-reported responding in preschoolers. *Developmental Psychology, 25,* 490–498.

El-Sheikh, M., Cummings, E. M., & Reiter, S. (in press). Preschoolers' responses to interadult conflict: The role of experimentally manipulated exposure to resolved and unresolved arguments. *Journal of Abnormal Child Psychology.*

Emery, R. E. (1982). Interparental conflict and the children of discord and divorce. *Psychological Bulletin, 92,* 310–330.

Emery, R. E. (1988). *Marriage, divorce, and children's adjustment.* Newbury Park, CA: Sage.

Emery, R. E. (1989). Family violence. *American Psychologist, 44,* 321–328.

Emery, R. E. (1994). *Renegotiating family relationships.* New York: Guilford Press.

Emery, R. E., Fincham, F. D., & Cummings, E. M. (1992). Parenting in context: Systemic thinking about parental conflict and its influence on children. *Journal of Consulting and Clinical Psychology, 60,* 909–912.

Fantuzzo, J. W., DePaola, L. M., Lambert, L., Martino, T., Anderson, G., & Sutton, S. (1991). Effects of interparental violence on the psychological adjustment and competencies of young children. *Journal of Clinical and Consulting Psychology, 59,* 258–265.

Feldman, S., & Downey, G. (1994). Rejection sensitivity as a mediator of the impact of childhood exposure to family violence on adult attachment behavior. *Development and Psychopathology, 6,* 231–247.

Fincham, F. D., & Osborne, L. N. (1993). Marital conflict and children: Retrospect and prospect. *Clinical Child Psychology, 13,* 75–88.

Folkman, S. (1991). Coping across the life span: Theoretical issues. In E. M. Cummings, A. Greene, & K. Karraker (Eds.), *Life-span developmental psychology: Perspectives on stress and coping* (pp. 3–20). Hillsdale, NJ: Erlbaum.

Gordis, E. B., Margolin, G., & John, R. (1997). Marital aggression, observed parental hostility, and child behavior during triadic family interaction. *Journal of Family Psychology, 11,* 76–89.

Grych, J. H., & Fincham, F. (1990). Marital conflict and children's adjustment: A cognitive-contextual framework. *Psychological Bulletin, 108,* 267–290.

Grych, J. H., & Fincham, F. (1993). Children's appraisals of marital conflict: Initial investigations of the cognitive-contextual framework. *Child Development, 64,* 215–230.

Grych, J. H., & Fincham, F. (in press-a). Children's adaptation to divorce: From description to explanation. In I. N. Sandler & S. A. Wolchik (Eds.), *Handbook of children's coping with common stressors: Linking theory, research, and intervention.* New York: Plenum Press.

Grych, J. H., & Fincham, F. (in press-b). Developmental psychopathology and children's adjustment to divorce: Towards more developmentally informed interventions. In W. K. Silverman & T. H. Ollendick (Eds.), *Developmental issues in the clinical treatment of children and adolescents.* Needham Heights, MA: Allyn & Bacon.

Grych, J., Seid, M., & Fincham, F. (1992). Assessing marital conflict from the child's perspective: The children's perceptions of interparental conflict scale. *Child Development, 63,* 558–572.

Harold, G. T., & Conger, R. D. (1997). Marital conflict and adolescent distress: The role of adolescent awareness. *Child Development, 68,* 333–350.

Harold, G. T., Fincham, F. D., Osborne, L. N., & Conger, R. D. (1997). Mom and Dad are at it again: Adolescent perceptions of marital conflict and adolescent psychological distress. *Developmental Psychology, 33,* 333–350.

Harrist, A., & Ainslie, R. (in press). Marital discord and child behavior problems: Parent–child relationship quality and child interpersonal awareness as mediators. *Journal of Family Issues.*

Hennessy, K., Rabideau, G., Cicchetti, D., & Cummings, E. M. (1994). Responses of physically abused children to different forms of interadult anger. *Child Development, 65,* 815–828.

Holden, G. W., & Ritchie, K. L. (1991). Linking extreme marital discord, child rearing, and child behavior problems: Evidence from battered women. *Child Development, 62,* 311–327.

Hubbard, R. M., & Adams, C. F. (1936). Factors affecting the success of child guidance clinic treatment. *American Journal of Orthopsychiatry, 6,* 81–103.

Jaffe, P. G., Wolfe, D. A., & Wilson, S. K. (1990). *Children of battered women.* Newbury Park, CA: Sage.

Jaffe, P. G., Wolfe, D. A., Wilson, S. K., & Zak, L. (1986). Family violence and child adjustment: A comparative analysis of girls' and boys' behavioral symptoms. *American Journal of Psychiatry, 143,* 74–77.

Johnston, J. R., & Roseby, V. (1997). *In the name of the child.* New York: Free Press.

Jouriles, E. N., Barling, J., & O'Leary, K. D. (1987). Predicting child behavior problems in maritally violent families. *Journal of Abnormal Child Psychology, 15,* 165–173.

Jouriles, E. N., Bourg, W., & Farris, A. (1991). Marital adjustment and child conduct problems: A comparison of the correlation across samples. *Journal of Consulting and Clinical Psychology, 59,* 354–357.

Jouriles, E. N., & Farris, A. M. (1992). Effects of marital conflict on subsequent parent–son interactions. *Behavior Therapy, 23,* 355–374.

Jouriles, E. N., Murphy, C. M., Farris, A. M., Smith, D. A., Richters, J. E., & Waters, E. (1991). Marital adjustment, parental disagreements about child rearing, and behavior problems in boys: Increasing the specificity of the marital assessment. *Child Development, 62,* 1424–1433.

Jouriles, E. N., Murphy, C. M., & O'Leary, K. D. (1989). Interspousal aggression, marital discord, and child problems. *Journal of Consulting and Clinical Psychology, 57,* 453–455.

Jouriles, E. N., Norwood, W. D., McDonald, R., Vincent, J. P., & Mahoney. A. (1996). Physical violence and other forms of marital aggression: Links with children's behavior problems. *Journal of Family Psychology, 10,* 223–234.

Katz, L. F., & Gottman, J. (1993). Patterns of marital conflict predict children's internalizing and externalizing disorders. *Development Psychology, 29,* 940–950.

Katz, L. F., & Gottman, J. M. (1995a, April). *Marital conflict and child adjustment: Father's parenting as a mediator of children's negative peer play.* Paper presented at the biennial meeting of the Society for Research in Child Development, Indianapolis, IN.

Katz, L. F., & Gottman, J. M. (1995b). Vagal tone predicts children from marital conflict. *Development and Psychopathology, 7,* 83–92.

Katz, L. F., & Gottman, J. (1997, April). *Positive parenting and regulatory physiology as buffers from marital conflict and dissolution.* Paper presented at the biennial meeting of the Society for Research in Child Development, Washington, DC.

Kerig, P. (1996). Assessing the links between interparental conflict and child adjustment: The Conflicts and Problem-Solving Scales. *Journal of Family Psychology, 10,* 454–473.

Kerig, P. (1997, April). *Gender and children's coping efforts as moderators of the effects of interparental conflict on children.* Paper presented at the biennial meeting of the Society for Research in Child Development, Washington, DC.

Kerig, P., Cowan, P. A., & Cowan, C. P. (1993). Marital quality and gender differences in parent–child interaction. *Developmental Psychology, 29,* 931–939.

Laumakis, M. A., Margolin, G., & John, R. S. (1998). The emotional, cognitive, and coping responses of preadolescent children to different dimensions of marital conflict. In G. W. Holden, R. Geffner, & E. N. Jouriles (Eds.), *Children exposed to marital violence: Theory, research, and applied issues* (pp. 257–288). Washington, DC: American Psychological Association.

Lazarus, R. S., & Folkman, S. (1984). *Stress, coping, and appraisal.* New York: Springer.

Lindahl, K., & Malik, N. (1997, April). *Linking marital conflict and children's adjustment: An assessment of dyadic and triadic family processes.* Paper presented at the biennial meeting of the Society for Research in Child Development, Washington, DC.

Mahoney, A., Boggio, R., & Jouriles, E. (1996). Effects of verbal marital conflict on subsequent mother–son interactions in a child clinical sample. *Journal of Clinical Child Psychology, 25,* 262–271.

Mahoney, A., Lape, L., Query, L., & Wieber, J. (1997, April). *Mothers' and fathers' reliance on overt and covert strategies to manage marital conflict: Links with child behavior problems.* Paper presented at the biennial meeting of the Society for Research in Child Development, Washington, DC.

Margolin, G., Christensen, A., & John, R. (1996). The continuance and spillover of everyday tensions in distressed and nondistressed families. *Journal of Family Psychology, 10,* 304–321.

Myers, R. L. (1997). *Relations between marital conflict, children's internal working models of parental relations, and the quality of their long-term episodic memory of interadult conflict.* Unpublished masters' thesis, West Virginia University, Morgantown.

O'Brien, M., Margolin, G., John, R. S., & Krueger, L. (1991). Mothers' and sons' cognitive and emotional reactions to simulated marital and family conflict. *Journal of Consulting and Clinical Psychology, 59,* 692–703.

O'Brien, M., Bahadur, M., Gee, C., Balto, K., & Erber, S. (1997). Child exposure to marital conflict and child coping responses as predictors of child adjustment. *Cognitive Therapy and Research, 21,* 39–59.

Osborne, L. N., & Fincham, F. D. (1996). Marital conflict, parent–child relationships, and child adjustment: Does gender matter? *Merrill-Palmer Quarterly, 42,* 48–75.

Reiter, S., & El-Sheikh, M. (1996). *Does the resolution of interadult conflict ameliorate children's arousal and distress across covert, verbal, and physical disputes?* Manuscript submitted for publication.

Rogers, M. J., & Holmbeck, G. N. (1997). Effects of interparental aggression on children's adjustment: The moderating role of cognitive appraisal and coping. *Journal of Family Psychology, 11,* 125–130.

Shifflett-Simpson, K., & Cummings, E. M. (1996). Mixed message resolution and children's responses to interadult conflict. *Child Development, 67,* 437–448.

Sroufe, L. A., & Rutter, M. (1984). The domain of developmental psychopathology. *Child Development, 55,* 17–29.

Sroufe, L. A., & Waters, E. (1977). Attachment as an organizational construct. *Child Development, 48,* 1184–1199.

Stocker, C., Stall, M., & Ahmed, K. (1997, April). *Maternal emotional expressiveness: Does it mediate the link between marital and sibling relationships.* Paper presented at the biennial meeting of the Society for Research in Child Development, Washington, DC.

Towle, C. (1931). The evaluation and management of marital status in foster homes. *American Journal of Orthopsychiatry, 1,* 271–284.

West, M. O., & Prinz, R. J. (1987). Parental alcoholism and childhood psycho-pathology. *Psychological Bulletin, 102,* 204–218.

Wilson, B. J., & Gottman, J. M. (1995). Marital interaction and parenting. In M. H. Bornstein (Ed.), *Handbook of parenting: Vol. 4. Applied and practical considerations of parenting* (pp. 33–55). Mahwah, NJ: Erlbaum.

Wolfe, D. A., Jaffe, P., Wilson, S., & Zak, L. (1985). Children of battered women: The relation of child behavior to family violence and maternal stress. *Journal of Consulting and Clinical Psychology, 53,* 657–665.

4

Children as Invisible Victims of Domestic and Community Violence

Joy D. Osofsky

> Children need to be safe and secure at home to develop a positive sense of self necessary to their growing into healthy, productive, caring adults; children need to be safe in their communities to be able to explore and develop relationships with other people; and children need to be safe at school in order to successfully learn.
>
> Position Statement on Violence in the Lives of Children.
> (National Association for the Education
> of Young Children, 1993)

In the United States, levels of violence have reached epidemic proportions and, for many years, this country has been the most violent developed country in the industrialized world. Public figures and average citizens have expressed growing concern about the effects of violence on children as homicide rates in the United States have soared in recent years (Rosenberg, 1994). Children are exposed to violence at an alarming rate every day of their lives in their homes and on the streets (see Osofsky, 1995b; Osofsky & Fenichel, 1994). Homicide has been the second leading cause of death among all 15- to 24-year-olds for many years, and it has now become the second leading cause of death among children 10 to 19 years old. For elementary school children, ages 5–14, homicide is now the third leading cause of death (Children's Defense Fund, 1996). The number of youth committing homicide has increased more than 150% between 1985 and 1993; the rate of known homicide offenders ages 14 to 17 has climbed from 16.2 per 100,000 in 1990 to 19.1 per 100,000 in 1994 (Herbert, 1996). A Louis Harris poll of 2,000 teenagers from suburban and rural areas showed that 1 in 8 youths, and almost 2 in 5 from high-violence neighborhoods, said they carried a weapon for protection. One in 9, and more than 1 in 3 in high-violence neighborhoods, said they had cut class or stayed away from school because of fear of crime (Appelbone, 1996).

In this chapter, I begin by reviewing current studies on the overall effects of violence exposure on children. Both similarities and differences in responses to community and domestic violence are discussed. I present material on how children's reactions may be influenced by their individual characteristics and developmental factors and what is known about the developmental sequelae of violence exposure on children. In the next section, I discuss how community and domestic violence exposure may affect parents and influence their ability to care for and nurture their children effectively. Moving to a broader systems response to violence in our society, I briefly describe the role and responses of law enforcement officials to children and families exposed to violence and discuss an intervention program with the police. Finally, in the concluding section of the chapter, I discuss directions for future research and public policy recommendations that would affect children, parents, and communities.

Before proceeding, it is necessary to define what is meant by *community violence* and *domestic violence*. *Community violence* refers to violence exposure that occurs in neighborhoods and on streets outside of the home. *Domestic violence* refers to violence that occurs between family members or people who are intimate with each other, either at home or outside the home. Differentiating children's exposure may become particularly complex when they are exposed to violence between family members or those who are intimate with each other and when the violence between them has spread outside of the boundaries of the home. Children are exposed to violence in their homes and in their communities every day, and violence affects them whether they are victims or witnesses. Although many people continue to want to believe that most community violence is between strangers, this is not the case. Most violent behavior is the result of arguments that develop between people who know each other, often those who are intimate with each other. These unresolved arguments then can erupt into severe violence. Frequently, homicide and violence occur in the home and involve family members or other people living in the household. Community violence, including drive-by shootings and random killing on the streets, not infrequently emanates from family or neighborhood feuds that are re-solved, if only temporarily, by a revenge killing. Thus, it is often difficult to separate the different effects of domestic and community violence on children.

More than half of the police calls for service in many communities are for domestic disturbances, many of which are witnessed by children. Countless numbers of children whom one never hears about, and for whom the police do not receive calls, are exposed to physical and verbal abuse between their parents or caretakers several times a week. Carlson (1984) has reported that at least 3.3 million children witness parental abuse each year, including such behaviors as hitting, slapping, and fatal assaults with guns or knives. This figure may well be an underestimate. Too often children are invisible or silent victims. To date, however, relatively little research has focused on the effects of domestic violence on children or the interface between community and domestic violence exposure.

A THEORETICAL PERSPECTIVE

A theoretical perspective is needed that can encompass the complexity of the developmental issues when children witness violence. A systems approach that takes into account not just the child but the interrelated connections that link the child and his or her community offers such a useful framework. My work in the community (Osofsky, 1997) and that of others (Groves & Zuckerman, 1997; Marans & Cohen, 1993; Murphy, Pynoos, & James, 1997) focuses on agents that can effect changes in systems (e.g., police, schools, and community agencies), which may then be available to help children and families who are traumatized by violence. Such an approach can assist in developing prevention and intervention efforts. A developmental framework that includes both psychodynamic and social learning theory principles may provide a useful background for influencing the types of training and techniques that may be most helpful in counseling children and educating parents, teachers, police, and others about violence, its effect on children, and what may be the most effective intervention approaches.

A helpful developmental perspective for understanding how exposure to violence may affect children comes from Erik Erikson's early writings in *Childhood and Society* (1963) concerning the development of trust and the crucial role that it plays in forming healthy relationships. Trust develops early and is primarily contingent on the infant's relationship with his or her caregiver. If the infant learns to trust in earlier relationships, particularly with the primary caregiver, then a firm foundation is formed for later relationship building. In contrast, mistrust can develop as a result of a single trauma or from chronic environmental stress. Emotional unavailability of parents or inconsistent, continual negative, or abusive behavior may lead to the infant or young child not developing basic trust (Egeland & Erickson, 1987). In this theoretical framework, it is important to consider the effect on a child of growing up in a home marked by instability and violence and a poverty-stricken neighborhood with drug trading and violence. It is likely that consistent relationships leading to the development of basic trust may be lacking—unless a child is lucky enough to identify a stable figure in his or her life despite the stressful and difficult environment.

Another theoretical perspective relevant to an understanding of the effects of violence exposure on children is social learning theory. According to Bandura and Walters (1963), aggressive behavior is acquired and sustained through observational learning, direct experience, and influences on self-regulation. Bandura (1983) has proposed that "people are not born with preformed repertoires of aggressive behavior. They must learn them" (p. 4). Children learn and imitate what they see and experience. Bell (1995) has suggested that children who are exposed to domestic and community violence are at much higher risk of becoming both perpetrators and victims of violence. Social learning theory with its emphasis on observational learning, imitation, and modeling would support this idea.

CHILDREN'S EXPOSURE TO VIOLENCE IN THEIR COMMUNITIES AND THEIR HOMES

A number of studies have been done in recent years on children's exposure to community violence; to date, however, there have been no longitudinal follow-up reports of long-term outcomes. Much of the increase in violence in the United States (which has doubled since the 1950s) has been among adolescents and young adults, ages 15 to 24 years (Blumstein, 1995). Although homicides decreased slightly in 1995, many criminologists believe this reflects a demographic trend in the adolescent and young adult population. A recent report estimated that the number of teenagers in the population is expected to increase substantially in the next 6 to 8 years and that the crime rate also will rise as a consequence (Blumstein, 1995). Although outcomes of exposure to community and domestic violence for children may have considerable similarities, a number of authors have also commented that community violence exposure may affect children differently than exposure to domestic violence (Bell & Jenkins, 1993; Garbarino, 1992; Jenkins & Bell, 1994; Marans & Cohen, 1993; Osofsky, 1995a, 1995b; Pynoos, 1993; Richters, 1993).

Recent data on community violence exposure indicate that children are being exposed to violence at high rates in many inner-city neighborhoods. In a survey of 6th, 8th, and 10th graders in New Haven in 1992, 40% reported witnessing at least one violent crime in the past year (Marans & Cohen, 1993). Very few of the children escaped some exposure to violence, and almost all of the 8th-grade students knew someone who had been killed. In Los Angeles, it was estimated in 1986 that 10% to 20% of the homicides committed were witnessed by children; undoubtedly, that figure has increased dramatically in the past decade (Pynoos & Nader, 1993). In a study of African American children living in a Chicago neighborhood, one in four had witnessed a shooting and one-third reported that they had seen a stabbing (Bell & Jenkins, 1991, 1993). Even more surprising, reports of witnessing among these 2nd, 4th, 6th, and 8th graders were not related to age. Yet another study showed that children's social and emotional adjustment in the classroom was related to the presence of social support in their lives, regardless of the level of violence in the community or the amount of exposure (Hill, 1995).

Although few studies have documented the relationship between community and domestic violence exposure, two recent studies shed some light on this issue. Richters and Martinez (1993) gathered interviews from 165 mothers of children ages 6 to 10 living in a low-income neighborhood in Washington, DC. In an attempt to gather similar data in New Orleans, Osofsky, Wewers, Hann, and Fick (1993) included interviews with 53 African American mothers of children ages 9 to 12 in a low-income neighborhood, which police statistics showed to have higher violence rates than the Washington neighborhood. Fifty-one percent of the New Orleans fifth graders and 32% of the Washington, DC children reported being victims of violence; 91% of the New Orleans children and 72% of the Washington children had witnessed some type of violence. Both studies also found significant relations between children's reported exposure to community violence and intrafamily conflict as measured by the Conflict Tactics Scale (Straus, 1979). The variables of violence in the home seemed particularly potent, and in the Osofsky et al. (1993) study, the Conflict Tactics Scale and age at which parenting began accounted for 54% of the variance in Child Behavior Checklist (Achenbach & Edelbrock, 1983) scores indicating that mothers who reported more family violence began their parenting earlier and reported more behavior problems in their children.

Whereas few studies have made the distinction between domestic and community violence, the Richters and Martinez (1993) and Osofsky et al. (1993) studies highlight the importance of including measures to determine how being raised in a violent home versus a violent neighborhood may, separately or in combination, affect children. Some evidence suggests that witnessing domestic violence may have more dire effects because children are exposed to violence by their parents, on whom they depend for stability and nurturance. However, the limited number of controlled research studies and the paucity of clinical follow-up that has been done highlight the crucial need for more work in this area.

It is well known that many homicides and incidents of severe violence occur in the home; however, less attention has been placed on how such exposure to violence may affect children. As discussed in the introduction to this volume, approximately 25% to 39% of American women are beaten at least once in the course of intimate relationships (Pagelow, 1984). How much of this violence occurs in the presence of children is unknown.

Unfortunately, the available data show a much higher incidence of child abuse and neglect when women are battered. Again, prevalence rates have been presented in the introduction to this volume. To restate the problem briefly, in homes where domestic violence occurs, children are physically abused and neglected at a rate 15 times higher than the national average (Senate Judiciary Committee Hearing 101–939, as cited in Massachusetts Coalition, 1995). However, few controlled studies have focused on the effects of domestic violence on children, and public policy initiatives have been almost nonexistent in this crucial area. Despite the suggestion that exposure to domestic violence as contrasted with community violence may be more devastating for children, because of their familiarity and relationship with the perpetrator or victim (Augustyn, Parker, Groves, & Zuckerman, 1995; Groves & Zuckerman, 1997), what is known about immediate symptoms and effects on development, at least for the short term, appears to be similar for exposure to severe community and domestic violence. Much more work is needed on short- and long-term effects on children as well as the effects of exposure to acute and chronic violence. It is also crucial that the impact at different developmental periods be included in the evaluation process.

DEVELOPMENTAL IMPACT OF COMMUNITY AND DOMESTIC VIOLENCE EXPOSURE ON CHILDREN

The impact on children of exposure to community and domestic violence depends on many factors, including the age of the child, frequency and type of violence exposure, characteristics of the neighborhood (including degree of community resources), amount and quality of support provided by caregivers and other significant adults, experience of previous trauma, proximity to the violent event, and familiarity with the victim or perpetrator (Pynoos, 1993). How much a child perceives or remembers a violent experience affects the presence or absence of symptoms and the circumstances under which they are likely to occur (Drell, Siegel, & Gaensbauer, 1993). Because the studies related to the effects of domestic violence exposure on children have been reviewed in the introduction to this book, I discuss relevant developmental factors briefly in this section.

Adolescent problems related to violence exposure have generally received the most attention in research and clinical work and in the media; however, the effects on younger children as witnesses or victims can be devastating. Very young children may be partially protected from exposure to a traumatic incident because they do not fully appreciate the potential danger. Yet, it is important not to ignore or de-emphasize young children's reactions to violence exposure. A number of studies have documented that infants and toddlers are likely to exhibit emotional distress, immature behavior, somatic complaints, and regressions in toileting and language (Drell et al., 1993; Jaffe, Wolfe, & Wilson, 1990; Margolin, 1995; Osofsky & Fenichel, 1994; Pynoos, 1993). Furthermore, the potential protective influence for young children of not being totally aware of what has happened appears not to be the case when severe trauma has occurred (e.g., when they witness the murder of one of their parents). Posttraumatic stress symptoms including sleeplessness, disorganized behavior, and agitation are often observed even if they are downplayed by caretakers and others in their environment. Similar symptom patterns have been reported for exposure to significant community and domestic violence. In survey data, Fick, Osofsky, and Lewis (1997) have found that both parents and police perceive witnessing violence against a parent to have a much greater impact on a child than violence against a stranger. For these reasons, it is possible to speculate that exposure to less significant incidents of domestic violence may also have a considerable impact on children, potentially leading to more negative outcomes and more severe symptoms.

As noted, there is growing evidence that children who witness extreme trauma such as a street murder or parental homicide commonly show signs of posttraumatic stress disorder similar to adults who have been exposed to war (Burman & Allen-Meares, 1994; Groves, Zuckerman, Marans, & Cohen, 1993; Osofsky, Cohen, & Drell, 1995; Pynoos, 1993; Pynoos & Nader, 1993). However, as law enforcement officials and others deal with the perpetrators and victims, relatively little attention is usually focused on these children. In Black and Kaplan's (1988) study of 28 child witnesses from 14 families (ages 1½ to 14 years) in which the father killed the mother, delays in referrals for treatment for the children ranged from 2 weeks to 11 years. Pynoos (1993) reported delays ranging from 1 month to several years; referrals coming after a year often showed a more serious diagnostic picture. My clinical experience has been consistent with these reports with delays in referrals, few preventive intervention programs, and children frequently receiving treatment long after the traumatic incident and only after serious behavior problems have been identified. There is general agreement that much more information and data are needed on the extent and implications of exposure to family violence, exposure at different developmental stages, and exposure to different types of violence (Margolin, 1995; Zuckerman, Augustyn, Groves, & Parker, 1995).

For future research in this area, special care needs to be paid to the methodologies used and the generalizability of findings from experimental studies. For example, the studies of Cummings and Zahn-Waxler (1992) have found that even expressions of anger between parents negatively affect children's emotions and behavior. However, questions have been raised about the degree to which the experimental situations in the studies are representative of real-life circumstances. Much of the direct knowledge on the effects of domestic violence on children has been obtained by interviewing parents or sometimes older children living in shelters (Margolin, 1995). The data are confounded by these children having experienced multiple traumas in addition to violence exposure. For example, most of these children have just undergone a significant loss, are living in a new and strange environment with a traumatized parent, and are living with other traumatized children and parents. Further compounding the concerns about the accuracy of the reports of family violence is that parents rarely agree about whether violence has occurred; they agree even less when they are asked if their child has been exposed (Jouriles, Pfiffner, & O'Leary, 1988; Margolin, 1987; O'Brien, John, Margolin, & Erel, 1994). Interrater agreement between children and parents about whether the child has witnessed domestic violence is also low. When children who live in families where there has been documented violence are interviewed, they often can give detailed reports about the violence that their parents assumed went unnoticed (Jaffe et al., 1990).

In general, parents tend to underestimate the extent to which their children may be exposed to both community and domestic violence. This finding is to be expected for several reasons, including children's fearfulness and attempts to be unseen while observing, parents' wishes that their children have not been exposed, and defensiveness regarding the potential exposure. When older children, who are more reliable reporters, are questioned about both community and domestic violence exposure, they usually report a much higher level. In determining the effects on children, information is needed on their actual exposure and their perceptions about family violence (Grych, Seid, & Fincham, 1992; Margolin, 1995; O'Brien et al., 1994).

An additional risk factor for children exposed to domestic violence is that it can become part of an intergenerational cycle of violence (Bell, 1995). In a study of 10,036 elementary and high school children in inner-city Chicago, Shakoor and Chalmers (1991) found that children and adolescents who witnessed violence and had been victims of violence were more likely to become perpetrators of violence than those who were not exposed. Another study of 536 children in grades 2, 4, 6, and 8 linked children's physical aggression with witnessing family violence, primarily spouse abuse (Jenkins & Thompson, 1986). A recent report for the Massachusetts Coalition of Battered Women Service Groups (1995) is informative about what children learn when they witness domestic violence: (a) Violence is an appropriate way to resolve conflicts, (b) violence is a part of family relationships, (c) the perpetrator of violence in intimate relationships often goes unpunished, and (d) violence is a way to control other people.

It is possible and even likely that early and repeated exposure to family violence may be a precursor to later violent adolescent and adult behaviors. Bell (1995) has elaborated about the impact of exposure to violence on later negative outcomes: "We have not fully conceptualized the impact of exposure to violence on children compared with other groups such as veterans of the Korean and Vietnam Wars" (p. 8). Children and adolescents who have witnessed violence are themselves victims and experience high amounts of stress. Furthermore, Bell believed that exposure to violence leads to more high-risk behaviors in youth. As Margolin (1995) has emphasized, children see aggression, and (more significantly) they learn how aggression may be applied in intimate relationships. Thus, children may come to view violence as an acceptable way—perhaps the only way—to resolve conflicts and may learn to rationalize the use of violence because they know nothing else.

Witnessing domestic and community violence may not be perceived as life-threatening, but it is still disturbing enough to cause distress. For example, in at least one study (Sternberg et al., 1993), children who were exposed to domestic violence but were not abused reported more depressive features than a nontraumatized group; moreover, the group that was exposed to domestic violence but was not abused did not differ in the severity of depressive features when compared to children who had been abused.

In our (Osofsky et al., 1995) clinical experience with elementary school-age and younger children exposed to repetitive family violence, we frequently observe disturbances in school behavior, mixed feelings toward parents when positive affect is mingled with anger, and difficulties in forming later relationships. With severe violence including witnessing or experiencing a homicide of a loved one, questions must be raised not only about the immediate reactions, but also about how the children will react over time. For example, how will they deal with the meaning of death when they come to understand it more fully during preadolescence? How will children deal with aggression, sexuality, and intimacy when they reach adolescence? How will they deal with relationships and parenting during adulthood?

Effects of Violence Exposure on Parenting

It is important to recognize that parents or caregivers are often traumatized in addition to the children. Parents who realize that they may not be able to protect their children from violence are likely to feel anxious, frustrated, and helpless (Osofsky & Fenichel, 1994). They often fear for their own and their children's safety. When parents witness violence or (in the case of domestic violence) are themselves victims of violence, they may have difficulty being emotionally available, sensitive, and responsive to their children. As victims of domestic violence, mothers' problems take on another dimension. They may become so preoccupied with safety and survival that they cannot be mindful of their children's needs. They may develop posttraumatic stress disorder symptoms and depression. As they numb themselves to the violence in their lives, they may be unable to be empathic about the effect on their children. (See Holden, Stein, Ritchie, Harris, & Jouriles, 1998, this volume, for a contrasting point of view.)

Parents must receive the support they need to cope with their own trauma so that they are then able to be more comfortable in dealing with their children's fears and problems. If children are raised by parents who are constantly fearful, they often lack a sense of basic trust and security that is the foundation of healthy emotional development. For traumatized parents, unfortunately, their children's distress frequently acts as a reminder for the parents of what they wish to forget and, therefore, may reawaken fears contributing to their difficulty in attending to their children's distress. Another way that parents may react is to become overprotective, or, if extremely traumatized themselves, they may expect their children to protect them. It is important to recognize that living in a violent environment may lead to chronic unrelieved stress. Because domestic violence most often affects the mother, the goal of ending violence against women has important implications for protecting children.

The Role of Law Enforcement Officials for Children Exposed to Violence

Academic and policy circles are engaged in spirited debate over the role of law enforcement in domestic violence incidents (Buzawa & Buzawa, 1993; Gelles, 1993; Pate & Hamilton, 1993). The police are usually the first on the scene in responding to community and domestic violence. Often forgotten by the feuding parents and other adults are the children living in violent homes and communities who are exposed to violence almost every day of their lives. Steinman (1989) found that children are present during almost half of all battering incidents.

In addition to children's exposure to this violence perpetrated by family members whom they love and trust, what is the impact on children of watching authority figures such as police officers coming into their homes to investigate or control a domestic dispute, especially if they also act in an insensitive and harsh way to the fighting parents? What does it mean to a young child to see his or her father being taken away in handcuffs? Law enforcement's response to these situations can teach children a variety of lessons. With an appropriate response, children can learn that someone in authority cares about their welfare.

Police responses to children's exposure to violence may be crucial for prevention because police are usually the first to arrive on the scene to respond to community or family violence. For these reasons, my colleagues and I and many others working with this problem, particularly in New Haven, Boston, Los Angeles, Chicago, and Washington, DC, have been developing educational and preventive intervention programs involving the police (see Bell, 1995; Groves & Zuckerman, 1997; Marans & Cohen, 1993; Murphy, Pynoos, & James, 1997; and Osofsky, 1995a, 1997, for descriptions).

To develop an earlier and better system of referrals for children exposed to violence and to stimulate community-based intervention programs, my team in New Orleans through the Department of Psychiatry at Louisiana State University Medical Center has been developing a collaborative effort with the local police to provide an educational program for police trainees and officers on the effects of violence on children and to integrate it with 24-hour mental health crisis referral and consultation services for children. Because of the size of the city, the level of violence, and the needs of the community, we decided initially to develop a model program in one of two police districts with the highest level of violence in the city. As part of the program, we carried out a needs assessment related to violence, including domestic violence and safety in the neighborhood, with 353 police officers, 250 children, 60 parents, and 68 teachers. The 250 elementary school children, ages 8–12, reported that they trusted police officers as the first people they would go to if they were lost or needed help. Because such trust seems to occur less often during adolescence, we are now trying to understand possible developmental shifts and some of the other important factors influencing this later lack of trust. In addition, through the program, we are supporting the development of more understanding between the police and the families being served.

Results from both the police and parent surveys showed strong beliefs about domestic violence. A majority of law enforcement officers in this study reported that domestic disputes are the most dangerous situations they face. Many officers reported believing that women are just as dangerous as men in this situation. They described domestic violence situations as unpredictable and chaotic. The police in our study reported that domestic violence is a serious component of the community violence with which they are dealing. Although all officers agreed that children would be traumatized by seeing their mother beaten by either the father or a stranger, most of them felt that the trauma would be greater if the perpetrator was the father. In our study, 43% of the officers with less experience (defined as less than 5 years on the job) considered exposure to domestic violence to be more serious for children in comparison to the 32% of more experienced officers. This finding suggests that over time, some officers may no longer appreciate, or perhaps become immune to, the seriousness of the effect of domestic violence on children. Officers also responded that the trauma to a child of witnessing his or her sibling being beaten would be greater if the perpetrator was a parent.

The findings from this survey were very helpful for our educational and intervention programs. Police need to be educated about children as victims of violence and about the negative effects of witnessing violence. Children are often forgotten when the police enter a spouse abuse situation. However, police attitudes toward the violence and the victims are critical to protect the children. The need to fight crime and arrest is often difficult to blend with providing help for the most vulnerable in need of services.

Perhaps of most importance, police officers report feeling more comfortable and supported when intervening when they have more education about dynamics of violent and abusive families and developmental issues including children's responses to violence exposure and conflict resolution. They also report that when they are involved in crisis situations involving children, they appreciate having information to offer about referral services for children. We have been impressed by the generally positive responses of the police to the educational programs, their wishes to learn more about children, and their use of the referral system when it is consistently available and staffed by familiar professionals. With increased training of officers about domestic violence situations and alternative ways to respond, the police have the opportunity to develop more proactive and helpful strategies for interacting with the community and dealing with children who witness both community violence and domestic disputes.

CONCLUSIONS

Directions for Future Research

In this chapter, I have emphasized the crucial issue in this violent society of recognizing children as the invisible victims. Many children are exposed to violence in their homes and communities almost every day of their lives. Although relatively little comparative research is available on the effects of community as compared to domestic violence exposure on children, one may draw some parallels and likely differences in responses. The symptom patterns in children following exposure to violence, be it domestic or community, are likely to be similar. In the most benign situations, temporary sleep disturbances, increase in activity and aggression, and interference with concentration may occur, depending on developmental factors and intensity of exposure. Following exposure to severe violence, whether community or domestic, children often show at least some symptoms of posttraumatic stress disorder accompanied by symptoms of re-experiencing of the event, avoidance or numbing, or hyperarousal. The effects for children are influenced by proximity to the event, familiarity with the victim or perpetrator, and chronicity of violence exposure, among other factors. The aversive effect on children of comparable levels of violence exposure may be greater for family than community violence. Thus, a less severe incident of domestic violence exposure will result in negative outcomes for children. For parents, domestic violence may also take even more of a toll and affect significantly their ability to be emotionally available to their children. Available research suggests that the combination of domestic and community violence exposure seems to lead to the most negative outcomes for both children and parents. It is time that we pay attention to this problem, place more focus on how these children may be affected, and develop appropriate prevention and intervention efforts.

Future studies should address long-term outcomes of violence exposure, differentiating exposure to community and domestic violence and controlling for the severity of the event as well as mediating factors such as interventions and support available to the children and family. There is also an urgent need to learn more about protective factors for children exposed both to community and domestic violence. Only a small percentage of exposed children are likely to become either violent perpetrators or victims. What are the factors that may protect some of these children? To date, little research has been done on protective factors for children exposed to violence; however, growing interest in the study of resiliency, or the ability to deal positively with adversity, may be helpful in understanding factors that may mitigate the effects of violence exposure (Garmezy, 1993; Hawkins, 1995). The presence of social support appears to be an important protective factor for children exposed to violence (Hill, 1995), just as it has been shown consistently to be a protective factor for other high-risk, high-stress groups such as adolescent mothers (Brooks-Gunn & Chase-Lansdale, 1995; Osofsky, Hann, & Peebles, 1993). In a recent study of consequences of domestic violence, however, it had been hypothesized that a positive relationship between parent and child might buffer children, but in one study, this was not the case (McCloskey, Figueredo, & Koss, 1995). This is an important research area to pursue in future research.

It would be helpful if future studies made an effort to quantify the dose of domestic violence in that the severity of exposure may have a significant impact on outcomes for the child. If possible, data should be gathered independently from both the parent and child. For example, the Conflict Tactics Scale, a widely used measure of family conflict (Straus, 1979), does not help to describe the children's perceptions of the violence and their immediate reactions (Fantuzzo & Lindquist, 1989). Furthermore, studies are needed on the different effects on the child and parent of placement in a shelter as compared to other alternatives for battered women and their children. Systematic studies are also needed on the impact of exposure at different developmental stages and, again, on longer term impact.

Long-term outcome studies also are urgently needed to be able to determine the effects of different types of interventions and treatments for children exposed to violence. Studies should include a recognition of differential outcomes depending on the earlier symptoms and diagnostic understanding of the child. Only with data from such studies can one develop meaningful and effective preventive intervention and treatment programs for children exposed to violence.

Public Policy Recommendations
for Parents and Communities

In recent articles on the effects of community and domestic violence exposure on children (Osofsky, 1995a, 1995b), I recommended public policy initiatives that are needed to help children and families living with community and domestic violence. Given the importance of these public policy initiatives, I reemphasize some recommendations that I believe are urgently needed at the present time.

- A family-centered and community-centered approach to the prevention of violence and the treatment of its aftermath is needed that builds on strengths within the community.
- A broad campaign is needed by media, policy makers, and child development specialists to change attitudes toward violence and tolerance of violent behavior.
- Education should be made available to parents, educators, law enforcement officials, and others about how violence can affect children and alternative approaches to violence.

REFERENCES

Achenbach, T. M., & Edelbrock, C. S. (1983). *Manual for the Child Behavior Checklist and Revised Child Behavior Profile*. Burlington: University of Vermont.

Appelbone, P. (1996, January 12). Crime fear is seen forcing changes in youth behavior. *New York Times*, p. A6.

Augustyn, M., Parker, S., Groves, B. M., & Zuckerman, B. (1995). Children who witness violence. *Contemporary Pediatrics, 12,* 35–57.

Bandura, A. (1983). Psychological mechanisms of aggression. In R. G. Green & E. I. Donnerstein (Eds.), *Aggression: Theoretical and empirical reviews* (Vol. 1, pp. 1–40). San Diego, CA: Academic Press.

Bandura, A., & Walters, R. H. (1963). *Social learning and personality development*. New York: Holt, Rinehart & Winston.

Bell, C. (1995). Exposure to violence distresses children and may lead to their becoming violent. *Psychiatric News, 6,* 8, 15.

Bell, C., & Jenkins, E. J. (1991). Traumatic stress and children. *Journal of Health Care for the Poor and Underserved, 2,* 175–185.

Bell, C., & Jenkins, E. J. (1993). Community violence and children on Chicago's Southside. *Psychiatry, 56,* 46–54.

Black, D., & Kaplan, T. (1988). Father kills mother: Issues and problems encountered by a child psychiatric team. *British Journal of Psychiatry, 153,* 624–630.

Blumstein, A. (1995, August). Why the deadly nexus? *National Institute of Justice Journal* (no. 229), 2–9.

Brooks-Gunn, J., & Chase-Landsdale, P. L. (1995). Adolescent parenthood. In M. H. Bornstein (Ed.), *Handbook of parenting: Vol. 3. Status and social conditions of parenting* (pp. 113–150). Mahwah, NJ: Erlbaum.

Burman, S., & Allen-Meares, P. (1994). Neglected victims of murder: Children witness to parental homicide. *Social Work, 39,* 28–34.

Buzawa, E. S., & Buzawa, C. G. (1993). The impact of arrest on domestic violence. *American Behavioral Scientist, 36,* 558–574.

Carlson, B. E. (1984). Children's observations of interparental violence. In A. R. Roberts (Ed.), *Battered women and their families: Intervention strategies and treatment programs* (pp. 147–167). New York: Springer.

Children's Defense Fund. (1996). *The state of America's children.* Washington, DC: Author.

Cummings, E. M., & Zahn-Waxler, C. (1992). Emotions and the socialization of aggression: Adults' angry behavior and children's arousal and aggression. In A. Fraczek & H. Zumley (Eds.), *Socialization and aggression* (pp. 61–84). New York: Springer-Verlag.

Drell, M., Siegel, C., & Gaensbauer, T. (1993). Posttraumatic stress disorders. In C. Zeanah (Ed.), *Handbook of infant mental health* (pp. 291–304). New York: Guilford Press.

Egeland, B., & Erickson, M. F. (1987). Psychologically unavailable caregiving. In M. R. Brassard, R. Germain, & S. N. Hart (Eds.), *Psychological maltreatment of children and youth* (pp. 110–120). New York: Pergamon Press.

Erikson, E. (1963). *Childhood and society* (2nd ed.). New York: Norton.

Fantuzzo, J. W., & Lindquist, C. U. (1989). The effects of observing conjugal violence on children: A review and analysis of research methodology. *Journal of Family Violence, 4,* 77–94.

Fick, A. C., Osofsky, J. D., & Lewis, M. L. (1997). Police and parents' perceptions and understanding of violence. In J. D. Osofsky (Ed.), *Children in a violent society* (pp. 261–276). New York: Guilford Press.

Garbarino, J. (1992). *Children in danger: Coping with the consequences of community violence.* San Francisco: Jossey-Bass.

Garmezy, N. (1993). Children in poverty: Resilience despite risk. In D. Reiss,

J. E. Richters, M. Radke-Yarrow, & D. Scharf (Eds.), *Children and violence* (pp. 127–136). New York: Guilford Press.

Gelles, R. J. (1993). Constraints against family violence: How well do they work. *American Behavioral Scientist, 36,* 575–586.

Groves, B., & Zuckerman, B. (1997). Interventions with parents and community caregivers. In J. D. Osofsky (Ed.), *Children in a violent society* (pp. 183–201). New York: Guilford Press.

Groves, B., Zuckerman, B., Marans, S., & Cohen, D. (1993). Silent victims: Children who witness violence. *Journal of the American Medical Association, 269,* 262–264.

Grych, J. H., Seid, M., & Fincham, F. D. (1992). Assessing marital conflict from the child's perspective: The Children's Perception of Interparental Conflict Scale. *Child Development, 63,* 558–572.

Hawkins, J. D. (1995). Controlling crime before it happens: Risk-focused prevention. *National Institute of Justice Journal, 229,* 10–18.

Herbert, B. (1996, March 4). In trouble after school. *New York Times,* p. A15.

Hill, H. (1995, April). *Community violence and the social and emotional adjustment of African American children.* Poster presented at the biennial meeting of the Society for Research in Child Development, Indianapolis, IN.

Holden, G. W., Stein, J. D., Ritchie, K. L., Harris, S. D., & Jouriles, E. N. (1998). The parenting behaviors of battered women. In G. W. Holden, R. A. Geffner, & E. N. Jouriles (Eds.), *Children exposed to marital violence: Theory, research, and applied issues* (pp. 289–334). Washington, DC: American Psychological Association.

Jaffe, P. G., Wolfe, D. A., & Wilson, S. K. (1990). *Children of battered women.* Newbury Park, CA: Sage.

Jenkins, E. J., & Bell, C. C. (1994). Violence exposure, psychological distress, and high risk behaviors among inner city high school students. In S. Friedman (Ed.), *Anxiety disorders in African-Americans* (pp. 76–88). New York: Springer.

Jenkins, E. J., & Thompson, B. (1986, August). *Children talk about violence: Preliminary findings from a survey of Black elementary school children.* Paper presented at the 19th Annual Convention of the Association of Black Psychologists, Oakland, CA.

Jouriles, E. N., Pfiffner, L. J., & O'Leary, S. G. (1988). Marital conflict, parenting, and toddler conduct problems. *Journal of Abnormal Child Psychology*, *16*, 197–206.

Marans, S., & Cohen, D. (1993). Children and inner-city violence: Strategies for intervention. In L. Leavitt & N. Fox (Eds.), *Psychological effects of war and violence on children* (pp. 281–302). Hillsdale, NJ: Erlbaum.

Margolin, G. (1987). The multiple forms of aggressiveness between marital partners: How do we identify them? *Journal of Marriage and Family Therapy*, *13*, 77–84.

Margolin, G. (1995, January). *The effects of domestic violence on children*. Paper presented at the Conference on Violence against Children in the Family and Community, Los Angeles, CA.

Massachusetts Coalition of Battered Women Service Groups. (1995, December). *Children of domestic violence* (Working report). Boston: Author.

McCloskey, L. A., Figueredo, A. J., & Koss, M. P. (1995). The effects of systemic family violence on children's mental health. *Child Development*, *66*, 1239–1261.

Murphy, L., Pynoos, R. S., & James, C. B. (1997). The trauma/grief focused group psychotherapy module of an elementary school-based violence prevention/intervention program. In J. D. Osofsky (Ed.), *Children in a violent society* (pp. 223–255). New York: Guilford Press.

O'Brien, M., John, R. S., Margolin, G., & Erel, O. (1994). Reliability and diagnostic efficacy of parents' reports regarding children's exposure to marital aggression. *Violence and Victims*, *9*, 45–62.

Osofsky, J. D. (1995a). Children who witness violence: The invisible victims. In *Social Policy Reports* (Vol. 9, no. 3). Ann Arbor, MI: Society for Research in Child Development.

Osofsky, J. D. (1995b). The effects of violence exposure on young children. *American Psychologist*, *50*, 782–788.

Osofsky, J. D. (Ed.). (1997). *Children in a violent society*. New York: Guilford Press.

Osofsky, J. D., Cohen, G., & Drell, M. (1995). The effects of trauma on young children: A case of 2-year-old twins. *International Journal of Psychoanalysis*, *76*, 595–607.

Osofsky, J. D., & Fenichel, E. (Eds.). (1994). *Hurt, healing, and hope: Caring for infants and toddlers in violent environments.* Arlington, VA: Zero to Three/National Center for Clinical Infant Programs.

Osofsky, J. D., Hann, D. M., & Peebles, C. (1993). Adolescent parenthood: Risks and opportunities for mothers and infants. In C. Zeanah (Ed.), *Handbook of infant mental health* (pp. 106–119). New York: Guilford Press.

Osofsky, J. D., Wewers, S., Hann, D., & Fick, A. (1993). Chronic community violence: What is happening to our children? *Psychiatry, 56,* 36–45.

Pagelow, M. D. (1984). *Family violence.* New York: Praeger.

Pate, A. M., & Hamilton, E. E. (1993). Formal and informal deterrents to domestic violence: The Dade county spouse assault experiment. *American Sociological Review, 57,* 691–697.

Pynoos, R. S. (1993). Traumatic stress and developmental psychopathology in children and adolescents. In J. M. Oldham, M. B. Riba, & A. Tasman (Eds.), *American Psychiatric Press review of psychiatry* (Vol. 12, pp. 205–238). Washington, DC: American Psychiatric Press.

Pynoos, R. S., & Nader, K. (1993). Issues in the treatment of posttraumatic stress in children and adolescents. In J. P. Wilson & B. Raphael (Eds.), *The international handbook of traumatic stress syndromes* (pp. 535–549). New York: Plenum Press.

Richters, J. E. (1993). Community violence and children's development: Toward a research agenda for the 1990's. In D. Reiss, J. E. Richters, M. Radke-Yarrow, & D. Scharf (Eds.), *Children and violence* (pp. 7–21). New York: Guilford Press.

Richters, J. E., & Martinez, P. (1993). The NIMH Community Violence Project: Children as victims of and witnesses to violence. In D. Reiss, J. E. Richters, M. Radke-Yarrow, & D. Scharf (Eds.), *Children and violence* (pp. 7–21). New York: Guilford Press.

Rosenberg, M. S. (1994, January). *Violence prevention: Integrating public health and criminal justice.* Presentation at the United States Attorneys' Conference, Washington, DC.

Shakoor, B., & Chalmers, D. (1991). Co-victimization of African American children who witness violence and the theoretical implications of its effect on their cognitive, emotional, and behavioral development. *Journal of the National Medical Association, 83,* 233–238.

Straus, M. A. (1979). Measuring intrafamilial conflict and violence: The Conflict Tactics Scales. *Journal of Marriage and Family, 41,* 75–88.

Steinman, M. (1989). The effects of police responses on spouse abuse. *American Journal of Police, 8,* 1–19.

Sternberg, K. J., Lamb, M. E., Greenbaum, C., Cicchetti, D., Dawud, S., Cortes, R. M., Krispin, O., & Lorey, F. (1993). Effects of domestic violence on children's behavior problems and depression. *Developmental Psychology, 29,* 44–52.

Zuckerman, B., Augustyn, M., Groves, B. M., & Parker, S. (1995). Silent victims revisited: The special case of domestic violence. *Pediatrics, 96,* 511–513.

PART TWO

Research

5

Using Multiple Informants to Understand Domestic Violence and Its Effects

Kathleen J. Sternberg, Michael E. Lamb,
and Samia Dawud-Noursi

COLLECTING AND EVALUATING INFORMATION

After nearly 30 years of research, researchers should have a good understanding of domestic violence and its effects on child development. No one doubts that domestic violence is harmful to children or that the psychological distress they experience should often be manifest in behavior problems, of course, yet the reported behavioral and psychological characteristics of abuse victims and witnesses vary considerably across studies. For example, Aber, Allen, Carlson, and Cicchetti (1989) found that physically abused children had more behavior problems than children in comparison groups, whereas other researchers reported no such differences (Kravic, 1987; Wolfe & Mosk, 1983). Likewise, Jaffe, Wolfe, Wilson, and Zak (1986) found that children who were exposed to parental violence had higher levels of behavior problems than children in comparison groups, whereas the same researchers found no such differences in another study (Wolfe, Zak, Wilson, & Jaffe, 1986). How can such traumatic events have such inconsistent effects on children's development?

In this chapter, we discuss several methodological issues in an attempt to explain why the established link between violence in the family and children's behavior problems appears weaker than might be expected. Because other reviewers and critics have focused at length on such factors as inadequate control groups, small sample sizes, and the degree to which the severity, frequency, and type of abuse are specified (Aber & Cicchetti, 1984; Lamphear, 1985; National Research Council, 1993), here we focus on methodological issues that have been given less consideration in the empirical literature. The primary focus of this chapter is the importance of including multiple informants when conducting research on family violence and its effects on children. Unfortunately, most researchers concerned with the effects of domestic violence have obtained information from only one person about both the history of family violence and the children's behavior problems. Only recently have some researchers come to recognize the problems caused by reliance on a single source of information. We also suggest that the failures to distinguish among types of family violence and carefully to document the diverse types of maltreatment to which some children are exposed may yield inconsistencies in the apparent effects of domestic violence.

We begin the chapter by showing how difficult it is to determine what types of violence have occurred in families. We proceed to argue that the judicious use of multiple informants can help researchers obtain more reliable portraits of the patterns of violence in individual families. We then review studies that have explored discrepancies among informants concerning the behavior of children in violent families and review the challenges involved in integrating information from multiple informants. In the final substantive section, we describe an ongoing longitudinal study to illustrate how researchers can use multiple informants to collect information about both independent (histories of child and spouse abuse) and dependent (e.g., behavior problems, depression) measures.

Child Maltreatment Histories

Traditionally, researchers interested in abused children relied on protective service records to distinguish between physically abusive and nonabusive families. Unfortunately, however, these records typically comprise second-hand information that is rarely complete, and this poses difficulties when assigning children to abuse and comparison groups. Indeed, researchers have shown in several recent studies how useful it is to obtain information about child maltreatment from multiple sources.

Kaufman and her colleagues (Kaufman, Jones, Stieglitz, Vitulano, & Mannariono, 1994), for example, examined the histories of 56 children from 30 poor families who were all receiving services from child welfare agencies because the children had been maltreated. By supplementing the information in the protective caseworkers' files with information from parents, medical records, and clinical observations, Kaufman et al. were able to create more complete pictures of the children's histories of maltreatment. Specifically, the additional information allowed the researchers to identify types of abuse that had not previously been reported and to document histories of abuse that were more severe than those reported by caseworkers.

In another study, McGee and her colleagues (McGee, Wolfe, Yuen, Wilson, & Carnochan, 1995) examined multiple perspectives on the histories of 180 adolescents. Adolescents, their caseworkers, and researchers were asked to identify perpetrators and rate the presence and severity of five types of maltreatment (physical, sexual, and emotional abuse; neglect; and exposure to family violence) on 4-point Likert scales with response options ranging from *not at all* to *severe*. Adolescents confirmed the caseworkers' reports in approximately 75% of the cases, but some interesting disagreements, which varied depending on the type of maltreatment, also emerged. Approximately 20% of the adolescents reported incidents of maltreatment that were unknown to the caseworkers. In addition, the adolescents often denied exposure to types of maltreatment reported by the social workers (family violence, 16%; emotional maltreatment, 15%; and neglect, 29%). Interestingly, the adolescents' reports of maltreatment were better predictors of behavior problems, as reported by both parents and the adolescents themselves, than were the caseworkers' reports.

Although Finkelhor and Dziuba-Leatherman (1994) did not ask multiple informants about individual histories, comparisons of survey responses obtained from two thousand 10- to 16-year-old children with those obtained from adults provide interesting insights regarding the type of information children can provide and underscore the value of obtaining information from multiple informants, even when attempting to assess the incidence of family violence. Twenty-seven percent of the girls and 30% of the boys they surveyed reported that their parents used corporal punishment in the last year, whereas 71% of the girls and 78% of the boys had experienced corporal punishment at some time in their lives. In addition, slightly less than 1% of the children reported a more serious incident (punching, slapping, kicking, hitting with an object, or threatening with a weapon) in the last year, and 2% reported at least one such prior incident of maltreatment. Children reported more assaults by nonparent family members (5%) and non-familial perpetrators (22%) than by parents; two-thirds of the youth reported disclosing the assault to someone, but only 25% had reported the assaults to authorities. In earlier surveys of parents, Straus and Gelles (1990) reported higher levels of parent-to-child violence, although differences in the ages of the target children (10 to 16 years in the Finkelhor survey, 3 to 17 years in the Straus and Gelles surveys), the source of data, and the definitions of abusive events preclude direct comparison of the results. The discrepancies nonetheless show how difficult it is to develop accurate estimates of child abuse and underscore the value of obtaining information from multiple informants.

Violence Between Parents

As in the case of child maltreatment, researchers concerned with children's exposure to spousal violence traditionally have relied on single informants. Although numerous researchers have documented an association between children's exposure to spousal conflict and child maladjustment, the association between the two factors is not as consistent as one might expect. Perhaps in part the lack of consistency across studies can be explained by the methods used to assess spousal conflict and children's exposure to the conflict (O'Brien, John, Margolin, & Erel, 1994; Sternberg, 1997). Because of logistical constraints, researchers interested in children who were exposed to spousal violence have recruited their samples primarily from battered women's shelters. In these settings, mothers are relied on as the primary (and often sole) informants about their and their children's exposure to spouse and child abuse. Researchers using samples from battered women's shelters rarely ask children directly to describe their experiences and almost never interview their fathers or father figures (see Sternberg, 1997, for a discussion of this topic). Concerns about the objectivity of abused women and the dangers of relying on single informants to learn about the extent and nature of family violence have prompted researchers to explore the reliability of spousal reports concerning marital violence.

In the first study designed to explore this issue, Szinovacz (1983) used the Conflict Tactics Scale (Straus, Gelles, & Steinmetz, 1980) to interview 103 couples recruited from the community. Men and women were separately interviewed about their own and their spouses' violent behavior toward one another. The level of agreement among spouses was low, particularly when Szinovacz focused on individual behaviors rather than overall levels of violence. Interestingly, the partners were more likely to agree about husband-to-wife violence than about wife-to-husband violence, and more violent incidents were described when the researchers relied on both reports rather than on either partner's report alone. Szinovacz discussed a number of reasons why spouses might underreport their violent behavior and emphasized that more complete reports would be obtained if both individuals were routinely questioned, particularly when each knows that his or her partner is being asked similar questions.

In a similar vein, Jouriles and O'Leary (1985) administered the Conflict Tactics Scale (Straus et al., 1980) to couples entering marital therapy ($n = 65$) and a community sample ($n = 37$). They found poor to moderate agreement between spouses, particularly about specific events. As in the Szinovacz study, husbands tended to report lower levels of violence toward their wives than their wives reported receiving. In a recent study comparing husbands' and wives' reports of marital violence, however, approximately 40% of the incongruities between spouses' reports reflected the underreporting of aggression by both men and women (Langhinrichsen-Rohling & Vivian, 1994). Nevertheless, all researchers agree that the apparent prevalence of spousal violence varies depending on whether husbands or wives are informants, particularly when agreement about specific violent incidents is at issue.

The possible unreliability of the partners' reports regarding the incidence of spousal violence is at least matched by the unreliability of parents' reports regarding their children's experiences as witnesses. Although researchers did not initially inquire systematically about the whereabouts of children during violent fights between their parents, the results of recent studies suggest that children often see or overhear these disagreements or confrontations between parents. Parents often underestimate the extent to which their children are exposed to marital violence, however. Hughes, Parkinson, and Vargo (1989) reported that children were either in the same room or in a room adjacent to the assault 90% of the time, whereas 58% of the women studied by Dobash and Dobash (1984) reported that children were present during assaults by their husbands. In another study, 25% of the 8- to 11-year-old children interviewed described having witnessed spousal violence at least once in their lives (O'Brien et al., 1994). Although spouse abuse has traditionally been considered a threat to the welfare of women, these data suggest that significant numbers of children are directly exposed to spousal violence. This realization has begun to foster dialogue between researchers interested in child and spouse abuse, although for the most part, the two types of violence continue to be studied independently.

In summary, a review of the literature reveals numerous reasons why single informants provide a limited picture of family violence. Although motivated distortions of reality sometimes explain the divergent reports, they may not be the most important factors. In some cases, adults may be unaware that their children witness or overhear incidents of spousal violence, and children may not always report child abuse by one parent to the other. In addition, individuals may not view specific events similarly, and as a result, one informant may define an act as abusive whereas the other person considers it normative. Agency case records represent a particularly problematic source of information for researchers. At best, they represent a source of second-hand information that is not systematically documented. The available evidence also raises serious questions about the exclusive reliance on mothers for information about the history of family violence and its effects on children. Only recently have researchers begun to identify the methodological and interpretive risks associated with this practice, underscoring the importance of obtaining information from multiple sources, including fathers and children.

Multiple Perspectives on Children's Behavior Problems

In the previous section we reviewed the risks of relying on single informants to understand children's histories of maltreatment and exposure to family violence. Questions have also been raised about the tendency to rely on one source of information when assessing the impact of family violence on children's adjustment. Although mothers or teachers have traditionally been the sole informants about children's behavior and adjustment (Fantuzzo & Lindquist, 1989), there is now persuasive evidence that these and other informants often disagree. This has fostered discussion about the importance of obtaining information about children's behavior and adjustment from multiple informants (Achenbach, McConaughy, & Howell, 1987).

In the past, agreement and disagreement among mothers, fathers, teachers, children, and mental health professionals with respect to children's behavior problems were viewed as manifestations of interobserver (un)reliability, with discrepancies among informants believed to reflect inaccuracy, error, or bias on the part of one or more of the informants. Many scholars thus sought to identify the "optimal informant" and explored the specific deficiencies and strengths of each potential informant (Achenbach et al., 1987; Loeber, Green, Lahey, & Stouthamer-Loeber, 1989; Reid, Kavanagh, & Baldwin, 1987). Only recently have these issues been reformulated, with many of the same researchers noting that, far from reflecting inaccuracy or "interrater unreliability," the discrepancies among informants may be extremely important in themselves (Achenbach et al., 1987; Reid et al., 1987). Some of the disagreements among informants have thus been attributed to differences in perspective, whereas others have been attributed to differences in the children's behavior across contexts and relationships

(Richters, 1992; Tein, Roosa, & Michaels, 1994). Unlike "objective" observers who are trained to code children's behavior in specific contexts, mothers, fathers, teachers, and mental health workers observe and interact with children in diverse, partially overlapping contexts and thus should not be expected to report the same behaviors and behavior problems. Unlike objective observers, furthermore, parents, teachers, mental health workers, and peers have different relationships and investments in these children, which by definition prevent them from being objective. Children themselves are widely underused as informants, even when they have the requisite developmental capacity.

Disagreements and differences of perspective among informants are of particular concern when examining the effects of family violence on children's adjustment. When parents are variously the victims of spouse abuse, the perpetrators of physical abuse, or the partners of child abusers, their perceptions of their children's behavior problems may vary (Wolfe et al., 1986; Wolfe, Jaffe, Wilson, & Zak, 1985). Such parents may project their own frustrations or guilty feelings onto their children, and distressed mothers are known to evaluate their children's behavior more harshly than objective observers do (Brody & Forehand, 1986; Hughes, 1988; Hughes & Barad, 1983; Kazdin, Moser, Colbus, & Bell, 1985). Abusive parents also appear more likely than other parents to attribute negative motives to their children's behavior (Bauer & Twentyman, 1985; Larrance & Twentyman, 1983) and more likely than independent observers to view their children's behavior as problematic (Reid et al., 1987). Even within the nonabusive range of parental behavior, more aggressive and hostile mothers tend to have more negative views of their children and their dispositions (MacKinnon-Lewis, Lamb, Arbuckle, Baradaran, & Volling, 1992).

The dangers of relying on battered women as the sole informants about their children's behavior problems were illustrated by O'Keefe (1994). O'Keefe interviewed 185 women who resided in battered women's shelters about the mothers' and fathers' aggression toward their children, marital aggression, and children's behavior problems. Although mothers' reports of their own child-directed aggression predicted children's behavior problems, father-to-child aggression (as reported by mothers) did not. Indeed, even though father-to-child violence was reportedly more severe than mother-to-child violence, it appeared to have little impact on the children's adjustment.

Unfortunately, O'Keefe's design typifies a widespread approach to research on battered women and their children, with mothers being the primary informants regarding both independent and dependent variables. O'Keefe's report is unique and laudable because she recognized and discussed the problems inherent in exclusive reliance on battered women as informants. We can only speculate about the interpretive problems that plague comparable studies in which researchers are less circumspect and self-critical. In the section that follows, we review our own ongoing research in some depth, using our practices, decisions, and findings to illustrate the importance and value of considering systematically multiple sources of evidence regarding domestic violence and its effects.

THE ISRAELI DOMESTIC VIOLENCE STUDY

In our study, Israeli mothers, fathers, teachers, peers, and children provided information about the behavior of children who were either victims of physical child abuse, witnesses of spouse abuse, both victims and witnesses, or neither victims nor witnesses. The study was undertaken in Israel because we were able to recruit a relatively large sample while avoiding some of the methodological problems that often plague research on domestic violence in the United States. Specifically, most researchers have studied abused children from single-parent families and/or children living with their mothers in battered women's shelters. In such contexts, it is difficult, if not impossible, to distinguish the effects of domestic violence from the effects of such potentially traumatic events as parental separation or divorce, relocation, or poverty. In addition, many children may have been both victims of child maltreatment and witnesses of spousal violence, although few researchers have made efforts to distinguish the effects of these quite distinct experiences. In our study, by contrast, all children were drawn from the case files of social welfare agencies, and the families were matched with respect to size, ethnicity, religious practices, and socioeconomic status. All children were still living with both of their biological parents during the first wave of data collection and had never been placed outside the home or lived in a shelter. Exhaustive efforts were made to recruit groups of children with known degrees of exposure to different forms of family violence so that comparisons could be made among the groups identified above. In this regard, we sought and obtained information from all family members and official records so as to create as comprehensive as possible a view of each family's history of violence.

The current report is based primarily on the first wave of data collection in a longitudinal study designed to explore the effects of child and spouse abuse on a wide range of developmental outcomes, including children's behavior problems, depression, relationships with family members, children's attributions about peers and parents, children's self-concepts, children's perceptions of their social networks, relationships with their peers, and their academic performance (Sternberg et al., 1993; Sternberg et al., 1994; Sternberg & Dawud-Noursi, 1996). Preliminary results from later waves of data collection are also introduced as we attempt to demonstrate the importance of obtaining information from multiple informants when evaluating children for clinical and empirical purposes.

Method

Sample

The sample, comprising one hundred and ten 8- to 12-year-old ($M =$ 10 years and 7 months) children (61 boys) and their parents, was recruited with the assistance of social workers from the Departments of Family Services in Jerusalem and Tel Aviv, Israel. The social workers referred all families that met our selection criteria. To obtain a homogeneous sample, the sample was limited to lower class, two-parent families of Jewish origin. We excluded the following groups of children from the study: children who were mentally retarded, children who were victims of sexual abuse, children whose parents were mentally retarded or had diagnosed psychiatric disorders, and children who were victims only of psychological maltreatment or neglect.

The families included in this study were representative of the Jewish social welfare population with respect to ethnic origin (75% had parents born in Middle Eastern or North African countries) and background characteristics. On average, mothers and fathers in this study had completed 9.4 years of formal education. All children lived with their biological parents and had an average of three siblings. The four groups did not differ with respect to background characteristics sometimes related to abuse and its effects (including socioeconomic status, apartment size, unemployment, stressful life events, birth order, birth complications, and chronic or serious health problems).

Data Gathering

One of the project interviewers, naive with respect to family history, contacted the parents by phone and asked them to participate in a research project concerned with the effects of stressful life circumstances on children's development. Upon consent, an appointment was made for two female researchers, both naive with respect to the family's history, to visit the home and conduct interviews with the child and his or her parents. The mother and father were separately interviewed by one researcher while another interviewed the child. During these interviews, both parents and the target children independently described the children's behavior problems using appropriate versions of Achenbach's Child Behavior Checklist (CBCL; Achenbach & Edelbrock, 1983, 1987).

After obtaining permission from the Department of Education, the school principals, and the classroom teachers, three female research assistants visited the children's classrooms and administered the questionnaires to the teachers and their pupils. The administration occurred at least 2 months after school began to ensure that children and teachers would have had sufficient opportunity to become familiar with one another. To ensure confidentiality and anonymity, the target children were not identified to either research assistants or the teachers, who were asked to complete the Teacher Report Form (TRF) of the Achenbach CBCL (Achenbach & Edelbrock, 1986) concerning the target children and two randomly selected children of the same gender. In addition, the teachers were asked to rate all of the children in the home-room class on the Teacher Rating Scale on Peer Relations developed by

Morison (1982). Three research assistants administered the Revised Class Play (RCP; Masten, Morison, & Pellegrini, 1985) to all the children in the classroom of the target child, while teachers completed the questionnaires in the school lounge. In Phase I, data were collected from all of the mothers and children, 77% of the fathers (child abuse, 85%; spouse abuse, 75%; abused witness, 77%; and comparison, 71%) and 57% of the teachers and classroom peers. Unfortunately, principals of a number of schools refused to participate in the study for religious reasons, insisting that by participating in the study they would be required to make negative comments about children's behavior, a practice they considered morally unacceptable.

Two to three years after these data were collected, school records (including the detailed reports compiled by school psychologists) were obtained through the Department of Education, and the children's current homeroom teachers were asked to rate both the target children and randomly selected classmates (Phase II). Shortly thereafter, the families were recontacted by a researcher who was unaware of the children's history or earlier responses. Separate interviews were then scheduled with the children, mothers, and fathers (Phase III). The adolescents averaged 14.5 years of age at the time they were interviewed in Phase III. (Note, however, that several of the adolescents and their parents had not yet been interviewed by the time this chapter was written.)

Measures

History of family violence. The initial classification of families into the four groups (child abuse only, spouse abuse only, both child and spouse abuse, neither child nor spouse abuse) was made by social workers from the Department of Social Services. The initial measure we developed for classifying families involved a 50-item inventory of specific acts of abuse. Social workers were asked to indicate whether either parent had directed such acts toward the other or toward the target child. To our surprise, however, the social workers were unable to answer these specific questions despite their close contact with the families. Instead, they provided us with vague descriptions of child or spouse abuse. In light of these difficulties, we revised our instrument and asked the case workers to provide detailed descriptions of at least one incident of domestic violence in the past 6 months. If the child was identified as an abused witness, the social workers were asked to describe one incident of physical abuse by a parent as well as one incident of spousal violence. In addition, the social workers were asked questions about the severity and history of violence and about any developmental problems the children were having.

Although the social workers were our primary informants, the information they provided was supplemented by interviews with the parents and children. Specifically, husbands' and wives' responses to questions on the Areas of Change Questionnaire (ACQ; Margolin, Talovic, & Weinstein, 1983) about hitting one another as well as mothers' and children's responses in semistructured interviews were used to corroborate the social workers' reports. For purposes of our initial analyses, we considered as valid any detailed reports of violence and the family was classified accordingly, even when the incidents in question were not reported by the other informants. Both children and parents reported incidents of domestic violence not reported by the social workers.

The sample was thus divided into four groups for purposes of analysis. Three groups of children who had experienced some form of chronic domestic violence (with at least one incident in the previous 6 months) were compared with each other and with children in a matched comparison group. Group I (child abuse; $n = 33$; 18 boys) included children who had experienced physical abuse by one or both parents. Group II (spouse abuse; $n = 16$; 8 boys) included children who had witnessed physical violence between their parents but were not themselves abused. Group III (abused witnesses; $n = 30$; 21 boys) included children who had both witnessed and been physically abused by one or both parents. Group IV (comparison; $n = 31$; 14 boys) comprised a group of children who had neither observed nor been victims of physical violence, but were matched with the other groups on a variety of demographic variables.

Unfortunately, because we did not comprehensively interview all informants about child and spouse abuse in Phase I, it was difficult to evaluate systematically the discrepancies and pattern of responses provided by different informants. (We expanded this aspect of the study in Phase III.) As in Phase I, social workers were asked to complete questionnaires about violent incidents that had been reported to them between Phases I and III, with special focus on incidents that had occurred in the past year. We were able to obtain detailed information from social workers about only 48% of the families, however, in part because many of the families were no longer under the supervision of the original welfare department or caseworker and there was no new information on file. It was thus especially important to obtain detailed information about child and spouse abuse from mothers, fathers, and children themselves. To collect information about the history of violence in these families we used a qualitative interview originally developed by Suzanne Salzinger (1993) to interview adults about family disagreements. We adapted this questionnaire so it could also be used with children and translated the parent and child versions to Hebrew. The questionnaire begins with a discussion of minor disagreements and ends with inquiries about "more serious disagreements" and "the worst disagreement ever." This format encourages children and adults to describe specific events, which provides the interviewer with a more comprehensive picture of their experiences.

To facilitate the illustrative and preliminary analyses included in this chapter, we used the informants' responses to the Family Interaction Questionnaire (Salzinger, 1993) to complete the Conflict Tactics Scale (Straus et al., 1980) concerning each of the dyadic relationships of interest (mother to father, father to mother, mother to child, father to child). For purposes of the present analyses, reports of incidents more serious than item 10 on the Conflict Tactics Scale ("slapping") were used to identify the relationship as violent, at least as reported by that informant.

Evaluation of behavior problems. Mothers, fathers, teachers, and the target children themselves were asked to evaluate the target children's behavior problems on relevant versions of Achenbach's Child Behavior Checklists, namely the CBCL (Achenbach & Edelbrock, 1981, 1983), the TRF (Achenbach & Edelbrock, 1986), and the Youth Self Report (YSR; Achenbach & Edelbrock, 1987), respectively. Each informant was asked to respond to approximately 100 questions (the exact number varied somewhat depending on the specific version concerned) describing the child's behavior in the past 6 months. All items were answered on a 3-point Likert Scale (*not true of me, somewhat true of me, very true of me*), with responses combined to yield scores on two broad-band scales (the Internalizing and Externalizing Behavior Problem Scales) for both boys and girls, an index of total behavior problems (Total Behavior Problem Scale) and a number of narrow band scales. Achenbach and Edelbrock (1987) proposed that *T* scores of 70 or above (which correspond to the upper 2% of scores in the standardization sample) reflect clinically significant problems, whereas *T* scores greater than or equal to 63 indicate a need for clinical intervention. The Hebrew translations of these questionnaires were used to interview all participants.

Preliminary Analyses: Shedding Light on Methodological Issues

Agreement and Disagreement About Family Violence Histories

In this section, we discuss preliminary patterns of agreement and disagreement between mothers, fathers, and children about the occurrence of child and spouse abuse.

The preliminary analyses reported here for illustrative purposes are based on 38 families in which all three informants had been interviewed. In only 7 of the families was there perfect agreement among informants about the abusive behavior of each of the parents (one triad agreed there was abuse by the fathers toward the mother and vice versa, and six triads reported no abuse by either parent). In 19 other cases, all three informants agreed about one parent's behavior toward the child but disagreed about the other parent's behavior. In 18 cases, all informants agreed about the father's behavior (two triads agreed abuse was present; whereas 16 triads agreed abuse was absent), whereas in 22 cases, all the informants agreed about the mother's behavior (four triads agreed abuse was present; 18 triads agreed abuse was absent). Three mothers reported abusing their children, whereas their husbands and children did not report any maltreatment, and two other mothers claimed that both parents abused the target children whereas their partners and children reported no abuse. Six mothers claimed that their husband had abused the target child, but this was denied by both the father and the child. Three fathers admitted abusive acts not reported by the other informants, and three fathers denied an abusive act reported by the other informants.

Stated differently, we thus found that seven fathers and children agreed about their relationships whereas their wives disagreed (one dyad reported abuse; six dyads reported no abuse). Mothers and children agreed with each other about their relationship but disagreed with fathers in three cases (three mother–child dyads reported abuse). Fathers and mothers agreed with each other but not with the child about the parents' behavior in three cases (two triads agreed mother was not abusive; one triad agreed father was not abusive). In 13 families, fathers and children disagreed about their relationship (10 fathers did not report abuse reported by children; three fathers reported abuse not reported by children). Mothers and children disagreed about their relationship in 12 cases. In 5 of these families, mothers reported abusing 24 children who did not report being abused, whereas 7 children reported having been abused by mothers who reported no such maltreatment. In 12 other families, data were available from fathers and children but not from mothers. Nine of these dyads agreed there was no violence in their relationship, whereas one pair agreed that the father abused the child. In one case, the child reported abuse not reported by his father.

Correspondingly, data were available from 26 mothers and children but not from fathers. Thirteen of these mother–child dyads agreed: Two dyads reported child abuse by mothers, whereas 11 dyads agreed abuse did not occur. In the 11 cases where mothers and adolescents disagreed, 8 mothers reported abuse not reported by their children, and 3 children reported abuse not reported by their mothers.

These preliminary data reveal surprisingly high levels of disagreement among mothers, fathers, and children regarding the occurrence of parent-to-child violence. What about the independent accounts of spousal violence? Unfortunately, our preliminary analyses regarding spouse abuse involve only 38 families in which reports from all three informants are currently available. Both parents and their children agreed regarding the occurrence of spousal violence in 17 of the 38 cases (13 triads agreed that violence was absent, 2 agreed that both partners were violent, 1 agreed that the mother was violent, and 1 agreed that the father was violent). In 13 other families, both spouses and the target child agreed that the mothers were not violent.

The results of these preliminary analyses strongly underscore the importance of obtaining data from multiple informants. Had we asked only mothers or social workers to identify the occurrence of child or spouse abuse, as is usually the practice in research on domestic violence, the picture we obtained would have been quite different. Furthermore, some of the patterns of disagreement contradicted conventional wisdom. Fathers agreed with their children more often than mothers did, for example, and not only in cases where abuse was reportedly absent. Our analyses also illustrate how difficult it is to obtain information about family violence from multiple informants when researchers do not know what really happened and thus cannot decide who is the "best" or most accurate reporter. Informants disagree for many different reasons, and thus lack of agreement should not be considered simply as an issue of reliability or unreliability. Instead, methods should be developed whereby information provided by different informants can be integrated so that children can be assigned to different experimental groups for research purposes. Presumably, increased precision in the assignment to such groups will permit clearer insight into the effects of violence on children.

Divergent Perspectives in Reporting Children's Behavior Problems

Unfortunately, discrepancies between reports by different informants do not end with the independent variable, as we demonstrate in this section. We used a series of multivariate analyses to examine group differences in behavior problems as reported by mothers, fathers, teachers, and the target children themselves in Phase I with the initial group assignments used for purposes of analysis (Sternberg et al., 1993). When the target children provided information about their behavior problems, respondents in the child and abused witness groups reported significantly more internalizing and externalizing behavior problems than

Table 1

Group Differences in Children's, Parents', and Teachers' Reports of Behavior Problems in Phase I

Reporter and scales	Child abuse	Spouse	Abused witnesses	Comparison
Children				
N	33	16	30	31
Internalizing (YSR)				
M	54.73$_a$	50.63$_c$	56.30$_{bc}$	48.61$_{ab}$
SD	9.92	9.55	9.30	7.82
Externalizing (YSR)				
M	49.48$_a$	46.88	49.37$_b$	41.39
SD	12.20	9.47	10.34	9.92
Mothers				
N	33	16	30	31
Internalizing (CBCL)				
M	63.18	68.06	66.83	62.48
SD	9.85	9.18	10.99	8.49
Externalizing (CBCL)				
M	61.42$_{ab}$	67.88$_{ac}$	68.77$_{bd}$	59.39$_{cd}$
SD	11.28	8.36	9.20	10.02
Fathers				
N	28	12	23	22
Internalizing (CBCL)				
M	63.71	64.08	63.09	63.27
SD	9.82	11.12	9.60	7.11
Externalizing (CBCL)				
M	65.46	62.08	61.61	60.73
SD	9.82	14.19	11.00	6.61

Reporter and scales	Child abuse	Spouse	Abused witnesses	Comparison
Table 1 *(Continued)*				
Teachers				
N	16	9	13	19
Internalizing (TRF)				
M	66.56	67.44	62.08	65.42
SD	8.52	9.33	8.45	9.78
Externalizing (TRF)				
M	66.81	66.11	60.92	59.84
SD	8.67	8.80	7.32	6.70

Note. Similar subscripts denote contrasts significant at the .05 level. CBCL = Child Behavior Checklist; TRF = Teacher Report Form; YSR = Youth Self Report.

children in the comparison group (see Table 1). By contrast, mothers of children in the spouse and abused witness groups reported more externalizing behavior problems than did mothers of children in the comparison group (see Table 1). Although the mothers of children in the child abuse group assigned higher scores to their children on these dimensions than mothers of comparison group children did, none of these differences was significant. Mothers who were abused had a similar but nonsignificant tendency to rate their children as having more problems on the internalizing dimension. When fathers and teachers were the informants, there were no significant group effects on either the internalizing or externalizing dimensions (see Table 1).

Chi-square analyses were then conducted to compare the numbers of children in each group who had T scores of 63 or above (the 10th percentile) on the YSR and maternal CBCL and were thus deemed to have problems serious enough to warrant clinical intervention (Achenbach & Edelbrock, 1987). When children were the informants, analyses revealed significant differences only on the Internalizing Behavior Problem Scale. Abused children were more likely to assign themselves scores in the intervention range than were children in the spouse abuse and comparison groups (see Table 2). One-fourth of the children who experienced physical abuse assigned themselves scores of sufficient magnitude to suggest the need for clinical intervention. When mothers were the informants, mothers of children in the abused witness and spouse abuse groups assigned their children scores above 63 on the Externalizing Behavior Problem Scale. Differences on the Internalizing Behavior Problem Scale were not statistically significant. According to mothers, therefore, most of the children in this sample were in need of clinical intervention for internalizing and externalizing problems, whereas the children themselves recognized a much smaller need for significant concern. When fathers and teachers were the informants, the chi-square analyses revealed no significant group differences. Once again, it seemed that perceptions of children's behavior problems varied substantially depending on the informants' perspectives.

Although we continue to distill and collect Phase II and III data, we have conducted preliminary analyses on the basis of the responses of 58 children, their mothers, and their teachers. When Phase I abuse status was used as the independent variable, analyses of variance revealed no group differences in the mothers' and children's reports of the target children's behavior problems in Phase III. The absence of group differences may well reflect the considerable number of changes in family circumstances that took place between the two phases of data collection, including multiple separations, entry by many of the children into boarding schools some distance from their families, and, presumably, changes in their exposure to family violence. When current abuse status (according to the children) was used as an independent variable, multivariate analyses of variance (MANOVA) revealed significant group differences in children's reports of their behavior problems and a comparable though nonsignificant trend on the teachers' reports (see Table 3).

Chi-square analyses were again conducted to evaluate the percentage of children in the intervention range. The 10 children who reported being abused in the past 6 months were more likely to report extensive internalizing and externalizing problems than comparison children were (see Table 4). When mothers and teachers were the in-

Table 2

Group Differences in the Percentages of Children With Reported Behavior Problems in the Intervention Range, Phase I

Scale	Child (n = 33)	Spouse (n = 16)	Abused witness (n = 30)	Comparison (n = 31)	$X^2(3)$	p
Youth Self Report						
Internalizing	27	6	27	3	9.80	.02
Externalizing	15	0	10	3	4.71	.20
Maternal Report of Child Behavior Checklist						
Internalizing	61	75	77	58	3.41	.33
Externalizing	49	75	77	36	13.62	.01

Table 3

Group Differences in Children's, Parents', and Teachers' Reports of Behavior Problems in Phase II by Reports of Violence in Phase II

Reporter and scale	Child abuse	Spouse	Abused witnesses	Comparison
Mothers (CBCL)				
N	15	3	12	20
Internalizing				
M	58.87	67.00	63.75	56.85
SD	7.37	5.57	13.78	10.38
Externalizing				
M	59.47	49.67	58.83	53.60
SD	9.59	11.37	9.92	10.66
Teachers (TRF)				
N	19	14	25	24
Internalizing[a]				
M	61.67	70.50	63.75	58.42
SD	11.70	9.14	6.80	8.77
Externalizing				
M	59.11	51.75	62.83	57.00
SD	11.29	9.70	7.81	9.65
Children (YSR)				
N	6	4	12	28
Internalizing[b]				
M	55.37	46.50	56.25	47.75
SD	10.86	10.47	8.92	8.13
Externalizing				
M	55.50	38.25	55.75	47.75
SD	13.04	6.24	11.65	8.32

Note. CBCL = Child Behavior Checklist; TRF = Teacher Report Form; YSR = Youth Self Report. [a]$F = 3.76$, $p < .10$. [b]$p < .05$.

Table 4

Group Differences in the Percentages of Children With Reported Behavior Problems in the Intervention Range, Phase II

Scale	Child ($n = 17$)	Spouse ($n = 5$)	Abused witnesses ($n = 12$)	Comparison ($n = 29$)	$X^2(1)$	p
Youth Self Report						
Internalizing	19	17	25	3	4.45	.04
Externalizing	38	0	25	26	5.86	.02
Total	31	0	25	3		
Maternal Report of Child Behavior Checklist						
Internalizing	60	60	42	29	.49	.49
Externalizing	20	20	75	36	.27	.16
Total	30	40	67	39		
Teacher Report Form ($n = 48$)						
Internalizing	44	50	46	28	.26	.26
Externalizing	50	25	37	20	.40	.25
Total	44	25	55	20	.39	.25

formants, however, there were no group differences in the proportion of children in the intervention range. Once again, therefore, these preliminary results underscored the effects of informant identity on the results and thus on the apparent effects of domestic violence.

Agreement and Disagreement Among Informants

After examining group differences in parents', teachers', and children's perceptions of the target children's behavior problems, it is also interesting to examine the pattern of agreement across informants. Analyses using Pearson product–moment correlations revealed surprisingly low agreement across informants on the internalizing and externalizing scales of the behavior problem checklists (CBCL, YSR, and TRF) in Phase I (see Table 5). An examination of the data suggested that there was little agreement among informants and that agreement was particularly low regarding reports of internalizing problems. Coefficients of agreement were not systematically better in any of the four groups. Levels of agreement between children and their mothers, fathers, and teachers were lower than for similar groups of informants studied by other researchers, although the levels of agreement between teachers and parents were similar (Achenbach et al., 1987). Preliminary analyses of the data obtained in Phase III revealed substantially higher levels of agreement, however (see Table 6). As before, agreement regarding externalizing problems was especially good.

Interpretations and Implications

In the past few years researchers have begun to realize the limitations of relying on single informants to assess the occurrence of domestic violence and its effects on children. The preliminary results reported in this chapter highlight the importance of obtaining information from multiple informants about both independent and dependent variables in studies focusing on child maltreatment and exposure to family violence. They also raise many interesting questions about how reports from different informants should be evaluated and integrated to yield the most accurate and complete picture of children's exposure to violence and of their behavioral adjustment.

Table 5

Agreement Among Informants in Phase I: Pearson Product–Moment Correlations

Dimension and informant	Mother	Father	Teacher
Internalizing			
Child			
r	.19	.01	.07
n	110	85	57
Mother			
r		.24	.00
n		85	57
Father			
r			.09
n			47
Externalizing			
Child			
r	.19	.24	.11
n	110	85	57
Mother			
r		.30	.32
n		85	57
Father			
r			.38
n			47

Perspectives on History of Family Violence

In Phase I, we relied primarily on the social workers' reports to assign children to different abuse groups. Information from interviews with the children and parents revealed incidents of child abuse unknown to the social workers. Likewise, we discovered discrepancies between descriptions of family violence provided by different infor-

Table 6
Agreement Among Informants in Phase II:
Pearson Product–Moment Correlations

Dimension and informant	Mother	Teacher
Internalizing		
Child		
r	.28*	−.02
n	61	57
Mother		
r		−.03
n		49
Externalizing		
Child		
r	.29*	.51**
n	61	57
Mother		
r		19†
n		49

*$p < .05$. **$p < .001$. †$p < .10$.

mants. These discrepancies prompted us to interview multiple informants about family violence systematically in subsequent phases of the study. In Phase III we thus obtained information from mothers, fathers, and the adolescents themselves using the same instrument. Preliminary analyses of data based on reports of child and spouse abuse by two or three informants suggest that the information provided by children and fathers often enriches the picture painted by mothers or teachers. Although it is difficult to integrate the information provided by the different informants, researchers clearly should be encouraged to collect information from as many perspectives as possible when attempting to conduct research on the specific and different effects of various forms of family violence. Our data suggest the importance of asking all informants to describe specific events of child and spouse abuse that were experienced or reported to them. Detailed descriptions improve the understanding of what happened, provide a context for the events, and facilitate the examination of reports across informants.

Perspectives on Child Adjustment

Divergent perspectives were also found when informants were asked to evaluate the impact of family violence on children. In Phase I, victims and abused witnesses were more likely than children in the comparison group to report internalizing and externalizing behavior problems. These children acknowledged that they behaved in ways likely to get them in trouble with significant others (i.e., parents and teachers) and reported behaviors revealing that they felt sad, unwanted, and less healthy than their peers. In fact, children from the child abuse and abused witness groups were significantly more likely to obtain scores in the intervention range on the internalizing scale of the YSR than were the children in the comparison group.

Mothers painted very different pictures of the children in the various groups. On the CBCL, mothers who were abused by their husbands (spouse and abused witness groups) reported more externalizing behavior problems than did mothers of children in the comparison group and a similar trend on the internalizing dimension approached significance. Thus, mothers reported effects of domestic violence on their children only when they were the victims of spousal violence. When their children alone were victimized, mothers did not report more behavior problems than mothers of children in the comparison group.

Interpreting Divergent Reports

Discrepancies in the patterns of group differences reported by the mothers and children raise many interesting questions about how one should interpret information provided by different informants. We had originally predicted that the children in the abused witness group would have the most problems and that they would be followed by children in the child abuse, spouse abuse, and comparison groups, respectively. We did not expect to find that group differences varied systematically depending on the informants' identity or that mothers of physically abused children and mothers of children in the comparison group would report similar levels of problematic behavior. It may be that the mothers of abused children in this sample were less sensitive to the behavior problems displayed by their children or that they preferred not to recognize signs of the damage wrought by abusive parental behavior. It was also surprising that the two groups of mothers who reported the highest levels of behavior problems were those who were themselves abused. Perhaps these mothers were so taxed by their own distress that "negative filters" compromised their ability to provide accurate information about their children's behavior.

Of course, one must consider the type of biases that might cloud children's reports of their own behavior problems as well. Loeber and his colleagues (1989) have suggested that children tend to underreport, acknowledging fewer symptoms than other informants. Although this pattern was replicated in this study—mothers, fathers, and teachers all reported higher rates of behavior problems than the children did—it is important to underscore the unique information provided by the children. Children were the only informants to identify group differences on the internalizing dimension, with approximately one quarter of the child abuse victims assigning themselves internalizing scores high enough to suggest the need for intervention. Other researchers have also found that children are more likely than their parents to report internalizing problems (Earls, Smith, Reich, & Jung, 1988; Kazdin et al., 1985; Reich & Earls, 1987).

By contrast, fathers of children who were victims and/or witnesses of physical abuse were no more likely to report problem behaviors than fathers of children in the comparison group. There are several possible explanations for this. Because fewer fathers than mothers and children responded to the CBCL, there may not have been sufficient statistical power to detect group differences in their reports. It is also possible that the fathers were not sufficiently familiar with their children's problems, were unused to describing their children's development and functioning, or had difficulty completing standardized measures, or that the children exposed to domestic violence did not in fact display more behavior problems than their counterparts in the comparison group. Before concluding that fathers are unlikely to be sources of useful information, however, we need to develop alternative ways of obtaining information from them about their children (Lamb, 1997). Perhaps open-ended interviews, in which fathers are asked to describe their children in their own words, would elicit more informative descriptions than the standardized questionnaires used in our study. Fathers' perspectives are especially important when, as in this study, fathers are the primary perpetrators of abuse (Sternberg, 1997). In Phase III of our study, we thus attempted to use more innovative ways of collecting information from fathers about their relationships with their children.

Somewhat surprisingly, teachers and peers agreed in Phase I that the target children's behavior in the classroom was not affected by their exposure to domestic violence. Other researchers have reported that abuse affects school behavior and peer relationships (Dodge, Bates, & Pettit, 1991; Kaufman & Cicchetti, 1989; Salzinger, Feldman, Hammer, & Rosario, 1993), although Dodge et al. (1991) found that teachers' and peers' reports of increased aggression were not confirmed by "objective" observers of classroom and playground behavior.

Our results underscore the importance of obtaining reports from multiple informants concerning children's adjustment and raise questions about how to integrate this information. Because there is no absolute yardstick by which one can measure children's behavior problems, we can only speculate about the meaning of discrepancies among informants. At the very least, however, these discrepancies illustrate the dangers implicit in relying on only one informant, however valuable and unique his or her perspective on the child's functioning. Had we relied on any one source of information, the results and conclusions of this study would have been very different. It is possible that some of the inconsistencies across studies of children from violent families can be attributed to the reliance on only one informant and the associated failure to consider the factors that influence their judgments, observations, and reports.

By comparing evaluations provided by mothers, fathers, teachers, classmates, and the children themselves, we have illustrated some of the "biases" that may characterize each of these informants as well as some of the unique contributions they can make to our understanding of both family violence and children's behavior problems. Instead of searching for the "optimal informant," we suggest that extensive efforts be made to examine the unique perspectives of different family members and to develop techniques for combining their reports into meaningful and comprehensive pictures of violence and adjustment. Loeber and his colleagues (1989) have suggested, for example, that contingency analyses may help determine which informants provide the best information about specific aspects of the children's development. Structured diagnostic interview procedures that provide a "decision tree" for weighing the input of different informants (Reich & Earls, 1987) might also be helpful. Tein et al. (1994) have recommended using multitrait, multimethod techniques for analyzing data from multiple informants. As we learn more about how specific factors like depression or abuse influence evaluations, it may also become possible to explore their contribution systematically. In addition, longitudinal studies like ours can help determine whether certain reports from different informants are especially useful for predicting future adjustment in specific domains. In the current study, mothers, fathers, teachers, peers, and the children themselves were asked to provide information about children who were victims or witnesses of domestic violence. By obtaining information from multiple sources, we hoped to ensure a more comprehensive appraisal of the children's adjustment. Each informant was believed to provide valuable information about the target children's behavior, supplementing the reports made by other informants.

CONCLUSIONS

In this chapter we have attempted to illustrate the importance of using multiple informants as one way of improving our understanding of how violent experiences in the family affect children's development. Collecting detailed information from multiple informants about a wide range of maltreatment experiences and violence in the home should help researchers establish a more accurate and comprehensive method of assessing violence as an independent variable. Likewise, obtaining information from multiple informants about behavior problems and other symptoms displayed by children should help professionals measure the effects of violence on children's adjustment more reliably. A clearer understanding of the scope and nature of children's violent experiences coupled with a more comprehensive description of their adjustment should improve researchers' ability to predict how violent experiences in the home affect children's development.

We undertook the study in Israel so that we could disentangle the effects of child and spouse abuse while simultaneously distinguishing the effects of family violence from the effects of other traumatic events. Would the results reported in this chapter have differed had the study been conducted in the United States? We suspect not. Although no other researchers have yet been able to mount as comprehensive a study of informants as that reported here, many researchers have reported findings that are consistent with those reported here, and none have obtained contradictory findings (Kaufman et al., 1994; Jouriles & O'Leary, 1985; McGee et al., 1995; Szinovacz, 1983). In addition, the Achenbach scales have since been standardized in Israel, where they are widely used in clinical and research contexts, suggesting that they constitute valid measures of behavior problems as they do in the United States (Zilber, Auerbach, & Lerner, 1994). For these reasons, we believe that the results reported in this chapter are also of relevance to researchers and practitioners in the United States.

REFERENCES

Aber, J. L., Allen, J. P., Carlson, V., & Cicchetti, D. (1989). The effects of maltreatment on development during early childhood: Recent studies and their theoretical, clinical, and policy implications. In D. Cicchetti & V. Carlson (Eds.), *Child maltreatment: Theory and research on the causes and consequences of child abuse and neglect* (pp. 579–619). Cambridge, England: Cambridge University Press.

Aber, J. L., & Cicchetti, D. (1984). The socio-emotional development of maltreated children: An empirical and theoretical analysis. In H. Fitzgerald, B. Lester, & M. Yogman (Eds.), *Theory and research in behavioral pediatrics* (Vol. 2, pp. 147–199). New York: Plenum Press.

Achenbach, T. M., & Edelbrock, C. S. (1981). Behavioral problems and competencies reported by parents of normal and disturbed children aged four through sixteen. *Monographs of the Society for Research in Child Development, 46*(Serial number 188).

Achenbach, T. M., & Edelbrock, C. S. (1983). *Manual for the Child Behavior Checklist and Revised Child Behavior Profile.* Burlington: University of Vermont.

Achenbach, T. M., & Edelbrock, C. S. (1986). *Manual for the Teacher's Report Form and Teacher's Version of Behavior Profile.* Burlington: University of Vermont, Department of Psychiatry.

Achenbach, T. M., & Edelbrock, C. S. (1987). *Manual for the Youth Self-Report and Profile.* Burlington: University of Vermont.

Achenbach, T. M., McConaughy, S., & Howell, C. T. (1987). Child/adolescent behavioral and emotional problems: Implications of cross-informant correlations for situational specificity. *Psychological Bulletin, 87,* 213–232.

Bauer, W. D., & Twentyman, C. T. (1985). Abusing, neglectful, and comparison mothers' responses to child-related and non-child-related stressors. *Journal of Consulting and Clinical Psychology, 53,* 335–343.

Brody, G. H., & Forehand, R. (1986). Maternal perceptions of child maladjustment as a function of the combined influence of child behavior and maternal depression. *Journal of Consulting and Clinical Psychology, 54,* 237–240.

Dobash, R. E., & Dobash, R. P. (1984). The nature and antecedents of violent events. *British Journal of Criminology, 24,* 269–288.

Dodge, K. E., Bates, J. E., & Pettit, G. S. (1991). Mechanisms in the cycle of violence. *Science, 250,* 1678–1683.

Earls, F., Smith, E., Reich, W., & Jung, K. (1988). Psychopathological consequences of a disorder in children: Findings from a pilot study incorporating a structured diagnostic interview. *Journal of the American Academy of Child and Adolescent Psychiatry, 27,* 90–95.

Fantuzzo, J. W., & Lindquist, C. U. (1989). The effects of observing conjugal violence on children: A review of research methodology. *Journal of Family Violence, 4*, 77–94.

Finkelhor, D., & Dziuba-Leatherman, J. (1994). Children as victims of violence: A national survey. *Pediatrics, 94*, 413–420.

Hughes, H. (1988). Psychological and behavioral correlates of family violence in child witnesses and victims. *American Journal of Orthopsychiatry, 58*, 77–90.

Hughes, H., & Barad, S. (1983). Psychological functioning of children in a battered women's shelter: A preliminary investigation. *American Journal of Orthopsychiatry, 53*, 525–531.

Hughes, H. M., Parkinson, D., & Vargo, M. (1989). Witnessing spouse abuse and experiencing physical abuse: A "double whammy?" *Journal of Family Violence, 4*, 197–209.

Jaffe, P., Wolfe, D. A., Wilson, S. K., & Zak, L. (1986). Family violence and child adjustment: A comparative analyses of girls' and boys' behavioral symptoms. *American Journal of Psychiatry, 143*, 74–77.

Jouriles, E. N., & O'Leary, K. D. (1985). Interspousal reliability of reports of marital violence. *Journal of Consulting and Clinical Psychology, 53*, 419–421.

Kaufman, J., & Cicchetti, D. (1989). Effects of maltreatment on children's socioemotional development: Assessments in a day-camp setting. *Developmental Psychology, 25*, 516–524.

Kaufman, J., Jones, B., Stieglitz, E., Vitulano, L., & Mannariono, A. P. (1994). The use of multiple informants to assess children's maltreatment experiences. *Journal of Family Violence, 9*, 227–248.

Kazdin, A. E., Moser, J., Colbus, D., & Bell, R. (1985). Depressive symptoms among physically abused and psychiatrically disturbed children. *Journal of Abnormal Psychology, 94*, 298–307.

Kravic, J. N. (1987). Behavior problems and social competence of clinic-referred abused children. *Journal of Family Violence, 2*, 111–120.

Lamb, M. E. (Ed.). (1997). *The role of the father in child development* (3d ed.). New York: Wiley.

Lamphear, V. S. (1985). The impact of maltreatment on children's psychosocial adjustment: A review of the research. *Child Abuse and Neglect, 9*, 251–263.

Langhinrichsen-Rohling, J., & Vivian, D. (1994). The correlates of spouses' incongruent reports of marital aggression. *Journal of Family Violence, 9,* 265–283.

Larrance, D. T., & Twentyman, C. T. (1983). Maternal attributions and child abuse. *Journal of Abnormal Psychology, 92,* 449–457.

Loeber, R. M., Green, S. M., Lahey, B. B., & Stouthamer-Loeber, M. (1989). Optimal informants on childhood disruptive behaviors. *Developmental Psychopathology, 1,* 317–337.

MacKinnon-Lewis, C., Lamb, M. E., Arbuckle, B., Baradaran, L. P. F., & Volling, B. (1992). The relationship between biased maternal and familial attributions and the aggressiveness of their interactions. *Development and Psychopathology, 4,* 403–415.

Margolin, C., Talovic, S., & Weinstein, C. D. (1983). Areas of Change Questionnaire: A practical approach to marital assessment. *Journal of Consulting and Clinical Psychology, 51,* 944–955.

Masten, A., Morison, P., & Pellegrini, D. (1985). A revised class play method of peer assessment. *Developmental Psychology, 21,* 523–533.

McGee, R. A., Wolfe, D. A., Yuen, S. A., Wilson, S. K., & Carnochan, J. (1995). The measurement of maltreatment: A comparison of approaches. *Child Abuse and Neglect, 19,* 233–249.

Morison, P. (1982). *Teacher rating scales on peer relations.* Minneapolis: University of Minnesota Press.

National Research Council. (1993). *Understanding child abuse and neglect.* Washington, DC: National Academy Press.

O'Brien, M., John, R. S., Margolin, G., & Erel, O. (1994). Reliability and diagnostic efficacy of parents' reports regarding children's exposure to marital aggression. *Violence and Victims, 9,* 45–62.

O'Keefe, M. (1994). Linking marital violence, mother-child/father-child aggression, and child behavior problems. *Journal of Family Violence, 9,* 63–78.

Reich, W., & Earls, F. (1987). Rules for making psychiatric diagnoses in children on the basis of multiple sources of information: Preliminary strategies. *Journal of Abnormal Child Psychology, 15,* 601–616.

Reid, J. B., Kavanagh, K., & Baldwin, D. V. (1987). Abusive parents' perceptions of child problem behaviors: An example of parental bias. *Journal of Abnormal Child Psychology, 15,* 457–466.

Richters, J. E. (1992). Depressed mothers as informants about their children: A critical review for the evidence for distortion. *Psychological Bulletin, 112,* 485–499.

Salzinger, S. (1993). *Family Interaction Questionnaire.* Unpublished manuscript, New York State Psychiatric Institute, New York.

Salzinger, S., Feldman, R., Hammer, M., & Rosario, M. (1993). The effects of physical abuse on children's social relationships. *Child Development, 64,* 169–187.

Sternberg, K. J. (1997). Fathers, the missing parents in research on family violence. In M. E. Lamb (Ed.), *The role of the father in child development* (3d ed., pp. 284–308, 392–397). New York: Wiley.

Sternberg, K. J., & Dawud-Noursi, S. (1996). Effects of domestic violence on children's behavior problems: Multiple perspectives. In R. Tessier, G. M. Tarabulsy, & L. S. Éthier (Eds.), *Dimension de la maltraitance* [Dimensions of maltreatment, pp. 25–42]. Québec, Canada: Les presses de l'Université du Québec.

Sternberg, K. J., Lamb, M. E., Greenbaum, C., Cicchetti, D., Dawud, S., Cortes, R. M., Krispin, O., & Lorey, F. (1993). Effects of domestic violence on children's behavior problems and depression. *Developmental Psychology, 29,* 44–52.

Sternberg, K. J., Lamb, M. E., Greenbaum, C., Dawud, S., Cortes, R. M., & Lorey, F. (1994). The effects of domestic violence on children's perceptions of their perpetrating and nonperpetrating parents. *International Journal of Behavioral Development, 17,* 779–795.

Straus, M. A., & Gelles, R. J. (1990). *Physical violence in American families: Risk factors and adaptations to violence in 8,145 families.* New Brunswick, NJ: Transaction Publishers.

Straus, M. A., Gelles, R. J., & Steinmetz, S. K. (1980). *Behind closed doors: Violence in the American family.* New York: Doubleday/Anchor.

Szinovacz, M. E. (1983). Using couple data as a methodological tool: The case of marital violence. *Journal of Marriage and the Family, 45,* 663–644.

Tein, J., Roosa, M. W., & Michaels, M. (1994). Agreement between parent and child reports on parental behaviors. *Journal of Marriage and the Family, 56,* 341–355.

Wolfe, D. A., Jaffe, P., Wilson, S. K., & Zak, L. (1985). Children of battered women: The relations of child behavior to family violence and maternal stress. *Journal of Consulting and Clinical Psychology, 5,* 657–665.

Wolfe, D. A., & Mosk, M. (1983). Behavioral comparisons of children from abusive and distressed families. *Journal of Consulting and Clinical Psychology, 51,* 702–708.

Wolfe, D. A., Zak, L., Wilson, S. K., & Jaffe, P. (1986). Child witnesses to violence between parents: Critical issues in behavioral and social adjustment. *Journal of Abnormal Child Psychology, 14,* 95–104.

Zilber, N., Auerbach, J. G., & Lerner, Y. (1994). Israeli norms for the Achenbach Child Behavior Checklist: Comparison of clinically-referred and non-referred children. *Israeli Journal of Psychiatry and Related Sciences, 31,* 5–12.

6

Correlates of Adjustment in Children at Risk

Timothy E. Moore and Debra J. Pepler

In this chapter, we describe the findings from a research project exploring the impact of stressful or conflictual family environments on latency-aged children. During the last two decades, numerous studies have demonstrated that children's adjustment disorders are strongly associated with chronic stressful events in the family. These include but are not limited to child abuse (Zigler & Hall, 1989), wife battering (Jaffe, Wolfe, & Wilson, 1990), nonviolent marital conflict (Emery, 1989; Grych & Fincham, 1990), and homelessness (Masten, 1992; Rescorla, Parker, & Stolley, 1991).

As discussed in the introductory chapter of this book, children in shelters for battered women have been found to exhibit high levels of both externalizing and internalizing behaviors. At the same time,

This research was supported by grants from the Ontario Ministry of Community and Social Services, the Social Sciences Research Council of Canada, and Glendon College Research Funds. We are indebted to the mothers and children who participated in this research, often at a difficult time in their lives. We are grateful to the shelter and hostel staff who supported our research efforts throughout the duration of the project. We appreciate the dedication and commitment of the women who have staffed this project: Joy Andres, Mila Buset, Joanne Cummings, Gabrielle Bautz, Liz Hammond, Dana Harrison, Helen Luhaorg, Michele Kates, Teresa MacDonell, Catherine McDermott, Reet Mae, Laurie Malabar, Christina Stroud, Janice Waddell, Brenda Weinberg, and Lisa Weiser.

they tend to exhibit lower levels of social competence. However, as Wolfe and Jaffe (1991) noted, this population is somewhat heterogeneous, with no clear pattern of adjustment difficulties (see Hughes & Luke, 1998, this volume). Systematic studies of homeless children are scarce. However, some evidence suggests that these children are at increased risk for developmental delays, depression, learning difficulties, and behavioral problems (Bassuk & Rubin, 1987; Masten, 1992; Rescorla et al., 1991). Various forms of maltreatment (e.g., physical abuse, sexual abuse, and observation of marital violence) may share important similarities in terms of the impairments they induce (Wolfe & Jaffe, 1991). Rutter (1983) has speculated that the negative effects of stressful events on children may be multiplicative rather than additive. When adverse living conditions are also accompanied by frequent bouts of physical violence, the impact on children can be particularly acute. Homeless children are demonstrably "at risk," as are the children of battered women and those from broken marriages. By comparing children in these different populations, we hope to make a start toward elucidating the specific influence of family violence on children's psychological adjustment and toward discovering both the unique and shared effects of various types of maltreatment and disadvantage.

One of the problems in interpreting research on family violence pertains to the difficulty of distinguishing between general predictors of child psychopathology and those that are specifically associated with domestic violence. For example, psychological tension and inadequate parenting may contribute to adjustment difficulties, rather than the presence of physical violence per se. A substantial amount of evidence indicates that nonviolent parental conflict, including divorce, often has a negative effect on children (Hetherington & Clingempeel, 1992; Long & Forehand, 1987). Thus, children exposed to family violence may be subjected to a number of stressors similar to those of children whose parents have been feuding or battling (nonviolently) in the course of becoming separated or divorced. Hershorn and Rosenbaum (1985) found that children from nonviolent but discordant families did not differ from children of battered women on measures of conduct or on incidence of personality problems. When physical violence between parents becomes chronic within a family, it is highly probable that a host of other factors are also present that predispose children to adjustment difficulties (e.g., disrupted routines, minimal contact with one or both parents).

Maternal adjustment is a factor that may mediate children's adjustment. Battered women often report numerous somatic complaints, higher anxiety levels, and more symptoms of depression. They are at risk for developing mental health problems, which in turn may affect their children (Wolfe, Jaffe, Wilson, & Zak, 1985). It is thus important to assess the relative physical and psychological stability of the mother as a potential mediating factor relating to child adjustment. Another confounding factor in the research relates to the nature of shelters for battered women as crisis-oriented facilities. Most of the mothers in a shelter are there for a relatively short time while they seek alternative living arrangements. The transient and stressful nature of their stay may influence their (and their children's) psychological stability. When tests are administered to shelter residents, it is not clear whether test results are attributable to the violence that preceded their seeking the shelter, the stresses of residing in a shelter, or some combination of the two. For example, Wolfe, Zak, and Wilson (1986) found that children of former shelter residents were rated by their mothers as more socially competent than children of current residents, even though former residents were more "disadvantaged" than current residents. Emery, Kraft, Joyce, and Shaw (1984) reported that mothers perceived their families to be more cohesive 4 months after seeking residence at a shelter than they were when help was first sought. Moreover, mothers judged their children as having significantly fewer internalizing problems at follow-up. Fantuzzo et al. (1991) showed that shelter residents who had been exposed to interparental physical and verbal aggression exhibited higher levels of internalizing problems than a comparable group of children who resided at home.

Researchers studying *resilience*—the process of adapting to adversity—hypothesize that the negative consequences of familial violence may be attenuated by the presence of certain psychological processes within the child or alternatively magnified by others (Garmezy,

1985, 1993; Rutter, 1987). Similarly, features of the family environment may either mitigate or exacerbate adjustment difficulties. Children might vary in their adjustment profiles as a function of individual capacities or protective factors within the family. Rutter (1987) suggested that "task accomplishment" (broadly defined) can improve self-esteem and self-efficacy. If so, then perhaps academic success can serve as a protective experience. An internal control orientation is another potential protective factor. Gender is a third factor that may mediate children's responses to witnessing assaults on their mothers. Although Davies and Cummings (1994) concluded that current findings were equivocal with respect to the relative vulnerability of boys and girls to marital conflict, some studies of children from violent families have found that a higher proportion of girls than boys were in the clinical range on the Child Behavior Checklist (e.g., Christopoulos et al., 1987; Davis & Carlson, 1987; Hughes, Parkinson, & Vargo, 1989; Sternberg et al., 1993). Allison and Furstenberg (1989) reported that the well-being of girls was more adversely affected than that of boys as a result of marital dissolution.

Children's sense of emotional security, which they derive from their parents, may be undermined when they are exposed to marital conflict. Without a secure emotional foundation, they are less able to meet the challenges of everyday life. The consequences of emotional instability may be evident in children's school performance, social interactions, and overall adjustment (Davies & Cummings, 1994). It is possible that abused wives who are nevertheless able to maintain a positive relationship with their children provide a protective buffer that attenuates the negative outcomes that would otherwise occur.

Are some negative outcomes uniquely associated with exposure to family violence, compared to other types of maltreatment? Are boys and girls similarly affected by exposure to family aggression? Are there child characteristics or family factors that mediate children's adjustment to stressful living conditions? In this chapter we describe some of the main findings from an ongoing research project designed to answer these questions.

METHOD

Participants

Participants were children in the age range of 6 to 12 years and their mothers. Data were collected on 113 children of mothers residing in several shelters for battered women (shelter group), 82 children of mothers residing in housing hostels (homeless group), 82 children from single-parent (mother-only) homes (single group), and 100 children from two-parent nonviolent homes (two-parent group). Shelter and homeless residents were recruited by means of notice-board announcements posted in the residences and through resident staff soliciting their participation. Single- and two-parent families were recruited through notice board announcements at shopping centers and through city and neighborhood newspapers. *Nonviolent families* were defined as those in which the mother reported no incidence of physical violence between adult partners since the child was 24 months old. Mothers were given a remuneration of $20 plus $5 per child. In a few cases, language difficulties precluded mothers' participation, and perforce, their children's.

Demographic characteristics of each group are presented in Table 1.

Procedure

Individual interviews were conducted separately and simultaneously for mothers and children. Single- and two-parent families were tested either in separate rooms in the psychology department or in the family's home; shelter mothers and children were tested at the shelter within 3 weeks of their arrival. Homeless mothers and their children were interviewed in the housing hostels. The research was described to the participants as a survey of family problem-solving tactics and child development. A brief description of the testing instruments was provided to mothers expressing interest in participating. Consent was obtained by explaining to mothers that they could terminate the interview at any point and that confidentiality of the data was assured, with the proviso that the researchers were required by law to report any suspected instances of child abuse to child welfare authorities.

Table 1
Descriptive Characteristics of Families

Characteristic	Shelter ($n = 73$)	Homeless ($n = 55$)	Single mothers ($n = 57$)	Two-parent families ($n = 59$)
Child's age	9.4	9.4	8.9	9.2
Child gender				
Male	52	41	38	50
Female	61	41	44	50
Mother's health (GHQ)[1]				
M	14.2$_a$	10.4$_b$	3.7$_c$	4.0$_c$
SD	8.4	8.2	4.9	4.8
Mother's education				
% with < grade 9	16	18	3	0
% with post-high school	22	21	61	78
% completed college	0	4	23	51
Mean number of children in family[2]	2.49$_a$	2.61$_a$	2.03$_b$	2.54$_{ab}$
Family income (in $1,000s)[1]				
M	21.8$_a$	15.0$_b$	22.0$_a$	41.3$_c$
SD	12.9	10.0	14.6	12.5
% earning < $20,000	51	88	56	7
% earning > $40,000	7	4	13	60
Marital status				
% with partner	100	29	0	100
% single[3]	0	71	100	0

Note. Means with different subscripts within a row differed from one another significantly. GHQ = General Health Questionnaire.
[1]$p < .01$.   [2]$p < .05$.   [3]Divorced, separated, widowed, or single.

The measures described below were completed by all participating mothers and their children. The interviews typically required between 60 and 90 minutes.

Measures

The mothers' test battery consisted of the following measures:

1. Family Information Form (FIF). The FIF was used to obtain demographic data, socioeconomic status, marital history, family health history, and mothers' perceptions of sources of stress and support for members of the family. Some of the questions were adapted from the Ontario Child Health Study (Offord et al., 1987).

2. Conflict Tactics Scale (CTS). The CTS (Straus, 1979) provided a measure of the use of verbal aggression and physical violence between family members during the previous year. Conflict tactics were assessed between parents, between each parent and each child in the target age range, and between children. The CTS is the standard instrument used by researchers of family violence to gauge the nature and extent of violence in the home (e.g., Christopoulos et al., 1987; Hughes, 1988). To establish the amount of family violence to which children are exposed, mothers indicated how often interparental violence was seen or heard by the children. Mothers also indicated the frequency and severity of abusive parent-to-child behaviors. Six verbal aggression items were presented: insulted or swore at other; sulked—refused to talk about it; stomped out of the room or house; did or said something to spite other; threatened to hit or throw something at other; and threw, smashed, hit, or kicked something. The physical aggression items were as follows: threw something at other; pushed, grabbed, or shoved; slapped; kicked, bit, or hit with a fist; hit or tried to hit with something; beat up; choked; threatened with a gun or knife; and used knife or gun.

3. General Health Questionnaire-30 (GHQ). The GHQ (Goldberg & Hillier, 1979) is a self-report measure designed to assess general psychological health or illness in individuals in a community. The instrument focuses on interruptions in normal functioning or the appearance of new symptoms of a distressing nature. Mothers were instructed to report on whether they had recently (i.e., in the past few weeks) ex-

perienced a particular symptom. The 4-point response scale ranges from *less than usual* to *much more than usual*. Scores of greater than 5 are indicative of serious health problems. Scores of 10 or greater comprise the clinical range (i.e., reflect a need for immediate professional help).

4. Child Behavior Checklist (CBCL). Mothers' perceptions of their children's behavior problems during the previous 6 months were assessed using the CBCL (Achenbach & Edelbrock, 1983), which yields standardized (*T* score) scores for Internalizing, Externalizing, and Total Behavior problems and Social Competence. The CBCL has been widely used by investigators in diverse areas of research and has frequently been used specifically to measure the nature and extent of behavioral problems in children from violent homes. A Teachers' Report Form (TRF) was administered for children in the two-parent and single-mother groups. Because of the confidentiality of the location of shelter families and the transience of homeless families, we were not able to contact teachers for a behavioral rating. Therefore, the TRF was amended for use by child care workers and administered, when possible, to shelter or housing staff for children in these groups.

The following tests were administered to the children:

1. Wide Range Achievement Test—Revised (WRAT-R). The WRAT-R (Jastak & Wilkinson, 1984) was designed to measure scholastic achievement ranging from kindergarten to college. The measure consists of three scales: Reading, Spelling, and Arithmetic. Only the Reading and Arithmetic subscales were used for this study. The Reading subscale measures the child's ability to recognize letters and read words in isolation (i.e., out of context). The Arithmetic subscale assesses the child's ability to recognize and read numbers, solve math problems orally, and perform written computations. Individual performances are compared to standardized age norms with a mean of 100 and a standard deviation of 15.

2. Digit Span (Wechsler Intelligence Scale for Children–Revised; WISC-R). The Digit Span is a subtest of the WISC-R (Wechsler, 1974). It is a measure of attention and short-term memory. It comprises two tasks: Digits Forward and Digits Backward. There are two series for

each sequence length. The Digits Forward task requires the child to remember a series of three to nine numbers that have no logical relationship to each other. The Digits Backward task requires the child not only to remember from two to eight numbers but also to reorganize the numbers in reverse order. Raw scores are converted to scaled scores and compared to age norms. A scaled score of 10 is considered average.

3. Children's Locus of Control Scale. This scale (Nowicki & Strickland, 1973) was designed to measure children's perceptions of their power to control or cause effectual change in their environment. Those with an internal control orientation feel that they can change what happens around them, whereas those with an external orientation feel themselves to be victims of circumstance and powerless to change their situation. Test–retest correlations for administration of the Children's Locus of Control Scale 6 weeks apart ranged from .63 to .71. Split-half reliabilities ranged from .63 to .68 (Nowicki & Strickland, 1973).

RESULTS

There were two stages in the data analysis for this study. First, group comparisons were conducted with 4 (Group) × 2 (Gender) analyses of variance (ANOVAs). For group comparisons on academic variables, mothers' education was entered as a covariate. Second, within-group regression analyses were conducted to examine the predictors of children's adjustment.

Demographic Variables

Table 1 presents data and significance tests for the four groups on a number of characteristics. As expected, mothers' health differed markedly between groups according to risk status as measured by the GHQ. A majority of shelter and homeless mothers had scores in the clinical range (68% and 51%, respectively, compared to 15% and 12% for mothers in the single- and two-parent families).

A similar pattern of differences was found for maternal education, with higher levels of schooling in the single- and two-parent families. Homeless mothers' incomes were the lowest, followed by those of mothers in the shelter and single groups. Incomes of the two-parent families were almost double those of the shelter and single groups.

Conflict Tactics

Table 2 displays the group means and significance tests for the Verbal and Physical Aggression subscales of the CTS. Interparental and parent-to-child tactics were assessed according to mothers' reports. Shelter family fathers were reported to use more verbally aggressive and more violent problem-solving tactics with their children and with their partners than fathers in any of the other groups. Group differences with respect to mothers' tactics were more varied. Shelter mothers reported that they used more verbal and physical aggression with their partners than mothers in the other groups. Mothers' Verbal Aggression scores with their children did not differentiate the groups and did not interact with gender. Shelter mothers reported that they were somewhat more physically aggressive with their children than mothers in the two-parent nonviolent families; however, they were no more punitive than mothers in the other two comparison groups, nor were the absolute levels of mother-to-child Physical Aggression especially high. Similarly, father-to-child Physical Aggression was higher among shelter fathers than it was in the other groups, but again these levels were not high, nor were shelter group fathers more punitive than shelter mothers.

Adjustment

Corroborating Mothers' Reports

To validate mothers' ratings of their children's behavior problems, we mailed CBCLs to teachers and child care workers. These independent ratings of children's adjustment were available for approximately 28% of the total sample. For shelter and homeless groups, child care workers from the residences filled out the TRF version of the CBCL. Children in the two-parent and single groups were rated by their teachers. The overall correlation between mothers' and independent raters' reports of children's adjustment was .32, $r(105) = .32$, $p < .001$. We compared the mean scores for total behavior problems provided by mothers with the

Table 2

Conflict Tactics Scale Subscale Scores

| | | Shelter | | | Homeless | | | Single | | | Two-parent | | |
Aggression	n	M	SD	n	M	SD	n	M	SD	n	M	SD	F
Verbal													
Mother to father	89	12.7$_a$	9.0	27	9.9$_b$	8.0	—	—	—	100	6.7$_b$	5.7	14.97****
Father to mother	89	24.5$_a$	7.6	27	12.2$_b$	8.9	—	—	—	100	5.7$_c$	6.3	160.32****
Father to child	81	12.2$_a$	9.7	26	7.1$_b$	7.9	—	—	—	100	4.4$_b$	5.0	22.98****
Mother to child	112	8.3	6.8	82	9.4	7.9	82	7.7	5.7	100	6.3	5.4	3.48
Physical													
Mother to father	89	5.3$_a$	7.9	27	3.0$_{ab}$	6.1	—	—	—	100	1.3$_b$	1.3	12.1****
Father to mother	89	21.3$_a$	13.3	27	3.5$_b$	6.1	—	—	—	100	1.2$_b$	0.8	128.9****
Father to child	81	5.2$_a$	4.7	26	2.7$_b$	3.4	—	—	—	100	2.5$_b$	1.9	14.9****
Mother to child	112	5.0$_a$	4.1	82	4.9$_{ab}$	3.8	82	4.5$_{ab}$	4.8	100	3.7$_b$	2.8	2.5

Note. Means with different subscripts within rows differed from one another at $p < .01$; mother-to-child physical aggression differed at $p < .05$.

p values refer to univariate main effects. ****$p < .001$.

corresponding mean scores from child care workers or teachers. Shelter mothers' ratings of their children were significantly higher than the child care workers'. None of the other comparisons was significant. In the shelter group, the correlation between mothers' and child care workers' ratings was .59 ($df = 32$, $p < .001$). Because the independent ratings were relatively few in number, the subsequent analyses are based on the mothers' reports.

Table 3 shows the group means for boys and girls on the CBCL summary scales for Internalizing problems, Externalizing problems, and Social Competence. Group $\times$ Gender univariate analyses revealed a main effect of group on all three summary scales. The interaction for Total Behavior Problems shown in Figure 1 typifies the Group $\times$ Gender differences found for both the Internalizing and Externalizing scales. According to mothers' reports, shelter girls were conspicuously and significantly more poorly adjusted than shelter boys. Gender differences in the other three groups were not significant, and in the case of children of single mothers, differences were in the other direction. The means for shelter and homeless girls differed significantly from the means for girls in the two-parent families for Internalizing, Externalizing, and Total scores.

To further explore the pattern of gender differences, children in the homeless group were partitioned into those who had witnessed violence (ever) and those who had not. Homeless families were screened initially to ensure that they had not witnessed or experienced any physical violence within the previous year. We thought it possible, however, that some of these families had had episodes of violence at some point in their past. If so, violence may be implicated in the adjustment profiles of children in the homeless and shelter groups.

Figure 2 compares boys and girls in the shelter group to those in the homeless group when prior exposure to violence is taken into account. Forty-eight of the 78 homeless children had witnessed violence in the past (24 boys, 24 girls). Of the 34 children who had not been exposed to family violence, 16 were boys and 18 were girls.

Although the interaction shown in Figure 2 was not statistically significant, planned comparisons showed that girls in the shelter

Table 3

Standardized Scores for CBCL Internalizing, Externalizing, and Social Competence (Group × Gender)

								Group							
	Shelter			Homeless			Single			Two-parent				
CBCL Subscale	n	M	SD	n	M	SD	n	M	SD	n	M	SD	F
Internalizing													
Boys	52	57.5_{ab}	8.9	41	58.2_a	10.14	38	55.8_{ab}	10.6	50	51.0_b	8.6	5.62***
Girls	61	63.9_a	10.1	41	61.41_a	10.99	44	54.5_b	9.2	50	52.9_b	8.8	15.3****
Total	113	60.9_a	10.0	82	59.8_a	10.64	82	55.1_b	9.8	100	52.0_b	8.7	18.23****
Externalizing													
Boys	52	56.4_{ab}	8.9	41	58.02_a	11.83	38	56.9_{ab}	12.1	50	51.7_b	9.9	3.29
Girls	61	61.3_a	10.1	41	61.49_a	9.76	44	55.3_b	9.6	50	51.0_b	7.9	14.50****
Total	113	59.1_a	9.9	82	59.76_a	10.91	82	56.1_a	10.8	100	51.4_b	8.9	14.05****
Social Competence													
Boys	51	39.6_a	10.8	41	46.12_{ab}	16.97	36	47.8_b	17.0	48	51.8_b	11.6	6.52****
Girls	61	40.9_a	13.1	41	42.37_a	13.4	44	46.3_{ab}	8.4	49	51.6_b	10.0	8.82****
Total	112	40.3_a	12.1	82	44.24_{ab}	15.3	80	47.0_{ab}	12.9	97	51.7_b	10.8	14.51****

Note. Means with different subscripts within rows differed significantly. CBCL = Child Behavior Checklist.
****$p < .001$.

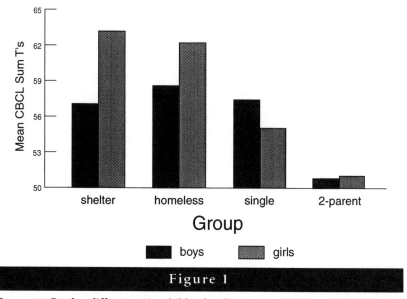

Figure 1

Group × Gender differences in children's adjustment. CBCL = Child Behavior Checklist.

and homeless violent groups had significantly higher scores than boys. In the homeless nonviolent group, girls' and boys' scores did not differ. Similar analyses performed on the Externalizing and Internalizing scales revealed the same pattern. These gender differences persisted when children were classified according to the clinical range cutoff scores (Achenbach & Edelbrock, 1983). Fifty-three percent of the shelter girls and 68% of the girls from the homeless violent group obtained scores within the clinical range (>90th percentile) on the Total Behavior Problems Scale, compared to 12% and 21% of the boys, respectively. Boys and girls in the homeless nonviolent group were comparable in terms of the percentage in the clinical range (35% and 33%, respectively).

As Table 3 shows, shelter and homeless children obtained significantly lower Social Competence scores than in the two-parent group, indicating that the former are more socially isolated and less engaged in school and community activities.

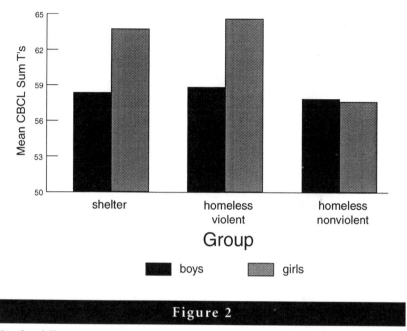

Figure 2

Gender differences in children's adjustment for shelter and homeless groups. The homeless group is partitioned according to presence or absence of prior violence in the family. CBCL = Child Behavior Checklist.

Children's Measures

Table 4 compares the group means for the Reading and Math subscales of the WRAT-R and the means on the Digit Span and Locus of Control tests. Shelter children had a significantly more external control orientation than the two-parent group children. The Digit Span scores of the shelter and homeless groups were significantly lower than that of the single and two-parent groups. The means of the homeless children on the Reading and Math tests are particularly noteworthy: They are more than one standard deviation below grade level, even when adjusted for mothers' education. There were no noteworthy differences on any of these measures when homeless violent and homeless nonviolent children were compared.

Table 4

Scores for Locus of Control, Digit Span, Reading, and Math

| | Group | | | | | | | | | | | | |
| Variable | Shelter | | | Homeless | | | Single | | | Two-parent | | | F |
	n	M	SD	n	M	SD	n	M	SD	n	M	SD	
Locus of Control	112	8.2_a	3.6	79	7.4_a	3.5	82	7.0_{ab}	3.6	100	5.9_b	3.6	7.5****
Digit Span	112	8.7_a	3.1	80	8.9_a	5.0	81	10.2_b	3.5	99	10.5_b	3.1	6.1**
Reading	111	90.42_a	18.3	79	83.7_c	21.5	81	94.4_a	19.7	99	102.6_b	8.7	11.51****
Math	112	86.23_{ab}	12.8	82	82.16_a	15.6	82	91.98_b	16.8	99	92.94_b	15.8	7.54****

Note. Group means for Reading and Math were adjusted after covarying mothers' education. Means with different subscripts within rows differed significantly.
**$p < .01$. ****$p < .001$.

Child Victims of Physical Aggression

Previous researchers have suggested that children who are both victims and observers of physical aggression are more poorly adjusted than those who have witnessed interparental violence (Hughes, 1988). According to mothers' reports, all but nine children in the shelter group had witnessed violence during the last year, and all children had witnessed violence at least once during the last 3 years. Children were identified as victims if their mothers reported harsh forms of corporal punishment (e.g., threw something at child; pushed, grabbed, shoved child; and kicked, bit, or hit with a fist) on the parent-to-child Physical Violence scales of the CTS. Forty percent of the children in the shelter group (46 of 114) had been the victims of parental violence within the last year. A 2 (Child Gender) × 2 (Victimization Status) univariate analysis revealed no main effect of Victimization Status and no interaction with Child Gender for Internalizing, Externalizing, and Total Behavioral Problem scores ($Fs < 1$ in all cases) for the children in the shelter group. The CTS yields a score that reflects the frequency of parent-to-child physical abuse during the previous year. Correlations between these scores (for each parent) and the CBCL adjustment measures did not approach significance (rs ranged from $-.10$ to $.12$).

Predicting Adjustment

To appraise the relative strengths of the associations between adjustment and various familial factors, we conducted stepwise regression analyses within each group. The homeless group was omitted from this analysis because of its heterogeneous nature (i.e., previous exposure to violence). Variables entered into the regression analyses varied somewhat by group because of the different family compositions in groups. In the shelter and two-parent groups, child's gender, mother's health, father-to-mother Physical Aggression, interparental Verbal Aggression (both parents combined), parent-to-child Physical Aggression (both parents combined), and mother- and father-to-child Verbal Aggression were regressed on children's adjustment, using the Total Behavior Problems scores as the adjustment measure. In the single group, child's gender, mother's health, mother-to-child Physical Aggression, and mother-to-child Verbal Aggression were entered. Table 5 reports the squared semipartial correlations (sr^2s) and the partial R^2s for the variables entered. The former is a measure of the unique contribution of that variable as a proportion of total variance in adjustment. For example, .19 (see Table 5) is the amount by which R^2 would be reduced if mother-to-child Verbal Aggression were not included in the equation. The Partial R^2s (column 2) represent the incremental changes in R^2 with successive additions of variables correlated with adjustment.

Table 5
Regressions on Children's Adjustment (Total Behavior Problems)

Variable	sr^2 (unique)	Partial R^2
Shelter group		
Mother-to-child verbal aggression	.19****	.43****
Gender	.08***	.10***
Father-to-mother physical aggression	.06***	.05***
Mother's health (GHQ)	ns	.04*
Two-parent group		
Mother-to-child verbal aggression	.08****	.25****
Mother's health (GHQ)	.06*	.08***
Single-parent group		
Mother-to-child verbal aggression	.07*	.21****
Mother's health (GHQ)	.04*	ns

Note. For shelter group, $df = (7, 64)$, $R^2 = .64$***, and adjusted $R^2 = .60$; for two-parent group, $df = (7, 75)$, $R^2 = .34$***, and adjusted $R^2 = .28$; and for single-parent group, $df = (4, 68)$, $R^2 = .26$***, and adjusted $R^2 = .22$. GHQ = General Health Questionnaire.
*$p < .05$. ***$p < .005$. ****$p < .001$.

Mother-to-child Verbal Aggression contributed significantly to adjustment in all groups and accounted for the largest unique proportion of the variance in all groups. Gender of child was a predictor only in the shelter group. Mothers' health was a modest predictor in all but the shelter group. Shelter mothers' health was uniformly poor (see Table 1). It is therefore possible that there was too little variability in shelter mothers' health for this factor to manifest a strong statistical association with adjustment.

To further investigate the association between mothers' Verbal Aggression and Adjustment, we divided the mothers into high and low Verbal Aggression subgroups, according to the CTS scores. Low Verbal Aggression was defined as scores of 3 or less on the CTS, and High Verbal Aggression consisted of scores of 10 or greater. Mothers in the homeless violent group were combined with the shelter mothers, and those in the homeless nonviolent group were reassigned to either the single- or two-parent group. A 3 (Group) $\times$ 2 (Verbal Aggression) ANOVA was then conducted, using the Sum Ts as the dependent measure. The results are displayed in Figure 3, where mean Total Behavior scores are plotted against Group (violent, single, and two-parent) and levels of mothers' Verbal Aggression (high, low). There was a main effect of group, $F(1, 232) = 15.14$, $p < .0001$, and a main effect of verbal aggression, $F(1, 232) = 79.72$, $p < .0001$. Higher levels of Verbal Aggression were generally associated with poorer adjustment, and this effect was most pronounced for the violent group, as shown by the significant interaction, $F(2, 232) = 4.69$, $p < .01$.

DISCUSSION

As Wolfe and Jaffe (1991) have observed, maltreatment does not leave a uniform mark on all children who experience it. On the other hand, different forms of abuse may be similar in terms of the adjustment disorders and impairments that they bring about. Children of battered women show a variety of stress-related disorders (Hughes, 1988; Hughes et al., 1989; Sternberg et al., 1993). The data reported here confirm these findings and also replicate both the gender differences

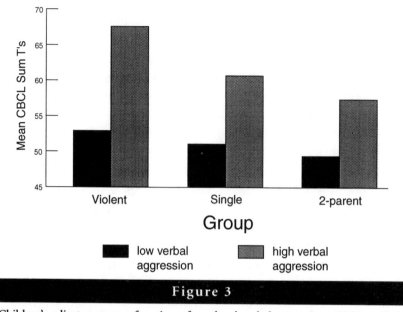

Figure 3

Children's adjustment as a function of mothers' verbal aggression. CBCL = Child Behavior Checklist.

on the CBCL and the lack of adjustment differences between child victims and observers of violence reported by Sternberg et al. (1993).

Wolfe et al. (1985) showed that the type and severity of violence toward mothers accounted for a significant amount (10%) of the variance in adjustment problems in witnessing children, but systemic family factors (e.g., mothers' health, income) accounted for a greater (19%) proportion of the variance. In our samples, low income levels, less education, frequent moves, and relatively poor maternal health characterized both shelter and homeless families. Children in the homeless group who had been exposed to violence, albeit more than a year prior to testing, were similar to shelter children in terms of the extent of behavioral and emotional problems, including a conspicuous gender difference. It is possible that daughters of abused women learn to emulate the undercontrolled behaviors of their mothers—behaviors that occur in response to the violence of their partners. In violent homes the prohibitions against assaulting women are violated. Consequently early gender socialization may be atypical (Hughes et al., 1989). For these girls, receiving or perpetrating aggression may not be perceived to be dissonant with the female role.

The data from the homeless children are consistent with those from other recent studies (e.g., Masten, 1992; Rescorla et al., 1991). Both shelter and homeless children share a number of familial and contextual variables that predispose these populations to conduct problems, emotional upset, and lower levels of social functioning. Both populations are heterogeneous, however, with significant numbers in both samples showing remarkably good adjustment, despite exposure to multiple stressors.

Some investigators have expressed concern that abused women may be unreliable evaluators of their children's behavior (Sternberg et al., 1993; see Sternberg, Lamb, & Dawud-Noursi, 1998, this volume). For that subset of children for which we were able to collect independent ratings, shelter mothers provided more negative ratings than did child care workers who rated the same children, although the correlation between the two sets of ratings was quite high, $r(32) = .59$, $p < .001$. Two factors may be contributing to the discrepancy between the mothers' and shelter workers' assessments. First, the mothers' well-being may influence their ratings of children's adjustment. For example, depressed mothers may tend to perceive the behavior of their children more negatively than mothers who are not depressed (Brody & Forehand, 1986). On the other hand, Richters and Pellegrini (1989) and McCloskey, Figueredo, and Koss (1995) have challenged the depression-distortion hypothesis. It is also possible that child care workers who are involved with distressed children on a daily basis may "drift" in their perceptions of what is normative or may see a more limited sample of behavior. Regardless of the biases inherent in ratings of child behavior problems, converging evidence of the difficulties experienced by children in the shelter and homeless samples comes from assessments of the children themselves. Children's scores on measures of Locus of Control and academic performance were related to the putative degree of risk within their families.

The data reported here do not indicate that academic performance is affected in some unique way by exposure to family violence. It is likely that school-related difficulties are a result of disrupted routines, unpredictable and upsetting family dynamics, and maternal stress rather than exposure to violence per se. The school difficulties are nevertheless severe for a substantial proportion of these children, and the deficits persist several months after mothers have moved from the shelters (Andres & Moore, 1995). It is possible that the poor performance of shelter children on these cognitive measures is a reflection of fundamental deficiencies in basic academic skills, as opposed to their temporary suppression brought about by shelter residency and the precipitating violence. If so, educational planning and intervention should be included in the programming provided to children from violent families.

Although we had expected that the severity of father-to-mother physical violence would be a major predictor of adjustment among shelter children, mother-to-child verbal aggression was a much stronger predictor. This finding was consistent with Jouriles, Barling, and O'Leary's (1987) study of the predictors of child behavior problems resulting from marital violence. Vissing, Straus, Gelles, and Harrop (1991) have also reported that parent-to-child verbal aggression was more closely tied to children's behavior problems than was physical aggression. Inasmuch as verbal aggression may accompany and precede episodes of wife abuse, it is possible that maternal verbal aggression may serve as a conditioned stimulus that triggers anxiety and distress in children, even in the absence of any physical conflict. Baum, O'Keefe, and Davidson (1990) have described an explanatory model whereby sporadic or infrequent traumatic experiences can produce chronic levels of stress. The duration of a traumatic event may be extended beyond its actual time span if the victim (or witness) reexperiences the event by virtue of intrusive imagery. The uncertainty and ambiguity that characterize the social dynamics in homes where spouse abuse occurs may render mothers' verbal aggression a powerful conditioned stimulus. Shelter group fathers were reportedly even more verbally abusive than were mothers to their children; however, fathers' verbalizations were not associated with adjustment. As the primary caretaker, mothers' comments may be more potent than fathers', and when verbalizations are negative they may have more adverse consequences (Patterson, 1982; Pianta, Egeland, & Sroufe, 1990).

It is also possible that children with more behavior problems elicit higher levels of verbal aggression from their mothers (Rutter, 1994). The fact that maternal verbal aggression was associated, to some degree, with adjustment difficulties in all groups is consistent with this perspective. In the case of children exposed to marital violence, mothers' verbal aggression may augment or exacerbate preexisting emotional susceptibility brought about by witnessing interparental violence. Rutter (1990) has shown that good parent–child relationships were protective for children living in disharmonious homes. Physically abused mothers may become too exhausted, distressed, and distracted to provide their children with the necessary attention, discipline, and affection. Consequently, the mother–child relationship suffers (Jenkins & Smith, 1990). High levels of verbal aggression may be a reflection of mothers' deteriorating physical and psychological resources. Verbal aggression is therefore a possible mechanism whereby maladaptive outcomes are intensified in children who are at risk because of violence in the home (Rutter, 1994).

CONCLUSIONS

The present study adds to the understanding of adjustment problems of children in families at risk by identifying the particular risk for daughters of abused women, academic difficulties related to family risk factors, and the importance of mothers' verbal aggression in children's adjustment problems. Inasmuch as the strongest findings of our study rely on dependent measures obtained exclusively from mothers, the conclusions should be interpreted conservatively. To move beyond a reliance on mothers' ratings of children's behavior problems and to supplement our understanding of mother–child dynamics, we are currently videotaping the interactions between mothers and their children in a variety of problem-solving situations. We are also collecting follow-up data in an attempt to appraise the persistence of the symptoms observed during children's shelter and hostel residence.

The key role that mothers' behaviors play in their children's adjustment has been described elsewhere. McCord (1983) found that maternal affection was the critical variable related to boys' delinquent offending. Herrenkohl, Egolf, and Herrenkohl (1997) showed that mothers' hostile interactions with their preschool children predicted subsequent assaultive behavior in late adolescence. Mothers' punitiveness and irritability were related to conduct problems of children in divorced families (Hetherington, Cox, & Cox, 1978). Patterson (1986) has also described how mothers' hostile and inconsistent parenting relates to boys' antisocial behavior. In our study, mothers' reports of using verbal aggression in conflicts with their children carried the most variance in the prediction of children's adjustment problems. Some mothers, despite horrific experiences of abuse at the hands of their partners, were able to maintain positive parenting strategies with their children. The children of these mothers were likely to be the most well-adjusted in the samples. Although we do not intend to lay the blame for adjustment problems at the feet of the mothers, they appear to be the gatekeepers for their children's health. In addition to addressing societal concerns about wife assault, homelessness, and poverty, mothers need help in raising the next generation of children.

REFERENCES

Achenbach, T. M., & Edelbrock, C. S. (1983). *Manual for the Child Behavior Checklist and Revised Child Behavior Profile.* Burlington: University of Vermont, Department of Psychiatry.

Allison, P. D., & Furstenberg, F. F. (1989). How marital dissolution affects children: Variations by age and sex. *Developmental Psychology, 25,* 540–549.

Andres, J., & Moore, T. E. (1995, March). *The adjustment of child witnesses to spousal abuse: A follow-up study.* Poster presented at the biennial meeting of the Society for Research in Child Development, Indianapolis, IN.

Bassuk, E. L., & Rubin, L. (1987). Homeless children: A neglected population. *American Journal of Orthopsychiatry, 57,* 279–286.

Baum, A., O'Keefe, M. K., & Davidson, L. M. (1990). Acute stressors and chronic response: The case of traumatic stress. *Journal of Applied Social Psychology, 20,* 1643–1654.

Brody, G. H., & Forehand, R. (1986). Maternal perceptions of child maladjustment as a function of the combined influence of child behavior and maternal depression. *Journal of Consulting and Clinical Psychology, 54,* 237–240.

Christopoulos, C., Cohn, D. A., Shaw, D. S., Joyce, S., Sullivan-Hanson, J., Kraft, S. P., & Emery, R. E. (1987). Children of abused women: Adjustment at time of shelter residence. *Journal of Marriage and the Family, 49,* 611–619.

Davies, P. T., & Cummings, E. M. (1994). Marital conflict and child adjustment: An emotional security hypothesis. *Psychological Bulletin, 116,* 387–411.

Davis, L. V., & Carlson, B. E. (1987). Observation of spouse abuse: What happens to the children? *Journal of Interpersonal Violence, 2,* 278–291.

Emery, R. E. (1989). Family violence. *American Psychologist, 44,* 321–328.

Emery, R. E., Kraft, S. P., Joyce, S., & Shaw, D. (1984). *Children of abused women: Adjustment at four months following shelter residence.* Paper presented at 92nd Annual Convention of the American Psychological Association, Toronto.

Fantuzzo, J. W., DePaola, L. M., Lambert, L., Martino, T., Anderson, G., & Sutton, S. (1991). Effects of interparental violence on the psychological adjustment and competencies of young children. *Journal of Consulting and Clinical Psychology, 59,* 258–265.

Garmezy, N. (1985). Stress-resistant children: The search for protective factors. In J. E. Stevenson (Ed.), *Recent research in developmental psychopathology* (pp. 598–611). New York: Pergamon Press.

Garmezy, N. (1993). Children in poverty: Resilience despite risk. In D. Reiss, J. E. Richters, M. Radke-Yarrow, & D. Scharf (Eds.), *Children and violence* (pp. 127–36). New York: Guilford Press.

Goldberg, D. P., & Hillier, V. F. (1979). A scaled version of the General Health Questionnaire. *Psychological Medicine, 9,* 139–145.

Grych, J. H., & Fincham, F. D. (1990). Marital conflict and children's adjustment: A cognitive-contextual framework. *Psychological Bulletin, 108,* 267–290.

Herrenkohl, R. C., Egolf, B. P., & Herrenkohl, E. C. (1997). Preschool antecedents of adolescent assaultive behavior: A longitudinal study. *American Journal of Orthopsychiatry, 67,* 422–432.

Hershorn, M., & Rosenbaum, A. (1985). Children of marital violence: A closer look at the unintended victims. *American Journal of Orthopsychiatry, 55,* 260–265.

Hetherington, E. M., & Clingempeel, W. G. (1992). Coping with marital transitions. *Monographs of the Society for Research in Child Development, 57*(2–3, Serial No. 227), 1–242.

Hetherington, E. M., Cox, M., & Cox, R. (1978). The aftermath of divorce. In J. H. Stevens & M. Mathews (Eds.), *Mother/child, father/child relations* (pp. 149–176). Washington, DC: National Association for the Education of Young Children.

Hughes, H. M. (1988). Psychological and behavioral correlates of family violence in child witnesses and victims. *American Journal of Orthopsychiatry, 58,* 77–90.

Hughes, H. M., & Luke, D. A. (1998). Heterogeneity in adjustment among children of battered women. In G. W. Holden, R. A. Geffner, & E. N. Jouriles (Eds.), *Children exposed to marital violence: Theory, research, and applied issues* (pp. 185–221). Washington, DC: American Psychological Association.

Hughes, H. M., Parkinson, D., & Vargo, M. (1989). Witnessing spouse abuse and experiencing physical abuse: A "double whammy?" *Journal of Family Violence, 4,* 197–209.

Jaffe, P., Wolfe, D., & Wilson, S. K. (1990). *Children of battered women.* Newbury Park, CA: Sage Publications.

Jastak, S., & Wilkinson, G. S. (1984). *Wide range achievement test.* Wilmington, DE: Jastak Associates.

Jenkins, J. M., & Smith, M. A. (1990). Factors protecting children living in disharmonious homes: Maternal reports. *Journal of the American Academy of Child and Adolescent Psychiatry, 29,* 60–69.

Jouriles, E. N., Barling, J., & O'Leary, K. D. (1987). Predicting child behaviour problems in maritally violent families. *Journal of Abnormal Child Psychology, 15,* 165–173.

Long, N., & Forehand, R. (1987). The effects of parental divorce and parental conflict on children: An overview. *Developmental and Behavioral Pediatrics, 8,* 292–295.

Masten, A. S. (1992). Homeless children in the United States: Mark of a nation at risk. *Current Directions in Psychological Science, 1,* 41–44.

McCloskey, L. A., Figueredo, A. J., & Koss, M. P. (1995). The effects of systemic family violence on children's mental health. *Child Development, 66,* 1239–1261.

McCord, J. (1983). A forty-year perspective on effects of child abuse and neglect. *Child Abuse and Neglect, 7,* 271–278.

Nowicki, S., & Strickland, B. R. (1973). A locus of control scale for children. *Journal of Consulting and Clinical Psychology, 40,* 148–154.

Offord, D., Boyle, M., Szatmari, P., Rae-Grant, N., Links, P., Cadman, D. I., Byles, J. A., Crawford, J. W., Blum, H. M., Byrne, C., Thomas, H., & Woodward, C. (1987). Ontario child health study: Six month prevalence of disorder and rates of service utilization. *Archives of General Psychiatry, 44,* 832–836.

Patterson, G. R. (1982). *Coercive family process: A social learning approach* (Vol. 3). Eugene, OR: Castalia.

Patterson, G. R. (1986). Performance models for antisocial boys. *American Psychologist, 41,* 432–444.

Pianta, R. C., Egeland, B., & Sroufe, L. A. (1990). Maternal stress and children's development: Prediction of school outcomes and identification of protective factors. In J. Rolf, A. Masten, D. Cicchetti, K. Nuechterlein, & S. Weintraub (Eds.), *Risk and protective factors in the development of psychopathology* (pp. 215–235). Cambridge, England: Cambridge University Press.

Rescorla, L., Parker, R., & Stolley, P. (1991). Ability, achievement, and adjustment in homeless children. *American Journal of Orthopsychiatry, 61,* 210–220.

Richters, J., & Pellegrini, D. (1989). Depressed mothers' judgements about their children: An examination of the depression-distortion hypothesis. *Child Development, 60,* 1068–1075.

Rutter, M. (1983). Stress, coping, and development: Some issues and some questions. In N. Garmezy & M. Rutter (Eds.), *Stress, coping, and development in children* (pp. 1–41). New York: McGraw-Hill.

Rutter, M. (1987). Psychosocial resilience and protective mechanisms. *American Journal of Orthopsychiatry, 57,* 317–331.

Rutter, M. (1990). Commentary: Some focus and process considerations regarding effects of parental depression on children. *Developmental Psychology, 26,* 60–67.

Rutter, M. (1994). Family discord and conduct disorder: Cause, consequence, or correlate? *Journal of Family Psychology, 8,* 170–186.

Sternberg, K. J., Lamb, M. E., Greenbaum, C., Cicchetti, D., Dawud, S., Cortes, R. M., Krispin, O., & Lorey, F. (1993). Effects of domestic violence on children's behavior problems and depression. *Developmental Psychology, 29*, 44–52.

Sternberg, K., Lamb, M., & Dawud-Noursi, S. (1998). Using multiple informants to understand domestic violence and its effects. In G. W. Holden, R. A. Geffner, & E. N. Jouriles (Eds.), *Children exposed to marital violence: Theory, research, and applied issues* (pp. 121–156). Washington, DC: American Psychological Association.

Straus, M. A. (1979). Measuring intrafamily conflict and violence: The Conflict Tactics (CT) scales. *Journal of Marriage and the Family, 41*, 75–88.

Vissing, Y. M., Straus, M., Gelles, R. J., & Harrop, J. W. (1991). Verbal aggression by parents and psychosocial problems of children. *Child Abuse and Neglect, 15*, 223–238.

Wechsler, D. (1974). *Manual for the Wechsler Intelligence Scale for Children.* New York: Psychological Corporation.

Wolfe, D. A., & Jaffe, P. (1991). Child abuse and family violence as determinants of child psychopathology. *Canadian Journal of Behavioral Science, 23*, 282–299.

Wolfe, D. A., Zak, L., & Wilson, S. (1986). Child witnesses to violence between parents: Critical issues in behavioral and social adjustment. *Journal of Abnormal Child Psychology, 14*, 95–104.

Wolfe, D. A., Jaffe, P., Wilson, S. K., & Zak, L. (1985). Children of battered women: The relation of child behavior to family violence and maternal stress. *Journal of Consulting and Clinical Psychology, 53*, 657–665.

Zigler, E., & Hall, N. W. (1989). Physical abuse in America: Past, present, and future. In D. Cicchetti & V. Carlson (Eds.), *Child maltreatment: Theory and research on the causes and consequences of child abuse and neglect* (pp. 38–75). New York: Cambridge University Press.

7

Heterogeneity in Adjustment Among Children of Battered Women

Honore M. Hughes and Douglas A. Luke

Concern regarding the psychological adjustment of children of battered women has intensified within recent years as more evidence has become available supporting the negative impact of witnessing marital violence (Cummings & Davies, 1994; Emery, 1989; Fincham, 1994; H. M. Hughes & Fantuzzo, 1994; Rossman, Hughes, & Hanson, in press). In general, research findings indicate that witnessing parental violence is a traumatic experience for children. These results are detailed by other authors elsewhere in this volume. At this point, there is solid evidence for the negative impact on children of witnessing spouse abuse. Suggestions have been made that it is now time to do more than document these detrimental effects, to investigate in closer detail many of the factors that are related to adjustment. These variables are important because they likely mediate or moderate the impact of exposure to parental violence on children's psychological functioning (e.g., Fincham, 1994; H. M. Hughes, 1991, 1997). One way to do so, and at the same time to consider children's problems in more depth,

We thank the children, women, and staff at the Project for Victims of Family Violence for their participation in this study.

is to examine the possibility that these children manifest a range of difficulties, both in presence and intensity. If some of these youngsters show good adjustment and others exhibit poor functioning, the identification of factors associated with each type of behavioral and emotional adjustment would help when planning interventions.

The impetus for examining heterogeneity in adjustment for children of battered women in the present study comes from two sources. One source is the percentage of children in shelter samples who have behavior problem scores (often on measures such as the Child Behavior Checklist; CBCL; Achenbach & Edelbrock, 1983) above the cutoffs indicating a need for clinical services. Several researchers have investigated the proportions of children in shelter samples who have behavior problem checklist scores above these levels. Depending on the gender of the child, the type of violence experienced, and the T score used as the cutoff, the percentages reported range from 25% to 65%, with, on the average, approximately 40% to 45% of the children falling above that cutoff (e.g., Christopoulos et al., 1987; H. M. Hughes, Parkinson, & Vargo, 1989; Sternberg et al., 1993; Wolfe, Zak, Wilson, & Jaffe, 1986). By comparison in terms of base rates, approximately 25% of children in comparably low-income families have scores within the clinical range (Burns, Patterson, Nussbaum, & Parker, 1991). Thus, a substantial portion of shelter children are reported by their mothers as being in need of clinical treatment. In accordance with the above, at least two groups of children are likely to be seen: one in which the children's scores are above the cutoff, and another group of children who receive scores below the cut-off and are not reported as having substantial problems.

Given the above findings, it seems possible that differences in individual children's adjustment are being obscured by group averages, when in fact some youngsters may be doing quite well and others faring poorly. It would be instructive to know more about both the children who are not reporting distress and those who are experiencing difficulties. The results mentioned above lead one to expect that when children are grouped by similarities and differences in behavior, at least two groups of children emerge: those who are reported to be experiencing emotional or behavioral problems (or both) and those who seem to be relatively nondistressed. If separate groups can be distinguished on the basis of differences in problem levels, this then would have important implications for the use of a variety of interventions with these children.

Another source of information relevant to an investigation of heterogeneity in adjustment is the literature on multiple informants. A number of researchers in this area have found that they often obtain different results depending on who is asked, the child or the parent (e.g., H. M. Hughes, 1988; H. M. Hughes et al., 1989; McCloskey, Figueredo, & Koss, 1995; Sternberg et al., 1993; see Sternberg, Lamb, & Dawud-Noursi, 1998, this volume). It is not unusual for the child and parent to have different views regarding the presence of children's distress (Achenbach, McConaughy, & Howell, 1987; H. M. Hughes, 1995). The child may deny distress and the parents may exaggerate, or vice versa. Another feasible reason for this discrepancy is that parents are thought to be better reporters of externalizing behaviors (e.g., Loeber, Green, Lahey, & Stouthamer-Loeber, 1991), and children better reporters of their internal experiences (e.g., W. M. Reynolds, 1993). In the present study it was possible to examine each reporter's view of the children's adjustment (because mothers' reports of externalizing-type problems were obtained) and children's descriptions of their internalizing type of problems and levels of self-esteem.

Thus, a number of subgroups of children and women may be found, in which (a) the mothers report that the children are distressed, whereas the children do not; (b) the children report that they are distressed, whereas the mothers say the children are not; (c) both mothers and children report children's distress; or (d) both informants report that the children are not distressed. The purpose of the study reported here was to examine a sample of children of battered women to ascertain whether there is indeed heterogeneity in their individual levels of adjustment. Because we expected to find subgroups within the overall data set, we used cluster analysis to group children on the basis of their patterns of psychological functioning. At least two distinct subgroups, and possibly four, were expected to emerge from this sample of children.

Cluster analysis is a classification technique used for forming homogeneous groups within complex data sets (Borgen & Barnett, 1987). It provides for grouping people on the basis of similarities and differences in their profiles across a set of variables; thus, it assists researchers in examining which people have similar characteristics based on more than one variable or data point. In this way, the technique emphasizes diversity rather than highlights central tendencies (Rapkin & Luke, 1993). Participants can be sorted into groups on the basis of more than one variable, so that a "profile" for each person is constructed from the specific factors of interest. For example, one person may be high on one scale, have low scores on another measure, and have medium level scores on a third instrument. The aim of this procedure is to create a number of subgroups in which people within the cluster have very similar combinations or profiles of scores, while at the same time differing from the profiles of people in the other clusters. Thus, cluster analysis sorts people with similar profiles of scores on the variables into separate groups such that cluster members' profiles are maximally similar to others in the cluster and maximally different from group members' profiles in the other clusters.

Cluster analysis has a long history of use in the psychiatric and clinical literature in a variety of situations. For example, it has been used successfully to classify people with dual diagnoses (Luke, Mowbray, Klump, Herman, & BootsMiller, 1996), the homeless (Humphreys & Rosenbeck, 1995), and persons who abuse substances, especially alcohol (S. O. Hughes, 1992); to create taxonomies of treatment environments and other organizational settings (Luke, Rappaport, & Seidman, 1991; Prince & Moos, 1975); and to examine the characteristics of diagnostic systems (Blashfield, 1983; Gara, Rosenberg, & Goldenberg, 1992). To date, there have been relatively few empirical examples of applying cluster analytic methods to families (for one notable exception, see Alexander & Schaeffer, 1994).

METHOD

Participants

Participants were 58 pairs of mothers and their oldest child who were residing in a shelter for battered women in the rural midwestern part of the country. The children's ages ranged from 6 to 12 years; the mothers' ages ranged from 20 to 50 years. There were 26 girls and 32 boys, and the average child's age was approximately 9 years. The majority of the families were of European American origin, with only 8 of the families of a different ethnic group (a mixture of African American, Hispanic, Asian, and Native American). The average adult female resident was 31 years old, had 12 years of formal education, and remained at the shelter for 11 days (range = 1 to 35 days). This was a low-income group of women, with 65% living in households of 4 people where the annual income was approximately $12,000. On average, the duration of the most recent abusive relationship was approximately 7 years, with the violence taking place over 5 years of that time.

From the larger shelter population, participants were selected on the basis of duration of residence and willingness to participate in the project. Approximately two-thirds of the families were not included because they remained at the shelter for less than 3 days. Prior residents of the shelter were excluded (approximately 15 women) if they had two or more previous stays, or if, in the case of second-time residents, the initial visit had occurred within the year preceding possible project participation. Approximately 5% of the eligible shelter women declined to participate; an additional 10% agreed to take part but did not follow through on completing the measures.

The shelter sample was further subdivided on the basis of abuse status (whether the children had witnessed physical violence between their parents or had been both victims of and witnesses to violence). In the shelter sample, 50% of the children had been physically abused, according to reports from their mothers. In addition, verification of physical abuse was obtained from the shelter staff workers (shelter staff conducted a thorough intake interview with the women regarding violence occurring in the family, with the appropriate social service agency notified as necessary). If there was a discrepancy between reports, children were classified according to the staff member's judgment.

The women filled out the Conflict Tactics Scale: Husband–Wife form (CTS; Straus, 1979, 1987) to obtain an estimate of the violence between the adults. As a check on the accuracy of the description "exposed," the mothers were asked where the children were when the fighting between the two adults took place. All of the children in the exposed group were either present in the same room and saw the fighting or were in an adjacent room and heard the physical conflict. The same was true of 90% of the exposed-abused children.

Measures

Behavioral problems, anxiety level, self-esteem, and depressive symptoms of children were assessed using parent and child self-report measures. Two different behavior problem instruments were used in two different investigations, with the data collected in two waves over a period of 4 years (H. M. Hughes, 1988; H. M. Hughes et al., 1989). In addition, an important aspect of the family environment was obtained by measuring the mothers' mental health.

Eyberg Child Behavior Inventory (ECBI)

The ECBI (Eyberg & Ross, 1978; Robinson, Eyberg, & Ross, 1980) was completed by mothers of children between the ages of 3 and 12 years to assess externalizing conduct disorder-type problems. Each of 36 behavioral items, drawn from case records of conduct problem children, is identified as problematic or nonproblematic and rated for frequency. The Problem Score (PS) is the number of items acknowledged as problematic on a yes–no scale (range = 0–36), and the Intensity Score (IS) is the sum of the frequency ratings (range = 36–262). Support for the measure's reliability, validity, and factor structure is provided by Eyberg and Ross (1978) and Robinson et al. (1980). Raw scores were used in the analyses.

CBCL

The CBCL (Achenbach & Edelbrock, 1983) is a 120-item measure of behavior problems and social competence. The 113 items of the behavior problem scale provide a rating of the broadband factors of Externalizing and Internalizing behaviors, based on descriptions of behaviors (e.g., "steals at home," "unhappy, sad, depressed"). Mothers rate the behaviors with regard to how well the questions describe their child. For the seven items on the Social Competence scale, parents are asked to list usual social, school, and leisure activities of their child and to indicate the quality and frequency with which their child performs the activity. The Total Behavior Problem Score is a combination of the Externalizing and Internalizing items, plus 10–12 additional items that did not load on either broadband factor.

The CBCL manual provides extensive evidence for its reliability and validity. Raw scores for the three behavior problem and the Social Competence scales were transformed into T scores and percentiles. One of the advantages of the CBCL is that the T scores allow comparisons across gender and age. T scores were used in the present study.

Children's Depression Inventory (CDI)

The CDI (Kovacs, 1983) was given to children 8 years and older. This 27-item self-report measure was designed to assess the presence and severity of depressive symptomatology such as sadness, anhedonia, suicidal ideation, and sleep and appetite disturbance. Each item contains three choices, scored in severity from 0 to 2, resulting in a range of 0–54 for total scores. The scale has acceptable internal consistency, significant item-total correlations, and adequate test–retest reliability (Kovacs, 1983). Normative data are available (Finch, Saylor, & Edwards, 1985; Kovacs, 1983). Total raw scores were used in the analyses in the current investigation.

Revised Children's Manifest Anxiety Scale (RCMAS)

Anxiety of school-age children (6 to 12 years) was measured using the RCMAS (C. Reynolds & Richmond, 1984). This 37-item self-report measure consists of statements that are answered *yes* or *no* by the child. Questions were read to 6- to 8-year-old children. Affirmative answers to identified items are summed to yield a Total Anxiety score, a Lie scale score, and three subscales. Evidence for the scale's reliability and validity in assessing "trait" anxiety and normative data are provided by

C. Reynolds and Paget (1981) and C. Reynolds and Richmond (1984). Raw total scores were used in the analyses.

Piers–Harris Children's Self-Concept Scale

The Piers–Harris 80-item inventory (Piers, 1984) has a yes–no format and was presented in written form to children ages 9 years and older. The scale yields a total self-esteem score and scores on six self-concept clusters. The manual (Piers, 1984) provides support for the scale's psychometric adequacy. Only the total self-esteem raw scores were used in the data analysis.

McDaniel–Piers Young Children's Self-Concept Scale

The McDaniel–Piers 40-item forced-choice inventory (McDaniel & Piers, 1976) was orally presented to younger (6- to 8-year-old) school-age children. A total self-concept score and three subscale scores are obtained. Evidence for the scale's reliability and validity was presented by H. M. Hughes (1984). The total self-esteem raw scores were used in the data analysis.

CTS–Husband-Wife Form

The CTS was used to assess the types and level of violence between the adult partners (Straus, 1979). The women were asked how many times in the past year they engaged in a certain behavior, rating it on a 7-point scale from 0 (*never*) to 6 (*more than 20 times*). According to Straus, the first three items comprise the Reasoning subscale, and the next seven items are part of the Verbal Aggressiveness subscale. Examples of items that comprise this latter scale include "threaten to throw something at the other" and "insulted or swore at the other." The Violence subscale consists of the last 8 items on the scale, ranging from "threw something at the other person" to "used a knife or a gun." The Physical Violence scores range from 0 to 48. Straus presented data regarding the scale's factor structure, reliability, validity, and normative data. In this study, women were requested to indicate how many times in the past year they engaged in a particular behavior toward their partner; the same was measured for their partner toward them.

Beck Depression Inventory (BDI)

Mothers completed the BDI (Beck & Steer, 1984), a 21-item scale developed to assess behavioral manifestations of depression. Each BDI item consists of several self-evaluative statements reflecting differing levels of depression and is rated on a 4-point scale from 0 to 3. The weights of alternatives chosen by the respondents are summed to yield a total score, with high scores reflecting higher depression. Scores range from 0 to 63. The manual provides extensive reliability and validity information.

State-Trait Anxiety Inventory–Form Y (STAI)

The STAI (Spielberger, Gorsuch, Lushene, Vagg, & Jacobs, 1983), completed by the women, consists of 40 items, each of which is rated on a 4-point scale. Separate scores for state and trait anxiety are obtained, with higher scores indicating higher anxiety. The manual provides evidence for the reliability and validity of the two scales.

Procedure

Mothers and children were tested at the shelter by a clinical psychology graduate student between 3 and 5 days after entry. The project was explained to the women, and permission for their participation and that of their children was obtained. Informed consent was handled by carefully explaining to the mothers and to the children above the age of 6 that the questions they would be asked would be somewhat personal and that they might feel uncomfortable. They were told they were free to discontinue participation at any point, and confidentiality of the results was emphasized.

After a brief rapport-building interview, mothers completed the inventories and checklists independently. Occasional questions raised by the women were answered, but few required assistance. Children were tested individually in a different room. In addition to the measures described above, mothers completed forms that contained questions about their history of domestic violence, previous problems with and negative experiences of their children, and demographic information. The inventories took between 20 and 40 minutes for the children to complete, whereas the checklists and questionnaires required between 60 and 90 minutes of the mothers' time. Each mother received $15 as compensation for her participation, and children were given a small toy. These two previously collected samples (H. M. Hughes, 1988; H. M. Hughes et al., 1989) were combined and the mother–child pairs used in the present analyses were drawn from this pool on the basis of the availability of data from the children on the measures of interest to this study.

Variables

To provide a broad context for examining the impact on children of witnessing spouse abuse, a number of potentially influential factors related to the family, the situation, the mother, and the children were included. The variables used in the following analyses are made up of these four different types of factors, which were chosen and grouped together on the basis of their conceptual distinctiveness. One group of variables contained family demographic information, including the child's gender and age and the mother's age, educational level, and household income.

The second group of factors was composed of family violence variables. These included whether the child was physically abused and the duration and frequency of the abuse. The length of time the mother lived with her partner, the length of time over which her abuse occurred, and the frequency with which she was hurt were also variables of interest. In addition, two sets of three CTS scores (Reasoning, Verbal Aggression, and Physical Aggression) were also examined; one set was based on those tactics directed from mothers to their partners, and the other was from the partners to the mothers.

Measures of the children's psychological functioning comprised the third group of factors. The mother-reported externalizing-type behavior problems included CBCL Externalizing subscale T scores and ECBI Problem and Intensity Scale raw scores. Internalizing-type distress, as assessed through child report, included total raw scores from the RCMAS and the CDI. Self-esteem of children based on their report was measured with the total raw scores from the McDaniel–Piers (ages 6–8) and the Piers–Harris (ages 9–12).

The fourth group of variables was composed of measures of mothers' psychological functioning. Three scores were used including the BDI total and the State and Trait total scores from the STAI.

To examine several areas of functioning, three types of child adjustment variables were selected from the third group of factors mentioned above with which to conduct the cluster analysis: behavior problems, anxiety, and self-esteem. Other variables in the four groups of factors listed above were used to describe and validate the clusters obtained.

Standardization of Cluster Variables

Because the scaling of variables influences a cluster analysis, the scores used in the analysis were standardized so that all variables were on a similar scale (Borgen & Barnett, 1987). Thus, the scores for the behavior problems, distress, and self-esteem measures were converted to z scores with a mean of 0 and a standard deviation of 1. In addition, this standardization procedure allowed the researchers to combine the samples in which different behavior problem measures were used and to join the two age groups of children because self-esteem had been measured with different instruments.

To make the scores from the two behavior problem scales as similar as possible, only the Externalizing score from the CBCL was used (ECBI measures conduct problem behaviors). In addition, to increase the similarity to the way the Externalizing scale is scored, the ECBI PS and IS scores were added together to obtain reports of both the presence and intensity of problems. This summed score was then standardized.

Cluster Analysis Procedure

After the clustering variables of behavior problems, internalizing distress, and self-esteem were selected, a hierarchical agglomerative cluster analysis method was chosen (Aldenderfer & Blashfield, 1984). Squared Euclidean distance was used as the proximity measure because it takes into account pattern, level, and scatter of the data (Skinner, 1978). Ward's Method was selected for the clustering algorithm because it maximizes within-group homogeneity (Borgen & Barnett, 1987). All cluster analysis procedures were carried out using SPSS-Version 7.0 for

Cluster Scree Plot

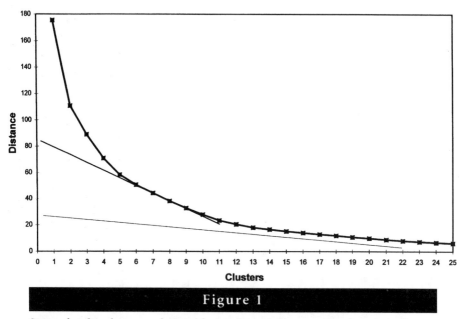

Figure 1

Scree plot for cluster analysis with number of clusters plotted against distance between clusters.

Windows (SPSS, 1995). Selection of the optimum number of clusters for this sample was based on an examination of the dendogram and the inverse scree plot, on whether cases in the different clusters differed from each other on the other variables assessed, and on whether the clusters made theoretical sense (Rapkin & Luke, 1993).

RESULTS

As can be seen in Figure 1, the scree plot shows the number of clusters plotted against the distance between the clusters when they are joined together. The best solution for the analysis (i.e., choosing the number of clusters) is based on the point where a jump in the numbers is seen. When a marked increase in the distance between clusters is noted, this signifies that information is lost when those two clusters are combined.

Table 1

Five-Cluster Solution: z Scores for Behavior, Anxiety, and Esteem

Cluster	Behavior		Anxiety		Esteem	
	M	SD	M	SD	M	SD
Cluster 1: Hanging in There ($n = 21$)	−0.25	0.69	0.38	0.68	−0.07	0.47
Cluster 2: Doing Well ($n = 15$)	−0.60	0.81	−1.16	0.32	0.99	0.28
Cluster 3: High Behavior Problems ($n = 9$)	1.03	0.69	−0.49	0.57	0.66	0.24
Cluster 4: High General Distress ($n = 9$)	0.79	0.88	1.39	0.30	−1.05	0.43
Cluster 5: Depressed Kids ($n = 4$)	−0.77	0.61	0.56	1.28	−2.20	0.84

The numbers jump at four, which indicates that the five-cluster solution is the best; information would be lost if the clusters were combined into four clusters.

Description of Clusters

On the basis of the scree plot, dendogram, and interpretability, a five-cluster solution was chosen. Table 1 presents the results of the cluster analysis, including the name selected to describe the cluster, the cluster mean scores, the standard deviations, and the number of children in each cluster. High z scores on behavior problems and anxiety indicate difficulties, whereas low esteem scores reflect low self-esteem. Five clearly different patterns of distress and problems are evident, which are illustrated in the profiles of the clusters seen in Figure 2. Based on the clustering variables, the four predicted patterns were obtained, with the nondistressed subgroup splitting into two clusters to reveal five patterns. Thus, there is indeed a subgroup of children, consisting of the first two clusters, who are not reported by mother or child to be ex-

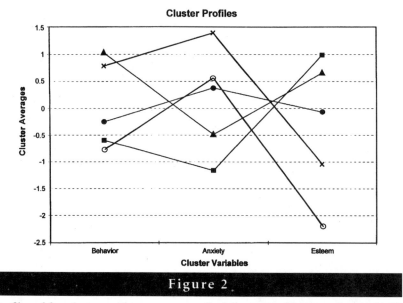

Figure 2

Profiles of five clusters with mean z scores for behavior problems, anxiety, and self-esteem. Filled circles = Hanging In There; filled squares = Doing Well; filled triangles = Behavior Problems; × = General Distress; open circles = Depressed.

periencing many difficulties. However, another subgroup of children who seem to be distressed also emerged. The last three clusters contain children for whom either the children or the mothers indicated that the children were having problems emotionally or behaviorally. Additional characteristics that further differentiate the clusters are discussed in the validation section.

Few Problems

The five-cluster solution using the three clustering variables (Table 1) revealed that the children in the "Hanging In There" cluster have an average number of problems, some mild anxiety symptoms, and an average level of self-esteem. This is the largest cluster, incorporating approximately 36% of the children. Children in the second largest cluster, "Doing Well," have a low number of behavior problems, report no anxiety, and have rather high levels of self-esteem (hence the name chosen for this group). Together, these first two groups of children make up 62% of the sample. This finding suggests that a number of young-sters in shelters may experience some, but not substantial, distress as a result of their situation.

Definite Difficulties

A considerable portion of the youngsters are described as experiencing (and report themselves to be experiencing) emotional or behavioral difficulties. Youngsters in the "High Behavior Problems" cluster are characterized as having high levels of behavioral difficulties, even though they report low anxiety and moderately high self-esteem levels. In the "High General Distress" cluster, the children's problems are ex-pressed both behaviorally and emotionally, and they experience low self-esteem. In contrast, the children in the "Depressed Kids" cluster have low levels of behavior problems; their distress is expressed emo-tionally with moderately high anxiety and very high levels of depression. However, because of the size of this last cluster, this finding must be considered quite tentative. Clusters of nine are not atypical in cluster analyses, but four is too few for the results to be very reliable.

Validation of Clusters

Both analysis of variance and chi-square tests were used to distinguish among the clusters on the basis of the other variables included. As mentioned previously, three of the four groups of factors used in de-scription and validation consisted of family demographics, family vio-lence variables, and measures of mothers' psychological functioning. In addition, one of the measures of the children's adjustment, the CDI, was included as a descriptor to assist with validation of the clusters.

Although many variables examined did not differ significantly among the clusters, a number of important factors did differ. These are discussed individually below. The factors that did not significantly dif-ferentiate among the subgroups included the following: (in the demo-graphic variables) gender of the children, household income, and moth-ers' employment, although ages of the children and mothers were marginally significant; and (in the family violence variables) physical abuse of the children, the frequency with which mothers were hurt, and

CTS variables (with one exception). Furthermore, the mothers' State-Trait scores showed no differences among the groups.

A general description of the clusters using the validating variables is provided in Table 2. There are some differences noted in the mean ages of children and mothers, with both family members in the Depressed Kids cluster being somewhat older. The youngsters in Cluster 5 were on average 11.9 years old, as opposed to the children in the other clusters (on average, 9.2 years old). The mean age for these mothers was 40, approximately 10 years older than mothers in the other four clusters.

The last column in Table 2 illustrates the reporters' perspectives, where, as predicted, diverse patterns of reported distress were found. All four of the predicted groups were obtained. More is said about this in the Discussion.

On a measure of the children's depression levels (CDI), large differences among the clusters are seen (Table 3 and Figure 3), especially in the High General Distress cluster and where the children report high levels of internalizing distress (anxiety and depression). Figure 3 provides the box plot for the CDI. The box contains 50% of the scores; the "whiskers" on the lines extending from either end of the box illustrate the range in scores; the darker line within the box indicates the median score for that box; and one outlier in Cluster 1 is indicated by the small circle. It is interesting to note that the mean score for the CDI in the standardization sample is 9, and the cutoff indicating the top 10% of the sample is 19 (Finch et al., 1985; Kovacs, 1983). As can be seen in Table 3, children in both the High General Distress and Depressed Kids clusters have depression scores at that high level.

Also included in Table 3 are mean scores from the mothers' reports of their depressive symptoms (BDI). In contrast with the CDI, the BDI scores were highest in the High Behavior Problems and the High General Distress clusters. The mothers in Cluster 3 obtained the highest BDI scores, closest to the severe range (severe = 30; Beck & Steer, 1984). This cluster had also been predicted, whereby the mothers reported the children to have behavior problems and the children did not note emotional or behavioral difficulties.

Table 2

Description of Five-Cluster Solution: Demographic Variables and Informants' Perspective

Cluster	Child gender		Mean child age (months)*	Mean mother age (years)*	Presence of physical abuse		Reporters' perspective
	Male	Female			Yes	No	
Cluster 1: Hanging in There	10	11	111	30	13	8	Both O.K.
Cluster 2: Doing Well	10	5	104	32	6	9	Both fine
Cluster 3: High Behavior Problems	5	4	105	28	4	5	Mom sees problems
Cluster 4: High General Distress	5	4	108	29	5	4	Both see problems
Cluster 5: Depressed Kids	2	2	143	40	1	2	Kid sees problems

*Marginally significant.

Table 3

Scores for Validation Variables That Significantly Differentiated Among the Clusters

Cluster	CDI[a]		BDI[b]		Mom's CTS Verb Aggr[c]		Months with partner[d]		Months of abuse[e]		Mom's education[f]	
	M	SD	M	SD	M	SD	M	SD	M	SD	M	SD
Cluster 1: Hanging in There (n = 21)	9.7	6.1	17.1	11.2	10.4	6.4	81.4	56.0	47.4	50.0	3.2	1.6
Cluster 2: Doing Well (n = 15)	2.6	2.9	15.7	9.0	13.0	7.2	86.6	51.0	75.6	49.1	2.9	1.4
Cluster 3: High Behavior Problems (n = 9)	5.7	3.8	28.1	11.8	19.7	6.1	74.9	39.2	51.0	46.5	2.6	1.1
Cluster 4: High General Distress (n = 9)	18.6	9.1	23.8	12.5	19.3	9.2	65.5	43.5	43.4	27.5	2.4	.92
Cluster 5: Depressed Kids (n = 4)	24.7	9.0	9.8	7.2	10.7	5.9	194.0	34.5	172.3	25.2	6.0	2.0

Note. CDI = Children's Depression Inventory; BDI = Beck Depression Inventory; CTS Verb Aggr = Conflict Tactics Scale–Verbal Aggression score.
[a]$F(4, 22) = 9.09, p = .000, \eta^2 = .623.$ [b]$F(4, 49) = 3.03, p = .018, \eta^2 = .212.$ [c]$F(4, 34) = 2.76, p = .043, \eta^2 = .246.$ [d]$F(4, 49) = 4.04, p = .007, \eta^2 = .248.$ [e]$F(4, 49) = 5.63, p = .001, \eta^2 = .315.$ [f]Educational level category 3 indicates high school graduate and 6 indicates 3+ years of college; $F(4, 49) = 4.34, p = .004, \eta^2 = .270.$

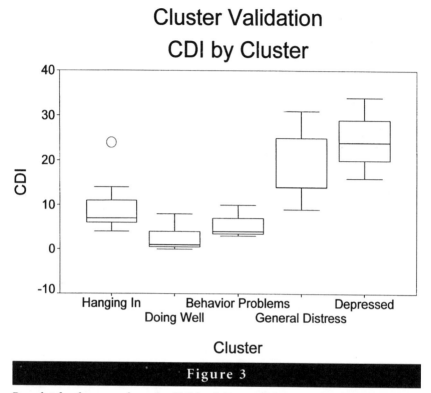

Figure 3

Box plot for the scores from the Children's Depression Inventory (CDI). (The circle indicates an outlier in Cluster 1.)

In the High General Distress cluster (Cluster 4), higher BDI scores are also seen for the women, though the scores are closer to a moderate level of symptoms (moderate = 25; Beck & Steer, 1984). Thus, in this cluster, there is agreement among sources related to distress. The mothers note that the children have behavior problems, and the children themselves describe internalizing distress and low self-esteem. Moreover, the mothers also admit to depressive symptoms.

In contrast, the mothers in the Depressed Kids subgroup have the lowest BDI scores of any of the clusters, even lower than the women in the first two reasonably well-functioning subgroups. This is discussed in greater detail later.

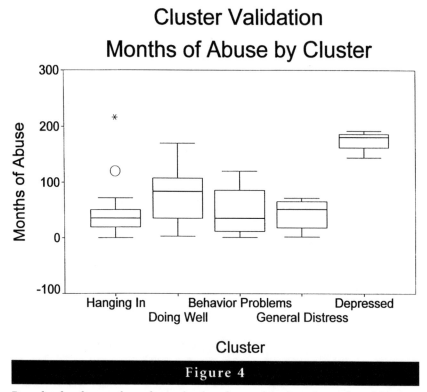

Figure 4

Box plot for the number of months that the mothers have been abused by their most recent partner. (The asterisk reflects an extreme outlier.)

Regarding family violence variables that significantly differentiated among the clusters (see Table 3), scores on the CTS Verbal Aggression from the mothers to their partners were the highest for the High Behavior Problems and High General Distress clusters (Clusters 3 and 4). Therefore, it appears that not only are the mothers in those clusters depressed, but they also admit to using more verbal aggression than the mothers in the other subgroups.

Several additional family violence variables also demonstrated significant differences among clusters. Months with partner and months of abuse both show few differences among the clusters, with the exception of the Depressed Kids cluster (see Table 3). Figure 4 illustrates the notable difference on the months of abuse variable between the Depressed Kids and the other four groups. (Box plot indicators are the same as in Figure 3.) In Clusters 1 through 4, time with partner ranges from 5.5 to 7 years, whereas abuse ranges from 3.5 to 6.25 years. However, the most substantial difference is seen with the Depressed Kids group, where time with partner is 16 years, and time of abuse 14 years. For these children, who are approximately 12 years old, the abuse clearly began before they were born. This seems to be less likely true for the children in the other four clusters and may play a prominent role in the poor adjustment of the youngsters in the Depressed Kids cluster.

DISCUSSION

Results from these analyses indicated that subgroups of children indeed emerged from this sample of children of battered women. The five-cluster solution was judged to be the best, because it was established through the scree plot, other variables showed the children in the groups to differ in important ways, and it made the most theoretical sense. Thus, variations in distress levels and heterogeneity in adjustment were found to exist within this group of youngsters.

These findings of heterogeneity in functioning correspond with results previously obtained in the recent literature. As mentioned earlier, a number of researchers found, on average, 40–45% of their sample to be above the cutoff for needing clinical intervention. Results from the present study are consistent with this. In this sample, 60% of the children were found to be in the not distressed or very mildly distressed groups, and 40% were in the clusters indicating difficulties.

These results are tentative and provide suggestions for future research and implications for intervention. These findings support the idea that there are subgroups of families within shelters, families whose adjustment varies depending on a number of factors. Clearly it is important to conduct additional cluster analyses with larger groups of battered women and their children to see how well the five-cluster solution found here can be replicated.

With a larger sample, it would be possible to investigate the stability of the Depressed Kids cluster. Whereas the other four clusters contained enough children to give confidence in the findings, the depressed subgroup included only four children, so it is hard to know whether that group would emerge from another sample. However, evidence from the validation procedures points to the very notable differences between these children and the others, adding to the likelihood that this cluster is not an artifact of this particular sample.

Possible Mediators of Adjustment

Regarding some of the factors that contributed to differences in adjustment among the children, some speculative thoughts can be put forth. A number of factors that may mediate or be associated with children's psychological functioning have been identified previously as possible sources of influence. These include both child-related and situational–contextual factors (H. M. Hughes, 1991, 1997; H. M. Hughes & Graham-Bermann, in press); the assumption is that all of the factors discussed below interact in some fashion. Child factors consist of characteristics of individual children that are relatively stable and more like "traits." For example, qualities such as temperament, self-esteem, cognitive abilities, coping skills, locus of control, age, and gender are important to consider regarding their role in an individual child's psychological functioning.

Situational–contextual factors include two types: (a) those situational variables that are more directly related to the children, such as their past experience with violence, perceived emotional climate in the family, parenting skills of the parents, mental health of the parents, and social support; and (b) those that are less directly related to the child, such as the frequency, intensity, duration, content, and resolution of the marital conflict.

Examining the clusters of children and women in terms of these mediators could provide some clues regarding differences among the children. Possible explanations for the adjustment of children in Cluster 5 (Depressed Kids) likely involve interactions among all three types of mediators, though one of the most notable differences among the groups was in duration of the abuse. These youngsters in the Depressed

Kids cluster, who are approximately 12 years old, have been exposed to the abuse of their mothers their entire lives (because the abuse has been ongoing for 14 years). Regarding the emotional climate in the family and parenting skills of the women, the mothers' adjustment in this cluster would lead one to speculate that these women may have found some way to cope with the chronicity of the 14 years of abuse, because these four women do not describe feelings of distress on the self-report measures. Fincham, Grych, and Osborne (1994) pointed out that when women are abused, parents' responses to the conflict may be either overt hostility or withdrawal and neglect of the children. Though highly speculative, perhaps the latter has occurred in the Cluster 5 families, in which the women have withdrawn to cope with the chronicity of the abuse. As a result, they have provided little emotional support for their children, who describe themselves as quite distressed. In support of this, there is some evidence that uninvolved parenting can lead to distress in children and substantial problems with attachment (Baumrind, 1991). Moreover, Kaslow, Rehm, and Siegel (1984) found that higher levels of depression in school-age children were related to decreased psychological availability of the parents.

Another potential influence comes from the individual child variables. Children differ in their attributional styles, and research has indicated that children of battered women also vary in their feelings regarding the extent to which they feel that they have control over their parents' behavior. Rosenberg and Rossman (1990) found that the children of battered women in their sample who felt they had some control over their parents' behavior and little control over their own fared worst in terms of their adjustment. Perhaps the children in the Depressed Kids cluster, who are substantially older than the other children in the sample, feel that they either have or should have some control over the occurrence of spouse abuse. Because they clearly cannot control their parents' behaviors or the abuse, they become anxious and depressed and have very low self-esteem.

Similar mediating factors are likely at work in the other two clusters of children with problems and feelings of distress. Demographic descriptions of the other two distressed groups are nearly identical, as are the mothers' levels of functioning. Cluster 3, High Behavior Problems, is made up of approximately even numbers of boys and girls as well as abused and nonabused children; however, these youngsters do not admit to feeling distress even though their mothers report them to have behavior problems. The women in Cluster 3 seem to be rather clearly distressed based on their BDI scores, which are two standard deviations above the mean of the normative sample (Beck & Steer, 1984), and are at the upper end of the moderate range of depressive symptoms. These women also report Verbal Aggressiveness scores on the CTS, which are at the 95th percentile (Straus, 1979), indicating substantial levels of yelling directed toward their male partners.

In contrast, both children and mothers in Cluster 4, High General Distress, report high levels of behavior problems and distress. Mothers in Cluster 4 endorse levels of depressive symptoms and verbal aggression that are very similar to those of mothers in Cluster 3. However, the children in Cluster 4, as opposed to those in Cluster 3, are reporting feelings of anxiety and low self-esteem. In terms of demographics, Cluster 4 youngsters, similar to those in Cluster 3, are evenly split between boys and girls and abused and nonabused. Thus, there are few obvious differences between the children, their mothers' adjustment, or their circumstances that would lead one to understand why one group of children experiences internalized distress and another does not, when that latter groups' mothers are reporting them to have externalizing-type problems.

Clearly, the main differentiation between the two clusters is in the children's reports of their distress levels. Children in Cluster 3 describe themselves as experiencing low levels of anxiety and moderately high self-esteem, whereas the children in the High General Distress cluster characterize themselves as distressed. Cluster 4 youngsters' feelings of anxiety are the highest among all the clusters, they experience low self-esteem, and their levels of depressive symptoms are above the cutoff for substantial difficulties (at the 10th percentile).

What are some of the explanations for these differences seen in child-reported adjustment, given that the patterns on the descriptive and validating variables are so similar? Examining the situational–

contextual factors for Clusters 3 and 4, it is apparent that the duration of the abuse for each cluster is also similar. This is true in terms of both the proportion of time this most recent relationship has been abusive and the percentage of the children's lives this abuse has been occurring. In both clusters the relationship has been abusive for 65–70% of its length, and the duration of spouse abuse in this most recent relationship has been approximately 40–50% of the lives of the children.

Another situational–contextual factor related to emotional climate and parenting skills, which also seems to be operating similarly in each of these clusters, is that the women in both are reporting high levels of depressive symptoms. Though parenting style was not assessed in the present study, evidence from other research indicates that depression often interferes with good parenting, with a negative impact on the children of depressed women (Downey & Coyne, 1990; Webster-Stratton & Hammond, 1988). Moreover, the women's CTS scores are very high, indicating high levels of yelling directed toward the male partner, some of which could "spill over" to their interactions with their children (Fincham et al., 1994). Moore and Pepler (1998, this volume) also describe spouse-abusing families as ones in which substantial amounts of yelling take place, including at the children. In their study, verbal aggression of the mother toward her children was related to behavior problems in the children. Thus, spouse abuse often contributes to ineffective parenting, a finding also obtained by McDonald and Jouriles (1991).

In terms of factors that might have operated differently in each cluster, parenting styles of either the women or the men in the families may have influenced the children's adjustment in some unknown way. Literature from child psychopathology indicates that parenting styles that result in internalizing problems and those that are related to externalizing difficulties are likely to show some important differences. Loeber and Stouthamer-Loeber (1986) characterized parenting associated with disruptive behavior disorders as involving low levels of parental involvement, poor supervision, and harsh and inconsistent disciplinary practices. It may be that children in Cluster 3 have experienced this style of parenting. In contrast, symptoms of depression and anxiety in children are associated with a parental style of inadequate affection and excessive parental control (Gerlsma, Emmelkamp, & Arrindell, 1990). Perhaps the children in Cluster 4, who experience internalizing and externalizing problems, have been subjected to both types of parenting, including both excessive control and low levels of involvement. As support for this conjecture, in studies conducted by Holden and Ritchie (1991) and Chew (1997), battered women describe their parenting styles as quite inconsistent, with the women being very strict when the man was present and lax when alone with their children.

Other possible child-related factors in these differences that one could consider are those of attributional style and feelings of control over the spouse abuse. It may be that the Cluster 3 children are externalizers and attribute responsibility for problems externally. Therefore, they do not feel a sense of control over the spouse abuse, and their externalization in this situation is probably adaptive. Perhaps the children who are in Cluster 4 are those who attribute causes for events more internally than the Cluster 3 youngsters; thus, they feel more responsibility for the spouse abuse, which may contribute to their feelings of distress. Inconsistent parenting plus a depressive attributional style could put the Cluster 4 children at risk for experiencing negative affect, though undoubtedly there are interactions among all of the factors mentioned above.

A factor not to be overlooked and related to child characteristics is denial on the part of the children, especially the youngsters in Clusters 1, 2, and 3, where the children are not reporting distress. Perhaps the children were reporting honestly, or they might have been denying their feelings of depression, anxiety, and low self-esteem. One check on this latter hypothesis is to examine the Lie scale scores from the RCMAS. When this was done, none of the children in any of the clusters had elevated scores, with no differences in mean scores seen among the clusters. Another speculation involves the possibility that the children were engaging in "healthy denial." Children in Clusters 2 and 3 may be denying problems, which might be a sign that the youngsters are engaging in healthy defensiveness (Rosenberg & Rossman, 1990; Shirk, 1988).

Clinical Implications

Future research will provide answers regarding the stability of these clusters. Assuming that this five-cluster solution is replicated, two aspects of the clinical implications from these findings are noteworthy. One is related to reports from different informants and the other to recommendations regarding intervention.

Perspective of Informant

When mothers and children agree regarding emotional or behavior problems, implications for intervention are clear. It is when children and mothers disagree on either the presence or absence of distress in the children that the assessment is more complex and clinicians are uncertain regarding ways to respond to the reports. H. M. Hughes (1995) summarized suggestions made by Achenbach et al. (1987); Phares, Compas, and Howell (1989); and Stanger and Lewis (1993), all of whom recommend that researchers and clinicians use both adult and child perspectives, rather than assuming that one reporter is "accurate" and the other "inaccurate." The latter authors also propose that requiring reports of problems above the cutoffs from at least two of the sources would add to the certainty that the child is actually distressed. This level of agreement could be taken as a signal that a particular child is more distressed than other children and a high priority for intervention. For example, in the present study, both children and mothers in Cluster 4 indicated that the children were experiencing high levels of emotional and behavioral problems. Thus, children and their mothers in that cluster would have highest priority for receiving intervention, especially because those mothers also reported high levels of depressive symptoms.

Recommendations for Intervention

Further research is needed to be able to make more specific suggestions for intervention, especially regarding mothers who would benefit from parenting skills training and children who need additional support. However, with the findings of heterogeneity in adjustment, one clearly evident recommendation is to base decisions on family members' individual needs. Some tentative thoughts with regard to provision of treatment are offered here, subject to revision when additional findings are available. Regarding suggestions for intervention, it may be helpful to think of these families in terms of their at-risk status, with the hanging in there and doing well groups at moderate risk because of their experiences with family violence. Members of these families would likely benefit from the usual interventions and programming found in shelters. Frequently, shelters with children's programs have educational groups for the children who have mild difficulties (H. M. Hughes & Marshall, 1995). Information regarding issues of responsibility for the family violence, safety planning, and nonviolent conflict resolution is often provided to the children, whereas the women are given information and suggestions regarding parenting (see Jaffe, Wolfe, & Wilson, 1990; Rosenberg & Rossman, 1990).

In contrast, the family members in the other three groups (High Behavior Problems, High General Distress, and Depressed Kids) would seem to be at substantially greater risk for emotional and behavioral difficulties and in need of additional intervention, services that are usually over and above the typical shelter programming. For shelter mothers who report both depressive symptoms and behavior problems with their children, this could indicate difficulties with discipline or in the parent–child relationship (or both). These mothers probably could use help with their parenting, though they also need intervention for their depression, likely before addressing parenting issues (H. M. Hughes, 1997; Webster-Stratton & Hammond, 1988). Webster-Stratton and Hammond emphasized the need to take any depression on the mother's part as a "signal" and to attend to her distress. According to these authors, intervention programs for mothers regarding parenting issues have not worked unless treatment was provided for her depression as well as the children's behavior problems.

Related to the children's distress, children clearly seem to respond differently when they are in violent situations, and interventions should be tailored to the specific needs of the children. For example, as previously mentioned, children's groups would likely be beneficial for youngsters with mild to moderate levels of problem behaviors (see Peled & Edleson, 1992). If the problems are more severe, especially if both child and mother report problems and distress on the child's part, additional attention to these children is definitely warranted. Referrals for assessment and appropriate interventions on an individual basis are essential to alleviate their distress (see H. M. Hughes, 1997).

Implications for Future Investigations

Several recommendations can be made regarding samples and constructs investigated. First, these analyses need to be replicated with larger groups of families, which would facilitate the use of more stringent validation procedures. For example, use of cluster analysis with larger samples would allow more rigorous reliability analyses such as use of split-half tests procedures (Borgen & Barnett, 1987; Rapkin & Luke, 1993). Plus, with additional family members in the analysis, some of the variables that were only marginally significant in the validation procedures, such as age of child and mother, might actually be significantly different. Moreover, any cluster that replicated Cluster 5 would add support to the importance of attending to the unique emotional needs of some of the older children who fit this profile.

Second, the majority of these participants were Anglo; whether similar clusters would be found within groups containing more ethnically diverse families is an interesting empirical question. Moreover, these were low-income families, and little is known about the adjustment of children in higher income families in which there is spouse abuse. Recruiting participants through nonshelter sources would also be very useful and provide information that could shed some light on whether there are differences between those families who seek assistance in shelters and those who do not.

In general in this area, it would be helpful for investigators to continue with a contextual approach to understanding exposure to family violence. For example, the present research has provided evidence for the importance of assessing children's functioning from more than one perspective, and therefore including both mothers' and children's reports. Also, it would be helpful to measure additional aspects of psychological functioning and adjustment, such as social competence, which is included on the CBCL. This would add another area of functioning to an assessment, in addition to self-esteem and emotional and behavioral distress, helping to provide a more complete picture of adjustment.

Also related to context, there is a need to continue to search for additional mediator and moderator variables. As demonstrated in the present research, a number of important mediating factors are likely to be influential. Additional research into possible mediating factors such as duration of abuse, parenting style, adjustment of mothers, and children's attributional style and sense of control could be very productive. Other equally important factors that need to be included in investigations are child-related variables such as age, gender, and abuse status (H. M. Hughes, 1997).

Researchers and clinicians need to attend to individual variability and the specific factors that contribute to adjustment in order to plan more individualized interventions designed for the identified needs of particular families. For example, as suggested by the results from the current study, the emotional climate of the family, including mothers' verbal aggressiveness and depression, are important to investigate. Moreover, the level of psychological abusiveness within the family makes a substantial contribution to adjustment and should not be overlooked (Jouriles, Norwood, McDonald, Vincent, & Mahoney, 1996). In addition, factors that operate in a protective fashion for youngsters also need to be included to provide a more complete understanding of children's functioning.

SUMMARY

In the current study, a more in-depth understanding of the impact on children of witnessing spouse abuse was obtained, with heterogeneity in the adjustment of children of battered women noted. Variables were identified that were associated with the children's distress, which included levels of mothers' depression, mothers' verbal aggressiveness, and the duration of the mothers' abuse. Cluster analysis was found to be a useful technique for identifying subgroups of children with a variety of patterns of adjustment. In addition, different groupings of variables were associated with those diverse patterns of distress. However, the particular cluster solution obtained awaits replication.

Variability and heterogeneity were found in both the distressed and nondistressed subgroups of children, even when the source of the information was taken into account. The five-cluster solution was validated to a reasonable extent, given the small sample, through validation criteria typically used with cluster analyses. Additional evidence supporting the five clusters was obtained from the descriptive differences among the clusters and from the fact that the solution made conceptual sense; if replicated, these five clusters then have important implications for intervention. The combinations of types of distress seen among the family members in the different clusters have the potential for providing clinicians with vital information related to both responding to the reports of different informants and planning individualized treatment approaches.

At this point, additional studies with larger, more diverse samples, examining various mediating factors which can influence aspects of adjustment and psychological functioning, are needed. Moreover, now that several of the variables which are likely to be associated with poor adjustment have been identified, such information linked with good functioning is also needed. Results from the present study provide useful data related to distress in family members who have experienced family violence. Further investigation into the question of variability in functioning among children of battered women, using cluster analysis and other sophisticated data analytic techniques, can help provide researchers and clinicians with a better understanding of possible reasons for this heterogeneity.

REFERENCES

Achenbach, T. M., & Edelbrock, C. S. (1983). *Manual for the Child Behavior Checklist and Revised Child Behavior Profile.* Burlington: University of Vermont.

Achenbach, T. M., McConaughy, S. H., & Howell, C. T. (1987). Child/adolescent behavioral and emotional problems: Implications of cross-informant correlations for situation specificity. *Psychological Bulletin, 101,* 213–232.

Aldenderfer, M. S., & Blashfield, R. K. (1984). *Cluster analysis*. Beverly Hills, CA: Sage.

Alexander, P. C., & Schaeffer, C. M. (1994). A typology of incestuous families based on cluster analysis. *Journal of Family Psychology, 8,* 458–470.

Baumrind, D. (1991). The influence of parenting style on adolescent competence and substance use. *Journal of Early Adolescence, 11,* 56–95.

Beck, A. T., & Steer, R. A. (1984). Internal consistencies of the original and revised Beck Depression Inventory. *Journal of Clinical Psychology, 40,* 1365–1367.

Blashfield, R. K. (1983). *The classification of psychopathology*. New York: Plenum Press.

Borgen, F. H., & Barnett, D. C. (1987). Applying cluster analysis in counseling psychology research. *Journal of Counseling Psychology, 34,* 147–162.

Burns, G. L., Patterson, D. R., Nussbaum, B. R., & Parker, C. M. (1991). Disruptive behaviors in an outpatient pediatric population: Additional standardization data on the Eyberg Child Behavior Inventory. *Psychological Assessment, 3,* 202–207.

Chew, C. (1997). *Parenting of battered women: A preliminary investigation*. Unpublished master's thesis. Saint Louis University, St. Louis, MO.

Christopoulos, C., Cohn, D. A., Shaw, D. S., Joyce, S., Sullivan-Hanson, J., Kraft, S. P., & Emery, R. E. (1987). Children of abused women: I. Adjustment at time of shelter residence. *Journal of Marriage and the Family, 49,* 611–619.

Cummings, E. M., & Davies, P. (1994). *Children and marital conflict: The impact of family dispute and resolution*. New York: Guilford Press.

Downey, G., & Coyne, J. C. (1990). Children of depressed parents: An integrative review. *Psychological Bulletin, 108,* 50–76.

Emery, R. E. (1989). Family violence. *American Psychologist, 44,* 321–328.

Eyberg, S. M., & Ross, A. W. (1978). Assessment of child behavior problems: The validation of a new inventory. *Journal of Clinical Child Psychology, 7,* 113–116.

Finch, A. J., Saylor, C. F., & Edwards, G. L. (1985). Children's Depression Inventory: Sex and grade norms for normal children. *Journal of Consulting and Clinical Psychology, 53,* 424–425.

Fincham, F. D. (1994). Understanding the association between marital conflict and child adjustment: An overview. *Journal of Family Psychology, 8*, 123–127.

Fincham, F. D., Grych, J. H., & Osborne, L. N. (1994). Does marital conflict cause child maladjustment? Directions and challenges for longitudinal research. *Journal of Family Psychology, 8*, 128–140.

Gara, M. A., Rosenberg, S., & Goldenberg, L. (1992). *DSM–III* as a taxonomy: A cluster analysis of diagnoses and symptoms. *Journal of Nervous and Mental Disease, 180*, 11–19.

Gerlsma, C., Emmelkamp, P. M. G., & Arrindell, W. A. (1990). Anxiety, depression, and perception of early parenting: A meta-analysis. *Clinical Psychology Review, 10*, 251–277.

Holden, G. W., & Ritchie, K. L. (1991). Linking extreme marital discord, child rearing, and child behavior problems: Evidence from battered women. *Child Development, 62*, 311–327.

Hughes, H. M. (1984). Measures of self-concept and self-esteem for children ages 3–12 years: A review and recommendations. *Clinical Psychology Review, 4*, 657–692

Hughes, H. M. (1988). Psychological and behavioral correlates of family violence in child witnesses and victims. *American Journal of Orthopsychiatry, 58*, 77–90.

Hughes, H. M. (1991, August). *Research concerning children of battered women: Clinical and policy implications.* Paper presented as part of the symposium State-of-the-Art Research in Family Violence: Practical Implications at the annual meeting of the American Psychological Association, San Francisco, CA.

Hughes, H. M. (1995, March). *Relationships between the affective functioning of mothers and children in shelters for battered women: Clinical implications.* Paper presented at the biennial meeting of the Society for Research in Child Development, Indianapolis, IN.

Hughes, H. M. (1997). Research concerning children of battered women: Clinical implications. In R. Geffner, S. Sorenson, & P. Lundberg-Love (Eds.), *Violence and sexual abuse at home: Current issues in spousal battering and child maltreatment* (pp. 225–244). New York: Haworth.

Hughes, H. M., & Fantuzzo, J. W. (1994). Family violence: Child. In R. T.

Ammerman, M. Hersen, & L. Sisson (Eds.), *Handbook of aggressive and destructive behavior in psychiatric patients* (pp. 491–508). New York: Plenum Press.

Hughes, H. M., & Graham-Bermann, S. A. (in press). Children of battered women: Impact of emotional abuse on adjustment and development. *Journal of Emotional Abuse.*

Hughes, H. M., & Marshall, M. (1995). Advocacy for children of battered women. In E. Peled, P. G. Jaffe, & J. L. Edleson (Eds.), *Ending the cycle of violence: Community responses to children of battered women* (pp. 97–105). Newbury Park, CA: Sage.

Hughes, H. M., Parkinson, D. L., & Vargo, M. C. (1989). Witnessing spouse abuse and experiencing physical abuse: A "double whammy"? *Journal of Family Violence, 4,* 197–209.

Hughes, S. O. (1992). Defining patterns of drinking in adolescence: A cluster analytic approach. *Journal of Studies on Alcohol, 53,* 40–47.

Humphreys, K., & Rosenbeck, R. (1995). Sequential validation of cluster analytic subtypes of homeless veterans. *American Journal of Community Psychology, 23,* 75–98.

Jaffe, P. G., Wolfe, D. A., & Wilson, S. K. (1990). *Children of battered women.* Newbury Park, CA: Sage.

Jouriles, E. N., Norwood, W. D., McDonald, R., Vincent, J. P., & Mahoney, A. (1996). Physical violence and other forms of marital aggression: Links with children's behavior problems. *Journal of Family Psychology, 10,* 223–234.

Kaslow, N. J., Rehm, L. P., & Siegel, A. W. (1984). Social-cognitive and cognitive correlates of depression in children. *Journal of Abnormal Child Psychology, 12,* 605–620.

Kovacs, M. (1983). *The Children's Depression Inventory: A self-rated depression scale for school-aged youngsters.* Unpublished manuscript, University of Pittsburgh, School of Medicine.

Loeber, R., Green, S. M., Lahey, B. B., & Stouthamer-Loeber, M. (1991). Differences and similarities between children, mothers, and teachers as informants on disruptive child behavior. *Journal of Abnormal Child Psychology, 19,* 75–95.

Loeber, R., & Stouthamer-Loeber, M. (1986). Family factors as correlates and predictors of juvenile conduct problems and delinquency. In N. Toney & N. Morris (Eds.), *Crime and justice* (Vol. 17, pp. 29–149). Chicago: University of Chicago Press.

Luke, D. A., Mowbray, C. T., Klump, K., Herman, S. E., & BootsMiller, B. (1996). Exploring the diversity of dual-diagnosis: Utility of cluster analysis for program planning. *Journal of Mental Health Administration, 23,* 298–316.

Luke, D. A., Rappaport, J., & Seidman, E. (1991). Setting phenotypes in a mutual help organization: Expanding behavior setting theory. *American Journal of Community Psychology, 19,* 147–167.

McCloskey, L. A., Figueredo, A. J., & Koss, M. P. (1995). The effects of systemic family violence on children's mental health. *Child Development, 66,* 1239–1261.

McDaniel, E. D., & Piers, E. (1976). The McDaniel–Piers Young Children's Self-Concept Scale. In O. G. Johnson (Ed.), *Tests and measurements in child development: Handbook II* (Vol. 2, pp. 1101–1102). San Francisco: Jossey-Bass.

McDonald, R., & Jouriles, E. N. (1991). Marital aggression and child behavior problems: Research findings, mechanisms, and intervention strategies. *The Behavior Therapist, 14,* 189–192.

Moore, T., & Pepler, D. (1998). Correlates of adjustment in children at risk. In G. W. Holden, R. A. Geffner, & E. N. Jouriles (Eds.), *Children exposed to marital violence: Theory, research, and applied issues* (pp. 157–184). Washington, DC: American Psychological Association.

Peled, E., & Edleson, J. L. (1992). Multiple perspectives on groupwork with children of battered women. *Violence & Victims, 7,* 327–346.

Phares, V., Compas, B. E., & Howell, D. C. (1989). Perspectives on child behavior problems: Comparisons of children's self-reports with parent and teacher reports. *Psychological Assessment, 1,* 68–71.

Piers, E. V. (1984). *Revised Manual for the Piers–Harris Children's Self-Concept Scale.* Los Angeles: Western Psychological Services.

Prince, R. H., & Moos, R. H. (1975). Toward a taxonomy of inpatient treatment environments. *Journal of Abnormal Psychology, 84,* 181–188.

Rapkin, B. D., & Luke, D. A. (1993). Cluster analysis in community research:

Epistemology and practice. *American Journal of Community Psychology, 21,* 247–277.

Reynolds, C., & Paget, K. (1981). Factor analysis of the Revised Children's Manifest Anxiety Scale for blacks, whites, males and females with a national normative sample. *Journal of Consulting and Clinical Psychology, 49,* 352–359.

Reynolds, C., & Richmond, B. (1984). *Manual for the Revised Children's Manifest Anxiety Scale.* Los Angeles: Western Psychological Services.

Reynolds, W. M. (1993). Self-report methodology. In T. H. Ollendick & M. Hersen (Eds.), *Handbook of child and adolescent assessment* (pp. 98–123). Boston: Allyn & Bacon.

Robinson, E. A., Eyberg, S. M., & Ross, A. W. (1980). The standardization of an inventory of child conduct disorders. *Journal of Clinical Child Psychology, 9,* 22–29.

Rosenberg, M. S., & Rossman, B. B. R. (1990). The child witness to marital violence. In R. T. Ammerman & M. Hersen (Eds.), *Treatment of family violence* (pp. 183–210). New York: Wiley.

Rossman, B. B. R., Hughes, H. M., & Hanson, K. L. (in press). Victimization of school-aged children. In B. B. R. Rossman & M. S. Rosenberg (Eds.), *Multiple victimization of children: Conceptual, developmental, research, and treatment issues.* Newbury Park, CA: Sage.

Shirk, S. R. (1988). Conclusion: Cognitive development and child psychotherapy. In S. R. Shirk (Ed.), *Cognitive development and child psychotherapy* (pp. 319–331). New York: Plenum Press.

Skinner, H. A. (1978). Differentiating the contribution of elevation, scatter and shape in profile similarity. *Educational and Psychological Measurement, 38,* 297–298.

Spielberger, C. D., Gorsuch, R. L., Lushene, R., Vagg, P. R., & Jacobs, C. A. (1983). *Manual for the State-Trait Anxiety Inventory: STAI (Form Y).* Palo Alto, CA: Consulting Psychologists Press.

SPSS, Inc. (1995). *SPSS-Base 7.0 for Windows Users Guide.* Chicago: Author.

Stanger, C., & Lewis, M. (1993). Agreement among parents, teachers, and children on internalizing and externalizing behavior problems. *Journal of Clinical Child Psychology, 22,* 107–115.

Sternberg, K. J., Lamb, M. E., Greenbaum, C., Cicchetti, D., Dawud, S., Cortes, R. M., Krispin, O., & Lorey, F. (1993). Effects of domestic violence on children's behavior problems and depression. *Developmental Psychology, 29*, 44–52.

Straus, M. A. (1979). Measuring intrafamily conflict and violence: The Conflict Tactics (CT) Scales. *Journal of Marriage and the Family, 41*, 75–88.

Straus, M. A. (1987, October). *The Conflict Tactics Scales: An evaluation and new data on validity, reliability, norms, and scoring methods.* Paper presented at the meeting of the National Council on Family Relations, Durham, NC.

Webster-Stratton, C., & Hammond, M. (1988). Maternal depression and its relationship to life stress, perceptions of child behavior problems, parenting behaviors, and child conduct problems. *Journal of Abnormal Child Psychology, 16*, 299–315.

Wolfe, D. A., Zak, L., Wilson, S., & Jaffe, P. (1986). Child witnesses to violence: Critical issues in behavioral and social adjustment. *Journal of Abnormal Child Psychology, 14*, 95–104.

8

Descartes's Error and Posttraumatic Stress Disorder: Cognition and Emotion in Children Who Are Exposed to Parental Violence

B. B. Robbie Rossman

A six year-old little girl, Janie, is staying with her mother in a shelter for battered women. Janie has just thrown her drawing in the waste basket. The shelter children's counselor retrieves the drawing, smooths it out and asks Janie to tell her about it. Janie says that it is a picture of a little girl drowning. The counselor suggests that they try to save the girl by rowing a boat out and throwing her a rope or a buoy. Janie tells the counselor that they can't save her, because no one can see her.

(Adapted from the slide series "Eyewitness: Children's Views of Violence Against their Mothers," St. Paul, MN: Whispers.)

This is a poignant illustration of the thoughts and feelings of help-lessness and sadness experienced by many children who have grown up in parentally violent families. The little girl is making an error

Research was supported by National Institute of Mental Health Grant R03 MH41051–01, two grants from W. T. Grant Foundation funds of the Developmental Psychobiology Research Group, and an Academic Research Center grant from the Psychology Department of the University of Denver.

in judgment, however: In normal circumstances, many drownings are prevented by the actions described by the counselor. Why is Janie making this error? She is expressing an action plan (do nothing) guided by cognition and emotion. Perhaps she has learned that in a parentally violent family her well-being is overshadowed by the engagement of her caretakers in intense battles. She is invisible. Her thinking (no hope) appears to be informed by past experience (no rescue) and emotion (sadness, giving up).

The purpose of this chapter is to explore the relationship of cognition and emotion for children exposed to severe and repetitive parental violence. I argue that cognition and emotion become strongly linked in guiding behavior in these circumstances because they are life-threatening. Both cognitive process and content may be shaped by a child's exposure to frightening circumstances, and this may be reflected in his or her behavior and by changes at the level of neuropsychological process and structure.

WHY COGNITION AND EMOTION?

Cognition comprises very powerful underlying processes. Try to imagine life without the ability to think, reason, learn, or remember, or at least without the ability to do this effectively. René Descartes would be cheering efforts to examine the importance of cognitive factors in shaping the form and adaptive goodness of children's response to exposure to parental violence. Descartes (1637) wrote that the control of more primitive urges by thought and reason was an important part of what made us human. The supremacy of cognition over affect for adaptive functioning was clear. However, this mind–body dualism was in error. Theory and research now suggest that cognition may not be profitably studied in isolation (cf. Damasio, 1994).

In examining cognitive content in this chapter, my focus is on schemas or models children have developed from their experience to represent their understandings of their interpersonal world. These understandings help them interpret incoming stimulation, provide places to store it for future use, predict what may happen next, and guide subsequent behavior. These schemas include perceptual, emotional, causal, and behavioral information. Language or representational thought is not required, because infants and toddlers exhibit memory for perceptual–motor schemas and attachment relationships laid down prior to the advent of formal representation (Howe & Courage, 1993).

What schema content do children in violent families construct in their search for constancies in their informational environment? They may learn that interactions between their caregivers can be dangerous and that some coping strategies are successful in either stopping or avoiding these interactions or reducing the fear associated with them. Children may learn that physical power is required to get needs met and that their needs are not likely to get met during parent conflicts. Thus, children may learn coping strategies of avoidance or aggression and strategies that do not depend on other people. If the cues to caretaker aggressive interactions or the child's ability to avoid or stop them are variable, children may also learn that their safety is unpredictable, that contingencies do not exist between their behavior and its outcome, and that one needs to be continually prepared to take action. These schemas could assist a child in a violent environment and yet be maladaptive outside it, interfering with normal cognitive development.

In examining cognitive process in this chapter, I ask whether anything about how the perceptual–cognitive system works might be influenced by repetitive exposure to life threat. To what extent do frightening circumstances interfere with (a) the process of exploration needed to gain information about the world and build useful schemas, (b) the capacity to modify schemas to be consistent with incoming information, (c) the process of learning and performance per se, or (d) the development of skills for both the broad and narrow deployment of attention depending on situational requirements?

COGNITION, EMOTION, AND REPETITIVE TRAUMA

This linkage of cognition and emotion is part of a normal adaptive stress response process (Horowitz, 1986), which aids survival under conditions of threat to physical or psychological well-being, conditions labeled as *traumatic* (American Psychiatric Association, 1994). However, when it is sustained over long periods of time because of repetitive threat, there is prolonged dysregulation and the response may have negative physiological consequences and be generalized to circumstances beyond those of the initial threat. Here maladaptive consequences of a protective mechanism may emerge.

Potential maladaptive consequences are multiple and occur at different levels of psychological functioning. Physiologically, a prolonged stress response, or chronic posttraumatic stress reaction, has been linked to changes in the functioning of the hypothalamic-pituitary-adrenal axis and neurotransmitters (Charney, Deutch, Krystal, Southwick, & Davis, 1993; van der Kolk, 1994). Changes have been found in the levels of several neurotransmitters that have implications for behavior and coincide with symptoms characteristic of posttraumatic stress disorder (PTSD). These include elevations in adrenalin and noradrenalin; glucocorticoids like cortisol, endogeneous opiates, and dopamine; and a reduction in serotonin. Heightened adrenalin and noradrenalin create increased heart rate and blood flow, preparing the body and muscles for quick action, fight or flight, but also increased agitation and perhaps decreased attention deployment capacities. In addition, with prolonged arousal, receptors for these neurotransmitters appear to decrease in number, perhaps to help the body re-regulate arousal. Greater glucocorticoids help the body deal with injury through the reduction of inflammation but also have been found to be associated, at high levels, with the death of cells in the hippocampus, one site of memory processes. High levels of endogeneous opiates reduce pain but are also linked to interference with memory consolidation processes. Excess dopamine in the frontal cortex stimulates thought processes but has also been linked to hallucinatory activity in schizophrenia (Berquier & Ashton, 1991) through the usefulness of dopamine antagonist drugs for that disorder. This same process could facilitate the intrusions and reliving experiences of PTSD patients, an interference to ongoing thought and reality testing. Finally, reduced serotonin levels are related to decreases in the body's ability to regulate emotional arousal, indexed by the usefulness of serotonin reuptake blockers like fluoxatine (Prozac) for both depression and chronic PTSD.

Thus, prolonged threat to survival may leave the individual in a dys-regulated state, where perception, cognition, and emotional systems are functioning atypically (in part to compensate for dysregulation) and per-manent changes to brain structure are possible. This speculation and sup-portive research are based on the study of adult PTSD victims. It is not known what other changes might occur for children where brain devel-opment is still ongoing. However, there could be major consequences for ongoing cognitive and emotional behavior of traumatized children and perhaps for their developmental trajectories in these domains.

COGNITION, EMOTION, AND DEVELOPMENT

Attachment theory suggests that a young child normally works back and forth between exploration of the environment and checking in with an attachment figure. In times of stress, exploration is reduced and contact with a secure base is enhanced. If threat is prolonged and a secure base is uncertain, would the motivation for exploration be per-manently reduced? Would attention deployment change? Research with abused children suggests that this may be the case (Aber & Allen, 1987; Aber, Allen, Carlson, & Cicchetti, 1989).

Thus, exposure to repetitive trauma may have negative effects for the development of bonding and information search processes. Accord-ing to Piagetian theory, decreases in exploration would be detrimental (Piaget, 1952). Piaget proposed that processes of assimilation (modi-fying new information so that it will fit into existing schemas) and processes of accommodation (modifying existing schemas to fit new information) must be balanced for intelligence to develop normally. Cognitive control theory (Santostefano, 1985) also postulates a normal balance between the quick and accurate use of new information (like accommodation), called *sharpening*, and slow and inaccurate intake of new information (more like assimilation), called *leveling*. The devel-opmental trend is for younger children to level more, but the balance changes toward greater sharpening. He feels that these processes are used as tools to modulate level of arousal. This balance could develop differently for children who frequently experience high levels of arousal.

Therefore, it appears likely that repeated exposure to frightening experiences could interfere with the operation of normal perceptual–cognitive processes and contribute to the distortion of interpersonal schema content. These distortions and interferences could have a cascading effect with development, changing the cognitive and emotional resources available to children as they face new developmental tasks. It is easy to see how changes and delays in these systems would have ramifications for other developmental arenas such as behavior regulation and peer relationships.

CONCEPTUAL APPROACHES TO COGNITION–EMOTION INTERRELATIONSHIPS

Some conceptual–theoretical approaches address issues of how cognition–emotion interrelationships may underlie cognitive schema distortion in traumatic circumstances. Others speak to traumatic effects of this linkage for cognitive processes. Still others are relevant for both content and process. All of them, as discussed below, help explain how the context of experience may be integrally related to a child's creation of meaning and the cognitive tools he or she may have developed to do so.

Approaches Relevant for Cognitive Content Distortion

The somatic marker hypothesis, attachment theory, and models of children's social information processing (SIP) are useful in thinking about how cognitive content distortions may arise for children in violent families. The somatic marker hypothesis states that survival relevant information (information about pain and pleasure, positive and negative feeling) has a somatic marker (Damasio, 1994). This marker (e.g., fear, joy) attached to the "factual" information helps the person "remember" the pain or pleasure associated with events and can be used to guide behavior in similar situations.

Damasio developed this hypothesis through studying historical cases like that of Phyneas Gage, a railroad worker in the early 1900s whose forehead was accidentally punctured by a steel rod. He lived and still "knew" his job, but his behavior became more erratic and unwise. Damasio also studied patients in his lab like Elliot, who had a lesion in his ventromedial frontal cortex. Elliot got above-average scores on conventional tests of IQ and cognitive functioning but made poor decisions in living. Elliot seemed to have all the facts he needed to make these decisions but did not foresee the hedonic interpersonal and financial consequences of his actions. Damasio speculated that at least part of the operation of this somatic marker process takes place in the ventromedial frontal cortex but that other processes such as working memory (i.e., the type of on-line memory one uses for chess playing) may be involved. Thus, studying cognition alone may not be enough, because emotion may inform cognition and vice versa.

The content of interpersonal schemas is highlighted in attachment theory and the work of Mark Cummings and his colleagues. Attachment theory and research suggest that secure attachment to a caregiver is important for normal development (Bowlby, 1988) and that interpersonal conflict and abuse may interfere with this security (Crittenden & Ainsworth, 1989). Furthermore, the child's working models of abusive caregivers may need to contain defensive and unrealistically positive content, whereas other schemas acknowledge the potential danger in interpersonal interactions (Bretherton, Ridgeway, & Cassidy, 1990).

Cummings's work (e.g., E. M. Cummings & Davies, 1994) demonstrates that children's reactions to adult anger are tied to their emotional state and aspects of meaning and interpersonal schemas. Negative reactions are minimized when children see or understand that parents have reached adequate conflict resolution. However, children with maritally violent histories are more reactive to adult anger (J. S. Cummings, Pellegrini, Notarius, & Cummings, 1989). It has a different meaning–emotion association for them. The emotional security of these children is more severely threatened by conflict, and their responses are shaped by the scripts they have developed on the basis of their experience (Davies & Cummings, 1994). These scripts involve cognitive and emotional components, and Davies and Cummings argued that the hedonic tone of their emotional state plays a role in organizing their reaction to adult anger (Davies & Cummings, 1995). Children's negative emotional state was found to be related to greater distress and expectation for future conflict.

SIP models also contribute to the understanding of possible schema distortion for children in violent families. Crick and Dodge (1994) have constructed a model of how children process and act on social information. The SIP model is based on much research by Dodge and colleagues showing that boys labeled as aggressive in the classroom or those with harsh punitive disciplinary histories misinterpret ambiguous interpersonal situations as potentially threatening. They attribute hostile intent to the other party, prepare for danger by mobilizing aggressive coping strategies, have few other strategies available to them, and believe in the efficacy of those behaviors over nonaggressive strategies. This can result in misinterpretations, misattributions about others, and inappropriate action. They have labeled the misattributional part of this process as a display of hostile attributional bias, meaning the inappropriate expectation of aggression and aggressive outcomes from benign others.

Grych and Fincham (1990, 1993) provided a related conceptual approach. They proposed that children's reactions to marital discord depend on conflict characteristics, past experience with marital conflict, primary processing of the current conflict, and secondary processing to determine cause and coping strategies. Children's emotional state is thought to inform and be informed by the ongoing search for meaning, attribution, and needed action. The researchers noted that (particularly for young children) the emotional arousal associated with primary processing may interfere with further cognitive processing. Again, cognition and emotion are linked in children's reactions to parental anger.

Approaches Relevant for Changes in Cognitive Process

Conceptualizations helpful for understanding potential changes in cognitive processes for child witnesses come from the PTSD literature, SIP theory, cognitive control theory, and Piagetian approaches. Trauma researchers (e.g., van der Kolk, 1994) have pointed to important changes in brain function and structure that may occur with repeated traumatic exposure. As noted previously, these changes have strong implications for the dysregulation of the cognitive and affective systems of trauma victims.

In their SIP model, Crick and Dodge (1994) also suggested possible changes in information processing. They speculated that with heightened emotional arousal, "preemptive processing" takes place. Preemptive processing involves a restriction in the range of meanings sought and an invocation of prior scripts to use in present interpretations. Research of human learning and performance also tells us that there is an inverted U-shaped relationship between arousal level and behavior; too little or too much arousal is associated with poorer performance (Hebb, 1955). If a child frequently experiences high levels of emotional arousal, this could interfere with the goodness of his or her information processing.

A related mechanism may be contributing to this process: the dual information input system proposed by LeDeux (1992, 1994). He speculated that two information pathways exist: One is an emergency pathway from the thalamus to the amygdala where survival information is processed quickly but less accurately on the basis of only fragmentary stimulus information (e.g., a child in black pajamas may be misperceived as Viet Cong by a Viet Nam veteran suffering from chronic PTSD); and the second is a regular information pathway through the cortex to the amygdala that is slower but more accurate, requiring more well-defined stimulus information. LeDeux's formulation suggests that when potentially threatening cues are detected, partial information might be processed very quickly, leading to a maladaptive reaction. The balance between emergency and more careful information processing might be disrupted by the misperceived emotional significance of the information.

A final approach also suggests that both the intake of information and modifiability of schemas may be disrupted by trauma. As mentioned above, cognitive control theory provides ideas about how information intake and use strategies may be influenced by exposure to threat (Santostefano, 1985). Working from Lewinian field theory and his clinical experience and research, Santostefano theorized that internal emotion and arousal are managed through the unconscious operation of cognitive mechanisms. Processes of selective attention, field articulation, and leveling–sharpening are used to manage potentially threatening information and arousal. When a person levels information, he or she is taking it in more slowly and/or inaccurately to protect the self through an information avoidance strategy. A person who sharpens is presumably adopting a preparedness tactic to protect the self by using the information more quickly and/or accurately, an approach or vigilant strategy. Generally individuals operate around a midpoint on this dimension, balancing usage of the approach and avoidance strategies depending on situational requirements. Thus, a leveling–sharpening cognitive style also highlights the close working relationship of emotional and cognitive processes in potentially threatening circumstances, a style that could generalize inflexibly beyond those circumstances. Excess sharpening, possibly through LeDeux's emergency pathway, is useful only when the cues acted on match situational needs.

RESEARCH ON THE LINKAGE BETWEEN COGNITIVE CAPACITY AND CONTENT

Relatively little evidence bears directly on the cognitive functioning of children exposed to parental violence or how cognition and emotion might interrelate in shaping their adaptation. In terms of general cognitive performance, Pepler and Moore (1989) reported significantly lower school performance and lower reading and mathematics achievement scores for children exposed to parental violence. In addition, research in my lab found significantly lower verbal IQ scores for exposed children, and some early pilot work made us concerned about their cognitive functioning. However, the most relevant research providing information about cognitive functioning and the relation of cognition and emotion for traumatized children comes from the literature on child abuse.

Child Abuse Research of Cognitive Capacity and Content

Mirroring other child abuse findings (cf. Rossman, Hughes, & Hanson, in press), a recent study by Carrey, Butter, Persinger, and Bialik (1995) showed a group of 7- to 13-year-old abused children to have significantly lower IQ scores on the Wechsler Intelligence Scale for Children —Revised (Wechsler, 1974) than a comparison group, primarily because of their significantly lower Verbal IQ performance. This was a mixed-abuse group where about half of the children had experienced sexual abuse, one-fifth experienced physical abuse, and one-third experienced both. When baseline versus task responding was compared for the two groups, the abused group showed reduced physiological responsiveness during several tasks on indices such as heart rate, galvanic skin response, and pulse height. Both increased and decreased physiological response compared to baseline have been interpreted as indicating changes in emotional arousal. In addition, results from the longitudinal Mother–Child Interaction Project on high-risk mothers at the University of Minnesota have shown neglected and abused children to have poorer cognitive capacities at school age (Erickson, Egeland, & Pianta, 1989). Finally, the work by attachment and SIP researchers summarized above documents the linkage of past experience with aggression with distortion of interpersonal schemas and expectations.

Child Abuse Research of Cognitive Process

Evidence from Cicchetti's lab shows that abused preschool children as compared with nonabused comparison preschoolers level information, allowing them to detect fewer changes in a changing field (Rieder & Cicchetti, 1989). In addition, Fish-Murray, Koby, and van der Kolk (1987) found that abused children had deficits in terms of how they take in and use new information. On Piagetian tasks for accommodation skills they performed significantly more poorly than nonabused children. Abused children showed less flexible schemas across many content areas, with mathematical reasoning remaining the most intact. Thus, the child abuse literature is consistent with a picture wherein traumatic dysregulation and attempts to compensate unfold in atypical cognitive content and process.

RESEARCH WITH CHILDREN EXPOSED
TO FAMILY VIOLENCE

Little work has been done with children exposed to family violence to examine more specific aspects of their cognitive functioning or their level of posttraumatic distress or dysregulation. Based on prior theory and research, I reasoned that good targets to assess for child witnesses would be those that had to do with the content of their interpersonal schemas and their intake and manipulation of new information. Three questions were addressed: (a) Do children exposed to marital violence show higher levels of trauma symptoms than nonexposed children? (b) Do exposed children show differences in cognitive schema content and process as compared with nonexposed children? (c) What is the relation of parental violence exposure to trauma symptoms and cognitive functioning, and adaptive functioning?

For several years, parts of ongoing projects have been designed to allow examination of one or more of these questions. The following discussion summarizes what we did and what we found, in general across projects and with regard to specific tasks used in some projects but not others.

Method

Participants and Procedures

More than 400 children aged 4–13 years and their mothers participated across six projects. They came from families representing a range of marital discord from mild verbal arguing to severe and repeated marital violence. Families were recruited from the community, schools, and agencies, and the most violent families were recruited with the aid of nine shelters for battered women. Shelter children and mothers were interviewed in shelter for their safety and community children in the lab. In some projects, it was also possible to obtain data from nonviolent community fathers and from shelter children's counselors. We worked to exclude abused children from our community samples so that comparisons among community groups would not need to take abuse into account. This was done by use of cutoffs on the Child Abuse

Potential Inventory (Milner & Wimberley, 1980) or parental report of the existence of a child abuse report filed with Child Protective Services. However, because abused children are estimated to comprise 40–60% of child witnesses (Carlson, 1984), it seemed ecologically valid to include those children in most shelter samples. Abused children were identified in shelter by maternal and children's shelter counselor report regarding the existence of a filed abuse report. Children and mothers participated in individual interviews ranging from 1 to 2 hours in length and were compensated financially and with prizes for the children.

Depending on the needs of specific projects, children were recruited for one or more of the following exposure groups: (a) a nonabusive, nonviolence community group; (b) a nonabusive but maritally aggressive community group, where parental violence tended to be at a low level (e.g., pushing and shoving); (c) a nonabusive but maritally violent shelter group, where mothers were residing in shelter at the time of the interview; and (d) a child abusive and maritally violent shelter group. Using maternal report (or combined maternal and paternal report when available) on the Conflict Tactics Scales (Straus, 1979) for violence exposure group definition, the number of children fitting into each of these groups in the total sample is presented in Table 1.

Measures

Most measures presented here were obtained for all children and mothers. The types of measures obtained are discussed below.

Demographic measures. Several types of demographic measures were obtained through use of maternal report on a family information questionnaire. These measures were used to assess levels of family adversity and to control for group differences that emerged inadvertently. They included family socioeconomic status (SES) defined by the Hollingshead and Redlich Two-factor Index (Miller, 1977), minority status, number of negative family stressful life events during the past year that were not dependent on the child's behavior as measured by items from the Life Events Questionnaire (Garmezy, Masten, & Tellegen, 1984), residence in shelter, and age of child.

Table 1

Sample Description (N = 425)

Measure	Community		Shelter		p
	Nonexposed	Exposed	Exposed	Exposed and abused	
Age and gender					
4–7 years					
Boys	45	1	33	12	
Girls	55	4	32	11	
8–10 years					
Boys	35	5	20	8	
Girls	48	7	15	8	
11–13 years					
Boys	21	2	9	4	
Girls	17	16	17	0	
Subtotal	221	35	126	43	
Minority (%)	9_a	40_b	50_b	58_b	.00
CTS					
Verbal Aggression	1.15_a	3.58_b	3.87_c	3.69_b	.00
Physical Aggression	$.00_a$	$.81_b$	1.62_c	1.60_c	.00
Socioeconomic status	2.40_a	3.42_b	3.61_b	3.71_b	.00
Family stressors	$.06_a$	$.17_b$	$.23_c$	$.26_c$	.00

Note.   Means followed by different subscripts are significantly different at $p < .05$ using Newman–Keuls post hoc pairwise comparisons. Conflict Tactics Scale (CTS) scores are averaged across both partners.

Parental conflict and violence. The Conflict Tactics Scales (CTS; Straus, 1979) were administered to index interparental verbal and physical aggression. Mothers' reports for self and partner and (when available) community fathers' reports for self and partner were averaged to create separate verbal and physical aggression scores for each family as indicators of exposure. In addition, for LISREL modeling (Hayduk, 1987) the verbal and physical aggression scores were averaged, standardized, and combined with the child abuse indicator to construct a total family violence composite.

Measures of posttraumatic symptoms. For all children, PTSD subscale scores (Wolfe, Gentile, & Wolfe, 1989) from the Child Behavior Checklist (CBCL; Achenbach & Edelbrock, 1983) were calculated as raw score scale means. In addition, for some projects the PTSD Reaction Index (Pynoos et al., 1987) was administered to mothers, shelter counselors, and children. For children a 3-point frequency scale was used (ranging from *never have symptom* to *often*) with picture props for children ages 4–7 years. These items were also adapted for adult report about the child on a 5-point frequency scale (ranging from *never* to *most of the time;* Rossman, Bingham, & Emde, 1997).

Child cognitive functioning. To assess global cognitive capacity, most researchers include the Peabody Picture Vocabulary Test (PPVT), a measure of receptive language that is highly correlated with traditional IQ scores (Dunn, 1965). Most studies also include Santostefano's Leveling/Sharpening Shootout Test (Santostefano & Rieder, 1984) to assess the usage of leveling–sharpening style with a changing visual field. The task consists of 63 presentations of a picture of two cartoon-like cowboys standing in front of a saloon door. There are knives and guns in the picture as well as nonaggressive details such as the sun and a rain barrel. With every third presentation of the picture an aggressive or nonaggressive detail is omitted, these being balanced across trials and with regard to central versus peripheral position. Thus, 10 aggressive and 10 nonaggressive details are omitted across trials.

For the leveling–sharpening task, children do a warm-up task with a neutral picture where they learn to inform the interviewer whenever they think something about a picture has changed. In warm-up they are told about the correctness of their answers and are shown different versions of the picture side by side if needed until they understand the task. During the actual task children are not informed about accuracy and simply proceed through all 63 trials. Several scores are calculated, and the one reported here is the leveling–sharpening ratio where a high score reflects a greater number of trials needed to correctly detect omissions and over which omissions were never detected. This score was also calculated separately for aggressive and nonaggressive details to indicate performance with nonaggressive cues in the presence of aggressive cues and vice versa.

For LISREL modeling, the aggressive leveling–sharpening ratio score and a nonaggressive sharpening ratio (i.e., standardized and re-flected nonaggressive leveling–sharpening ratio) were tried. It was as-sumed that leveling of aggressive information and sharpening of non-aggressive information would represent avoidant protective strategies.

A Theory of Mind task, the M&M's task (Perner, Leekam, & Wim-mer, 1987) was used in several projects with 4- to 7-year-olds. For this task a child is shown an M&M's box and asked what is in it. The child guesses and is shown that it contains pencils that are put back in the box. The child is then asked to imagine that another child his or her age comes into the room and to predict what that child would say was in the box. The correct prediction of M&M's requires a cognitive per-spective taking shift that most kindergartners can perform.

Three other types of cognitive tasks were used in one project. Work-ing memory was assessed using the Counting Span Task (Case, Kurland, & Goldberg, 1982). Piagetian accommodation tasks for classification, correspondence, and conservation that had been used by Fish-Murray et al. (1987) were administered. Expectation of an aggressive outcome or aggressive bias was assessed by asking children to predict the out-come of neutral male–female adult videotaped conversations. When angry or aggressive outcomes were predicted for these neutral 1-minute interactions, aggressive bias was scored.

Measures of child adjustment. The main measure of adjustment was the CBCL (Achenbach & Edelbrock, 1983), which was completed by all mothers and some community fathers and shelter children's counselors. For the three samples where there were several informants for each child, problem behavior scales were constructed using the max-imum score method as recommended by Bird, Gould, and Staghezza (1992). This score is based on the premise that it is socially undesirable to report problem behaviors, so these generally are underestimated.

Thus, for each problem behavior item the most negative score across the informants is used. Corrected total, internalizing, externalizing, and aggressive behavior problem scores were calculated, omitting items that entered into the CBCL-PTSD scale to eliminate mechanical overlap of scales. Scores were calculated as raw score scale means as recommended by the authors for research including nonclinical samples. Social competence scores based on maternal report were calculated in the usual way. Maternal report was used here because information comprising this scale is better-known to a parent, and maternal report was available for all children. Maternal ratings of children's preschool or school performance were also obtained for most of the sample based on a 9-point rating scale ranging from *has many problems* to *does very well.*

Results

Group differences on demographic and parental conflict and violence measures were examined by performing exposure group (4) analyses of variance (ANOVAs). These suggested that minority status, CTS verbal and physical aggression between caregivers, and family stressful events were all significantly higher in the shelter witness groups, and SES levels were significantly lower (see Table 1). To control for these risk factors in examining PTSD and cognitive and adjustment measures, four violence group analyses of covariance (ANCOVAs) were calculated covarying SES, minority status, family stressors, and shelter residence. ANOVAs without the covariate were also calculated, and results are noted when different (see Table 2).[1]

Trauma Symptoms

An ANCOVA of CBCL-PTSD subscale scores showed that all child witness groups had significantly higher symptomatology than the nonexposed children. This pattern was replicated in maternal report data

---

[1]It can be argued that these covariates, which are co-linear with parental violence in many studies, are part of an ecological package of influence, and that controlling these covariates is overly conservative, removing real exposure variance in addition to nuisance variance and leaving the researcher looking at a different phenomenon. Although I acknowledge the validity of this argument, I have tried to follow a somewhat more conservative strategy by presenting both sets of results but focusing on covariance results.

Table 2

Analyses of Covariance of Group Differences

| | Adjusted group means | | | | |
| | Community | | Shelter | | |
Measure	Nonexposed	Exposed	Exposed	Exposed and abused	p
CBCL-PTSD	.33$_a$	.54$_b$	.50$_b$	.44	.01
RI-PTSD	1.82$_a$	2.26$_b$	2.57$_b$	2.35$_b$	.00
PPVT-IQ	100.83	91.39	102.00	99.81	.34†
Leveling–sharpening					
Ratio	19.74	18.67	23.11	23.57	.08†
Aggression ratio	16.72$_a$	14.62$_a$	21.53$_b$	22.70$_b$	.03
M&M's task (%)	79	100	88	32	.00
Aggression bias (z)	−.37	.44	.28	.14	.06†
CBCL					
Total††	.28$_a$	.43$_b$	.41$_b$	.33$_a$	.01
% increase in clinical cutoff	.26$_a$	.51$_b$	.45$_b$	.28$_a$	.01
Internal††	.27	.39	.34	.28	.07†
% increase in clinical cutoff	.22$_a$	.49$_b$	.45$_b$	.44$_b$	.02
External††	.29$_a$	.45$_b$	.44$_b$	.35$_a$	.01
% increase in clinical cutoff	.17$_a$	.49$_b$	.45$_b$	.23$_a$	.00
Aggression††	.36$_a$	.57$_b$	.57$_b$	.46$_a$	.01
Social Competence	3.93	3.74	3.59	2.96	ns
School performance	6.97	7.01	5.96	5.68	ns†

Note. Socioeconomic status, life events, minority status, and shelter residence were co-varied. Means followed by different subscripts are significantly different at $p < .05$ using Newman–Keuls post hoc pairwise comparisons, and effects followed by one dagger (†) are significant when covariates are not used. Child Behavior Checklist (CBCL) scores are raw score scale means recommended for use when nonclinical samples are involved. Scores corrected by omitting Post-traumatic Stress Disorder (PTSD) subscale items are indicated by two daggers (††). RI = Reaction Index; PPVT = Peabody Picture Vocabulary Test.

from the PTSD Reaction Index. Child-report PTSD Reaction Index scores also showed this trend for noncovaried data. Thus, exposed children were showing higher levels of traumatic response, and support was found for one aspect of the cognition–emotion thesis.

Cognitive Functioning

An ANOVA of PPVT-IQ scores showed all child witnesses to be performing more poorly, but group differences were not significant in the covariance analysis, suggesting the importance of examining both. There was a trend in the ANCOVA for overall leveling–sharpening ratio scores to be higher for shelter witnesses, and an ANCOVA of aggressive and nonaggressive ratio scores revealed that shelter witnesses showed significantly greater leveling of aggressive but not nonaggressive cues.

An ANCOVA of M&M's perspective taking scores for the 4- to 7-year-olds revealed a significant group difference wherein exposed, abused shelter children were performing least well. Pairwise post hoc comparisons were not significant. Working memory performance and Piagetian task group differences were not significant, although exposed children tended to demonstrate poorer performance. There was a trend, significant in the noncovariance analysis, for aggressive bias to increase with greater exposure. Thus, greater violence exposure appears associated with poorer cognitive functioning, providing some support for the second part of the cognition–emotion thesis.

Measures of Adjustment

Total, externalizing, and aggressive problem scores, all corrected for PTSD, were significantly higher in the community and shelter nonabused groups, with the community nonexposed and abused shelter exposed children not differing significantly. It has been speculated that abused, exposed children work hard to control any disruptive behaviors at home, the site of abuse for most of these children (Rossman et al., 1991). Alternatively, mothers of abused children may find it more difficult to report disruptive child behaviors because of their guilt about the abuse. Internalizing problem adjusted means showed the same trend, which was significant without covariance. Not surprisingly, the percentage of children above clinical cutoff on total, internalizing, and

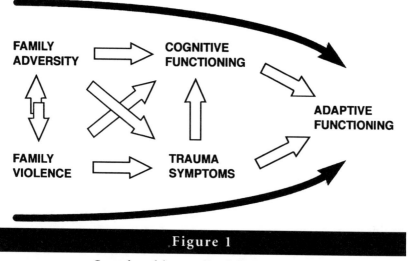

Figure 1

General model to predict child functioning.

externalizing problems was higher for child witnesses. Social competence and school performance both show nonsignificant declines with increased exposure, which increase in significance in noncovariance analyses, mimicking noncovariance findings of previous studies (cf. Jaffe, Wolfe, & Wilson, 1990). Exposed children tend to be showing poorer functioning on both problem and competence indices of adjustment.

Exposure, Cognitive Functioning, Trauma Response, and Adaptation

To examine the last question concerning the role of cognitive functioning and trauma response in mediating the relationship of family violence to indices of adjustment, LISREL procedures were used to compute path coefficients for a path model constructed to represent these relationships (see Figure 1). This model suggests that both general family adversity risk factors and specific trauma risk associated with exposure to family violence and abuse directly affect adjustment, children's level of traumatic response (PTSD symptoms), and their abilities to take in and use new information. In addition, it says that PTSD symptoms influence cognitive functioning. Finally, children's trauma response and poorer ability to deal with environmental information are assumed to influence their adaptive functioning. Thus, family adversity and family violence exposure were assumed to influence adaptive functioning directly and indirectly, as mediated by traumatic responding and cognitive functioning.

In examining the tests of this model, several warnings need to be issued. Because tests were not based on longitudinal data from at least three points in time (exposure at Time 1, cognitive functioning and trauma response at Time 2, and adaptive functioning at Time 3), it is not possible to infer causation; and it cannot be assumed that this model or subparts of it represent the best model for accounting for adaptive functioning. Subparts of this model were tested, and the only smaller model that fit equally well was one that did not include the direct pathways from family adversity and violence to child outcome. With these warnings in mind, we turn to results based on fitting the general path model for different indices of PTSD, cognitive functioning, and adaptive behavior.

Correlations among variables used in model testing are presented in Table 3. Model testing results shown in Figures 2–4 are based on the CBCL-PTSD subscale and nonaggressive sharpening as the cognitive index. For predicting CBCL total behavior problems, as shown in Figure 2, the model explains 86% of the variance in behavior problems ($R = .93$, $p < .01$). The left-hand side of the model suggests that the family adversity and family violence composites are significantly bidirectionally related to each other and that family adversity is directly and significantly predictive of lower cognitive functioning, but not PTSD.[2] Family violence is directly and significantly predictive of greater posttraumatic response, but not sharpening. So the traumatic response associated with family violence is not directly accounted for by variance in family adversity. Counter to expectation, traumatic response is negatively related to cognitive functioning, but it is not a significant contributor.

---

[2]Models that did not include younger child age in the family adversity composite and did not include child abuse in the family violence composite were also tested, and results were highly similar to those reported which did include these variables.

Table 3

Correlations Among Model Testing Variables

Measures	1	2	3	4	5	6	7	8	9	10	11	12
Fam. Adversity	—											
Fam. Violence	.66***											
Sharpen (nonagg)	-.34***	-.18**										
Level (agg)	.18**	.08	-.52***									
Agg Bias	.25**	.22*	-.02	.10								
CBCL-PTSD	.33***	.32***	-.02	-.16*	.17							
RI-PTSD	.62***	.49***	-.21**	-.02	.32***	.66						
CBCL-Tot. Prob.	.33***	.29***	-.04	-.15*	.24*	.91***	.63***					
CBCL-Int. Prob.	.30***	.27***	-.06	-.12	.19*	.90***	.61**	.94***				
CBCL-Ext. Prob.	.32***	.27***	-.05	-.13	.24**	.85***	.60***	.97***	.84***			
CBCL-Agg. Prob.	.32***	.28***	-.06	-.12	.25**	.82**	.61***	.95***	.83***	.96***		
CBCL-Soc. Comp.	-.20***	-.13**	.41***	-.38***	-.14	-.11*	-.22**	-.11*	-.10	-.13*	-.12*	
School Perform.	-.42***	-.40***	.10	-.06	-.21*	-.48***	-.56***	-.57***	-.44***	-.62***	-.54***	.13

Note. Significance levels are appropriate for sample size on which coefficient is based. Fam. = Family; agg = aggression; nonagg = nonaggression; CBCL = Child Behavior Checklist; PTSD = posttraumatic stress disorder; RI = Reaction Index; Tot. = total; Prob. = Problem; Int. = Internalizing; Ext. = Externalizing; Soc. Comp. = Social Competence; Perform. = Performance.
*p < .05. **p < .01. ***p < .001.

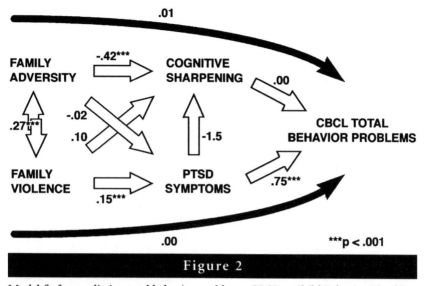

Figure 2

Model fit for predicting total behavior problems. CBCL = Child Behavior Checklist; PTSD = posttraumatic stress disorder.

Moving across the model to the right, the path coefficients also suggest that PTSD is a significant enhancer of CBCL total behavior problems (i.e., that greater traumatic response is associated with poorer total behavior regulation). Family adversity, family violence, and cognitive sharpening do not contribute directly and significantly to behavior problems.

Predicting social competence using this model presents a slightly different picture (see Figure 3). Note that intermediate path coefficients for the left-hand side of the model must be identical to those predicting behavior problems because they are the same variables used in the same model. For social competence the model explained 19% of the variance ($R = .44$, $p < .01$). Looking at the right-hand side of the model, results show that cognitive sharpening makes a significant contribution to differences among children in social functioning. This does not rule out the role of PTSD because a model without PTSD pathways fits significantly more poorly, indicating that these pathways make a contribution to prediction.

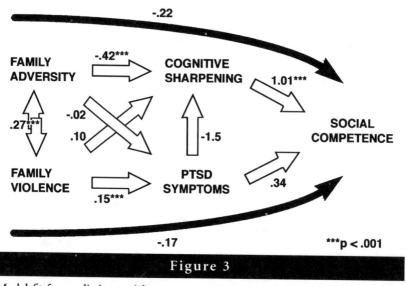

Figure 3

Model fit for predicting social competence. PTSD = posttraumatic stress disorder.

The path coefficients for predicting school performance again highlight the role of cognitive functioning (see Figure 4). The model explained 14% of the variance ($R = .37$, $p < .01$). Again looking at the right-hand side of the model, cognitive sharpening made a significant positive contribution to school performance, as might be expected. Traumatic response contributed negatively to school performance, but this linkage was not significant.

Model tests for the three adjustment measures were also done using maternal report on the Reaction Index for PTSD and the leveling ratio for aggressive cues or the aggressive bias score as indicators of cognitive functioning.[3] Results using aggressive cue leveling were similar, showing that it made a negative contribution to social and school functioning, but aggressive bias did not make significant contributions to prediction. Results for PTSD were also similar when the Reaction Index was used to predict behavior problems. However, Reaction Index PTSD path co-

---

[3]It should be noted that the sample was reduced from over 300 to about 100 when using aggressive bias and to about 200 when using the PTSD Reaction Index.

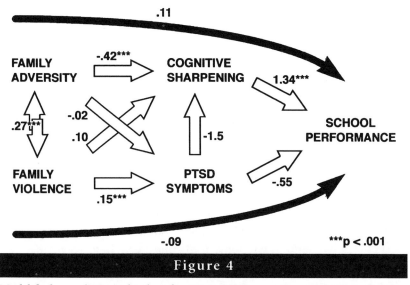

Figure 4

Model fit for predicting school performance. PTSD = posttraumatic stress disorder.

efficients were significant and positive for school and social functioning, a result discussed later.

Model tests using corrected internalizing, externalizing, and aggressive problem scores in place of total problems were also examined. Given the substantial relationship among these scales, it was not surprising that results were similar, with PTSD measures being the significant predictors.

Discussion

This discussion began with Janie, the little girl for whom prior trauma exposure may have linked cognition and emotion in a way that made it difficult for her to process new information and think well about current circumstances. She thought and felt that there was no help for the little girl in her drawing, because that little girl was invisible. Descartes thought and felt that reason and cognition provided the hope for humanity in overcoming basic emotional urges. They were both making errors in judgment, but errors no doubt consistent with their experience of the world. Both are examples of possible negative interactions between thought and affect. Positive interactions need to be noted as well, such as the surge of positive affect accompanying the "ah–ha" cognitive reaction that goes with creative discovery and supports further exploration, or the positive feelings of parents or clinicians as they guide children in developing a sense of personal mastery.

Returning to the negative side of a possible cognition–emotion interaction, we had investigated a thesis here that severe and repetitive exposure to parental violence could be related to both greater trauma symptomatology and poorer cognitive functioning, which could interact to leave a child in a less favorable position developmentally and adaptively. The several pieces of this thesis were examined individually and together. First, it was found that exposed children were showing higher levels of PTSD symptomatology, confirming one link. Next, the connection of exposure with poorer cognitive functioning received some support. This support was weak for expectations of aggression, a finding more robust in Mallah and Rossman's data (1997), but this occurred primarily for boys. There was also mild support for the connection of exposure with poorer cognitive processing, but this occurred mainly for younger children who had experienced both abuse and exposure to parental violence. This was consistent with the greater behavioral risk found for these "double whammy" children (Hughes, Parkinson, & Vargo, 1989). The third link of exposure with poorer behavioral adjustment was evidenced, replicating much past work with children exposed to parental violence (e.g., Hughes et al., 1989; Jaffe et al., 1990; McCloskey, Figueredo, & Koss, 1995; Sternberg et al., 1993). In all of these analyses, findings were stronger when variance accounted for by covariate risk factors in addition to violence exposure was left in the mix. This highlighted the close interplay among risk factors and parental violence in contributing to poorer functioning for children in violent lower SES families. The contribution of multiple risk factors clearly needs to be considered in research with children exposed to parental and other forms of violence.

Finally, the pieces of this thesis were combined into a model that allowed family risk factors and exposure to parental violence to have both direct effects on adaptive outcomes and indirect effects mediated through the link of cognitive functioning and PTSD physiological and emotional trauma reactions. Two results were surprising: Cognitive functioning indices and PTSD scores were not significantly linked; and a smaller model that fit the data equally well was one that did not include the direct links of family adversity and parental violence exposure with child adaptation, counter to previous expectation (e.g., Jaffe et al., 1990). The nonsignificant linkage between indices of cognitive functioning and PTSD in the model does not, however, rule out the possibility that this connection exists for several reasons: We may have selected the wrong measures, we may have the wrong model, and family adversity that contributes to cognitive functioning does include components with negative emotional features such as family life stressors and child abuse. The equally good fit of the smaller model without direct links suggested that, for our particular children and measures, variability in children's adaptation was accounted for by intermediate links of family adversity and violence through traumatic response and cognitive functioning. This finding does not tell us what a true causal test of this model using longitudinal data might show about the importance of the direct and intermediate (or indirect) pathways in the model. It does tell us that measurement of possible intermediate cognitive and affective process variables is probably important, just as work by Graham-Bermann, Levendosky, Porterfield, and Okun (1996) has shown that examination of intermediate maternal pathology and social network pathways may be important. Assessing the importance of intermediate variables is also useful because it may suggest additional targets for intervention research.

Findings from our tests of the larger interactive model showed PTSD symptomatology to contribute to behavioral problems and cognitive functioning to contribute to social and school performance. It is interesting that when a different measure of PTSD symptoms was used, symptomatology contributed positively to social and school performance. It is unclear what to make of this result, because it is based on a smaller number of children, and the two PTSD measures correlated significantly. However, Kiser, Heston, Millsap, and Pruitt (1991) have speculated about a possible protective role of PTSD in reaction to child abuse. Abused children with primary diagnosis of PTSD were found to be functioning better than abused children with other primary diagnoses.

Our overall model testing results, however, raise the possibility that there may be a dual influence process at work. They suggest, at least descriptively, that there may be a dual pathway mediator network wherein family violence does enhance traumatic response which does contribute to behavior problems (undercontrolled and overcontrolled) as one part of the process. It also appears that family adversity may interfere with the efficient taking in and processing of new information which, when working well, enhances social and school functioning. Leveling of aggressive cues and sharpening of nonaggressive information could be useful for children at times when they are operating in safe settings at school or with peers. This could allow them to minimize negative aspects of a relationship and attend to positive or neutral ones, thus sustaining positive interactions.

The dual pathway notion makes some sense in that cognitive functioning may reflect the child's developmental level and the total parenting environment. Better parenting, even within a violent family, and greater help with school and other learning tasks might compensate for the cognitive disruptions that could occur with family violence exposure. This is similar to the indirect parenting pathway suggested in other work (Jaffe et al., 1990; Jouriles, Pfiffner, & O'Leary, 1988). However, it appears that the distress reflected in traumatic responding is linked to family violence exposure and may be further expressed in the behavior problems observed mainly in the home by mothers, because they were the most used reporters. The home is a traumatic setting. It is unknown whether this linkage would be observed for ratings of behavior problems made in other settings like school.

IMPLICATIONS FOR WORK WITH CHILDREN EXPOSED TO FAMILY VIOLENCE

Much work remains to be done. However, the theory and research reviewed and reported here suggest that children exposed to repetitive family violence may have negative interaction expectations, may show difficulties taking in new information, and may not be as easily able as other children to modify their schemas. It appears that the leveling (avoidance) of trauma relevant information and sharpening of neutral information may have adaptive significance for better social and school functioning. However, research is needed to clarify this issue.

These results could mean that children exposed to parental violence, especially younger ones, placed in new learning situations would have more trouble than might be expected because they appear to avoid information more than other children their age. Because school performance and what can be learned in treatment and in living all depend on effective usage of new information, many aspects of these children's lives may be affected. The possibility that they have shifted the balance of style of information usage more toward avoidance could help explicate, for professionals working with exposed children, why these children appear to need many and frequent repetitions of new information before they appear to use it. They could need more trials at first, as Damasio's patient Elliot did and as Janie might, to change their schemas and styles to be more adaptive and flexible.

REFERENCES

Aber, J. L., & Allen, J. P. (1987). Effects of maltreatment on young children's socioemotional development: An attachment theory perspective. *Developmental Psychology, 23*, 406–414.

Aber, J. L., Allen, J. P., Carlson, V., & Cicchetti, D. (1989). The effects of maltreatment on development during early childhood: Recent studies and their theoretical, clinical and policy implications. In D. Cicchetti & V. Carlson (Eds.), *Child maltreatment: Theory and research on the causes and consequences of child abuse and neglect* (pp. 579–619). New York: Cambridge University Press.

Achenbach, T. M., & Edelbrock, C. S. (1983). *Manual for the Child Behavior Checklist and Revised Child Behavioral Profile.* Burlington: University of Vermont.

American Psychiatric Association. (1994). *Diagnostic and statistical manual of mental disorders* (4th ed.). Washington, DC: Author.

Berquier, A., & Ashton, R. (1991). A selective review of possible neurological etiologies of schizophrenia. *Clinical Psychology Review, 11*, 585–598.

Bird, H. R., Gould, M. S., & Staghezza, B. (1992). Aggregating data from multiple informants in child psychiatry epidemiological research. *Journal of the American Academy of Child and Adolescent Psychiatry, 31*, 78–85.

Bowlby, J. (1988). *A secure base.* New York: Basic Books.

Bretherton, I., Ridgeway, K., & Cassidy, J. (1990). Assessing internal working models of the attachment relationship. In M. T. Greenberg, D. Cicchetti, & E. M. Cummings (Eds.), *Attachment in the preschool years* (pp. 272–308). Chicago: University of Chicago Press.

Carlson, B. E. (1984). Children's observations of interparental violence. In A. R. Roberts (Ed.), *Battered women and their families* (pp. 147–167). New York: Springer.

Carrey, N. J., Butter, H. J., Persinger, M. A., & Bialik, R. J. (1995). Physiological and cognitive correlates of child abuse. *Journal of the American Academy of Child and Adolescent Psychiatry, 8*, 1067–1075.

Case, R., Kurland, D. M., & Goldberg, J. (1982). Operational efficiency and the growth of short-term memory span. *Journal of Experimental Child Psychology, 33*, 386–404.

Charney, D. S., Deutch, A. Y., Krystal, J. H., Southwick, S. M., & Davis, M. (1993). Psychobiological mechanisms of post-traumatic stress disorder. *Archives of General Psychiatry, 50*, 294–305.

Crick, N. R., & Dodge, K. A. (1994). A review and reformulation of social information-processing mechanisms in children's social adjustment. *Psychological Bulletin, 115*, 74–101.

Crittenden, P. M., & Ainsworth, M. D. S. (1989). Child maltreatment and attachment theory. In D. Cicchetti & V. Carlson (Eds.), *Child maltreatment: Theory and research on the causes and consequences of child abuse and neglect* (pp. 432–463). New York: Cambridge University Press.

Cummings, E. M., & Davies, P. T. (1994). *Children and marital conflict: The impact of family dispute and resolution.* New York: Guilford Press.

Cummings, J. S., Pellegrini, D., Notarius, C., & Cummings, E. M. (1989). Children's responses to angry adult behavior as a function of marital distress and history of interparent hostility. *Child Development, 60*, 1035–1043.

Damasio, A. R. (1994). *Descartes' error*. New York: G. P. Putnam.

Davies, P. T., & Cummings, E. M. (1994). Marital conflict and child adjustment: An emotional security hypothesis. *Psychological Bulletin, 116*, 387–411.

Davies, P. T., & Cummings, E. M. (1995). Children's emotions as organizers of their reactions to interadult anger: A functionalist perspective. *Developmental Psychology, 31*, 677–684.

Descartes, R. (1970). *The philosophical works of Descartes, vol. 1* (E. S. Haldame & G. R. T. Ross, Trans.). Cambridge, England: Cambridge University Press. (Original work published 1637)

Dunn, L. M. (1965). *Expanded manual for the Peabody Picture Vocabulary Test*. Circle Pines, MN: American Guidance Service.

Erickson, M. F., Egeland, B., & Pianta, R. (1989). The effects of maltreatment on the development of young children. In D. Cicchetti & V. Carlson (Eds.), *Child maltreatment: Theory and research on the causes and consequences of child abuse and neglect* (pp. 647–684). New York: Cambridge University Press.

"Eyewitness: Children's views of violence against their mothers." St. Paul, MN: Whispers.

Fish-Murray, C. C., Koby, E. V., & van der Kolk, B. A. (1987). Evolving ideas: The effect of abuse on children's thought. In B. A. van der Kolk (Ed.), *Psychological trauma* (pp. 89–100). Washington, DC: American Psychiatric Association.

Garmezy, N., Masten, A. S., & Tellegen, A. (1984). The study of stress and competence in children: A building block for developmental psychopathology. *Child Development, 55*, 97–111.

Graham-Bermann, S. A., Levendosky, A. A., Porterfield, K., & Okun, A. (1996). *The impact of woman abuse on children: The role of social relationships and emotional context*. Manuscript under review.

Grych, J. H., & Fincham, F. D. (1990). Marital conflict and children's adjustment: A cognitive–contextual framework. *Psychological Bulletin, 108*, 267–290.

Grych, J. H., & Fincham, F. D. (1993). Children's appraisals of marital conflict: Initial investigations of the cognitive–contextual framework. *Child Development, 64*, 215–230.

Hayduk, L. A. (1987). *Structural equation modeling with LISREL: Essentials and advances.* Baltimore: Johns Hopkins University Press.

Hebb, D. O. (1955). Drives and the C.N.S (conceptual nervous system). *Psychological Review, 62,* 243–254.

Horowitz, M. J. (1986). *Stress response syndromes* (2nd ed.) Northvale, NJ: Jason Aronson.

Howe, M. L., & Courage, M. L. (1993). On resolving the enigma of infantile amnesia. *Psychological Bulletin, 113,* 305–326.

Hughes, H. M., Parkinson, D. L., & Vargo, M. C. (1989). Witnessing spouse abuse and experiencing physical abuse: A "double whammy"? *Journal of Family Violence, 4,* 197–209.

Jaffe, P. G., Wolfe, D. A., & Wilson, S. K. (1990). *Children of battered women.* Newbury Park, CA: Sage.

Jouriles, E. N., Pfiffner, L. J., & O'Leary, S. G. (1988). Marital conflict, parenting, and toddler conduct problems. *Journal of Abnormal Child Psychology, 16,* 197–206.

Kiser, L. J., Heston, J., Millsap, P. A., & Pruitt, D. B. (1991). Physical and sexual abuse in childhood: Relationship with post-traumatic stress disorder. *Journal of the American Academy of Child and Adolescent Psychiatry, 30,* 776–783.

LeDeux, J. E. (1992). Emotion as memory: Anatomical systems underlying indelible neural traces. In S. Christianson (Ed.), *The handbook of emotion and memory: Research and theory* (pp. 269–288). Hillsdale, NJ: Erlbaum.

LeDeux, J. E. (1994, June). Emotion, memory, and the brain. *Scientific American,* 50–57.

Mallah, K., & Rossman, B. B. R. (1997). *Social information processing for children exposed to parental violence.* Unpublished manuscript, University of Denver.

McCloskey, L. A., Figueredo, A. J., & Koss, M. P. (1995). The effects of systemic family violence on children's mental health. *Child Development, 66,* 1239–1261.

Miller, D. (1977). *Handbook of research design and social measurement.* New York: Davis McKay.

Milner, J. S., & Wimberley, R. C. (1980). Prediction and explanation of child abuse. *Journal of Clinical Psychology, 36,* 875–884.

Pepler, D. J., & Moore, T. E. (1989, March). *Children exposed to family violence: Home environments and cognitive functioning.* Paper presented at the meeting of the Society for Research in Child Development, Kansas City, MO.

Perner, J., Leekam, S. R., & Wimmer, J. (1987). Three-year olds' difficulty with false belief: The case for a conceptual deficit. *British Journal of Developmental Psychology, 5,* 125–137.

Piaget, J. (1952). *The origins of intelligence in children.* New York: International Universities Press.

Pynoos, R. S., Frederick, C., Nader, K., Arroyo, W., Steinberg, A., Eth, S., Nunez, F., & Fairbanks, L. (1987). Life threat and posttraumatic stress in school age children. *Archives of General Psychiatry, 44,* 1057–1063.

Rieder, C., & Cicchetti, D. (1989). Organizational perspective on cognitive control functioning and cognitive–affective balance in maltreated children. *Developmental Psychology, 25,* 382–393.

Rossman, B. B. R., Bingham, R. D., & Emde, R. N. (1997). Symptomatology and adaptive functioning for children exposed to normative stressors, dog attack, and parental violence. *Journal of the American Academy of Child and Adolescent Psychiatry, 36,* 1–9.

Rossman, B. B. R., Heaton, M. K., Moss, T. A., Malik, N., Lintz, C., & Romero, J. (1991, August). *Functioning in abused and nonabused preschool witnesses to family violence.* Paper presented at the 99th Annual Convention of the American Psychological Association, San Francisco, CA.

Rossman, B. B. R., Hughes, H. M., & Hanson, K. L. (in press). The victimization of school-age children. In B. B. R. Rossman & M. S. Rosenberg, (Eds.), *The multiple victimization of children: Conceptual, developmental, research and clinical issues.* Binghamton, NY: Haworth Press.

Santostefano, S. (1985). *Cognitive control therapy with children and adolescents.* New York: Pergamon Press.

Santostefano, S., & Rieder, C. (1984). Cognitive controls and aggression in children: The concept of cognitive–affective balance. *Journal of Consulting and Clinical Psychology, 52,* 46–56.

Sternberg, K. J., Lamb, M. E., Greenbaum, C., Cicchetti, D., Dawud, S., Cortex, R. M., Krispin, O., & Lorey, F. (1993). Effects of domestic violence on children's behavior problems and depression. *Developmental Psychology,* *29,* 44–52.

Straus, M. A. (1979). Measuring intrafamily conflict and violence: The conflict tactics (CT) scales. *Journal of Marriage and the Family, 41,* 75–88.

van der Kolk, B. A. (1994). The body keeps score: Memory and the evolving psychobiology of post-traumatic stress. *Harvard Review of Psychiatry, 1,* 253–265.

Wechsler, D. (1974). *Manual for the Wechsler Intelligence Scale for Children—Revised.* New York: Psychological Corporation.

Wolfe, V. V., Gentile, C., & Wolfe, D. A. (1989). The impact of sexual abuse on children: A PTSD formulation. *Behavior Therapy, 20,* 215–228.

9

The Emotional, Cognitive, and Coping Responses of Preadolescent Children to Different Dimensions of Marital Conflict

Mark A. Laumakis, Gayla Margolin, and Richard S. John

With the advent of the second generation of research about the effects of marital conflict and violence on children, theoretical and empirical efforts have expanded from examining global linkages between marital conflict and children's outcomes to exploring children's immediate reactions to conflict. The objective of studying children's immediate reactions is to understand processes by which exposure to marital conflict and violence may lead to adverse effects over time. That is, by examining the different reactions to conflict that children experience, we may begin to construct models that explain why conflict is more stressful and leads to more devastating outcomes for some children than for others (Margolin, in press). In constructing such models, attention needs to focus on dimensions of the conflict itself, on dimensions reflecting characteristics of the child, and on the interaction

Preparation of this article was supported by National Institute of Mental Health Grant RO1 36595 awarded to Gayla Margolin and Richard S. John. We gratefully acknowledge the assistance of Barbara Rottman, who wrote and directed the conflict tapes used in this study, and David Jones, who served as sound technician. We also thank Diana Doumas, Louise Foo, Chandra Ghosh, Elana Gordis, Liza Halloran, Beth Leedham, and Betsy Morris who administered the procedures to the participants.

between conflict dimensions and child characteristics. One strategy for examining children's immediate reactions to conflict is to have children respond to audiotaped or videotaped samples of simulated marital conflicts. When the conflict cues are systematically controlled, one can see which conflict dimensions influence the intensity or nature of the children's reactions.

CHILDREN'S TWO-PHASE REACTIONS TO MARITAL CONFLICT

Theoretical models of children's responses to stressors have several common features. The reactions are said to take place across several modalities (e.g., affective, cognitive, coping) and to occur in at least two, if not more, phases (e.g., Crockenberg & Forgays, 1996; Gottman & Katz, 1989; Grych & Fincham, 1990; Lazarus & Folkman, 1984). More specifically, children initially attend to and interpret particular cues, becoming aware that an unpleasant event is occurring (Grych & Fincham, 1990). In making such determinations, they are interpreting both the external stimuli and their own internal cues (Crick & Dodge, 1994). This initial step thus entails the parallel processing of affective, cognitive, and physiological cues and the reciprocal feedback among these different cues. Hence the stressor, which in this case would be the marital conflict or violence, first elicits affective responses and cognitive appraisals. At the next step, children are focused on what they might wish to happen in the situation and what they might do to attain that objective. In this step the child is generating solutions and determining which to adopt. Although they do not test the entire model, empirical investigations of children's immediate reactions to marital conflict generally examine some combination of affective, physiological, cognitive, and coping reactions.

Researchers have learned about the initial stage of children's reactions to conflict from studying children's reactions to conflict between two adults, such as an experimenter and the child's mother, or from taped vignettes of male and female actors, or from observation of taped segments of the child's own parents (Crockenberg & Forgays, 1996; E.

M. Cummings, Ballard, & El-Sheikh, 1991; E. M. Cummings, Ballard, El-Sheikh, & Lake, 1991; E. M. Cummings, Simpson, & Wilson, 1993; El-Sheikh & Cheskes, 1995; El-Sheikh, Cummings, & Goetsch, 1989; Grych & Fincham, 1993). Taken as a whole, these studies provide evidence that witnessing conflict elicits negative affect in children, with high-intensity conflict eliciting more affect than low-intensity conflict. Anger, sadness, and fear are the primary affective reactions noted in analog studies on children's responses to simulated interadult anger, although some studies report a generalized distress reaction. Conflicts portraying physical aggression, as compared to less severe forms of anger, tend to elicit stronger negative emotions (E. M. Cummings, Vogel, Cummings, & El-Sheikh, 1989), although, as El-Sheikh and Cheskes (1995) reported, that may be reflected in a tendency to report less rather than more aggressive impulses. Likewise, conflicts in which the anger remains unresolved rather than resolved induce more distress in children (E. M. Cummings, Ballard, El-Sheikh, & Lake, 1991; E. M. Cummings et al., 1993; E. M. Cummings et al., 1989; Hennessy, Rabideau, Cicchetti, & Cummings, 1994).

Children's appraisals of the marital conflict reflect the way they interpret and evaluate the conflict they are witnessing, that is, the extent to which the child views the interaction as negative, threatening, and self-relevant (Grych & Fincham, 1990). In line with the Lazarus and Folkman (1984) model that cognitive processing mediates the impact of environmental events on individuals, E. M. Cummings, Davies, and Simpson (1994) examined how children's appraisals of marital conflict serve as mediators of the association between marital conflict and child adjustment. They found that appraisals of threat are stronger predictors of outcome for boys, whereas self-blame is a better predictor of outcome for girls. O'Brien, Margolin, John, and Krueger (1991) found that children's appraisals of the conflict (as reflected in criticisms, praise, and predictions about where the conflict might lead) were dimensions differentiating children's reactions to the conflict stimuli. Grych and Fincham (1993) reported that more intense conflict is associated with perceptions of greater threat and expectancies about conflict escalation. It is known that children experience both cognitive and emotional reactions to simulations of marital conflict and that these reactions are associated. Concerns about conflict escalation, for example, are related to reactions of emotional distress (Grych & Fincham, 1993).

At the second level of processing, children generally attempt to cope with the marital conflict. As contrasted with the initial stress response, coping is characterized by effortful, intentional, or purposeful physical or mental action (Lazarus & Folkman, 1984; Rudolph, Dennig, & Weisz, 1995). Children's coping generally takes two forms: (a) emotion-focused coping, which serves to regulate stressful emotions and includes strategies such as avoidance, distancing, and selective attention; and (b) problem-focused coping, which serves to manage or alter the problem through strategies such as intervening directly or generating alternative solutions (Lazarus & Folkman, 1984). The coping process is not limited to the action the child actually emits but also includes those strategies generated, considered, and perhaps rejected.

In accordance with the general coping literature, children's reactions to marital conflict reflect attempts to alter the problem itself and their own emotional state. Children's direct intervention into the marital conflict is a coping strategy more frequently endorsed by children with a history of exposure to physical aggression in marriage than by children exposed only to verbal conflicts or to low conflict (O'Brien et al., 1991). Direct intervention also was more frequently endorsed when the conflict involved child-related as opposed to adult-related topics (Grych & Fincham, 1993), when the conflict participants were adult–child as compared to adult–adult (El-Sheikh & Cheskes, 1995), or when the conflict portrayed unresolved, as contrasted with resolved, anger (E. M. Cummings, Ballard, El-Sheikh, & Lake, 1991; E. M. Cummings et al., 1993). Indirect intervention attempts, in which children attempted to resolve the conflict on their own without interrupting the parents, were common responses to conflicts that were high in intensity and related to child topics (Grych & Fincham, 1993). Children exposed to physically aggressive marital conflict, as compared to less severe marital conflict, not only suggested intervention strategies more frequently but also endorsed strategies designed to calm themselves or distance themselves from the conflict (O'Brien et al., 1991). Grych and Fincham (1993) also reported the importance of strategies involving distancing or ignoring the conflict when children were exposed to marital conflict. Although children's coping thus appears to be related to the intensity of the current conflict and their histories of conflict exposure, the nature of the coping response takes varied and sometimes contrasting forms ranging from directly intervening to distancing oneself from the conflict.

FACTORS AFFECTING CHILDREN'S REACTIONS TO MARITAL CONFLICT

Children's previous experience with marital conflict serves as a context for each stage of their reactions (Crockenberg & Forgays, 1996; Grych & Fincham, 1990), influencing their initial interpretations of the situation, their emotional and cognitive appraisals, and the type of response they select. From a theoretical standpoint, increased exposure to interparental conflict could lead to reactions indicative of either habituation or sensitization. The habituation hypothesis suggests that children exposed to greater amounts of marital conflict over time show decreased reactivity to conflict. The sensitization hypothesis, in contrast, posits that children who are exposed to greater amounts of marital conflict with time become more vulnerable to its effects. The data quite clearly support the sensitization hypothesis with respect to children's reactions to conflict. On an affective level, children who have been exposed over time to high conflict or physical violence in their homes tend to exhibit more distress when faced with new instances of conflict than do children without the exposure history (E. M. Cummings et al., 1989; J. S. Cummings, Pellegrini, Notarius, & Cummings, 1989; El-Sheikh, 1994). Similarly, children who themselves are physically abused respond with greater fear to interadult anger than do nonabused children (Hennessy et al., 1994). With respect to cognitive processing, boys exposed to marital violence compared to other forms of conflict were less likely to evaluate the new conflictual situations negatively, whereas from a coping perspective, the boys exposed to violence were more likely to consider intervening in the conflict (O'Brien et al., 1991). As concluded by O'Brien, Balto, Erber, and Gee (1995), the legacy of childhood exposure to violent interparental conflict may be the presence of extreme affective reactions and restricted abilities for cognitive processing.

Children's gender is another characteristic said to play a role, albeit somewhat mixed, in children's reactions to conflict (Davies & Cummings, 1994; Margolin, in press). Whereas some studies on global associations between marital violence and children's adjustment offer data supporting greater vulnerability in boys than in girls (Carlson, 1990; Doumas, Margolin, & John, 1994; Wolfe, Jaffe, Wilson, & Zak, 1985), other studies portray greater vulnerability in girls than in boys (Hughes & Barad, 1983; O'Keefe, 1994; Spaccarelli, Sandler, & Roosa, 1994; Sternberg et al., 1993). Attention to gender in studies of children's immediate reactions to conflict may help unravel these global associations. Davies, Myers, and Cummings (1996), for example, reported that, in response to adult conflict, girls reported more fear than boys, whereas boys suggested more direct interventions than did girls. With respect to coping, E. M. Cummings et al. (1994) suggested that boys may be more socialized than girls to respond to aggression with some type of direct intervention, whereas girls may be socialized to respond by taking blame for the marital conflict. Their data support gender differences in the way cognitions mediate the relationship between conflict exposure and child adjustment. Overall, however, with only a few studies examining gender as a variable of interest, relatively little is known about gender differences in children's immediate reactions. The goal of the present study is not only to examine whether boys and girls react differently to conflict but also to examine whether gender interacts with characteristics of the conflict stimulus or with history of conflict exposure.

A key contextual feature in understanding children's responses to marital conflict is the nature of the conflict itself, as reflected in intensity, resolution, and content. Considerable attention has focused on whether the conflict is resolved, with children clearly showing more emotional distress and negative appraisals to unresolved conflict (E. M. Cummings, Ballard, El-Sheikh, & Lake, 1991; E. M. Cummings et al., 1993; E. M. Cummings et al., 1989; Hennessy et al., 1994). Likewise, disagreements surrounding child topics, as opposed to adult topics, are particularly upsetting to children (Grych & Fincham, 1993). There is preliminary evidence that marital conflict containing physical aggression, as contrasted with verbal or nonviolent aggression, is associated with greater distress in children (E. M. Cummings et al., 1989), yet a number of unanswered questions remain. First, is it marital aggression per se that is upsetting to the children, or is it the implication that the marriage might end? As Katz and Gottman (1993) suggested, perhaps children are especially affected by severely hostile marital patterns because of what these patterns mean for the long-term prognosis of the relationship. Second, does physical aggression lead to distinctly different responses than do serious forms of verbal aggression? In the study reported in this chapter, we sought to disentangle these dimensions of marital conflict and to examine children's responses to distinct dimensions of marital conflict.

THE STUDY

The study reported below dismantles the marital conflict stimuli used in previous studies into unique elements that have yet to be examined empirically. In this study, we examined preadolescent children's emotional, cognitive, and coping responses to simulated marital conflicts portraying different conflict dimensions. In particular, we deconstructed several of the "scarier" elements of marital conflict, namely, name-calling, threats to leave the marriage, and physical aggression, and examined pre-adolescent children's reactions to these dimensions. In three separate vignettes, each of these three dimensions is paired with negative voice tones, a fourth but seemingly less severe negative dimension of marital conflict. Positive affect is presented in a fifth vignette, as a contrasting and constructive mode of conflict resolution. A sixth, no-conflict vignette is presented as a practice tape and control.

Our intention was to answer three questions about children's emotional, cognitive, and coping reactions to simulated marital conflict:

1. What dimensions of simulated marital conflict result in the greatest levels of emotional and cognitive reactivity in children, and how are conflict dimensions related to specific coping strategies?

2. Do children exposed to high versus low levels of marital conflict in their homes show differences in their emotional reactions and coping responses to and cognitive processing of simulated marital conflict?

3. Do boys and girls differ in their emotional reactions and coping response to and cognitive processing of simulated marital conflict?

We made the following hypotheses: (a) Simulated marital conflicts characterized by more intense styles of conflict, namely physical aggression and threats to leave, result in greater levels of emotional and cognitive reactivity in children, in comparison with simulated marital conflicts without these features; (b) children from high, as compared with low, conflict homes report and evidence greater cognitive and emotional reactivity to simulated marital conflict; and (c) both boys and girls are reactive to marital conflict stimuli, but it is expected that boys might be more likely to engage in direct intervention strategies whereas girls might be more likely to take responsibility for the marital conflict and to report more negative affect.

We used two methods to assess children's reactions to simulated conflict; both are largely unstructured, open-ended, and rely on the children's own words. Children's immediate cognitive processing was assessed through the Articulated Thoughts During Simulated Situations paradigm (ATSS; Davison, Robins, & Johnson, 1983; Davison, Navarre, & Vogel, 1995). This think-aloud cognitive assessment approach initially was used with adults but recently has been applied with children (Bice Pitts, 1993; O'Brien et al., 1991). In this procedure, children respond to a stimulus by speaking aloud, into a tape recorder, whatever thoughts come to mind. As Davison et al. (1995) suggested, this alternative is preferable to the use of predetermined, experimenter-selected categories to describe children's cognitive processing, because it creates the potential for a richer sampling of actual cognitions of interest. The second method of assessment, a questionnaire following the ATSS procedure, also relies on an open-ended approach to assess children's coping responses. Once again, children respond in their own words so that we do not suggest what possible coping strategies might be.

Method

Participants

The 74 children who participated in this study were drawn from a sample of families who previously had taken part in the Family Studies Project at the University of Southern California. Families who participated in the initial study were two-parent families having at least one child between the ages of 8 and 11. In addition, the families needed to meet the following criteria: (a) both adults were biological parents of the child or, if nonbiological, then the parent had resided with the child since the child was 2 years old; (b) the parents had a telephone; and (c) the parents read and spoke English fluently.[1] Ninety-one families (out of 123 who were invited) agreed to participate in the second phase of this study, which occurred approximately 18 months following the original study. Seventy-five children were eligible for the ATSS procedure because this was added to the protocol after 16 of the 91 families already had participated. The final sample size was 74 (40 girls and 34 boys), because one child declined to participate in part of the ATSS procedure. Ages of the children in the current sample, by the time of the second phase of the study, ranged from 9.4 to 13.4 years for girls ($M = 11.2$, $SD = 1.1$) and from 9.4 to 13.2 years for boys ($M = 11.4$, $SD = 1.2$). The ethnic composition of the sample was as follows: 68% Caucasian, 23% African American, and 9% from other groups.

Between group 2 (Conflict Exposure) $\times$ 2 (Gender) analyses of variance (ANOVAs) were run on the demographic variables. No main effects for conflict exposure or gender were found for father's age, mother's and father's years of education, family gross monthly income, child's age, or child's intelligence level as measured by the Information and Block Design subtest scores on the Wechsler Intelligence Scale for Children—Revised (WISC-R; Wechsler, 1974). A main effect for mother's age indicated that mothers in the low-conflict group were older than those in the high-conflict group, $F(1, 70) = 4.69$, $p < .05$. No

---

[1] For more details about the recruitment and description of this sample, see Gordis, Margolin, and John (1997).

effects were found for gender or for the interaction between conflict exposure and gender.

Procedures

The scripts used in the ATSS procedure were written by a professional screenwriter and performed by professional actors and actresses and were designed to capture distinct and powerful stimuli in interchanges lasting less than 2 minutes. The steps in developing the audiotapes included writing the scripts, recording pilot tapes, revising the scripts to better illustrate specific conflict dimensions, recording final performances by the actors, and dubbing in sound effects. Each tape was recorded with a different pair of actors and actresses.

Before children participated in the ATSS procedures and as part of overall consent for the study, both parents read verbatim transcripts of the conflict vignettes and gave consent for their child to participate in this part of the study. In addition, consent forms read directly to the child informed him or her of his or her right to cease participating at any point in the procedures.

When administering the ATSS procedures, the experimenter took the child into a specially arranged room, in which the child was visually isolated from the experimenter and any other distractions by a three-sided study carrel. The experimenter showed the child the equipment in the room, including the headphones, microphone, and tape recorder, and read aloud the following standardized set of instructions:

> You are about to listen to six conversations between a mom and a dad. Imagine you are at home in the bedroom and you over-hear this conversation between your mom and your dad. We want you to tell us what is running through your mind as you are hearing them. Really notice what you are thinking and feeling. You will hear a tone at the end of each conversation. At that time please say out loud whatever is going through your mind. Please try to be as open as possible with your thoughts, and try to fill up the whole time with as many of your thoughts and feelings as you can. Please stop when you hear the second tone.

> There are no right or wrong answers, so don't worry about what you say. Please do not retell the story or summarize what you just heard. Just tell us what you're thinking and how you are feeling. After 30 seconds, you will hear the tone again, signaling the time to talk is up. Any questions?

All participants first received a no-conflict practice tape to familiarize and orient them to the ATSS task. They received the remaining five tapes in randomized order.

The five randomized tapes (Margolin, Rottman, & Jones, 1992) portray the following different dimensions of conflict: positive affect, negative voice, name-calling, threats to leave, and physical aggression. The positive affect tape illustrates a definite disagreement in the content, but the spouse actors maintain a positive, light interactive style. In the negative voice tape, the spouses' disagreements are accompanied by loud, irritated, and angry voice tones. Negative voice tones also are present in the three remaining tapes, in combination with each of the "scary" dimensions of marital conflict—name-calling, threats to leave, and physical aggression. The name-calling tape included the use of demeaning, belittling language (e.g., dumb, jerk, ridiculous) by each of the spouses. In the tape portraying threats to leave, there is the clear message, following a heated argument, that the wife is getting out a suitcase, mumbling about getting a divorce, and slamming a door as she marches out of the room. In the tape portraying physical aggression, the conflict quickly escalates with sounds of clothes tearing and objects being knocked over and crashing to the floor in the scuffle, and fear is expressed in the wife's voice. All topics for these conflicts are fairly mundane and reflect common household issues such as taking the car for repair, scheduling conflicts between the spouses' plans for the upcoming Friday evening, and spending money on a nonessential sale item. Audiotapes were used as stimuli for the following reasons: to give children the opportunity to personalize the voices they heard, to decrease the salience of potentially distracting visual cues, and to emphasize salient audio cues in the interactions.

After hearing each tape, the participants had 30 seconds in which to articulate their thoughts and feelings, which were recorded on a separate cassette. A short, pleasant tone cued the participants when the 30-second interval began and ended. At the conclusion of each 30-second interval for articulating thoughts and feelings, the child completed the ATSS Follow-Up Questionnaire, which assessed children's emotional reactions and coping responses to the six simulated marital conflicts. Each child completed the questionnaire six times, once for each of the stimulus tapes.

Measures

Conflict exposure. The high versus low marital conflict distinction for this sample of children was made on the basis of scores on the child's version of the Conflict Tactics Scale (CTS; Straus, 1979). The CTS requires each child to report separately for mothers and fathers the extent to which she or he witnessed six forms of verbal conflict and eight forms of physical conflict. Examples of verbal conflict items include the following: How often does your mother or father: (a) insult or swear at the other one? (b) sulk and refuse to talk about it? and (c) do or say something to spite the other one? Examples of physical conflict items include the following: How often does your mother or father: (a) throw something at the other one? and (b) beat up the other one? Each item was rated for mothers and fathers and scored for each on a four-point scale: *never* (0); *once* (1); *a few times* (2); and *lots of times* (3). For the entire sample, scores on the verbal conflict subscale ranged from 0 to 26 ($M = 6.3$, $SD = 6.1$), and scores on the physical conflict subscale ranged from 0 to 10 ($M = 0.6$, $SD = 1.8$).

The criteria used to partition the sample of children into high-conflict and low-conflict groups were as follows: High-conflict children were those who endorsed any item on the physical subscale of the CTS or received scores of greater than or equal to 5 on the verbal subscale of the CTS; low-conflict children were those who received scores of less than 5 on the verbal subscale of the CTS and did not endorse any items on the physical subscale of the CTS. On the basis of these criteria, 35 children were assigned to the high-conflict group (19 girls, 16 boys), and 39 children were placed in the low-conflict group (21 girls, 18 boys). The high-conflict group differed significantly from the low-conflict group on verbal conflict subscale scores ($M = 10.8$, $SD = 6.0$

vs. $M = 2.3$, $SD = 1.7$), $t(72) = 8.00$, $p < .01$, and physical conflict subscale scores ($M = 1.2$, $SD = 2.4$ vs. $M = 0$, $SD = 0$), $t(72) = 2.85$, $p < .01$.[2]

Emotional data. The ATSS Follow-Up Questionnaire provides self-report data on emotional reactions. Emotional reactions are rated on a five-point scale, ranging from 0 (*not at all*) to 4 (*a lot*). Based on the results of an exploratory factor analysis with a varimax rotation, scores were collapsed into two summary categories of emotions. A positive emotional reaction score was calculated by summing each child's responses to two items: happy and hopeful. A negative emotional reaction score was calculated by summing each child's responses on five items: sad, scared or frightened, mad or angry, nervous or worried, and helpless. Cronbach's alpha for the positive emotion scale was .50; for the negative emotion scale, it was .92.[3]

Cognitive data. Each child's spontaneous and unedited responses[4] to the six ATSS tapes were transcribed and then coded using a modification of the O'Brien et al. (1991) system for coding ATSS audiotapes. The four codes used in this study, their definitions, and examples of each code are presented in Table 1.[5]

Three volunteer coders reviewed each transcript. The coders were blind to which stimulus tape was responded to and coded responses in random order. For each of the response categories, the three coders rated the response on a four-point scale, ranging from 0 (*not at all*) to 3 (*a lot*). Coders rated responses on the basis of a global consideration of the combined elements of the response, including its content, tone,

---

[2]The CTS subscale scores of the present sample match well with El-Sheikh's (1994) community sample, which were as follows: high-conflict group verbal aggression subscale score: $M = 12.32$, $SD = 5.95$; high-conflict group physical aggression subscale score: $M = .79$, $SD = 1.08$; low-conflict group verbal aggression subscale score: $M = 1.95$, $SD = 1.94$; low-conflict group physical aggression subscale score: $M = 0$, $SD = 0$.

[3]The item How surprised did you feel? loaded moderately on both the positive emotional scale and the negative emotional scale; hence, it was not included in subsequent analyses.

[4]For these analyses, $n = 71$; the audiotaped responses of three children could not be coded as a result of technical difficulties.

[5]A copy of the ATSS Follow-Up Questionnaire and the Cognitive Reactions Coding Manual and Coding Sheet can be obtained from the authors. With respect to the Cognitive Reactions Coding system, the following three codes from the O'Brien et al. (1991) system were not used: self-distraction, democracy, and autocracy; a negative outcome code was added.

Table 1

Coding System for Cognitive Reactions

Code Category	Definition	Example
Negative Evaluation	Reflects criticism specific to the incident on the tape directed toward the actors in the simulated conflicts	The husband is mean to the wife. That wife got too angry and she got her husband on the defensive right away.
Positive Evaluation	Reflects praise of the actors	They seem to be getting along nicely. Well, I think they're going pretty fine.
Negative Outcome	Pertains to pessimistic predictions about how the conflict will end	I feel like their marriage was gonna go down the drain. I don't think they're gonna stay together.
Positive Outcome	Pertains to optimistic predictions about how the conflict will end	It sounds like they're gonna have a nice time from now on. I'm sure that they'll be able to work out their finances so that both people are satisfied.

and the frequency of specific types of statements. Reliabilities for the codes were calculated using the intraclass correlation coefficient, as detailed by Shrout and Fleiss (1979). The resulting reliabilities were as follows: Negative Evaluation = .86, Positive Evaluation = .86, Negative Outcome = .88, and Positive Outcome = .91.

Coping data. Children's coping responses to the simulated marital conflicts were assessed through the following open-ended item from the ATSS Follow-Up Questionnaire: *If you overheard this discussion, what are all the things you would have done to deal with the situation?* Children were provided with space to suggest up to three coping responses, and their responses were transferred to coding sheets. All children were asked this question for each of the six tapes to maintain a standardized response procedure. However, only their responses to the name-calling, threats to leave, and physical aggression conflict tapes were coded and analyzed because the other three tapes did not present a situation that elicited coping responses.

Responses were coded by two coders who were blind to the child's gender and classification regarding previous exposure to marital conflict. Each response was coded into 1 of 15 mutually exclusive codes, which were subsequently collapsed into five final coping response categories.[6] These final categories and examples of each are presented in Table 2. Three of these categories (Intervention, Child-Directed Solution, and Seek Others) reflect problem-focused coping responses or attempts to change or manage some aspect of the environment that is causing the distress. Intervention comprises both verbal interventions, in which the children tell the parents to stop fighting, and physical interventions, in which the children use physical actions to interrupt the parents' conflict. Child-Directed Solution comprises suggestions and after-the-fact comments about what could have been done differently and specific solutions to the problem suggested by the child and to be executed by the child. Seek Others reflects children's efforts to seek assistance from peers, siblings, neighbors, or authority figures such as the police. The final two categories, Self-Protect and Express Feelings, reflect emotion-focused responses or attempts by the children to change or regulate their own emotional state. Self-Protect consists of actions in which the children withdraw or distance themselves from the situation, distract themselves by becoming involved in an activity, or in-

---

[6]The following 4 of the original 15 codes in the Coping Coding System were not used in the analyses: Blame Self, Blame Parents, I Don't Know, and Uncodeable–Irrelevant. The first two were dropped because of their low frequency of occurrence, and the last two were dropped because they were used simply to monitor the occurrence of such unusable responses. A copy of the Coping Coding Manual and Coding Sheet may be obtained from the authors.

Table 2

Coping Coding System

Category	Example
Intervention	I'd go in and try to stop them from fighting by talking to them about it.
	Try to stop them . . . try to not let the discussion go so far.
	Go over to mom, snatch her suitcase and hide.
	I would go in and tell them to stop shouting.
	I would first try to stop the man from breaking things.
	Try to pull dad off of mom.
Child-Directed Solution	I'd go get him some shirts.
	I would help clean the mess.
	Give my mom and dad some money.
	I'd tell the wife to leave if she ever experiences that again.
	I would tell my mom that the dad didn't mean it.
Seek Others	I would have tried to talk to someone.
	Call the police.
	Go visit my dog.
Self-Protect	Stay out of their way.
	I would have tried to go to sleep.
	Turn on the radio really loud.
	Not go downstairs because I could get hit with the shoes.
Express Emotions	Run to my room and cry.
	I would have felt scared.
	I would feel helpless.

dicate they would leave the couple alone and not become involved. Express Feelings captures children's direct and indirect expressions of emotion. Intraclass correlation coefficient reliabilities for these five categories were as follows: Intervention = .66, Child-Directed Solution = .74, Seek Others = .81, Self-Protect = .78, and Express Feelings = .78.

Results

Children's emotional and cognitive reactions to the simulated marital conflicts on the ATSS tapes were examined through 6 (Conflict Dimension) $\times$ 2 (Conflict Exposure) $\times$ 2 (Gender) repeated-measures multivariate analyses of variance (MANOVAs). Coping responses, examined only for three tapes, were analyzed through 3 $\times$ 2 $\times$ 2 analyses. Conflict Dimension was a repeated measure, whereas Conflict Exposure and Gender were between-subjects factors.

Emotional Reactions

Figure 1 (top panel) displays the means of the children's negative and positive emotional reactions to the six tapes of simulated marital conflict. The MANOVA revealed a significant main effect of Conflict Dimension for both negative emotional reactions, $F(5, 70) = 56.59$, $p < .01$, and positive emotional reactions, $F(5, 70) = 55.14$, $p < .01$. This main effect was further analyzed using a slight modification of Tukey's honestly significant difference (HSD) test of all pairwise comparisons (Gravetter & Wallnau, 1988). The HSD test indicated that children reported significantly more negative emotional reactions in response to the threats to leave and physical aggression tapes than in response to the negative voice and name-calling tapes, which, in turn, elicited more negative emotional reactions than either the nonconflictual simulation or the conflict with positive affect. The Tukey's HSD test on children's positive emotions indicated that children reported significantly more positive emotions in response to the nonconflictual pilot tape than in response to the conflict with positive affect, which, in turn, elicited more positive emotional reactions than any of the other tapes, which did not differ from each other. The MANOVA did not indicate any main effects or interactions for either Conflict Exposure or Gender on children's positive or negative emotional reactions.

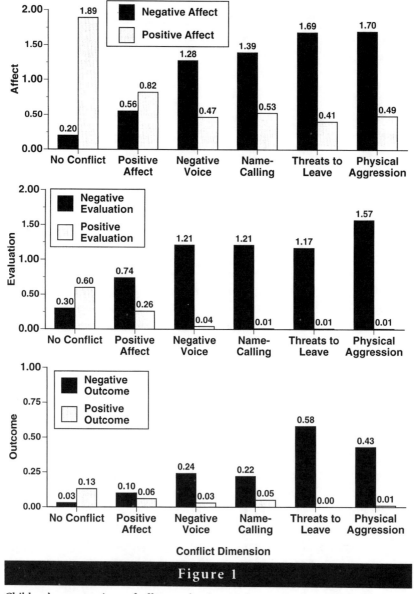

Figure 1

Children's mean ratings of affect, evaluation, and outcome by conflict dimension.

Cognitive Processing

Coded data were averaged across the three coders for each of the six ATSS tapes. The means of the children's responses for all four coded dimensions are plotted in the middle and lower panels of Figure 1.

The MANOVA on negative evaluation revealed a significant main effect of Conflict Dimension, $F(5, 67) = 54.15$, $p < .01$. The Tukey's HSD test indicated that children made the most negative evaluation statements about the conflict that included physical aggression. Furthermore, they evaluated the conflicts with negative voice, name-calling, and threats to leave more negatively than either the conflict with positive affect or the nonconflictual simulation. For negative evaluation, there also was a significant Conflict Exposure × Gender interaction, $F(1, 67) = 5.13$, $p < .05$, as well as a significant main effect for Conflict Exposure, $F(1, 67) = 4.14$, $p < .05$. Children from high-conflict homes tended to evaluate the tapes overall more negatively than did children from low-conflict homes. This result, however, essentially is due to the responses of boys exposed to high-marital conflict who responded to each of the six conflict tapes with more negative evaluations than did children in any of the other three groups. As seen in Figure 2, high-conflict boys responded with more negative evaluation than did low-conflict boys. High- and low-conflict girls had comparable mean scores on negative evaluation.

The significant main effect for conflict dimension on negative outcome, $F(5, 67) = 12.94$, $p < .01$, showed, through the post hoc analyses, that children predicted more negative outcomes for conflicts characterized by threats to leave and physical aggression than for any of the other conflicts. There were no interactions or main effects for gender or conflict exposure for negative outcomes.

Positive evaluation and positive outcome responses were quite rare across all six conflict dimensions, as is clear in Figure 1. On the original 0 to 3 scale, means for positive evaluation across the five conflictual tapes ranged from .01 to .26 and, for positive outcome, they ranged from .00 to .06. In addition, many of the cells in the 6 × 2 × 2 design yielded means of zero, indicating that all children in those cells re-

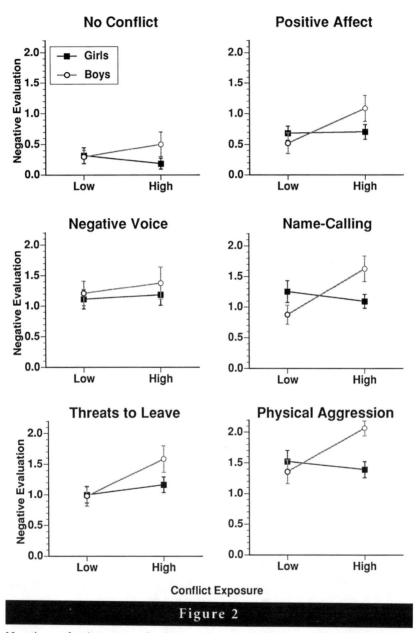

Figure 2

Negative evaluation means for boys and girls having low- and high-conflict exposure for six conflict tapes.

sponded with no positive evaluation or no positive outcome. Hence, no analyses could be run on these measures.

Coping Responses

Coded data were averaged across both coders for each of the ATSS tapes, and 3 (Conflict Dimension) × 2 (Conflict Exposure) × 2 (Gender) MANOVAs were used to examine children's coping responses to the name-calling, threats to leave, and physical aggression tapes. Across all children and across the three conflict tapes, the distribution of coping responses was as follows: Intervention = 22.0%; Child-Directed Solutions = 29.3%; Seek Others = 2.1%; Self-Protect = 21.8%; Express Emotions = 10.7%; and Other–Uncodeable = 14.0%. There were no main effects for conflict dimension, gender, or conflict exposure.

Figure 3 (top panel) displays the mean percentages of the children's suggestion of Intervention coping responses to the three "scary" dimensions of conflict. Visual inspection of this figure shows that boys exposed to high-conflict marriages are more likely to report an Intervention response than are children in any of the other three groups, particularly for the tape involving Physical Aggression. The MANOVA revealed a significant Conflict Exposure × Gender interaction for the Intervention coping response, $F(1, 67) = 5.96$, $p < .05$. This interaction indicated that boys from high-conflict homes report more Intervention responses than do girls from high-conflict homes. For children in low-conflict homes, boys and girls show similar percentages of Intervention responses.

The results for Child-Directed Solutions appear in the bottom panel of Figure 3. Here, high-conflict boys show the lowest overall mean score across tapes for behaviors reflecting the child's suggestions for actions on his or her part that would solve the problem. The MANOVA on Child-Directed Solutions revealed a significant Conflict Exposure × Gender interaction, $F(1, 67) = 5.73$, $p < .05$. This significant interaction indicated that, among the children from high-conflict homes, girls reported a greater percentage of Child-Directed Solutions in response to each of the three conflict tapes than did boys. Among the children from low-conflict homes, boys reported a greater percentage than girls of Child-Directed Solutions when the tape portrayed threats to leave,

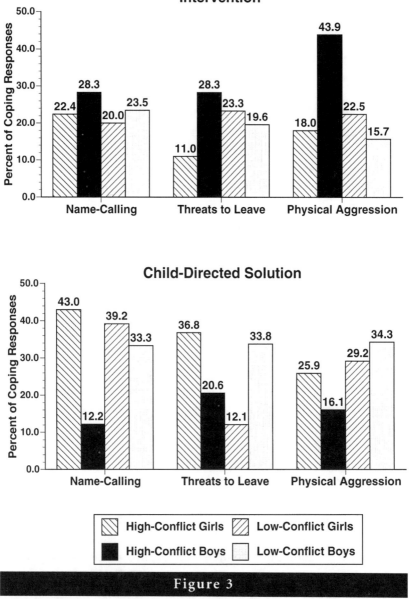

Figure 3

Percentage of intervention and child-directed coping responses for the tapes depicting name-calling, threats to leave, and physical aggression.

whereas low-conflict boys and girls reported quite comparable percentages of Child-Directed Solutions in response to the name-calling and physical aggression vignettes.

MANOVAs on the remaining three coping categories of Self-Protect, Seek Others, and Express Emotions revealed no significant main effects or interactions.

Discussion

With respect to the proposed two-phase model of how children deal with stress, this study portrays different patterns of findings for the first versus the second phase. In the processing of affective and cognitive cues, the most salient feature was the conflict dimension. For both negative and positive affect, and for the two negative cognitive appraisal variables, there was a main effect for the conflict dimension. For the most part, negative affect and negative cognitive appraisals were induced more by the physical aggression and the threat to leave vignettes than by the name-calling or negative voice vignettes. Nevertheless, the vignettes portraying name-calling and negative voice induced more negative affect and appraisals and less positive affect than did the positive affect and practice tapes indicating that even negative voice tones have a notable influence on children's emotions and appraisals.

In the second phase, in which the children generated coping responses, the most salient feature was the interaction between child gender and previous exposure to high conflict. Boys from high-conflict homes gave a higher percentage of direct intervention coping strategies than either high-conflict girls, low-conflict boys, or low-conflict girls. However, child-directed solutions, compared to other coping responses, were more prominent in girls from high-conflict homes than in boys from high-conflict homes, with boys and girls from low-conflict homes showing mean percentages approximately similar to one another.

Children's immediate affective and cognitive reactions to the tapes involving physical aggression and threats to leave support the current literature but also bring certain assumptions under closer scrutiny. These data vividly illustrate that, to understand children's reactions to conflict, attention needs to be directed to the features of the conflict

(E. M. Cummings, 1995; Grych & Fincham, 1990; Margolin, 1988). Why are physical aggression and threats to leave more upsetting than conflicts with name-calling and negative voice qualities? In the language of the emotional security hypothesis (Davies & Cummings, 1994), the key feature of these two scenarios is the implied impact on the child, by virtue of the potential for major disruption and change in the marriage and in family life as the child knows it. These data lead one to examine more closely the commonly stated assumption that exposure to marital aggression and violence is more upsetting than exposure to other forms of marital conflict. Whereas the data support the assumption that physical aggression is more distressing than some forms of verbal aggression, they reflect fairly similar levels of emotional distress with the threats to leave the marriage. The one difference between physical aggression and threats to leave is seen in children's negative evaluations. We speculate that, although children are made uncomfortable by the wife's decision to leave the marriage, they may not appraise it with the same negative judgments as they do the use of physical aggression. That is, children may be emotionally distressed and predict negative outcomes associated with the potential break-up of a marriage, but they also may be empathic to the decision. On the other hand, children may judge physical aggression quite harshly because it contradicts a social norm and turns what should be a safe environment for the child into one that is chaotic and dangerous (Margolin, in press).

There was support for the assumption that children's actual history of exposure to high versus low marital conflict affects their reactions, but always in the context of an interaction with children's gender. It thus appears that the effects of conflict exposure are different for boys and girls. The cognitive appraisal data suggest that boys from high-conflict homes evaluated the conflict situations more negatively than did boys from low-conflict homes. Girls from high- and low-conflict homes did not vary from each other but expressed less negative evaluation than did the high-conflict boys. The coping data show that boys from high-conflict homes also were more likely to offer coping suggestions that involve direct intervention than children in the other groups. These data for boys are thus consistent with the sensitization theories

(Davies & Cummings, 1994) that repeated exposure leads to more, rather than less, reactivity.

Yet questions remain. Why are high-conflict boys but not girls more likely to evaluate the vignettes negatively? Previous literature has suggested that boys are more likely than girls to be exposed to interparental conflict (Emery, 1982). Whereas that would be a potential explanation if we used parents' reports to determine the high- and low-conflict groups, in this study we used children's own reports of exposure. Gender analyses on children's mean scores of exposure reported in the high-conflict group indicated no differences for boys and girls. More likely, in this case, the difference between boys and girls is a function of either socialization or physiological processes. Boys may be given stronger messages than are girls about the inappropriateness of fighting, both verbally and physically, with the opposite sex. In addition, boys' own experiences in conflict with peers, siblings, and in the parent–child relationship may have sensitized them to anger and conflict. Overall, boys are more likely to be the target of aggression and to emit aggressive acts. Moreover, previous studies have indicated that boys are more likely than girls to be exposed to parent–child conflict (Jouriles & LeCompte, 1991; O'Keefe, 1994). Thus, boy's sensitization to conflict dimensions may result not only from exposure to marital conflict but also from their being the direct recipients of aggression in the parent–child relationship. As Gottman and Katz (1989) suggested, exposure to chronic conflict may condition certain physiological stress symptoms which then affect how the child deals with future conflict exposure. Hence, boys may be conditioned to be hypervigilant to cues of angry affect, have difficulty controlling the negative arousal that accompanies those cues, and thus evaluate the conflicts more harshly.

Similar explanations might be applied to the question of why high-conflict boys suggest direct intervention more than high-conflict girls. We find that, on average, close to 45% of the coping responses of high-conflict boys to the physical aggression tape involve direct intervention, which is twice as high as the rates of any other group. This percentage of direct involvement for high-conflict boys calls attention to this group of preadolescent boys not only as children exposed to conflict but also as participants in these intense conflicts. Preadolescent boys, who are increasingly aware of their own size and strength, may experience success in their attempts to disrupt their parents' arguments and may even see themselves as the mother's protector (Jaffe, Wolfe, & Wilson, 1990). That is, boys who live in high-conflict homes and who may even have intervened in interparental conflicts now may be likely to contemplate direct intervention strategies in response to the experimental task. To examine these explanations, additional studies are needed to determine how children's actual attempts to cope with conflict in the natural environment relate to their proposed coping strategies in a task such as this one.

This study adds to the literature that emotion-focused coping, in addition to problem-focused coping, is a common response to interparental anger. Emotion-focused coping accounts for a third of the children's coping strategies, although not varying by conflict dimension, conflict exposure, or gender. Emotion-focused coping strategies, which involve efforts to manage and regulate negative emotions, have been shown to develop primarily in late childhood and early adolescence (Compas, Banez, Malcarne, & Worsham, 1991). It has been suggested that the usefulness of either emotion-focused or problem-focused coping is a function of the fit between the stressor event and the coping strategy. Emotion-focused strategies tend to be a better fit for events appraised as uncontrollable, whereas problem-focused strategies are a better fit for controllable events (Forsythe & Compas, 1987). Specifically with respect to coping with interparental conflict, data indicate that children's beliefs regarding controlling their own arousal or distress through self-calming and avoidance, more than solving the problem, are associated with lower levels of problem behaviors (O'Brien, Margolin, & John, 1995; Rossman & Rosenberg, 1992).

There are several advantages to the experimental approach used here. To examine the effects of specific dimensions of conflict required the use of simulations of marital conflict to control the manipulation of the conflict dimensions (E. M. Cummings, 1995). The ATSS paradigm, designed specifically for the assessment of spontaneous cognitions (Davison et al., 1995), permitted the presentation of standardized marital conflict stimuli, ensuring that every child is exposed to identical marital conflicts. The ATSS assessment of cognitive appraisals and the post-ATSS questionnaire assessment of coping strategies allowed us to code the unedited words of the children, rather than have children respond to preselected categories. In addition, the use of children's self-reports about exposure to marital conflict, rather than parents' reports, avoids problems of overestimates or underestimates of the children's awareness of the marital conflict (Grych, Seid, & Fincham, 1992).

The paradigm of exposing children to audiotapes of simulated marital conflict raises issues regarding research ethics and design validity. Working from the premise that parents are the best judges of what would be inappropriately disturbing stimuli for their children, we asked them to read the transcripts of the vignettes as part of the consent procedures. No parent chose to exclude his or her child from this part of the study. Moreover, parents and children were told that the child could discontinue the procedures at any time and that payment to the family was not contingent on the child completing this aspect of the study. The audiotapes did elicit the anticipated reactions, but several parents and children spontaneously reported that these vignettes were less explicitly negative than what they sometimes see on television or in the movies. Although children were instructed to imagine that they overheard these discussions between their parents, this instruction was not intended to have children think that their parents actually were emitting these behaviors. Rather, this instruction was designed to create a situation similar to what a child experiences when he or she overhears a couple arguing, for example, at a friend's house, and then begins to think about what it would be like if that argument were occurring between his or her parents. In everyday life, children commonly observe situations and, using their imaginations, place themselves in those situations regardless of how likely they believe the situations to be. By using this instruction and by having audiotaped stimuli, instead of simply asking children what they would do if their parents behaved that way, we circumvented the situation of having children say that their parents never would exhibit those types of conflict behaviors.

Certain limitations of the research design must be noted. First, because of the restricted age range of the sample, our results do not permit us to make statements about developmental changes that might be operative in children's reactions to marital conflict across each of the domains assessed here. Particularly with regard to coping, such developmental changes may be of great significance (Compas et al., 1991; Rudolph et al., 1995). Second, this study did not include an assessment of children's outcomes, either concurrent or predictive. Thus, we do not know how the emotional, cognitive, and coping processes examined here relate to children's actual adjustment.

We designed this study to examine how specific dimensions of marital conflict affect multidimensional aspects of children's reactions. By isolating what we believe to be particularly salient dimensions of marital conflict, namely the use of negative voice tones, name-calling, threats to leave the marriage, and physical aggression, we found that these dimensions influence children's immediate reactions to conflict. Yet, in thinking about these data, we need to be mindful that the reactions themselves are not functional or dysfunctional. They are short-term reactions that are part of an ongoing process in children of learning to respond to stressors of the outside world. To better understand the role of the reactions examined here, we need to explore further how individual reactions lead to positive or negative consequences in the natural environment, and how these momentary reactions are shaped into long-term behavioral patterns.

REFERENCES

Bice Pitts, T. (1993). *Cognitive and psychophysiological differences in proactive and reactive aggressive boys.* Unpublished doctoral dissertation, University of Southern California, Los Angeles.

Carlson, B. E. (1990). Adolescent observers of marital violence. *Journal of Family Violence, 5,* 285–299.

Compas, B. E., Banez, G. A., Malcarne, V. L., & Worsham, N. (1991). Perceived control and coping with stress: A developmental perspective. *Journal of Social Issues, 47,* 23–34.

Crick, N. R., & Dodge, K. A. (1994). A review and reformulation of social information-processing mechanisms in children's social adjustment. *Psychological Bulletin, 115,* 74–101.

Crockenberg, S., & Forgays, D. K. (1996). The role of emotion in children's understanding and emotional reactions to marital conflict. *Merrill-Palmer Quarterly, 42,* 22–47.

Cummings, E. M. (1995). Usefulness of experiments for the study of the family. *Journal of Family Psychology, 9,* 175–185.

Cummings, E. M., Ballard, M., & El-Sheikh, M. (1991). Responses of children and adolescents to interadult anger as a function of gender, age, and mode of expression. *Merrill-Palmer Quarterly, 37,* 543–560.

Cummings, E. M., Ballard, M., El-Sheikh, M., & Lake, M. (1991). Resolution and children's responses to interadult anger. *Developmental Psychology, 27,* 462–470.

Cummings, E. M., Davies, P. T., & Simpson, K. (1994). Marital conflict, gender, and children's appraisals and coping efficacy as mediators of child adjustment. *Journal of Family Psychology, 8,* 141–149.

Cummings, E. M., Simpson, K. S., & Wilson, A. (1993). Children's responses to interadult anger as a function of information about resolution. *Developmental Psychology, 29,* 978–985.

Cummings, E. M., Vogel, D., Cummings, J. S., & El-Sheikh, M. (1989). Children's responses to different forms of expression of anger between adults. *Child Development, 60,* 1392–1404.

Cummings, J. S., Pellegrini, D. S., Notarius, C. I., & Cummings, E. M. (1989). Children's responses to angry adult behavior as a function of marital distress and history of interparent hostility. *Child Development, 60,* 1035–1043.

Davies, P. T., & Cummings, E. M. (1994). Marital conflict and child adjustment: An emotional security hypothesis. *Psychological Bulletin, 116,* 387–411.

Davies, P. T., Myers, R. L., & Cummings, E. M. (1996). Responses of children and adolescents to marital conflict scenarios as a function of the emotionality of conflict endings. *Merrill-Palmer Quarterly, 42,* 1–21.

Davison, G. C., Navarre, S. G., & Vogel, R. S. (1995). The articulated thoughts in simulated situations paradigm: A think-aloud approach to cognitive assessment. *Current Directions in Psychological Science, 4,* 29–33.

Davison, G. C., Robins, C., & Johnson, M. K. (1983). Articulated thoughts during simulated situations: A paradigm for studying cognition in emotion and behavior. *Cognitive Therapy and Research, 7,* 17–40.

Doumas, D., Margolin, G., & John, R. S. (1994). The intergenerational transmission of aggression across three generations. *Journal of Family Violence, 9,* 157–175.

El-Sheikh, M. (1994). Children's emotional and physiological responses to interadult angry behavior: The role of history of interparental hostility. *Journal of Abnormal Child Psychology, 22,* 661–678.

El-Sheikh, M., & Cheskes, J. (1995). Background verbal and physical anger: A comparison of children's responses to adult-adult and adult-child arguments. *Child Development, 66,* 446–458.

El-Sheikh, M., Cummings, E. M., & Goetsch, V. L. (1989). Coping with adults' angry behavior: Behavioral, physiological, and verbal responses in preschoolers. *Developmental Psychology, 25,* 490–498.

Emery, R. E. (1982). Interparental conflict and the children of discord and divorce. *Psychological Bulletin, 92,* 310–330.

Forsythe, C. J., & Compas, B. E. (1987). Interaction of cognitive appraisals of stressful events and coping: Testing the goodness of fit hypothesis. *Cognitive Therapy and Research, 11,* 473–485.

Gordis, E. B., Margolin, G., & John, R. S. (1997). Marital aggression, observed parental hostility, and child behavior during triadic family interaction. *Journal of Family Psychology, 11,* 76–89.

Gottman, J. M., & Katz, L. F. (1989). Effects of marital discord on young children's peer interaction and health. *Developmental Psychology, 25,* 373–381.

Gravetter, F. J., & Wallnau, L. B. (1988). *Statistics for the behavioral sciences* (2nd ed.). St. Paul, MN: West.

Grych, J. H., & Fincham, F. D. (1990). Marital conflict and children's adjustment: A cognitive–contextual framework. *Psychological Bulletin, 108,* 267–290.

Grych, J. H., & Fincham, F. D. (1993). Children's appraisals of marital conflict: initial investigations of the cognitive–contextual framework. *Child Development, 64,* 215–230.

Grych, J. H., Seid, M., & Fincham, F. D. (1992). Assessing marital conflict from the child's perspective: The Children's Perception of Interparental Conflict Scale. *Child Development, 63,* 558–572.

Hennessy, K. D., Rabideau, G. J., Cicchetti, D., & Cummings, E. M. (1994). Responses of physically abused and nonabused children to different forms of interadult anger. *Child Development, 65,* 815–828.

Hughes, H. M., & Barad, S. J. (1983). Psychological functioning of children in a battered women's shelter: A preliminary investigation. *American Journal of Orthopsychiatry, 53,* 525–531.

Jaffe, P. G., Wolfe, D. A., & Wilson, S. K. (1990). *Children of battered women.* Newbury Park, CA: Sage.

Jouriles, E. N., & LeCompte, S. H. (1991). Husbands' aggression toward wives and mothers' and fathers' aggression toward children: Moderating effects of child gender. *Journal of Consulting and Clinical Psychology, 59,* 190–192.

Katz, L. F., & Gottman, J. M. (1993). Patterns of marital conflict predict children's internalizing and externalizing behaviors. *Developmental Psychology, 29,* 940–950.

Lazarus, R. S., & Folkman, S. (1984). *Stress, appraisal, and coping.* New York: Springer.

Margolin, G. (1988). Marital conflict is not marital conflict is not marital conflict. In R. de V. Peters & R. McMahon (Eds.), *Social learning and systems approaches to marriage and the family* (pp. 193–216). New York: Brunner/Mazel.

Margolin, G. (in press). The effects of domestic violence on children. In P. Trickett & C. Schellengach (Eds.), *Violence against children in the family and community.* Washington, DC: American Psychological Association.

Margolin, G. (Executive Producer/Research Director), Rottman, B. (Writer/Director), & Jones, D. (Sound Engineer). (1992). *Quarreling couples: Five examples of conflict style* [Audiotapes]. (Available from Gayla Margolin, Department of Psychology, University of Southern California, Los Angeles, CA 90089-1061)

O'Brien, M., Balto, K., Erber, S., & Gee, C. (1995). College students' cognitions and emotional reactions to simulated marital and family conflict. *Cognitive Therapy and Research, 19,* 707–724.

O'Brien, M., Margolin, G., & John, R. S. (1995). The relationship between marital conflict, child involvement in marital conflict, and child adjustment. *Journal of Clinical Child Psychology, 24,* 346–361.

O'Brien, M., Margolin, G., John, R. S., & Krueger, L. (1991). Mothers' and sons' cognitive and emotional reactions to simulated marital and family conflict. *Journal of Consulting and Clinical Psychology, 59,* 692–703.

O'Keefe, M. (1994). Linking marital violence, mother–child/father–child aggression, and child behavior problems. *Journal of Family Violence, 9,* 63–78.

Rossman, B. B. R., & Rosenberg, M. S. (1992). Family stress and functioning in children: The moderating effects of children's beliefs about their control over parental conflict. *Child Psychology and Psychiatry, 33,* 699–715.

Rudolph, K. D., Dennig, M. D., & Weisz, J. R. (1995). Determinants and consequences of children's coping in the medical setting: Conceptualization, review, critique. *Psychological Bulletin, 118,* 328–357.

Shrout, P. E., & Fleiss, J. L. (1979). Intraclass correlations: Uses in assessing rater reliability. *Psychological Bulletin, 86,* 420–428.

Spaccarelli, S., Sandler, I. N., & Roosa, M. (1994). History of spouse violence against mother: Correlated risks and unique effects in child mental health. *Journal of Family Violence, 9,* 79–98.

Sternberg, K. J., Lamb, M. E., Greenbaum, C., Cicchetti, D., Dawud, S., Cortes, R. M., Krispin, O., & Lorey, F. (1993). Effects of domestic violence on children's behavior problems and depression. *Developmental Psychology, 29,* 44–52.

Straus, M. A. (1979). Measuring intrafamilial conflict and violence: The Conflict Tactics (CT) Scales. *Journal of Marriage and the Family, 41,* 75–88.

Wechsler, D. (1974). *Manual for the Wechsler Intelligence Scale for Children— Revised.* New York: Psychological Corporation.

Wolfe, D. A., Jaffe, P., Wilson, S. K., & Zak, L. (1985). Children of battered women: The relation of child behavior to family violence and maternal stress. *Journal of Consulting and Clinical Psychology, 53,* 657–665.

10

Parenting Behaviors and Beliefs of Battered Women

George W. Holden, Joshua D. Stein, Kathy L. Ritchie,
Susan D. Harris, and Ernest N. Jouriles

It is now well recognized that children living in families characterized by marital violence are victimized in a variety of ways. They are terrorized by hearing and seeing violent marital interactions. They are often subjected to a range of forms of psychological maltreatment, including being degraded, rejected, denied emotional responsiveness, and isolated from others (Geffner, 1996). Furthermore, they may be the recipients of physical abuse themselves: Studies are finding an overlap between marital violence and child physical abuse. Although determining the rate of co-occurrence of wife and child abuse is fraught with methodological problems, perhaps as many as 59% of children of battered women are also physically abused themselves (Appel, Angelelli, & Holden, 1997). In addition to these direct and indirect assaults on the children, maritally violent homes are often characterized by poverty, exposure to chronic community violence, high stress, and job and fam-

This work was supported by grants from the Hogg and H. F. Guggenheim Foundations. We thank Christina Cardenas, Kris Elliott, Leslie Gaines, Antonia Guerra, Sue Hall, Wendy London, Marcy Mayers, Jody Scott, Melanie Skipper, Shannon Sparks, Susan Tyroch, Deanna Watley, and Carrie Wilson for their help with data collection. A small portion of the data was previously reported in Holden and Ritchie (1991).

ily instability (Osofsky, 1995). In summary, children of battered women are exposed to a host of risks to healthy physical and psychological development.

Consequently, it comes as no surprise that research over the past 15 years has repeatedly documented that children of battered women are at high risk for developing behavior problems. One of the most remarkable findings from this body of research is the wide variability in child outcomes. Depending on the study, somewhere between 25% and 70% of children from maritally aggressive families manifest clinically significant behavior problems (McDonald & Jouriles, 1991). Some of the children from one sample may show extreme maladjustment in contrast to their peers, who share very similar family backgrounds but who appear to be largely unaffected by their exposure to the marital conflict and violence.

What accounts for this wide variation in responses? At least three types of variables are thought to be responsible: (a) the type and extent of the violence, (b) the child's characteristics, and (3) the parenting received by the child. Relatively speaking, most of the research addresses the effects of different types and extent of interspousal aggression (e.g., see Laumakis, Margolin, & John, 1998, this volume). For example, Jouriles, Norwood, McDonald, Vincent, and Mahoney (1996) have recently reported that not only physical marital violence is related to children's externalizing problems within maritally violent families. Other forms of marital aggression, such as verbal threats and hitting objects, were also found to be associated with children's problems after accounting for physical marital violence.

Some attention has also begun to be devoted to identifying those child characteristics that relate to severity of behavior problems. In particular, child gender (Jouriles & Norwood, 1995) and children's perceptions of control (Rossman, 1998, this volume; Rossman & Rosenberg, 1992) are two child variables that have been shown to affect children's behavioral adjustment. Other child characteristics that can protect children from some of the consequences of adverse environments, such as intelligence, school achievement, good peer relationships, or a close, positive relationship with an adult, have yet to be measured in the children of battered women.

To date, the third major variable believed to be associated with child behavior problems—parenting—has been largely neglected. Very few studies have included measures of parenting in violent homes or attempted to relate parenting variables to children's behavior problems. In this chapter, we intend to begin to remedy that deficiency by examining the parenting abilities of mothers who live in maritally violent homes.

PARENTING IN VIOLENT HOMES

In contrast to the paucity of attention that child rearing in maritally violent homes has received, considerable theoretical attention and empirical research have been devoted to the links between marital conflict (as opposed to violence), parenting, and children's functioning. This topic has been an active area of developmental and clinical psychological research for many years (Cummings, 1994; Emery, 1982).

Research has identified a variety of ways in which parenting, in the face of marital conflict, may be related to child adjustment. The simplest model but one that is incomplete at best is a direct effects explanation: Youth maladjustment results from modeling the conflict to which they are exposed (see Buehler, Krishnakumar, Anthony, Tittsworth, & Stone, 1994). That is, the aggressive, externalizing problems that some children exhibit derives from observing and then modeling their parents' interactions. Thus, some children may act aggressively toward peers because they have learned that aggression is a way to solve problems.

All the other explanations for the link between conflict and child behavior problems reflect some type of mediating factor. The most common explanation is that parental behavior is likely affected by marital conflict. For example, a negative marital interaction may "spill over" into child rearing and result in harsh and possibly aggressive behavior directed toward the child (Easterbrooks & Emde, 1988). In the case of battered women, a violent marital interaction may prime parents to interact in an aggressive manner with their children, because of such processes as emotional contagion or behavioral momentum.

Parental behavior may also be affected in more subtle ways, as a consequence of the parent's reaction to the conflict. Depression is a prime example of a variable that has been shown to affect parenting (Patterson, 1990). In some cases, the parent may not be consciously aware of the influence of the marital conflict on his or her parenting behavior. Another way in which marital conflict may affect parenting is intentional. According to the family systems concept of triangulation, an angry parent may choose to be uninvolved or engage in harsh parenting as a strategy for indirectly attacking or retaliating against the spouse.

There are several other possible links between family conflict, changes in parenting, and child adjustment. A variety of "third variable" explanations could also explain the link between marital conflict or violence and child adjustment. For example, a spouse may be socially inept in general, deficient in the necessary skills to avoid family conflict, or have personality characteristics (e.g., irresponsible, antisocial) that make him or her a poor spouse and incompetent parent. However, rather than try to assess the complex processes involved in the links between interspousal conflict, parenting, and child outcome, we limit our focus to an examination of the apparent effects of marital violence on parental behavior.

Investigators have suspected, and in some cases shown, that parenting is affected by interparent conflict in a variety of areas, including parental involvement, warmth and support, discipline and control, consistency, and monitoring (Buehler et al., 1994; Grych & Fincham, 1990). Among these variables, the most likely effect of marital violence is an increase in the amount of aggression directed toward the child. As far as maternal behavior is concerned, this aggression may develop in at least three ways. In the spill-over hypothesis, marital violence (with its accompanying negative emotion and possible physical aggression) may result in child-directed aggression. Alternatively, a social learning explanation might posit that mothers, who are victims of marital aggression, learn first-hand that aggression can be used to get one's way and therefore use it with their children. A third mechanism that could account for the relation between marital violence and mothers' child-directed aggression is stress. Stressed-out parents are more likely to engage in punitive, excessively harsh, and negative child-rearing behavior (Jaffe, Wolfe, & Wilson, 1990; Jouriles, Barling, & O'Leary, 1987; McLoyd, 1990).

Various researchers (e.g., Jaffe et al., 1990; Walker, 1979) have argued that in addition to becoming more aggressive, parenting is likely to become disrupted and diminished as a consequence of living in a violent relationship. Indeed, it is difficult to imagine that mothering is not affected in some way by living in such a hostile environment. Violence between parents is likely to be distracting at the very least; more likely it is consuming and debilitating. Attention and energy must be devoted to monitoring and assessing the partner's mood and propensity for violence, engaging in frequent verbal combat, and defending oneself and one's children against verbal and physical attacks. These mothers undoubtedly fear for their own physical safety. It is suspected that living in such a context makes women preoccupied with their own needs and not mindful of their children's needs, although there are some conflicting reports (e.g., Hilton, 1992). For one or all of these reasons, it is commonly thought that these mothers have difficulty being warm, emotionally available, consistent, and responsive to their children. Consequently, mothers who experience marital violence are likely to exhibit a deterioration in the quality of their parenting.

To date, the research available concerning child rearing in violent homes is extremely limited. Investigations have been almost exclusively focused on maternal behavior, with the exception of occasional reports by mothers or children about the batterers' child-rearing behavior. Most of the studies have focused on the hypothesis that batterers and mothers are more aggressive toward their children. For example, the most common information about violent men as fathers is that they are often violent toward their children. National survey data indicate that both fathers and mothers in families marked by recent spousal violence are two to five times more likely to use physical aggression with their children than parents in families not characterized by such violence (Straus & Gelles, 1990; Straus, Gelles, & Steinmetz, 1980). Moreover, the frequency and severity of violence toward women correlates positively with the frequency and severity of both mothers' and fathers' physical aggression toward children, particularly sons (Jouriles et al., 1987; Jouriles & LeCompte, 1991; Jouriles & Norwood, 1995; Straus et al., 1980). Thus, children in families characterized by frequent and severe violence toward women are at greater risk for experiencing both maternal and paternal physical aggression than children in nonmaritally violent families.

Little is known about the nature of fathering in violent homes. Most of the available information has been limited exclusively to comparing fathers' and mothers' aggression toward children. For example, when comparing the rates and severity of aggression toward children, it is typically found that batterers are more violent than the mothers. Jouriles and Norwood (1995) discovered that for the most part, both mothers and their children reported that fathers were more aggressive toward their children than mothers. Similarly, McCloskey, Figueredo, and Koss (1995) also used both mother and child reports to determine that children experience more aggression and abuse from fathers than from mothers. However, there is at least one conflicting report: O'Keefe (1994a) found that mothers reported that they had engaged in approximately as much aggression toward the children as the women reported their partners did.

Beyond child-directed aggression, little is known about parental behavior. One exception to that dearth of information comes from Holden and Ritchie (1991), who asked mothers to report on various types of paternal behavior. According to the mothers, violent fathers were significantly less involved with their children, less affectionate, and less likely to reason with their children than a group of comparison fathers (Holden & Ritchie, 1991). Interestingly, battered women did not uniformly condemn the quality of their partners' fathering. Almost 40% of the battered women reported that they thought their partners were at least "average" fathers. Whether at least some of the violent men are indeed adequate fathers remains an unanswered question until more data and convergent sources of information are collected.

Compared to the virtual absence of data on violent fathers, some information is available about maternal behavior in maritally violent homes. Most of these assessments have been limited to determining levels of aggression and violence directed toward their children. Using Straus's (1979) Conflict Tactics Scale (CTS), studies do find that battered women are aggressive and even violent with their children. For example, in one study of 185 mothers and their children, 44% of mothers reported that they hit their children with an object sometime in the past year (O'Keefe, 1994b). That study, however, did not include a comparison group. In a study that did include a nonviolent comparison group, abused and comparison mothers had similar levels of mother-to-child aggression (e.g., slapped, hit with object), according to the children's reports (McCloskey et al., 1995). Similarly, Hershorn and Rosenbaum (1985) found no difference in the degree of child-directed punitiveness between groups of maritally abused mothers, maritally discordant but not abused mothers, and satisfactorily married women.

One variable that appears to influence the extent of maternal aggression is child gender. Several reports indicate that boys are more likely to be the recipients of maternal aggression than girls within maritally violent families (Jouriles & LeCompte, 1991; Jouriles & Norwood, 1995). The reasons boys are more at risk is not yet fully understood. It could be that the boys remind their mothers of the fathers, that boys are more likely to identify with fathers, that boys intervene in marital conflict more frequently than girls and thus are more likely to be caught in the cross-fire, or that boys engage in higher rates of externalizing problems and misbehavior and thus, in the parents' eyes, warrant more physical punishment (see Jouriles & Norwood, 1995).

Very few other parenting variables have received any attention. We were able to locate only three published studies that reported information concerning maternal behavior beyond reports of mother-to-child aggression (Holden & Ritchie, 1991; McCloskey et al., 1995; O'Keefe, 1994a). However, most of those studies included only two or three maternal self-report variables, and in two of the studies, interpretation of those particular results is compromised. O'Keefe (1994a) assessed the quality of mother–child relationships as well as family variables such as family cohesion and adaptability but did not include a comparison group. In the other study, McCloskey and her colleagues (1995) had a comparison group but did not directly report their findings about the incidence of authoritarian and authoritative patterns of parenting.

To date, Holden and Ritchie (1991) assessed the greatest number of mothering variables. They found no difference between battered and comparison women in reported use of reasoning, physical affection, or physical punishment or on a composite of various negative child-rearing behaviors (e.g., power assertion). Differences were found in the amount of parenting stress experienced, inconsistency in child rearing, and on several observational variables (e.g., amount of conflict, attention directed toward child).

The amount of stress experienced appears to be a particularly important variable with regard to children's behavior problems. Wolfe, Jaffe, Wilson, and Zak (1985) found that maternal stress, as assessed by a negative life events survey and a questionnaire concerning the mothers' emotional and physical health, was the single most important predictor of child behavior problems. It accounted for 19% of the variance of scores on the Child Behavior Checklist (CBCL; Achenbach & Edelbrock, 1981). The predictive ability of stress is increased further when parenting stress is measured. Holden and Ritchie (1991) found that parenting stress (Abidin, 1986) predicted child behavior problems with an adjusted R^2 of .33. Given these high rates of stress and the link to child behavior problems, one untested explanation for the high rates of aggressive child-rearing behavior is that it is associated with maternal stress. Mothers may well be losing control and aggressing toward their children in response to the intense stress they are experiencing. Alternatively, maternal aggression may be used because of its dramatic ability to stop the ongoing child misbehavior in the short term. Perhaps this practice is adopted by mothers because it can help reduce their child-induced stress.

In summary, little research attention has been devoted to assessing the nature of parenting in maritally violent homes. Currently there is inadequate evidence to evaluate either of the two major hypotheses concerning how parenting may be directly affected by marital violence (increased aggression, diminished parenting). Although there is more evidence about the hypothesis of increased aggression, some of the reports are conflicting. To date, there has not been enough empirical evidence to evaluate the diminished mothering hypothesis.

In this chapter, we report results from three studies on the parenting of young children of battered women. Specifically, we examine parenting behavior, reported parenting behavior, behavioral intentions, and child-rearing beliefs to gain a better understanding of how marital violence may affect parenting. The first study was intended to broaden the empirical basis of our knowledge of the parenting of battered women. The second study expanded on the results of the first study in several ways. The final study was designed to address the question of the stability and change in battered women's parenting behavior and beliefs.

A STUDY OF BATTERED WOMEN'S CHILD-REARING BEHAVIORS AND BELIEFS

Our primary goal was to test two hypotheses about how mothering is affected by a maritally abusive relationship. First, we sought to evaluate whether mothers would exhibit more aggressive parenting as expressed by more aggressive behavior toward their children and more physical punishment. We anticipated that battered women would report more aggressive behavior toward their children than the comparison mothers. That aggression, we predicted, would be related to the mothers' stress level. Based on the previous work cited above, we also expected sons would receive more aggressive behavior from their mothers than daughters. The final hypothesis concerned diminished parenting. We expected mothers in violent relationships to engage in less warmth, emotional availability, and consistency than other mothers.

Comprehensive answers to these questions actually require a multiyear longitudinal design to track the developmental change in maternal behavior before and after her partner engages in violence. Because of considerations of time and expense, we opted to approximate that developmental process by comparing groups of battered mothers with community mothers sharing similar background characteristics except for the marital violence. We assumed that both groups of women were similar prior to becoming involved with their partners.

Another decision we made affecting the methodology was to rely mostly on verbal reports for assessing maternal behavior. To minimize the likelihood of reporting bias caused by social desirability, however, we used several methodological precautions. First, where possible, we designed questions and worded items so the desirable answer was not obvious. One way we did that was to ask questions about the frequency with which mothers engaged in various behaviors (e.g., "How often do you talk to someone about your child?"). Because it is unlikely that mothers know what is the appropriate or acceptable frequency of engaging in various child-rearing behaviors, as determined by community standards, mothers must base their responses on their own experience. Questions were also phrased to make a range of responses sound normative (e.g., "Some mothers hug and hold their children a lot. Other mothers don't. How often do you hug your child?"). To minimize the likelihood of eliciting socially desirable responses, a problem particularly common with global attitudes, we framed questions around specific, commonly occurring situations. Questions were posed about the mothers' most likely response to these situations. For example, mothers were asked how they would react when their child accidentally broke a glass while trying to help clean up.

Method

Sample

Thirty-seven battered women residing at a women's shelter and 37 comparison mothers from nonviolent marital relationships formed the sample. The comparison mothers were recruited from the community and matched on child's age, child's gender, race, and maternal and paternal education. (More details about the recruiting procedures and method can be found in Holden & Ritchie, 1991.) The mothers had at least one target child who was 2 to 8 years old. Seventeen of the 37 children from the shelter were girls; so were 18 of the 37 comparison children. Mothers were mostly Caucasian (57%) or Hispanic (35%); the average age was 30 years. The women generally were high school graduates, and 90% reported a family income of less than $30,000 per year.

Instruments and Procedure

Most parenting variables were assessed by a computer program, Computer-Presented Social Situations (CPSS; Holden, 1988), designed for this study. The CPSS involves simulating a day in their life by presenting a set of vignettes, chronologically arranged, about common family situations or child-rearing problems in order to collect maternal reports of behavior in the home. The CPSS included 107 questions concerning the mothers' child-rearing practices, their partners' parenting, their children's behavior, and common activities they engaged in (e.g., frequency of going out with children, children's bedtime routines). The key child-rearing variables assessed included how their days were structured, frequency of maternal affection, use of physical punishment, and other forms of discipline used (e.g., power-assertive techniques). Mothers also reported on their partners' behavior, including frequency of anger, aggression, affection, and involvement in child rearing. Fifty-two percent of the questions were answered on multiple-choice format, and the rest were responded to on 7-point Likert-type scales.

The computer-presented vignettes had several advantages over paper-and-pencil measures. First, the interactive nature of the computer program makes the task more engaging than filling out a questionnaire. Second, the text was personalized with the names of family members, and mothers could type in idiosyncratic responses if the available options did not correspond to their view. All but four mothers typed in their own response at least once ($M = 3$ responses to different items, range = 0 to 25), which were subsequently coded. This computer-based interview method has been found to provide a reasonably valid proxy for observed child-rearing behavior. For example, the agreement between observed parenting behavior in the supermarket and maternal responses to the same child-rearing situations assessed on a CPSS program 1 week later averaged 79% (see Holden, Ritchie, & Coleman, 1992).

The mothers also filled out several other questionnaires. Surveys related to parenting included the CTS and the 120-item Parenting Stress Index (PSI; Abidin, 1986). The CTS subscale of interest here was the 9-item Mother-to-Child Physical Violence scale (including such items as throw something at your child, push child, kick, & hit), which had an alpha of .56. The PSI had an alpha of .90 in this sample. Mothers also filled out the CBCL (Achenbach & Edelbrock, 1981) to provide an index of their children's behavior problems.

In addition to the computer procedure and questionnaires, mothers and children were observed interacting together. Systematic observations, lasting 10 minutes, involved the mother–child dyads in structured block play and then in free play. The observations were recorded on audiotape in addition to paper-and-pencil behavioral records. The five maternal variables observed included instructions, commands, asks child's opinion, initiates interaction, and attends. In addition, two interactional variables were coded: number of conflicts and times engaged in joint play. Mean percentage agreement, established on 15% of the observations, was .87 (κ = .84).

Battered women came from a shelter and comparison mothers responded to advertisements in local publications. Once recruited, battered women and their children participated in a vacant room at the shelter. Comparison mothers participated in their homes. None of the comparison women reported on the CTS that they had experienced any marital violence over the past year. All mothers received $15 for their participation, and the children received a toy.

Results

Home Environment

What is the nature of the child-rearing context for these children? Mothers reported that both they and their children were frequent targets of angry interchanges with their partners. Eighty-nine percent of mothers in violent marriages revealed that they were involved in marital arguments at least every few days. In contrast, only 16% of the nonviolent couples reported such a high rate of conflict, $\chi^2(1, N = 74)$ = 39.52, $p < .001$. The children were not oblivious to interparent conflict: According to the battered women, 78% of the children were aware of marital arguments "most" of the time. Only about 5% of the children were spared from actually observing the abusive incidents.

Paternal irritability was not just directed at mothers; most violent fathers became angry with their children every few days, according to the mothers. This rate is significantly higher than the rate of the comparison fathers who reportedly became angry less than once a week, $t(54) = 6.22$, $p < .01$.

How Is Mothering Affected by Living With a Violent Man?

Given this acrimonious climate, how is mothering affected? Several measures of aggressive child rearing are examined, followed by an examination of the diminished parenting hypothesis.

Mother-to-child aggression. The numbers of mothers who engaged in aggression toward their children differed. Almost all (92%) of the battered women reported they did engage in some aggression toward their children (one or more of the eight acts of physical aggression on the CTS), in contrast to 50% of the comparison women, $\chi^2(1, N = 74) = 16.56$, $p < .001$. Of the battered women who engaged in child-directed aggression, the mean CTS subscale score was 5.1 ($SD = 3.9$, range = 1 to 17), in contrast to the comparison mothers' mean of 5.6 ($SD = 3.5$, range = 1 to 15). The group differences were not significant as tested by a t test.

A second index of maternal aggression toward their children concerned the amount of corporal punishment. No significant group differences were found on reports of rates of spanking ($M_b = 3.9$, $M_c = 3.4$, *ns*) or use of other power assertive disciplinary techniques ($M_b = 13.8$, $M_c = 11.0$, *ns*). The data were further examined to test whether boys were the recipients of more aggression than girls. In contrast to expectations, no significant differences by gender of child were found on any of the physical aggression variables.

Battered women did report experiencing significantly more parenting stress than women in the comparison sample, $M_b = 164$, $M_c = 146$, $F(1, 65) = 10.68$, $p < .001$. For battered women, their parenting stress levels were at the 90th percentile in contrast to the comparison mothers' 55th percentile (see Abidin, 1986). Correlations between stress and mother-to-child violence supported the proposed link between stress and aggression toward children, with a positive but nonsignificant association between parenting stress and violence toward children, $r(26)$ = .27, $p < .20$.

Part of the source of the stress that mothers experienced was likely a result of the child's aggressive and noncompliant behavior. Battered women reported that their children hit them more frequently than the comparison sample reported, $F(1, 66) = 4.39$, $p < .05$.

Diminished mothering. The second major hypothesis was that battered women would exhibit a deterioration in their parenting, presumably as a consequence of living with a violent partner. Surprisingly, our data provide almost no support for that proposition. On the variable maternal affection, there was no significant group difference ($M_b = 6.8$, $M_c = 6.6$, *ns*).

Signs of diminished parenting were also searched for in the mothers' reports of the structure they provide for their children in their daily living. On a range of such questions, the results were similar: There was no evidence that battered women provided any less structure for or attention to their children than did comparison mothers on a variety of single questions (e.g., frequency of going out). In some cases, the mothers in violent marriages actually reported more structure. For example, a majority of battered women (74%) reported that they had a standard weekday bedtime for their children (with a modal time of 9:00 p.m.), in contrast to only 57% of the comparison women. This difference, however, did not differentiate the groups, $\chi^2(1, N = 74) = 2.13$, $p = .14$.

One potentially important aspect of mothering in a violent home that could reflect either diminished or supportive parenting was how the mothers interpreted or explained the violent incidents to their children. To assess that, we posed the open-ended question: "What do you say to your child after he/she becomes aware of a violent conflict?" Mothers' typed-in answers showed marked differences in how they explained a violent incident to their children. The two most common responses, each provided by about 20% of the mothers, was to tell their children that their father was angry with the mother and not the child or to explain to their children that their father was sick and needed help. Another 17% of the mothers indicated that after a violent incident they would reassure their children that they were okay. In contrast to those explanations, some mothers reported that they would offer other types of comments. These included threats ("You better behave before he hits you too") and excuses for the fathers' violent behavior ("It's not his fault"). This question was only a single item but it indicates that there are some potentially important differences in how mothers explain the violence to their children and hence, how the mothers assist or compromise their children's understanding of the violence.

One significant difference that did emerge concerned the amount of inconsistency in parenting. Battered women, compared with the matched mothers, indicated on the CPSS that they would modify their parenting behavior more in terms of changing their child-rearing behavior in the presence of their partner (M_b = 2.6, M_c = 2.0), $F(1, 65)$ = 5.49, $p < .05$. For example, some mothers reported they would become more strict with their children, although other mothers indicated they would be more permissive. The mothers reported that this inconsistency in child rearing was intended to minimize the likelihood that the fathers become irritable.

Observational data. Observations of the mothers interacting with their children provided converging support that the battered women did not differ dramatically from the comparison mothers. However, some subtle differences in the quality of interactions were detected. Two out of seven variables assessed showed significant group differences. Battered women attended less to their children (M_b = .14, M_c = .23), $F(1, 54)$ = 8.17, $p < .01$, and experienced more conflicts with their children than the comparison group (M_b = .08, M_c = .03), $F(1, 54)$ = 8.47, $p < .01$.

Mothers' Perceptions of Children's Behavior Problems

As has been repeatedly found in prior studies, battered women reported more behavior problems in their children than the comparison women. A multivariate analysis of variance (MANOVA) computed on the Externalizing and Internalizing scores of the CBCL indicated a significant group difference, $F(2, 58)$ = 3.27, $p < .05$. Follow-up analyses of variance (ANOVAs) indicated a significant group difference on Internalizing scores (M_b = 60.4, M_c = 54.3), $F(1, 56)$ = 6.45, p < .02, but not Externalizing scores (M_b = 57.8, M_c = 53.9).

Summary

This study resulted in several predicted as well as unexpected results. First, almost all of the battered women reported in engaging in violence toward their children, in contrast to just half of the comparison mothers. However, the levels of mother-to-child aggression for those mothers who did engage in it did not differ between groups. No evidence was found indicating that boys were more likely to be recipients of that aggression. However, as expected, battered women did report high levels of parenting stress, and stress was positively related (although not significantly) with mother-to-child aggression.

The major surprise of the study was that essentially no evidence of diminished parenting was found in the battered women, as compared to the matched community mothers. On a series of questions, the battered women as a group reported similar parenting practices as the community women. However, that finding was mostly based on single self-report items. A more comprehensive assessment of the diminished parenting hypothesis was clearly warranted before any tentative conclusions could be drawn. That some subtle interactional differences were found suggests that effects on parenting may be subtle and may not be readily accessible by maternal reports.

REPLICATION AND STUDY OF ETHNIC GROUP DIFFERENCES

A second study was conducted with two goals. First, it was designed to replicate and extend the central findings of the first study. Specifically, a second sample of mothers was sought to assess whether battered women were more likely to engage in aggressive behavior toward their children than comparison mothers. In addition, given the lack of differences concerning diminished parenting in the first study, we planned to conduct a more rigorous test of that hypothesis (and specifically of maternal warmth). In addition, mothers' emotional availability and use of positive reinforcement were suspected to be key variables that would reveal diminished parenting (if any existed).

A second goal was to test for ethnic or racial group differences in battered women. As has been pointed out in a review by Fantuzzo and Lindquist (1989), there is a dearth of knowledge about the cultural effects of race and ethnicity in these families. It is possible that racial or ethnic variation may affect the parenting variables or child outcomes. For example, O'Keefe (1994b) found that European American children had higher Externalizing scores than African American children. Thus, part of the intent of this study was to test for cultural variation. Toward that end, mothers and their children from European American, African American, and Mexican American groups (subsequently labeled as *ethnic groups* for the sake of clarity) were included. Given that we were unable to locate any information regarding how family violence may differentially affect the parenting of mothers from different backgrounds, we made no specific predictions.

Method

Participants included 30 battered women who were residing at a women's shelter and 28 comparison mothers from nonviolent families. These mothers were matched on the same characteristics as the first sample, although this sample was collected several years later. These mothers, who averaged 33 years of age, had at least one child between the ages of 3 and 7 years ($M = 61$ months, $SD = 9.8$ months). Thirteen of the children from the shelter and 12 of the comparison group were girls. In most cases the mothers were similar to the mothers in the first study, with the exception that this sample was tri-ethnic: 46% were European American ($n = 27$), 28% were Mexican Americans ($n = 16$), and 26% were African American ($n = 15$). There were no significant differences between the three groups on any background variables except for maternal education, $F(2, 47) = 5.52$, $p < .01$. The European American ($M = 11.9$) and African American ($M = 13.3$) mothers had significantly more years in school than the Mexican American mothers ($M = 10.9$). Almost all (96%) of the battered women and 86% of the community sample reported annual family incomes of less than \$30,000; no significant differences were found between the two groups on any background variable except the presence of marital violence.

A new CPSS was created for this study. It contained 63 questions designed to replicate and extend some of the findings from the first sample. All of the questions were responded to on 7-point Likert-type response scales. To measure aggression and diminished parenting more systematically, we created six subscales to assess (a) use of positive reinforcement with their children (seven items; $\alpha = .60$); (b) showing warmth (seven items such as frequency of hugging, kissing, saying "I love you"; $\alpha = .73$); (c) emotional availability (six items; $\alpha = .53$); (d) limit setting (eight items; $\alpha = .66$); (e) use of physical punishment (six items; $\alpha = .84$); and (f) beliefs in positive parenting (six items concerning importance of showing warmth to child, use of reasoning, use of rules and limits, allowing child to make some decisions by himself or herself, consistent discipline, and importance of a good marriage for a child's development; $\alpha = .43$). Because of the low alpha on the Beliefs subscale, each of the five questions was analyzed individually. Scales were also included to assess mothers' perceptions of the frequency of child misbehavior (9 items; $\alpha = .74$) and inconsistency in parenting (9 items) as measured by the amount of change the mother reports when the father is present as opposed to when the mother is alone. However, the internal consistency of the scale was very low ($\alpha = .34$), so those items were also analyzed individually.

As in the first study, the CTS was used to assess mother-to-child physical violence. However, that subscale had low internal consistency with this sample ($\alpha = .39$), so it should be evaluated with caution. The mothers also reported on their level of stress using the short form of the PSI (Abidin, 1991). This 36-item instrument had a high level of internal consistency ($\alpha = .92$) in this sample. The mothers also provided information about their levels of social support on the Inventory of Parents' Experiences (Crnic, Greenberg, Ragozin, Robinson, & Basham, 1983). This is a 26-item survey to assess sources of and satisfaction with social support from the community, friendships, and extended family. Twelve of the items formed a satisfaction scale and had an acceptable level of reliability ($\alpha = .83$). Finally, as in the first study, mothers filled out the CBCL (Achenbach & Edelbrock, 1981) to provide an index of their children's behavior problems.

Mothers and children were observed for 15 minutes in a room equipped with both in-bound but dull objects (a dish, a block) and tempting but off-bound objects (a typewriter, a robot toy) in a procedure previously developed (see Holden & West, 1989). The mothers were instructed to keep their children from playing with the off-bound objects. Maternal variables assessed, using laptop computers and the software program OBSERVE (Deni, 1992), included positive behaviors (acknowledging, redirecting, verbalizations, proactive managing, providing affectionate contact) and one negative behavior (prohibiting). Interrater reliability on the presence or absence of each behavior, assessed on 17% of the sample, averaged 93% (range = 84% to 100%).

Results

Replication

As in the first study, battered women reported that their children heard—or overhead—a great deal of the marital arguments. On average, children from violent homes heard two to six marital arguments per week. Forty percent of the mothers from violent homes indicated that their children overheard marital arguments more than once a day. In contrast, community mothers reported their children overheard an average of one to three arguments a month. The two groups differed significantly on this variable, $t(56) = 6.97$, $p < .001$.

Mother-to-child aggression. Ninety percent of the battered women in this study indicated that they did indeed use physical aggression with their children (as did battered women in the previous study). However, all but two of the comparison mothers also reported some child-directed physical aggression. The mean amount of aggression for the battered women who reported some aggression was 6.5 ($SD = 3.7$, range = 3 to 17), but this mean did not significantly differ from that of the comparison women ($M = 5.1$, $SD = 2.0$, range = 2 to 12).

Unlike the first study, an effect of child gender was found, $F(1, 54) = 4.26$, $p < .05$. Both battered women and comparison mothers were more likely to use physical aggression with their sons ($M = 6.4$, $SD = 4.1$, range $= 0$ to 16) rather than with their daughters ($M = 4.5$, $SD = 2.5$, range $= 0$ to 12).

No significant group difference was found on the spank subscale in the CPSS ($M_b = 20.4$, $M_c = 22.0$), $t(54) = .25$, ns. Part of the reason for that was undoubtedly the divergent orientations toward the use of corporal punishment. This variability was most evident in the mothers' response to a question about how likely they would be to spank their children after the child engaged in one particular type of misbehavior. About one-third (37%) of the mothers from violent homes reported "quite likely" or "very likely," in contrast to another third of the mothers who took the opposite stance and replied "quite unlikely" or "very unlikely."

Replicating results from the first study, battered women reported experiencing high levels of parenting stress. Although not quite attaining the conventional level of significance, the battered women reported more stress than the comparison mothers ($M_b = 85.5$, $M_c = 75.5$), $F(1, 54) = 3.52$, $p < .07$. The parenting stress levels were at the 85th percentile for the battered women and the 65th percentile for the comparison mothers (Abidin, 1991). These stress scores were significantly correlated with reports of aggression toward children, $r(58) = .32$, $p < .02$. With regard to social support, it was not surprising to find that the battered women reported lower levels of social support than the comparison women ($M_b = 28.2$, $M_c = 36.9$), $F(1, 52) = 27.2$, $p < .001$.

Diminished mothering. The diminished mothering hypothesis was more rigorously evaluated in this study than the prior one by assessing group differences on the four CPSS subscales. No group differences were found on three out of the four subscales (Warmth, Emotional Availability, Positive Reinforcement), $F(3, 53) = 1.15$, $p = .33$. For example, maternal warmth was partially assessed by five questions on the CPSS concerning the frequency with which they engaged in such behaviors as hugging, kissing, and laughing with the child. Both groups reported similar frequencies: The mean rate of hugging their children for both groups was 6.1 (range $= 3$ to 7), translating to 3 to 4 times a day for both groups. The only statistically significant group difference occurred on the limit setting subscale, $F(1, 54) = 5.58, p < .05$. Mothers in violent homes were less likely to set limits on a child's behavior than were the comparison mothers ($M = 33.5$ vs. $M = 37.8$), $F(1, 54) = 4.68$, $p < .05$. For example, mothers from violent homes reported that they were less likely to restrict TV viewing or stop the child from making a mess during a meal. The means for the composite variables are provided in Table 1.

Because emotional availability is a parenting commodity that is thought to suffer in violent homes, a range of questions was posed about it in the second CPSS program. Both groups of mothers shared the belief that it was very important to be available to the child when the child was upset ($M_b = 6.7$, $M_c = 6.3$). However, battered women recognized that they were not able to be emotionally available all the time. In response to the question "How often does an argument with your partner upset you so much that you have difficulty comforting your child?", battered women reported a frequency of two to three times a month in comparison to the other mothers' report of "almost never" ($M_b = 3.1$, $M_c = 1.5$), $t(56) = 4.20, p < .001$. The contrast between the battered women's beliefs about the importance of emotional availability and their reported frequency of being unavailable is depicted in Figure 1.

This occasional inability to render comfort is probably only a small portion of the story with respect to children's adjustment. What also might be an important maternal mediating variable, along with warmth, is the ways in which mothers help their children understand and think about the marital violence. As discussed above, mothers report that almost all of their children were aware of most of the violent marital conflict. In the battered women group, there was a nonsignificant but positive association between parenting stress and violence toward children, $r(28) = .33, p < .08$.

Whether battered women were more inconsistent in their parenting was examined with the nine individual questions. In contrast to the first study, no overall group effect was found for the items, $F(8, 49) = 1.71, p < .10$. Consequently we inferred that if there is an increased likelihood for abused mothers to modify their behavior in the presence

Table 1

Comparison Between Mothers in Violent Homes and the Community Group in the Replication Study

Parenting variable	Battered women		Community		F	p
	M	SD	M	SD		
Discipline and aggression						
Limit setting	3.5	7.4	37.8	6.2	5.58	<.02
Physical punishment	0.4	8.3	22.0	9.2	.65	ns
CTS spank–slap item	4.0	1.9	4.2	1.7	.34	ns
Diminished parenting						
Warmth and affection	40.8	5.6	40.8	5.7	.48	ns
Emotional availability	34.1	4.4	40.8	3.8	.59	ns
Positive reinforcement	38.5	5.9	36.3	6.6	1.75	ns
Beliefs in positive parenting						
Importance of						
being affectionate	6.8	0.4	7.0	0.2	2.71	<.10
reasoning	6.5	0.6	6.7	0.7	1.15	ns
a good marriage	6.5	1.0	6.7	0.6	.62	ns
using rules and setting limits	6.6	0.9	6.8	1.9	1.92	ns
consistent discipline	6.1	1.3	6.2	1.6	.04	ns
allowing child to make some decisions	5.9	1.0	6.0	1.3	.30	ns

Note. CTS = Conflict Tactics Scale.

of their partner, such change is not systematic. Rather, the modifications probably reflect intrafamily idiosyncratic considerations such that certain mothers change some behaviors, but the changes are not uniform across battered mothers.

The data regarding maternal beliefs provided evidence at the atti-

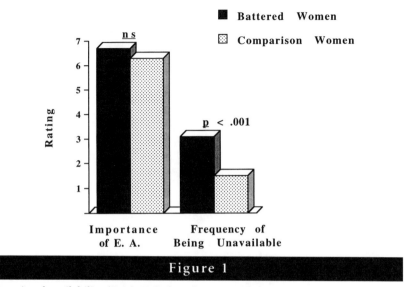

Figure 1

Emotional availability (E.A.): Beliefs and reported behavior.

tudinal level that the two groups of mothers did not differ greatly. In fact, there were no significant differences on any of the six belief measures that concerned the importance of such child-rearing practices as being affectionate, using reasoning, and letting the child make some decisions for himself or herself. The means can be found in Table 1.

Observation data. As in the first study, the observational data showed little difference between the battered and comparison mothers. Out of the five maternal variables examined (acknowledging, redirecting, proactive limit setting, providing affectionate contact, and prohibiting), only one group difference was significant. Battered women engaged in less proactive limit setting than the comparison group (M_b = 1.3, M_c = 1.9), $F(1, 53) = 4.67$, $p < .05$. This result reflects a modest difference indicating that battered mothers were somewhat less likely to make suggestions concerning activities their children could engage in with the in-bound objects.

Mothers' Perceptions of Children's Behavior Problems

With regard to mothers' perceptions of their children's behavior problems, there was an overall trend for group differences as assessed by a

MANOVA, $F(2, 55) = 2.81$, $p < .07$. ANOVAs computed on the two subscales revealed a significant group difference for Externalizing scores ($M_b = 58.6$, $M_c = 53.6$), $F(1, 56) = 5.67$, $p < .02$, and a trend for differences on Internalizing scores ($M_b = 60.9$, $M_c = 54.7$), $F(1, 56) = 3.63$, $p < .06$. Battered women also reported that their children engaged in significantly more misbehavior and were less compliant than the comparison children, as assessed by the CPSS subscale ($M_b = 43.4$, $M_c = 37.1$), $F(1, 56) = 7.42$, $p < .01$. Scores on the misbehavior subscale correlated significantly with Externalizing problem scores on the CBCL, $r(58) = .41$, $p < .001$.

Ethnic Group Differences

The second purpose of this study was to determine whether ethnicity had any systematic effect on the quality of parenting. This proposition was examined with a series of 2 (Group) × 3 (Ethnicity) MANOVAs or ANOVAs. Only one significant effect attributable to ethnicity was found. For example, there were no significant ethnic group effects for mother-to-child aggression on either the CTS subscale or the spank subscale on the CPSS. In the case of diminished parenting hypotheses, a Group × Ethnicity interaction was found on the four CPSS subscales, $F(8, 92) = 2.48$, $p < .05$. Follow-up ANOVAs indicated the only significant interaction occurred on the emotional availability subscale, $F(2, 51) = 9.11$, $p < .001$. Examination of the means indicated that the abused Mexican American mothers reported lower emotional availability scores ($M = 28.7$) than the other two groups of battered women or the comparison mothers ($Ms = 32.4$ to 36.2). No main effects for ethnicity were found, nor were there any significant ethnic group differences on the observational data or the CBCL data.

Discussion of the Two Studies

The data from these studies indicate that women who live with violent partners appear to be remarkably similar to comparison women on a variety of child-rearing indices. Although they live with frequent violence, the battered women in these two studies revealed few differences in parenting behavior compared with mothers from nonviolent marital relationships. These data also did not reveal that homes where marital violence occurred were cold or chaotic environments for the child, although they are indeed often hostile. Instead, using the comparison mothers as a baseline, battered women appear to be functioning rather normally in their parenting role. Across the two samples, on more than 10 child-rearing indices, battered women did not significantly differ from comparison mothers. On such variables as providing structure, showing warmth, being emotionally available, and positively reinforcing their children, mothers in maritally violent homes and mothers in the comparison homes reportedly engaged in very similar child-rearing behavior. This same null result has recently been reported with a sample of battered and comparison mothers from St. Louis, Missouri (Chew, 1996). These results appear to hold not only for White mothers but also for African American and Mexican American mothers.

The major exception concerns aggression directed toward their children. In the first study, 92% of the battered women admitted to engaging in some aggression directed toward their children, in contrast to 50% of the comparison mothers. In the second study, the comparable percentages were 90% and (surprisingly) 93%, respectively. These numbers are alarming and certainly provide additional support for the view that children of battered women are at risk for physically abusive behavior. However, it appears that at least in the second sample, the community mothers are not very different on this dimension of parenting. For example, the two groups of women did not differ from the comparison women on their reports of using corporal punishment. A similar finding was reported by McCloskey et al. (1995).

The discrepancy in the first study between group differences found in the mother-to-child CTS subscale score but not found on the spanking subscale may be attributable to the different determinants of those measures. Mother-to-child aggression by battered women appears to be at least partially driven by stress, as the positive correlation suggests. In contrast, use of corporal punishment reflects an instrumental, purposive child-rearing behavior (Holden, Coleman, & Schmidt, 1995). Consequently, the stress associated with marital violence may have relatively little effect on the frequency with which spanking is used. Although more information is needed about the context in which the mother-to-child violence occurs to evaluate that hypothesis, these data indicate that negative emotion-based aggression is somewhat more common in violent homes but that the reliance on corporal punishment as a disciplinary technique is not. Future research should further evaluate the role of stress and violence by examining the contexts in which child-directed aggression occurs.

One ambiguous result concerned child gender effects on maternal aggression. A significant effect attributable to gender was found in the second study but not the first. It may be that gender effects are not particularly powerful unless the sample includes older children or children from those families who experienced more extreme violence, as was the case in studies by Jouriles and LeCompte (1991) and Jouriles and Norwood (1995). Evidently, given the defining role that men play in violent homes, the role of child gender in differential maternal behavior merits considerably more attention in subsequent studies.

An expected but nevertheless disturbing result was the high rate of conflict in violent homes and awareness by the children of marital fights. These results were similar to other reports indicating that children are all too often privy to family arguments and violence (e.g., Hilton, 1992). Given the strong physiological reactions associated with being exposed to angry interactions (e.g., El-Sheikh, Cummings, & Goetsch, 1989), one wonders how this frequent hostility, directed toward either the mothers or the children, negatively affects the children's physiological as well as psychological development (see Rossman, 1998, this volume).

Several qualifications must be made about these results. First, although mothers from violent and matched-comparison homes did not differ on a variety of child-rearing measures, that does not mean that the quality of mothering was necessarily good or adequate. For instance, the frequency of use of corporal punishment is alarming. Furthermore, the question of what is "adequate" child rearing is difficult to determine. Ultimately, adequacy is best judged as a function of child outcomes. Given the high rates of child behavior problems in the violent homes, it could be argued that the mothers were not providing good-enough parenting to compensate for the toxic environment. Perhaps a mother in a maritally violent home needs to engage in certain parenting behaviors above and beyond what may be needed in nonviolent homes in order to be judged as adequate for that violent home context.

A second qualification concerns the wide individual differences among mothers. Although relatively few group differences were found between the battered and nonbattered women, it is clear that at least some mothers from each type of household were exhibiting poor parenting behavior. Such mothers are desperately in need of assistance in their child rearing. Given the low-income status of almost all of the mothers and the pervasive problems for both adults and children that accompany poverty (Huston, 1991), both groups of mothers are at risk for parenting difficulties. Furthermore, given the increased likelihood of emotional and more serious psychological problems associated with being battered, there is increased probability that parenting could be adversely affected (see Levendosky, 1996).

Several caveats concerning the results must also be acknowledged. First, the mothers from violent homes came from shelters. Shelter mothers may not be representative of women from violent homes who do not leave the batterer. A woman at the shelter may be unusual in that she took the initiative to leave the batterer. In fact, many mothers who leave the batterer do so because they are concerned about their children's well-being (Hilton, 1992). Consequently, it is possible that mothers at a shelter may be more child centered than mothers who remain with the batterer. Moreover, the results are limited to the child rearing of mothers of preschoolers and young school-age children. Perhaps more differences would be found in parents of older youth. In addition, the samples in the two studies comprised a total of 74 and 58 mothers, respectively. The sample size issue is perhaps of greatest concern in the ethnic group analyses.

Another limitation is the reliance on maternal self-reports. Although efforts were made to avoid self-report biases, more extensive observational data and data from multiple informants would strengthen our confidence in the results. At least three specific concerns about the reliance on self-report data need to be raised. First, it is possible that the CPSS method was not adequately sensitive to detect differences between the battered and comparison groups. However, given the ability of the method to confirm relations between maternal self-reports and observed behavior (Holden et al., 1992), we do not believe this is a likely explanation. Second, there may be group differences in subject reactivity to the procedures. Battered women may be more inclined to try to present a positive impression of their parenting behavior than the comparison women. For example, the mothers in the shelter were prohibited from using corporal punishment, and such directives could affect their reports. Alternatively, battered women may minimize, deny, or even be unaware of problems in their parenting. Any of these possibilities could result in a lack of between-group differences.

It is clear that future studies should attempt to assess a wider variety of parenting variables in multiple ways. It is possible that other parenting variables such as quality of attachment, extent of monitoring, or degree of involvement would reveal differences between battered women and nonabused mothers. More observational data from different contexts also are needed. Because several subtle interactional group differences were found, more observational research is needed. Moreover, converging information from the reports of other family members, such as fathers and older children, would provide a richer set of data.

The findings from these studies indicate that the major concern with the parenting of battered women lies in their child-directed aggression. Although such aggression is nondefensible, the data from this study indicate that it may be linked to the degree of stress they are experiencing. It can be hypothesized that a reduction in maternal stress, such as after she leaves the violent environment, should result in a decrease in child-directed aggression. An alternative hypothesis is that because aggression is a learned behavior, mothers may have established a habitual form of interacting with their children that includes aggression, and thus it remains stable over time. Only a longitudinal study can address that possibility. A study conducted over time could also test whether other aspects of maternal behavior changed. For example, it is possible (although unlikely) that battered women may become less involved with their children after leaving a violent household, because the protective allegiance that they may have formed in the face of assaults from the abusive father could fade when they are no longer living in that situation. Furthermore, a longitudinal study would provide valuable information for battered women about how children and mothers adjust to living without the batterer.

A SHORT-TERM LONGITUDINAL STUDY OF CHANGE IN THE PARENTING OF BATTERED WOMEN

A short-term longitudinal study was designed to track mothers for 6 months after leaving a shelter. Such data can begin to fill an important informational void about battered women's behavior over time. In particular, it can address the key question of whether mothers' child-directed aggressive behavior changes over time. We located only one longitudinal study of battered women and their children that has been reported in the literature. Giles-Sims (1985) interviewed 21 battered mothers with children under 18 years of age while at a shelter and 6 months later. Using the CTS, she found that almost all of the mothers admitted to engaging in some form of violence (e.g., pushing, slapping, spanking) toward their children at both times. With regard to the severe forms of violence (kicking, biting, hitting with object, beating up), there was indeed a considerable drop in the amount of violence to which children were subjected. Only about one-third of the children continued to receive such abusive treatment 6 months postshelter, although 62% of the mothers had reported using such behavior during the year prior to coming to the shelter. Thus, it appears that after leaving the shelter, mothers are less likely to engage in severe forms of violence directed to their children.

A second study that attempted to look at change over time was a cross-sectional study conducted by Wolfe, Jaffe, Wilson, and Zak (1986) that assessed 23 former residents, 17 current residents of shelters for battered women, and 23 nonviolent comparison families from the community. Although the authors made no assessments of maternal aggression, they did find that children of the former residents had no more behavioral or emotional problems than the community sample. Surprisingly, the scores of these children also did not differ significantly either from the scores of children currently residing in a shelter with their mothers. However, the former residents faced the greatest number of disadvantages (e.g., low income, single parent, frequent moves). Given the lack of group differences in terms of their behavior problems but their high level of current disadvantages, Wolfe and his colleagues inferred that children of battered women may be able to recover from their troublesome past once they are away from the violence. As they acknowledged, a longitudinal study rather than a cross-sectional one is necessary to address the issue of continuity and change in mothers' and children's behavior and adjustment.

On the basis of those two studies, and the results of the first two studies indicating the association between aggression toward children and stress, we expected battered women to show a significant decrease in their aggressive behavior directed toward their children. We also expected that both mothers and children would show improved adjustment over a 6-month period of time, simply as a result of being out of the violent environment. Maternal stress levels were expected to decrease significantly. Also of interest was whether different aspects of maternal behavior, namely disciplinary practices, would be modified after leaving the shelter.

Method

Sample

Fifty mothers temporarily residing at a shelter for battered women volunteered to participate. Each mother had at least one target child who was between the ages of 4 and 9 ($M = 5.7$ years). Twenty of the target children were girls and 30 were boys. The mothers had a mean age of 29 years and were from one of three ethnic groups: Hispanic (39% of the sample), Caucasian (32%), and African American (24%). Two mothers did not indicate their ethnicity.

A majority (69%) of the women were homemakers. The other mothers were employed full-time (15%) or part-time (10%) or were students (6%). Most (76%) of the women had a high school education, 8% had not graduated from high school, and 16% had some higher education. Fifty-four percent of the women in the study were divorced or separated at the time the study began. The remaining women had never married (26%), were currently married (18%), or were widowed (2%).

Of those women who reported on the occupation of their partners, a majority (62%) of the men were employed full-time, 23% worked part-time, and 15% were homemakers. Most (75%) of the men had a high school diploma, although 13% had an 8th grade education or less and 12% had attended college. As in the first study, the average family income was very low. Most (88%) of the women reported their annual family income to be less than $15,000. Another 8% had family incomes between $15,000 and $30,000; only two women reported an annual family income over $30,000.

Instruments and Procedure

Three types of data were collected: (a) measures of parenting and mother–child interaction, (b) measures of maternal functioning, and (c) measures of child functioning. The quality of mother–child interactions and parenting was assessed by four self-report instruments. As in the previous study, the mother-to-child aggression subscale from the CTS and the short form of the PSI were used. For our data to be comparable with findings from other studies, at Time 1, we instructed mothers to respond to the CTS in the standard way, that is, to report on tactics used over the past year. However, at the 6-month visit, they were asked to report on their conflict tactics used since they had last filled out the form.

To assess other types of child-rearing behaviors used in response to conflict, the Parental Responses to Child Misbehavior (PRCM; Holden et al., 1995) was given. This is a survey of the frequency, in an average week, of nine different types of disciplinary behaviors used in response to child misbehavior (e.g., reason, time out, spank–slap, yell). Response ratings range from 0 to 9 or more times per week. The survey Attitudes Toward Spanking (ATS) was also used to determine the degree to which spanking attitudes were linked with maternal practices. The

ATS is a 10-item Likert-type instrument that has been found to have good internal consistency and is correlated with behavioral reports of physical punishment (Holden et al., 1995). In this sample, the coefficient alpha was .76.

Maternal depressive symptoms were measured with the Beck Depression Inventory (BDI; Beck, Steer, & Garbin, 1988) and maternal self-esteem with the Rosenberg Self-Esteem Scale (Rosenberg, 1965). Finally, as in Study 1, mothers' perceptions of their children's behavior problems were assessed with the CBCL (Achenbach & Edelbrock, 1981).

Mothers and children also participated in an observation procedure similar to the one used in the second study. The observational codes were similar to those used in the second study. Because of equipment failure, experimenter error, or other problems, observational data from only 23 of the mothers are available at both times. Reliability was checked on 22% of the observations. The average percentage agreement for the child behavior codes was .88, with a kappa of .81. The comparable analyses for maternal codes were .85 and .67, respectively.

Participants were recruited at a shelter for battered women. An appointment was then made for them to come by cab to a research laboratory. To maintain contact with the mothers and assess how they were functioning, researchers made bi-weekly telephone calls to the mothers. Approximately 6 months after the first visit, mothers returned to the laboratory and went through the same procedures (Time 2). A taxi-cab ride was arranged if the mother did not have her own transportation. Following each visit, the children selected a toy from a toy box, and mothers received cash for their time ($25 after Time 1 and $50 after Time 2).

Results and Discussion

Rate of Completion

Eighteen of the mothers did not return for the 6-month visit. Consequently, 32 of the original 50 mothers and children (8 girls, 24 boys) remained in the study, resulting in an attrition rate of 36%. Of the 18 mother–child dyads who dropped out, 6 moved out of town, 6 declined to participate further, contact was lost with 5, and 1 child had moved in with his father. According to mothers' self-reports, five mothers (16%) who remained in the study moved back in with the batterer. It is likely that at least some of those mothers who dropped out of the study also moved back in with their batterers.

A series of tests were conducted to assess whether those mothers who dropped out differed significantly from those who completed the study. Out of the 29 comparisons conducted, significant differences were found on only three variables. Drop-outs were more likely to be homemakers ($z = 2.83$, $p < .05$), to have been in a shelter before ($z = 2.10$, $p < .05$), and to have children in a school or daycare setting for a shorter length of time, $t(49) = 3.44$, $p < .01$, in comparison to those who completed the study.

Maternal Behavior

How did mothers' behavior change across the 6-month period? As measured by the CTS, there was a significant decrease in the amount of child-directed aggressive behavior. In the year preceding the Time 1 assessment, 75% of the mothers ($n = 24$) admitted to using some sort of coercive child-rearing behavior with their children. The most common forms of aggression were pushing, grabbing, or shoving the child (63%), throwing, smashing, hitting, or kicking an object (53%), and throwing something at the child (47%). The group mean averaged 8.4 ($SD = 6.0$, range = 0 to 28). However, during the 6 months after leaving the shelter, only 11 mothers (34%) reported engaging in some form of aggression directed to their children. Stated differently, 15 mothers who had previously aggressed toward their children reportedly stopped by Time 2, nine mothers continued, two mothers started, and six mothers reported that they never engaged in aggression at either times. This was a significant change as assessed by a repeated measures categorical analysis, $\chi^2(1, N = 32) = 14.42$, $p < .001$ (SAS, 1990). The nine mothers who continued to aggress toward their children had an average CTS score of 6.5 at Time 2 ($SD = 8.4$, range = 1 to 30). There was no significant change from Time 1 to Time 2 in those mothers' CTS scores (adjusted to correct for the different time durations reported on).

To further examine stability and change in maternal behavior, we examined disciplinary responses to common child misbehaviors with the PRCM instrument. There were no significant changes in the average weekly reports of behavioral responses on the nine measures. For example, the reported rate of spanking or slapping during an average week before coming to the shelter was 1.9 (SD = .97); 6 months later, the reported rate was exactly the same (M = 1.9, SD = .65). These results are depicted in Figure 2. Convergent evidence for the stability of parental disciplinary behavior practices was found at the attitudinal level: There was a slight but nonsignificant decrease in positive attitudes toward spanking (M_{T1} = 34, M_{T2} = 29), $F(1, 31)$ = 2.63, p = .11. Thus, these data indicate that the mothers' habitual styles of disciplining and reacting to child misbehavior had not changed appreciably over the 6-month period.

As expected, parenting stress did show a significant decrease over time. At Time 1 the mothers reported being highly stressed, with their PSI averaging 91.7 (SD = 24). However, 6 months later, the mean parenting stress was 78.9 (SD = 24). This change was a significant decrease, $t(32)$ = −3.41, p < .01, and reflected a drop from the 90th to the 75th stress percentile (Abidin, 1991). To determine whether stress was related to frequency of child-directed aggression, we correlated the PSI and

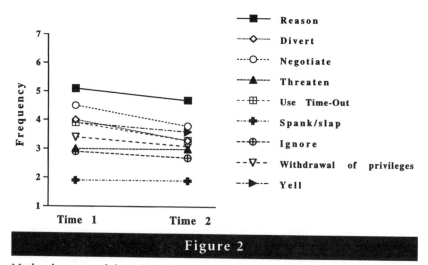

Figure 2

Mothers' reports of their disciplinary practices across 6 months.

CTS scales. At both assessment times there was a positive but nonsignificant association between stress and aggression toward children. At Time 1 the correlation was $r(32) = .25$, $p = .16$; six months later that relation was somewhat stronger, $r(32) = .31$, $p < .09$.

Maternal Functioning

Two measures of mothers' general level of functioning were used: depressive symptoms and self-esteem. The results provide a mixed picture of maternal adjustment. On the positive side, mothers reported a significant drop in the number of depressive symptoms. While at the shelter, mothers had an average of 13.9, but 6 months later the mean was 9.0, $t(30) = -3.06$, $p < .01$. However, there was an unexpected trend for a decrease in the mothers' self-esteem ($M_{T1} = 20.2$, $M_{T2} = 18.1$), $t(32) = 1.87$, $p = .07$. This decrease may reflect the significant financial and psychological hardships that many of these mothers found themselves in 6 months after leaving the shelter.

Mothers' Perceptions of Their Children's Behavior Problems

Mothers' reports of their children's behavior problems also showed significant change. A 2 (Time) × 2 (Scale) repeated measures ANOVA was computed on the Internalizing and Externalizing scores. The repeated-measures multivariate test for Time was significant, $F(2, 28) = 9.66$, $p < .001$. Follow-up t tests indicated significant differences for both the Internalizing ($M_{T1} = 56.5$, $M_{T2} = 50.2$), $F(1, 29) = 11.50$, $p < .01$, and Externalizing subscales ($M_{T1} = 61.2$, $M_{T2} = 54.3$), $F(1, 29) = 18.24$, $p < .01$. Despite the significant decreases, continuity in behavior problems could be detected as both Internalizing and Externalizing scores were significantly correlated, $rs(30) = .76$ and $.66$, $ps < .01$, respectively. That is, the children who were exhibiting the highest levels of behavior problems during shelter residence were also the children who were exhibiting the highest levels of behavior problems 6 months after shelter residence.

Using T scores of 67 or greater as a cutoff point indicating borderline clinical problems, 36% of the children had overall scores at this level at Time 1, in comparison to only 9% of the children 6 months later. Comparable percentages for Internalizing and Externalizing prob-

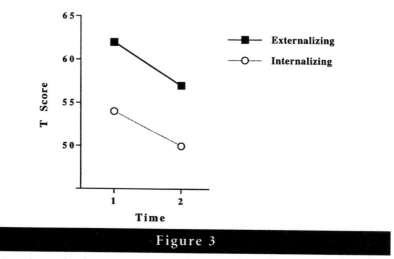

Figure 3

Changes in mothers' perceptions of their children's behavior problems across 6 months.

lems were 23% and 33% at Time 1 and 6% and 16% at Time 2. These were significant decreases as assessed by a repeated-measures categorical data analysis, $\chi^2(1, N = 30) = 13.49$, 12.68, and 9.27, $ps < .01$, respectively. The change in the Internalizing and Externalizing scores across the 6 months is graphed in Figure 3.

Behavioral Observations

The observations of mother–child interactions provided some convergent evidence of the improved quality of mother–child interaction. Six months after leaving the shelter there was a significant decrease in number of times the children were touching the off-bound toys ($M_{T1} = 7.2$, $M_{T2} = 4.4$), $t(22) = 2.29$, $p < .05$, and in their frequency of withdrawing from interactions with the mother ($M_{T1} = .83$, $M_{T2} = .19$), $t(22) = 2.64$, $p < .02$. Instead, there was a significant increase in the number of minutes the children played with the in-bound object ($M_{T1} = 4.8$, $M_{T2} = 6.9$), $t(22) = -3.73$, $p < .01$. There was also a significant increase in the number of children who expressed positive affect during the 15-minute observation. During the first observation, only 13% of the children were observed to laugh at least once. That percentage jumped to 38% six months later, a significant increase, $\chi^2(1, N = 29) = 5.26$, $p <$

.05. However, on other measures there was no significant change across time.

Summary

This study indicates that some aspects of maternal behavior change, whereas others stay the same. The most important finding was the significant reduction in the percentage of mothers who continued to aggress toward their children. More generally, mothers appear to be functioning considerably better 6 months after leaving a shelter. Their level of parenting stress and their depressive symptoms are down. Similarly, the mothers report that their children are also showing significantly fewer behavior problems. The observational data supported such a view by finding improved interactions across time. Interestingly, mothers reported no change in their disciplinary practices or their reliance on (or attitudes toward) corporal punishment.

In contrast to the cross-sectional results of Wolfe and his colleagues (1986), these results indicated that after 6 months, the children were significantly better off than they were while in the shelter. The fact that Wolfe's study was cross-sectional and the present one was longitudinal may account for the discrepant findings. Despite the relatively sanguine picture these results provide, the fact that there was a trend for a decrease in the mothers' reported levels of self-esteem is a reminder of the problems and hardships with which these families were dealing.

GENERAL DISCUSSION

The results of these three studies provide a better understanding of how child rearing may be affected by marital violence. These studies point to three findings concerning the parenting of mothers who are physically abused by their spouses. The most important result concerns the diminished parenting hypothesis. These data indicate that on the vast majority of measures assessing child-rearing behavior, battered women from a shelter do not differ significantly from nonabused community mothers. Contrary to a deficiency model of battered women, no evidence was found to indicate they were less affectionate, less proactive, less likely to provide structure for the child, or more punitive.

Across the first two studies, very little support was found for the diminished parenting hypothesis. For example, on only one index of parenting (limit setting) out of four subscales tested did the battered women show a significant difference from the other mothers. Given that most of these families are low to very low income, it appears that marital violence does not contribute over and above the effects of poverty. Nevertheless, these results are tempered by the reliance on self-report data and the finding that behavioral observations revealed some subtle interactional differences. The possibility that battered women denied, minimized, or were unaware of some of their parenting deficits cannot be ruled out.

A second general finding is that many of the mothers in violent marriages do indeed engage in aggressive behavior toward their children. However, community mothers also engage in child-directed aggression; there was relatively little difference between the battered and comparison mothers on the variable (see also Moore & Pepler, 1998, this volume). Furthermore, once the women leave the battering relationship, the number of women who continue to engage in aggression toward their children drops significantly.[1] This mother-to-child aggression was found to be positively associated (at least at the trend level) with parenting stress in all three studies.

The third major finding, stemming from the last study, concerns the evidence for both change and stability in the mothers and the children. On several different fronts, there appears to be significant improvement for the mothers and children 6 months after leaving the batterer. Mothers reported significant decreases in the rates of stress and depressive symptoms, and they perceived their children as having fewer behavior problems. Despite this positive finding, their low self-esteem scores suggest that the considerable problems and hardships the women undoubtedly continue to face should not be forgotten. Assistance and interventions on a variety of fronts evidently are seriously needed. However, that single but monumental act of extricating oneself

---

[1] Recall that five of the mothers returned to the batterer. That small number precluded a separate analysis. It appears though, from looking at those five cases, that they were in the calming stage of the cycle of violence (e.g., Walker, 1979).

from the violent relationship appears to have advantageous outcomes for the mothers. On the other hand, the data indicate little change in mothers' disciplinary responses over the 6-month time period, presumably because those behaviors are based on previously developed disciplinary habits and belief systems that have not been modified.

These conclusions are tentative and await replication and extension. There is much we do not yet know about the child rearing in violent homes. A limited number of child-rearing variables were assessed in these studies. Other variables, such as involvement, sensitivity, and monitoring, must be examined. Furthermore, the approach taken in the first study was that of testing for differences between group averages. Such comparisons do not do justice to the considerable within-group variability. For example, as was pointed out in the second study, about a third of the battered women endorsed physical punishment in response to one situation in contrast to another third that opposed its use. To be sure, all battered women do not parent alike. Some are performing at subpar levels and need assistance in their child-rearing practices, such as those mothers in the longitudinal study who continued to engage in aggression toward their children 6 months after leaving a shelter.

Another limitation of this work is that the data did not adequately capture the quality of the mother–child relationship. Mean frequencies do not reflect the way in which a mother may express love or warmth. Ritchie (1996) has argued that heightened levels of maternal warmth could reflect an adaptive maternal compensatory behavior, such that the mother may be trying to buffer her child from the hostile home climate. Alternatively, a mother who exhibits the same level of warmth may be engaged in a maladaptive enmeshment with her child. These data do not enable one to evaluate the quality of maternal warmth expressed or reveal the reasons underlying its expression. Such a determination awaits future research.

The most surprising results of this work are that so few differences were found between battered and comparison mothers. That does not mean that all the mothers were exhibiting model parenting behavior, as pointed out previously. Rather, the marital violence in itself did not appear to result in consistent group differences. Indeed, both groups engaged in some aggression directed toward children, although battered women were more likely to report doing this. As Straus and Gelles (1990) have made so clear, aggression and violence are endemic in many households.

The aggression toward the children can be partially explained by the bidirectional determinants of behavior. At least some of the child-directed aggression may be accounted for—though not excused—by the children's behavior. Just as parents respond negatively to stress, so too do their children. Given the high rate of child misbehavior and Externalizing problems in many of these children, at least some mother-to-child disciplinary interactions undoubtedly escalate to the point of violence. One mother from a maritally violent home reported that her 7-year-old overactive son was becoming abusive toward others and wanted to hurt people. When asked about the characteristics she liked the best about him, she poignantly wrote: "I'm so fed up with him right now, I can't think of any." It is not difficult to imagine how conflict between the two could escalate into aggressive behavior. Fortunately, 6 months later the mother reported that her son was no longer obsessed with hurting people and had fewer behavior problems. She too was exhibiting much less aggressive behavior toward him. That finding must be tempered with the realization that the children are still experiencing a number of behavior problems and are likely to in the future (Silvern et al., 1995). Nevertheless, most of the mothers and children were faring considerably better 6 months after leaving the shelter.

It should be kept in mind that parenting is not just affected by violence but can affect its consequences. As mentioned above, mothers may serve as buffers to protect children from violence or may attempt to compensate for it by providing extra warmth or support. Such evidence suggests that from the mothers' perspective, their children may not be "forgotten victims" but instead are a focal point of their attention and concern. More evidence for this view comes from the mothers who cited concerns over the negative effects on their children as the impetus for leaving the violent relationship (Hilton, 1992).

One of the provocative findings of this work comes from mothers' reports about what they say to their children after a violent incident. Clearly, some comments are constructive and may facilitate the children's understanding and living with a hostile and violent father. In contrast, other explanations may serve to further terrorize a child. Similarly, children's feeling of blame and responsibility as well as control or helplessness may be influenced by maternal comments (Rossman & Rosenberg, 1992). Thus, mothers' explanations of and interpretations about the violence may represent an important aspect of parenting and at the least warrants further investigation as a potentially important mediating influence on children's adjustment.

Future studies also should collect data from other informants (e.g., child, neighbors, and even partners) to provide converging evidence about the mothers' behavior (see Sternberg, Lamb, & Dawud-Noursi, 1998, this volume). Data about and from the children's fathers are needed as well. Investigations into how different violent environments (e.g., different types of batterers) and characteristics of the mothers (e.g., posttraumatic stress disorder) may affect or interact with their parenting behavior are also needed. Such work could help to explicate relations between marital violence, parenting, and children's behavior problems. For example, women married to antisocial batterers may develop different survival skills and compensatory parenting mechanisms than wives of family-only batterers (see Holtzworth-Munroe & Stuart, 1994).

In conclusion, this chapter sheds new light on the mothering that goes on in maritally violent households. The present work indicates that the view of abused mothers as deficient in parenting and highly aggressive may well be misguided. The results from this work and other recent studies (e.g., McCloskey et al., 1995) indicate that battered mothers as a group do not differ uniformly in their child-rearing practices from other women in their community. Perhaps the fundamental implication of this work is that it appears researchers should revise their orientations with regard to battered women. A search for pathologies of battered women and negative qualities of their parenting seems to be the wrong direction to pursue. Rather, the focus should be shifted to one that begins to recognize and document the strengths and coping strategies of these women. Investigations are needed into the proactive, strategic, adaptive, and compensatory behaviors that many of these mothers engage in to protect or even save their children from the detrimental effects of being reared in a maritally violent home.

REFERENCES

Abidin, R. R. (1986). *Parenting stress index* (2nd ed.). Charlottesville, VA: Pediatric Press.

Abidin, R. R. (1991). *Short form of the Parenting Stress Index.* Charlottesville, VA: Pediatric Press.

Achenbach, T. M., & Edelbrock, C. S. (1981). Behavioral problems and competencies reported by parents of normal and disturbed children aged four through sixteen. *Monographs of the Society for Research in Child Development, 46*(1, Serial No. 188).

Appel, A., Angelelli, M. J., & Holden, G. W. (1997). *The correspondence between wife and child abuse: A review.* Manuscript under review.

Beck, A. T., Steer, R., & Garbin, M. G. (1988). Psychometric properties of the Beck Depression Inventory: 25 years of evaluation. *Clinical Psychology Review, 8,* 77–100.

Buehler, C., Krishnakumar, A., Anthony, C., Tittsworth, S., & Stone, G. (1994). Hostile interparental conflict and youth maladjustment. *Family Relations, 43,* 409–416.

Chew, C. M. (1996, June). *Battered women and their ability to parent: A preliminary investigation.* Poster presented at the First National Conference on Children Exposed to Family Violence, Austin, TX.

Crnic, K. A., Greenberg, M. T., Ragozin, A. S., Robinson, N. M., & Basham, R. B. (1983). Effects of stress and social support on mothers and premature and full-term infants. *Child Development, 54,* 209–217.

Cummings, E. M. (1994). Marital conflict and children's functioning. *Social Development, 3,* 16–36.

Deni, R. (1992). *OBSERVE software v2.1 for the Macintosh: User's manual.* (Available from the author, 32 Merritt Drive, Lawrenceville, NJ 08648)

Easterbrooks, M. A., & Emde, R. N. (1988). Marital and parent–child relationships: The role of affect in the family system. In R. A. Hinde & J.

Stevenson-Hinde (Eds.), *Relationships within families: Mutual influences* (pp. 83–103). New York: Oxford University Press.

El-Sheikh, M., Cummings, E. M., & Goetsch, V. L. (1989). Coping with adults' angry behavior: Behavioral, physiological, and verbal responses in preschoolers. *Developmental Psychology, 25,* 490–498.

Emery, R. E. (1982). Interparental conflict and the children of discord and divorce. *Psychological Bulletin, 92,* 310–330.

Fantuzzo, J., & Lindquist, C. U. (1989). The effects of observing conjugal violence on children: A review and analysis of research methodology. *Journal of Family Violence, 4,* 77–94.

Geffner, R. (1996, June). *Linking intimate partner and child abuse fields: Psychological maltreatment of children exposed to family violence.* Keynote address presented at the Conference on Children Exposed to Family Violence, Austin, TX.

Giles-Sims, J. (1985). A longitudinal study of battered children of battered wives. *Family Relations, 34,* 205–210.

Grych, J. H., & Fincham, F. D. (1990). Marital conflict and children's adjustment: A cognitive–contextual framework. *Psychological Bulletin, 108,* 267–290.

Hershorn, M., & Rosenbaum, A. (1985). Children of marital violence: A closer look at the unintended victims. *American Journal of Orthopsychiatry, 55,* 260–266.

Hilton, N. Z. (1992). Battered women's concerns about their children witnessing wife assault. *Journal of Interpersonal Violence, 7,* 77–86.

Holden, G. W. (1988). Using computers for research into social relations. *Simulations/Games for Learning, 18,* 61–68.

Holden, G. W., & Ritchie, K. L. (1991). Linking extreme marital discord, child rearing, and child behavior problems: Evidence from battered women. *Child Development, 62,* 311–327.

Holden, G. W., Ritchie, K. L., & Coleman, S. (1992). The accuracy of maternal self-reports: Agreement between reports on a computer simulation compared with observed behavior in the supermarket. *Early Development & Parenting, 1,* 109–119.

Holden, G. W., Coleman, S., & Schmidt, K. L. (1995). Why 3-year-old children get spanked: Parent and child determinants in a sample of college-educated mothers. *Merrill-Palmer Quarterly, 41,* 431–452.

Holden, G. W., & West, M. J. (1989). Proximate regulation by mothers: A demonstration of how differing styles affect young children's behavior. *Child Development, 60,* 64–69.

Holtzworth-Munroe, A., & Stuart, G. L. (1994). Typologies of male batterers: Three subtypes and the differences among them. *Psychological Bulletin, 116,* 476–497.

Hughes, H. M., & Luke, D. A. (1998). Heterogeneity in adjustment among children of battered women. In G. W. Holden, R. A. Geffner, & E. N. Jouriles (Eds.), *Children exposed to marital violence: Theory, research, and applied issues* (pp. 185–221). Washington, DC: American Psychological Association.

Huston, A. C. (Ed.). (1991). *Children in poverty: Child development and public policy.* New York: Cambridge University Press.

Jaffe, P. G., Wolfe, D. A., & Wilson, S. K. (1990). *Children of battered women.* Newbury Park, CA: Sage.

Jouriles, E. N., Barling, J., & O'Leary, K. D. (1987). Predicting child behavior problems in maritally violent families. *Journal of Abnormal Child Psychology, 15,* 165–173.

Jouriles, E. N., & LeCompte, S. H. (1991). Husbands' aggression toward wives and mothers' and fathers' aggression toward children: Moderating effects of child gender. *Journal of Consulting and Clinical Psychology, 59,* 190–192.

Jouriles, E. N., & Norwood, W. D. (1995). Physical aggression toward boys and girls in families characterized by the battering of women. *Journal of Family Psychology, 9,* 69–78.

Jouriles, E. N., Norwood, W. D., McDonald, R., Vincent, J. P., & Mahoney, A. (1996). Physical violence and other forms of marital aggression: Links with children's behavior problems. *Journal of Family Violence, 11,* 223–234.

Laumakis, M. A., Margolin, G., & John, R. S. (1998). Emotional, cognitive, and coping responses of preadolescent children to different dimensions of mental conflict. In G. W. Holden, R. A. Geffner, & E. N. Jouriles (Eds.), *Children exposed to marital violence: Theory, research, and applied issues* (pp. 257–288). Washington, DC: American Psychological Association.

Levendosky, A. (1996, June). *Parenting in battered women: A developmental psychopathology approach.* Paper presented at the First National Conference on Children Exposed to Family Violence, Austin, TX.

McCloskey, L. A., Figueredo, A. J., & Koss, M. P. (1995). The effects of systemic family violence on children's mental health. *Child Development, 66,* 1239–1261.

McDonald, R., & Jouriles, E. N. (1991). Marital aggression and child behavior problems: Research findings, mechanisms, and intervention strategies. *Behavior Therapist, 14,* 189–192.

McLoyd, V. C. (1990). The impact of economic hardship on black families and children: Psychological distress, parenting, and socioemotional development. *Child Development, 61,* 311–346.

Moore, T. E., & Pepler, D. J. (1998). Correlates of adjustment in children at risk. In G. W. Holden, R. A. Geffner, & E. N. Jouriles (Eds.), *Children exposed to marital violence: Theory, research, and applied issues* (pp. 157–184). Washington, DC: American Psychological Association.

O'Keefe, M. (1994a). Adjustment of children from maritally violent homes. *Families in Society, 94,* 403–415.

O'Keefe, M. (1994b). Linking marital violence, mother–child/father–child aggression, and child behavior problems. *Journal of Family Violence, 9,* 63–78.

Osofsky, J. D. (1995). Children who witness domestic violence: The invisible victims [Monograph]. *Society for Research in Child Development, 9,* No. 3.

Patterson, G. R. (Ed.). (1990). *Depression and aggression in family interaction.* Hillsdale, NJ: Erlbaum.

Ritchie, K. (1996, June). *Maternal warmth in battered women: A theoretical perspective.* Paper presented at the Conference on Children Exposed to Family Violence, Austin, TX.

Rosenberg, M. (1965). *Society and the adolescent self-image.* Princeton, NJ: Princeton University Press.

Rossman, B. B. R. (1998). Descartes's error and posttraumatic stress disorder: Cognition and emotion for children who are exposed to parental violence. In G. W. Holden, R. A. Geffner, & E. N. Jouriles (Eds.), *Children exposed to marital violence: Theory, research, and applied issues* (pp. 223–256). Washington, DC: American Psychological Association.

Rossman, B. B. R., & Rosenberg, M. S. (1992). Family stress and functioning in children: The moderating effects of children's beliefs about their control over parental conflict. *Child Psychology and Psychiatry, 33,* 699–715.

SAS. (1990). *SAS/STAT guide for personal computers, Version 6* (4th ed.). Cary, NC: Author.

Silvern, L., Karyl, J., Waelde, L., Hodges, W. F., Starek, J., Heidt, E., & Min, K. (1995). Retrospective reports of parental partner abuse: Relationships to depression, trauma symptoms, and self esteem among college students. *Journal of Family Violence, 10,* 177–202.

Sternberg, K., Lamb, M. E., & Dawud-Noursi, S. (1998). Using multiple informants to understand domestic violence and its effects. In G. W. Holden, R. A. Geffner, & E. N. Jouriles (Eds.), *Children exposed to marital violence: Theory, research, and applied issues* (pp. 121–156). Washington, DC: American Psychological Association.

Straus, M. A. (1979). Measuring intrafamily conflict and violence: The Conflict Tactics Scale. *Journal of Marriage and the Family, 41,* 75–88.

Straus, M. A., & Gelles, R. J. (1990). *Physical violence in American families: Risk factors and adaptations to violence in 8,145 families.* New Brunswick, NJ: Transaction.

Straus, M. A., Gelles, R. J., & Steinmetz, S. K. (1980). *Behind closed doors.* Garden City, NY: Doubleday.

Walker, L. E. (1979). *The battered woman.* New York: Harper & Row.

Wolfe, D., Jaffe, P., Wilson, S., & Zak, L. (1985). Children of battered women: The relation between child behavior, family violence, and maternal stress. *Journal of Consulting and Clinical Psychology, 53,* 657–665.

Wolfe, D., Jaffe, P., Wilson, S., & Zak, L. (1986). Child witnesses to violence between parents: Critical issues in behavioral and social adjustment. *Journal of Abnormal Child Psychology, 14,* 95–104.

PART THREE

Applied Issues

11

Breaking the Cycle of Violence: Helping Families Departing From Battered Women's Shelters

Ernest N. Jouriles, Renee McDonald, Nanette Stephens,
William Norwood, Laura Collazos Spiller, and
Holly Shinn Ware

I n this chapter, we describe a multicomponent intervention to reduce conduct problems exhibited by children of battered women. We also present preliminary results of a treatment outcome study designed to evaluate the effectiveness of the intervention. The professional literature on children of battered women offers a number of suggestions for intervention and includes descriptions of several specific intervention programs. With a few notable exceptions, however, systematic evaluation of the efficacy of these suggestions and programs has not been undertaken. At best, this state of affairs may contribute to an inefficient use of scarce resources; at worst, it may result in children and families receiving ineffective or perhaps even harmful services. Moreover, many of the existing intervention programs for children of battered women appear to identify all children of battered women as needing intervention. That is, a child is identified as needing help on the basis of the behavior of the mother's batterer. This approach ignores what is known

This work was supported in part by grants from the National Institute of Mental Health (MH53380–01A1), the Texas Higher Education Coordinating Board, the Hogg Foundation, and the George Foundation.

about children's differential responses to stressors and suggests an inefficient use of resources by offering services to children who may not need or benefit from them. In this chapter, we delineate the background, theory, and data that provided the rationale for our intervention efforts with the children of battered women. We then describe the major components of our intervention and conclude with a presentation of our results, to date, documenting our program's effectiveness.

THE PROBLEM OF CHILDREN EXPOSED TO DOMESTIC VIOLENCE

Domestic violence toward women is neither a new nor a trivial phenomenon. Although one can only guess the historical prevalence, contemporary estimates indicate that between 12% and 50% of women in this country are victims of some form of physical violence from a husband or cohabiting male partner each year (Straus & Gelles, 1988), as discussed in the introductory chapter of this volume. Between 3% and 10% are estimated to be victims of repeated, severe assaults from an intimate partner (Straus & Gelles, 1988). It is no wonder, then, that violence toward women has captured the attention of researchers, policy makers, law enforcement agencies, and social welfare organizations and has given rise to programs to provide emergency services and temporary shelter to the victims of domestic violence and their dependent children. In Texas alone, 11,778 women and their 16,984 children sought refuge at battered women's shelters during 1994 (Texas Council on Family Violence, 1994). The physical assault of women by an intimate partner is clearly an all too common occurrence in the United States, and the provision of services for these women and children warrants high priority.

Over the past 20 years, researchers and service providers have begun to recognize that in families characterized by spousal violence, women are not the only victims; the children suffer as well. This recognition has led to a number of well-designed investigations of the problems experienced by these children. One pattern of problematic behavior consistently identified among the children is *conduct problems*, which refers to behavior characterized as aggressive, antisocial, and oppositional. Conduct problems are not the only area of dysfunction associated with exposure to spousal violence, and not all children exposed to such violence exhibit conduct problems. However, such problems have been repeatedly documented by cross-sectional research comparing samples of children of battered women to samples of children of nonviolent parents (for reviews of the empirical literature, see Jaffe, Wolfe, & Wilson, 1990; Kolbo, Blakely, & Engleman, 1996; McDonald & Jouriles, 1991). This research provides empirical confirmation of our observations based on interviews with more than 300 battered women with children, many of whom have expressed concern about their children's aggression, noncompliance, and hostility. The available evidence also indicates that marital violence is a more potent risk factor for child conduct problems than are nonviolent forms of marital conflict (e.g., verbal conflict or general marital discord; Fantuzzo et al., 1991; Jouriles, Murphy, & O'Leary, 1989; Rossman & Rosenberg, 1992). In other words, the association between the physical abuse of women and the frequency and severity of child conduct problems is not simply due to the nonphysical marital conflict (e.g., yelling, name-calling, verbal threats) that so often occurs in conjunction with spousal violence.

It is important to reiterate that conduct problems are not the only type of difficulties experienced by children of battered women. As the authors of the previous chapters in this volume suggest, many of these children experience a wide range of psychological adjustment problems, including anxiety, depression, and psychological trauma. Furthermore, although many children of battered women suffer from multiple clinical problems, those who are not exhibiting overt problems are often distressed by the violence and may display a variety of "subtle" symptoms, such as a passive acceptance of violence as a means of dealing with interpersonal conflict and stress (Jaffe, Sudermann, & Reitzel, 1992; Jaffe, Wilson, & Wolfe, 1986). In contrast, researchers have also identified a subgroup of children of battered women who appear surprisingly well adjusted despite their violent home environments (see Hughes & Luke, 1998, this volume). Such variability in responses to spousal violence is consistent with what is known about children's responses to stressful circumstances in general (Compas, 1987; Rutter, 1983). We believe that it is important to take this variability into account when designing and implementing intervention programs for the children of battered women. We also believe that careful assessment is necessary to determine the likelihood that a given individual or family will benefit from a given intervention.

Given the variability in children's responses to spousal violence, it is important to recognize that a single intervention (particularly a time-limited one) is not likely to address effectively the needs of each and every child with problems. Our decision to focus our intervention on the conduct problems exhibited by so many of these children was guided by a number of considerations. These considerations include the empirical literature summarized above, which documents high rates of significant conduct problems among the children of battered women, and the input we received directly from the mothers we interviewed. Most of the mothers recognized that their children had been affected by the violence, and many indicated multiple concerns about their children's emotional and behavioral adjustment. The problem voiced by mothers most frequently, however, and the one about which they seemed most concerned, was their children's increasingly defiant, aggressive behavior. Many also expressed concern that their children's behavior mirrored the aggression and hostility of the batterers.

Although many mothers were hopeful that their children's behavior would improve on separation from the batterer, we were less optimistic, given the available data on the stability of child conduct problems. Very few studies have directly addressed this question within samples of battered women, but some data suggest that children's conduct problems remain stable, even following the mother's separation from an abusive partner. Wolfe, Zak, Wilson, and Jaffe (1986) compared the level of behavior problems across three groups of boys and girls aged 4–13 years: (a) children who had been exposed to marital violence within the past 6 weeks and who were residing at a battered women's shelter; (b) children whose last exposure to marital violence was at least 6 months prior to the study, who were former residents of a battered women's shelter, and who were no longer living in a maritally violent home; and (c) children from the community who had not been directly exposed to marital violence. The mean level of conduct problems was almost identical across the current and former shelter groups and was approximately one-half of a standard deviation higher than the group that had not been exposed to violence. Although Wolfe and colleagues interpreted these data differently, it appears that the conduct problems exhibited by at least some of these children remain stable over time and do not simply disappear after mothers leave their batterers (see Holden, Stein, Ritchie, Harris, & Jouriles, 1998, this volume, for further discussion and some contradictory data).

Findings from several other sources corroborate the Wolfe et al. (1986) results. For example, retrospective data have consistently shown that boys' exposure to fathers' marital violence relates to spouse abuse in adult intimate relationships (Hotaling & Sugarman, 1986), and longitudinal data indicate that boys' exposure to fathers' marital violence is one of the few childhood factors that predict adult criminal activity (McCord, 1979). Furthermore, the literature on early-onset conduct disorder indicates notable continuity in aggressive and antisocial behavior from early childhood into adulthood (Moffitt, 1993; Patterson, Reid, & Dishion, 1992). In summary, a substantial amount of research converges to suggest that many children of battered women display increased levels of conduct problems, and such problems, when evident in early childhood, often predict aggressive and criminal behavior in adolescence and adulthood. These findings highlight the need for early identification and intervention specifically with those children of battered women who display elevated levels of aggressive and antisocial behavior.

THEORY AND DATA PERTAINING TO OUR INTERVENTION

Our intervention is designed specifically for families (mothers and children) who have recently sought refuge at a shelter for battered women, who are in the process of setting up a residence independent of the violent partners, and in which a child between the ages of 4 and 9 years exhibits aggressive/oppositional behavior. We recognize that by targeting women and children who have sought refuge at a shelter for battered women, we are capturing only a subset of families affected by battering. However, this subset is large in number, has a great many needs, and is often underserved. By focusing on children whose mothers are establishing residences independent of their abusive partners, we are narrowing the subset of families even further; however, our pilot work, clinical experience, and the experiences of other professionals in this area suggest that a very different intervention (with a different emphasis) would be necessary for families in which mothers return to their violent partners. Our reasons for targeting families with children exhibiting aggressive/oppositional behavior were presented above.

The content of our intervention was drawn from three domains: (a) Patterson and his colleagues' developmental model of antisocial behavior (Patterson, 1982; Patterson, DeBarsyshe, & Ramsey, 1989; Patterson et al., 1992), (b) the empirical literature on the treatment of child conduct problems, and (c) our experiences with mothers and their children departing from battered women's shelters. Below we summarize and integrate these domains, focusing on those aspects pertinent to developing an intervention for the children who are already exhibiting conduct problems and who live in families departing from battered women's shelters. Next, we describe the components of our intervention and discuss preliminary data pertaining to its effectiveness.

Patterson's Developmental Model of Antisocial Behavior

Drawing heavily on social learning theory principles (Bandura, 1973, 1986), Patterson's theory links specific parenting behaviors and stressful family conditions to the development of antisocial behavior in young children. According to Patterson et al. (1992):

> basic training for patterns of antisocial behavior prior to adolescence takes place in the home, and family members are the primary trainers. It begins with a breakdown of parental effectiveness in disciplinary confrontations . . . the child learns that his own aversive behaviors turn off the aversive behaviors

of other family members and may also directly produce positive reinforcers. (p. 11)

In other words, during early childhood children can learn that oppositional and aggressive behavior can "pay off." For example, a 5-year-old boy finds that the easiest way to get a toy from his younger brother is to pull it out of his brother's hands when his parents are not watching (and, hence, not likely to intervene). An emotionally drained mother gives in to her 3-year-old son's repeated refusal to go to bed, even though she has told him, several times, that he needs to go to bed immediately. A hurried mother opts not to battle with her 4-year-old daughter who is refusing to pick up her toys and picks them up herself instead, because it is faster and easier. These last two examples, familiar to any parent or child caregiver, demonstrate that giving in to the child's noncompliance or aggression also can pay off for the parent, in that giving in reduces parental distress and parent–child conflict. The pay-off for the caregiver, however, is typically short-lived. To the extent that giving in to the child is repeated over time, the child's persistence and noncompliance may become habitual. Some parents may also respond inconsistently to their children's demands, sometimes succumbing to the child's aversive tactics and sometimes either requiring compliance or punishing the child for defiance. Unfortunately, giving in to such behavior, whether consistently or inconsistently, serves to increase the likelihood that the child's defiance and aggression will continue and will be exhibited in other settings as well (e.g., with teachers and peers).

Many factors can contribute to ineffective or inconsistent parental discipline such as that described above. Such factors include parent characteristics (e.g., beliefs about parenting and child development, psychological resources of the parent), child characteristics (e.g., persistence), and contextual factors (e.g., social isolation, marital conflict, economic stress, cultural support for certain child behaviors or disciplinary techniques). In addition to Patterson, other theorists who study parenting and child maltreatment (e.g., Belsky, 1984; Cicchetti & Lynch, 1993) suggest that such factors converge and that the balance between stressors/risk factors and supports/resources determines the probability of breakdowns in parental discipline. Many of the contextual factors that act as stressors, such as marital conflict, financial difficulties, and social isolation, are characteristic of families in which mothers have sought shelter for themselves and their children because of domestic violence (Margolin, Sibner, & Gleberman, 1988; Peled & Edleson, 1994). For many women, seeking refuge at a battered women's shelter suggests that the personal and contextual stressors impinging on them vastly outweigh their available resources and supports. After all, women who seek refuge at battered women's shelters typically do so because they feel they have nowhere else to go. It is easy to see how such circumstances might contribute to diminished consistency and effectiveness in parenting.

For the children of these women, the direct training for child antisocial behavior described by Patterson includes the presence of aggressive role models. That is, in addition to breakdowns in parental discipline that teach children that aggressive and defiant behavior can pay off, many of these children are also exposed to explicit demonstrations of physically abusive and socially inappropriate interpersonal behavior. Jaffe, Wilson, and Wolfe (1986) suggested several lessons that children are likely to learn from such aggressive models: (a) aggression is an appropriate form of conflict resolution; (b) aggression is an appropriate means of stress management; and (c) sexism, as defined by an inequality of power and decision making, is to be encouraged. These proposed lessons are consistent with battered women's reports of their children's behavior problems.

Patterson and others (e.g., Conduct Problems Prevention Research Group, 1992) postulated further that the family environment that promotes children's antisocial behavior is characterized by inadequate parental support and encouragement for the development of prosocial behavior (e.g., emotional control, social skills, and academic readiness). In many families with conduct-disordered children, positive reinforcement for desirable child behavior is sorely lacking, as is academic or intellectual stimulation. Although some battered women try desperately to shield their children from the effects of marital violence, living in such an environment limits a child's opportunities to learn prosocial behavior. Our observations suggest that few battered women who seek refuge at shelters have the personal, social, or financial resources to facilitate a supportive environment for their children while simultaneously coping with the demands of a violent relationship.

A key assumption of Patterson's model is that the conduct problems of preschoolers lead to academic and social difficulties during the early school years; that is, early-onset conduct problems set the stage for later antisocial behavior. Specifically, as behavior problems and academic failure experiences accumulate, doors to other socialization opportunities close, and these children become more and more alienated from their better behaved peers. As a result of this alienation, such children may begin to associate with other rejected youths, who may encourage deviant and aggressive behavior. It also can be argued that children of battered women may have limited exposure to many important socialization opportunities and are at increased risk of peer rejection. For example, children of battered women often endure frequent moves and, subsequently, school changes (Christopoulos et al., 1987; Wolfe, Jaffe, Wilson, & Zak, 1985), some of which are prompted directly by battering episodes (e.g., family is evicted because of the violence). Repeated family moves can interfere substantially with both academic competence and friendships. Moreover, children of battered women are often reluctant to bring friends to their homes and may not feel able to talk openly about their home and family life with peers. Alternatively, if they do talk with friends or bring them into their homes, they may have to deal with the negative emotional consequences of recognizing or acknowledging that their family life is "different" from that of their peers.

Other mechanisms by which wife abuse and marital conflict compromise parenting have received a great deal of theoretical and empirical attention (Easterbrooks & Emde, 1988; Emery, 1982; Erel & Burman, 1995; Margolin, 1981). Theorists often invoke one of several versions of the "spillover" hypothesis, suggesting that the effects of marital conflict spill over into the parent–child relationship. One such version of this hypothesis suggests that marital conflict is a stressor that causes parents to become irritable, depressed, distracted, and emotionally drained and that it reduces parents' attentiveness and prosocial responsiveness to their children (Easterbrooks & Emde, 1988). This spillover hypothesis is consistent with the empirical literature indicating that wife abuse correlates with both mothers' and fathers' aggression toward children (Jouriles, Barling, & O'Leary, 1987; Jouriles & LeCompte, 1991; Jouriles & Norwood, 1995; O'Keefe, 1995; Straus & Gelles, 1990; Straus, Gelles, & Steinmetz, 1980) and with parenting inconsistencies between mothers and fathers (Holden & Ritchie, 1991).

A logical conclusion of the spillover hypothesis is that parenting should improve after the mother leaves the batterer. Although longitudinal data on families departing from battered women's shelters are sparse, and the data pertaining to parenting following separation from a batterer are fraught with methodological limitations, available evidence suggests that the percentage of women who are violent toward their children actually increases following shelter departure (Giles-Sims, 1985).[1] Although these findings might seem inconsistent with the spillover hypothesis, it is important to keep in mind that relationship conflict and stress often escalate following marital separation (Emery, Matthews, & Kitzmann, 1994; Maccoby & Mnookin, 1992). Indeed, the time following a separation is particularly dangerous for battered women (Browne, 1987); it is a time during which they are at increased risk of being stalked and battered, or even killed, by their former partners. In addition, these women are making the transition from dual- to single-parent households, an experience that is often very stressful even in the absence of continued relationship conflict. Thus, it does not appear that

---

[1] In chapter 10 (p. 317), the Giles-Sims (1985) study was cited as evidence for decreases in child abuse following shelter departure. The Giles-Sims study reported that the percentage of women who used any of the physically violent tactics on the Conflict Tactics Scale (Straus, 1979; throwing something at the child; pushing, grabbing, or shoving; slapping; kicking, biting, hitting with a fist; hitting or trying to hit with something; beating up; threatening with a knife or gun; and using a knife or gun) increased from 95.2% at Time 1 (when they came to the shelter) to 100% at Time 2 (6 months later). However, the percentage of women who reported physically abusive tactics with their children (kicking, biting, hitting with a fist; hitting or trying to hit with something; beating up; threatening with a knife or gun; and using a knife or gun) decreased from 61.9% to 38.1%. It is important to note that the Time 1 scores covered a 12-month period, whereas the Time 2 scores covered a 6-month period. Thus, the two sets of scores are not directly comparable.

mother–child interactions necessarily improve as a result of the mother's moving away from the batterer.

Interventions for Reducing Children's Conduct Problems

Training in parenting skills appears to be the most promising single treatment approach for reducing conduct problems among preadolescents (Kazdin, 1987), and there is some evidence that such interventions are more effective with children under 7 years than with older children (Dishion & Patterson, 1992; Reid, 1993). Parenting skills training interventions typically involve ten to twenty 45-minute sessions, which focus on teaching parents how to reduce negative child behaviors, increase positive child behaviors, and enhance parent–child communication. More than 100 clinical outcome studies have evaluated this approach, and many controlled studies have documented improvements in child behavior over the course of treatment (Kazdin, 1985). In addition, improvements often remain evident 1 year after treatment, and continued benefits of treatment have been documented for up to 4.5 years posttreatment (Baum & Forehand, 1981).

Although training in parenting skills tends to be less effective when parents are experiencing high levels of personal distress (Webster-Stratton & Hammond, 1990), the effectiveness of such an intervention can be enhanced tremendously when concurrent family stressors are addressed during the course of treatment (Miller & Prinz, 1990). Women in battered women's shelters often lack the resources necessary for "low-stress" lifestyles following shelter departure. Thus, it is often necessary to address maternal and family stressors that may influence parenting, as a prelude to, and often coincident with, addressing parenting skills.

Needs of Women Departing From Battered Women's Shelters

Most of the mothers and children departing from battered women's shelters have a wide range of needs that social and mental health service providers can help address. For example, many of the mothers we interviewed in shelters lacked occupational skills, had elevated levels of anxiety and depression, and had very few social or economic resources. These data are consistent with survey results indicating that access to resources and social supports is one of the most important needs of women seeking help from agencies serving battered women (Peled & Edleson, 1994). These data are also consistent with pilot work conducted prior to the development and evaluation of our intervention in which we followed 31 families who had set up residences independent of their violent partners. We found that 25 of these families attempted to establish a residence in a neighborhood that was unfamiliar to them (the women and children, not the batterers, are typically forced by the circumstances to leave their homes). Whereas the majority (22 out of 31) of these women attempted to establish new residences on their own (i.e., just the mother and the children living in the household), some moved in with friends or relatives (7 out of 31) or into transitional living centers (2 out of 31). Many were without a reliable means of transportation (14 out of 31 did not have access to a car, and most lived in areas with little or no public transportation), had no phone (16 out of 31), and lacked basic home furnishings (e.g., beds, chairs, dishes; 7 out of 31). Understandably, many of the women reported feeling isolated, lonely, hopeless, and depressed after leaving the shelter.

To our knowledge, Sullivan and colleagues are the only other investigators who have systematically evaluated an intervention that provides resources and support services to women exiting battered women's shelters (Sullivan, Campbell, Angelique, Eby, & Davidson, 1994; Tan, Basta, Sullivan, & Davidson, 1995). In their program, "advocates" were trained to help women obtain needed resources and expand their social networks (if the women desired) for 10 weeks following shelter departure. They found that women who received advocacy services expressed greater satisfaction with their social support at posttreatment compared to women who did not receive such services; however, these between group differences disappeared after 6 months (Tan et al., 1995). Consistent with the general literature on social support (Cohen & Wills, 1985; Robinson & Garber, 1995), these investigators found women's satisfaction with social support to be strongly related to their psychological adjustment.

Helping mothers with decision-making and problem-solving skills appears to be another method by which mothers' stress can be reduced (e.g., Nezu, 1986) and by which the effectiveness of child management skills training can be enhanced. This latter point was investigated directly with a small sample of single-mother families seeking services for child conduct problems (Pfiffner, Jouriles, Brown, Etscheidt, & Kelly, 1990). In this study, families were randomly assigned to one of two conditions: intensive parent training only and parent training plus social problem-solving skills training. The problem-solving skills were often taught in the context of helping these mothers obtain needed resources. Mothers in both conditions reported significant reductions in children's conduct problems posttreatment and at a 4-month follow-up assessment. However, only families who also received training in problem solving evidenced significant reductions on observational measures of deviant child behavior. Mothers in that group also reported significantly greater decreases in children's conduct problems at follow-up than did mothers who received intensive parent training only.

Summary

Patterson's model suggests that deficits or breakdowns in parental discipline and a lack of parental support for, and modeling of, prosocial behavior lead to conduct problems in early childhood. Stressful family conditions are postulated to contribute to deficits and breakdowns in parenting and characterize many families departing from battered women's shelters. In addition, certain stressors, such as wife abuse, directly communicate to children an acceptance of violence in the family. Patterson's model hypothesizes that patterns of antisocial behavior established during the preschool years set the stage for school and peer problems and severe antisocial behavior later in life. This implies that reductions in family stress and alterations in parenting during the preschool and early school years decrease the likelihood of future social adjustment difficulties and academic failure. Consistent with Patterson's model, providing parenting skills training to parents of preschoolers and young school-age children appears to be an effective intervention for reducing children's conduct problems. In addition, the empirical literature strongly suggests that attention must also be directed toward the reduction of concomitant family stressors for this intervention to be effective. With women and children departing from battered women's shelters, this might include offering emotional support, providing direct assistance in obtaining needed resources, and teaching mothers skills to help them obtain resources and reduce stress on their own. Finally, the intervention must fit the special needs and limited resources of the families (e.g., lack of transportation, phones).

INTERVENTION DESCRIPTION

Our intervention for reducing conduct problems among children of battered women is a multicomponent family intervention. As indicated earlier, it is designed specifically for mothers and their children who have recently sought refuge at a shelter for battered women and who are in the process of setting up a residence independent of the violent partners. In addition, it is designed for families in which at least one child between the ages of 4 and 9 years exhibits aggressive/oppositional behavior. There are two primary components to the intervention: (a) providing mothers and children with social and instrumental support and problem-solving skills, and (b) parent-training, that is, teaching child management and nurturing skills to mothers.

We conduct weekly in-home intervention sessions, which begin after shelter departure and continue for up to 8 months. Families are assigned to an intervention team consisting of a trained therapist and one or more advanced undergraduate or postbaccalaureate students. Therapists work primarily with the mothers (e.g., teaching parenting and problem-solving skills, providing support). The undergraduate and postbaccalaureate students serve as mentors for the children. They accompany therapists on all weekly home visits, provide positive support, and serve as prosocial role models for the children. They also serve as role models for the mothers, demonstrating appropriate child management and nurturing skills. Although they are trained to use the same skills we teach mothers, their primary role is similar to that of a "big brother" or "big sister"—they engage the children in fun activities and provide positive attention and affection.

We offer a home-based intervention, as opposed to a clinic- or school-based intervention, to make it possible for families to take advantage of these services. As noted above, more than 50% of the women at the women's shelters in which we were working lacked transportation. Shelter workers reported that few former shelter residents were able to take advantage of support groups offered by the women's centers (either at the shelters or at administrative offices), a clear indication that home-based services were needed. In addition, home-visitation has been endorsed by both the U.S. Advisory Board on Child Abuse and Neglect (1991) and the U.S. General Accounting Office (1992) as the single most critical element in a comprehensive approach to preventing child maltreatment. Home-based parent training is also likely to increase the use of newly acquired skills in the home environment (Stokes & Osnes, 1989) and can enhance general therapeutic efforts by giving clinicians a clearer picture of a family's circumstances.

Our intervention is designed so that the specific content of these two primary components (parenting skills and the provision of instrumental and social support and problem-solving skills) and the manner in which they are delivered can be tailored to the needs of individual families. That is, we systematically assess each mother's needs, beliefs, practices, and knowledge with respect to how she perceives her child's behavior and how she parents her child. At times, it has also been helpful to discuss some of the parenting beliefs and behaviors of the mother's relatives and friends, especially in situations where mothers rely on those individuals for advice and child care. In some cases, our staff have worked directly with relatives or friends who were involved in the care and discipline of a client's children. For example, one mother shared her apartment and child care responsibilities with her grandmother. At the request of the mother and grandmother, we included the grandmother in a number of sessions so that both mother and grandmother could respond to the family's children consistently. Throughout our intervention, services are customized for each family with careful consideration of the family's specific needs, resources, and circumstances.

Provision of Social and Instrumental Support and Problem-Solving Skills

The social and instrumental support component of our intervention is based on our pilot work and is similar to an advocacy intervention conducted by Sullivan and colleagues for women departing from battered women's shelters (Sullivan et al., 1994; Sullivan & Davidson, 1991; Sullivan, Tan, Basta, Rumptz, & Davidson, 1992; Tan et al., 1995). Again, our experiences with mothers who exit battered women's shelters and attempt to establish residences independent of their batterers indicated that these women endured many stressors related to their immediate circumstances, such as no transportation, limited income, and unsatisfactory housing with few home furnishings. Many of these stressors loomed so large that until they were at least partially resolved, the women had little or no time or attentional resources to focus on their children's behavior problems. Thus, our work with families often begins with providing emotional support to the women during their transition from the shelter and helping them obtain the physical resources and social supports necessary to ensure their ability to become self-supporting and remain independent of their batterers. Our staff help mothers obtain services available to them by gathering information about community resources (this includes services available to them through the women's shelters), modeling how to call potential resource providers for services, observing the mothers make similar calls, and providing them with encouragement and feedback. In addition, we regularly deliver clothing and small household items to the families, and we deliver furniture and food when necessary. In certain limited circumstances, we also transport mothers, if necessary (i.e., if the mother has no other means of transportation), to help them gain access to needed goods and services.

Following the work of D'Zurilla and Goldfried (1971), the social and instrumental support component of the intervention includes training mothers in decision-making and problem-solving skills.

Through direct instruction, practice, and feedback, mothers are taught how to identify problems, to prioritize problems, to generate several alternative solutions, and to evaluate the potential outcome of each solution to choose from among them. Throughout our intervention, mothers are guided in the use of these techniques to make decisions and resolve problems as they arise.

It should also be emphasized that an integral goal of our intervention is to provide mothers and children an opportunity to have an ongoing relationship with a warm and supportive person (the therapists and child mentors). We conceptualize this relationship as part of the support component of the intervention. Although such a relationship might be considered a part of all, or at least many, therapies, it warrants emphasis because many of the mothers and children in our project have commented to us that their relationship with our staff was the only truly accepting relationship they had ever had. The presence of an encouraging, dependable person in the lives of many of these families is particularly important, given that many have experienced repeated criticism, denigration, and rejection. Such experiences often cause feelings of hopelessness, self-doubt, and resentment which, in turn, are likely to interfere with the family's ability to make positive and enduring changes. Given the difficult circumstances and experiences of many of the families served by our program, our staff always try to take advantage of any opportunity to acknowledge the efforts and courage of mothers and children and to applaud their successes.

Parent Training

Training mothers in child management and nurturing skills is the central component of our intervention for reducing child conduct problems. Through direct instruction, practice, and feedback, mothers are taught skills with which to increase desirable child behavior, decrease undesirable child behavior, communicate more effectively with their children, and facilitate a more positive and warm mother–child relationship. This component of the intervention is based on a composite of programs by other researchers (Dangel & Polster, 1988; Forehand & McMahon, 1981; Wolfe, 1991). Mothers are also instructed how to provide a safe, healthy environment for their children and how to ensure safe, alternative child care arrangements. Specific skills taught include listening to children, giving contingent praise and positive attention, giving clear and appropriate directives, shaping positive child behavior, giving rewards and privileges, and using time out.

The child nurturing element of the skills training component is derived from the work of several researchers (Eyberg, 1988; Forehand & Long, 1996; Hembree-Kigin & McNeil, 1995; Wolfe, 1991) and includes effective ways of playing with, listening to, and comforting children. Mothers are encouraged to spend at least a few minutes of "together time" every day, if possible, playing with each child in the family. Because many mothers' communications with their children primarily involve admonitions, reprimands, or instructions, some mothers do not notice or may disregard their children's feelings and concerns. To help mothers develop effective listening/attending skills, our staff point out the differences between a listening/attending response (e.g., nonverbal responses such as a smile or a nod, a reflective statement such as, "You sound really hurt"), and other types of responses (e.g., interrupting, interrogating, blaming, lecturing). Because most of the children in families served by our project have been exposed to frightening and distressing experiences, it is especially important for mothers to be able to comfort and reassure them effectively. Mothers are asked to review how they typically reassure and console their children and, when necessary, are helped to develop appropriate ways of addressing their children's concerns and fears (e.g., reflecting the child's feelings in words, using a soothing tone of voice, taking time to give the child a warm hug and a few moments of undivided attention).

We make it clear to the mothers that they are not to blame for their children's conduct problems. We do not want mothers to assume that they are being taught child management and nurturing skills because their "failures" or "deficits" are responsible for their children's problems. Although the theory in which our intervention is based highlights the role of family members as the "primary trainers" of child antisocial behavior, the term *family members* encompasses a variety of individuals who may significantly influence a child's development (e.g., siblings, grandparents, relatives, or other individuals living with the family). Patterson's theory also suggests that a different pattern of mother–child interaction would have developed in a different family context (i.e., one that is not characterized by battering) and that aggressive models contribute to the development of aggressive child behavior. Furthermore, many factors not mentioned directly in Patterson's theory are also likely to contribute to the development of child conduct problems. Again, we do not view the mothers as the cause of their children's conduct problems, and we make this clear to them over the course of our intervention.

However, we do emphasize to mothers that they can help their children recover from the experience of living in a violent household (i.e., reduce their children's conduct problems) by altering the way they interact with their children. In other words, by altering patterns of mother–child interaction, we can change child behavior, irrespective of the factors that were originally responsible for the development of the child's problematic behavior. We recognize, though, that certain factors contributing to the development of antisocial behavior patterns may also limit the extent to which the behavior problems can be modified (e.g., neurological damage caused by a head injury). When this is the case, we help the mothers understand the reasons for their children's behavior patterns and work with them to set reasonable expectations for the outcome of our intervention.

Although we teach mothers parenting skills that are applicable to all of their preschool and school-age children, we simplify the process by selecting one child, a child identified as having problematic behavior, to focus on. That is, we use the child's behavior problems that the mother has identified as the point of entry for helping the mother develop the skills with which to foster the child's prosocial development, enhance her relationship with the child, and address the child's conduct problems. Because the child's behavior has been problematic for the mother, she is often motivated to learn new information and skills with hopes of resolving her child's problems. The skills we teach are described to the mothers as general skills that are appropriate both for normally developing children and for children with conduct problems, and the mothers are strongly encouraged to apply their newly learned skills with all of their young children.

PRELIMINARY OUTCOME DATA

At the time this chapter was submitted for publication, we had just initiated a large-scale evaluation study of the intervention described above. The data presented below describe our ongoing evaluation efforts and provide preliminary results on the effectiveness of our intervention. The evaluation of our intervention is based on data from families meeting the three inclusion criteria delineated earlier: (a) mothers and children have sought refuge at a shelter for battered women because of relationship violence (i.e., physical violence from an intimate partner during the past year), (b) mothers are in the process of setting up a residence independent of their violent partners, and (c) mothers have a child between the ages of 4 and 9 years who exhibits aggressive or oppositional behavior. Families are excluded if the mother or child is experiencing active psychotic symptoms or if the target child does not live with the mother when they leave the shelter. In addition, we do not yet have the resources to offer and evaluate services delivered to non-English speaking mothers; thus, these families are also excluded. To date, we have gathered data from 34 families. Demographic data describing these participants are presented in Table 1. Twelve of the women are White, 11 are Hispanic, 9 are African American, 1 is Asian American, and 1 identified herself as "other." As can be seen in Table 1, these families are very low-income and have very few resources.

Families are screened for eligibility to participate in this project and are offered the opportunity to participate during their residence at one of four Houston-area women's shelters. Project staff build rapport with potential participants by informally visiting with mothers and children, playing with the children, talking with the mothers about how they and their children are doing, and offering to help find information about resources. Families who meet our eligibility criteria are informed of the nature of the evaluation study, including random assignment, by project staff during their shelter residence. Over the course of this project, 36

Table 1			
Sample Description (_N_ = 34)			

Variable	_M_	_SD_	Frequency
Mother age (years)	28.62	4.7	
Education (years)	11.39	2.1	
Mother annual income (preshelter; $)	7,421	4,841	
Batterer income ($)	11,407	12,363	
Mother annual income (postshelter; $)	5,929	4,826	
Number of moves in past 24 months	3.6	2.3	
Target child age (years)	5.7	2.0	
No. of children in family	2.79	1.1	
Target child			
Boy			25
Girl			9
No. receiving government assistance (preshelter)			21
Batterer is biological father of target child			22

families have met the eligibility criteria for this evaluation study, and 34 of the 36 (94%) agreed to participate. We interpret this high participation rate as an indicator of the representativeness of our sample (with respect to families who meet our eligibility criteria) and of the need and desirability of these services.

This study is a true experiment in which families are randomly assigned to either an intervention or comparison condition. Families in the intervention condition receive the intervention services we described above. Families in the comparison condition are encouraged to use any existing community or shelter services they believe are useful to them, but they receive no intervention services through our program. No restrictions are placed on families' receipt of services from other sources. For sample retention purposes, we have monthly contacts with families in the comparison condition and help provide school supplies, Thanksgiving dinners, and birthday and Christmas presents for all participants.

All families participate in an initial comprehensive assessment (prior to their assignment to either the intervention or comparison condition) as soon as possible following their departure from the shelter. This assessment includes multiple measures of child conduct problems, mothers' parenting skills, and mothers' psychological distress, among other factors. In this chapter, we present data on five of our outcome measures: two indices of child conduct problems, two indices of mothers' parenting, and an index of mothers' psychological distress. Child conduct problems are assessed both by mothers' reports on the Externalizing Scale of the Child Behavior Checklist (CBCL; Achenbach, 1991) and by an in-home observational procedure, which involves a 40-minute videotape of each mother and her child during and shortly after a meal. The in-home observational procedure is also used to assess mothers' warmth and involvement with her child and her use of parenting skills (e.g., appropriate use of praise, issuing clear directives). Scores for antisocial child behavior and mothers' parenting are obtained using an adaptation of a coding system devised by Hetherington and Clingempeel (1986, 1992). We measure mothers' general psychological distress with the Symptom Checklist-90-Revised (SCL-90-R; Derogatis, 1977). Our assessments of family functioning are repeated at 4, 8, 12, and 16 months following the initial assessment.

At the time of publication of this chapter, 8-month data (i.e., 8 months following shelter departure) were coded for 18 of these 34 families. Eight of these families were in the intervention condition, and 10 were in the comparison condition. Because of the preliminary nature of our data and the small number of families in each condition who had completed their participation in the project, we do not present a formal statistical analysis of the data. However, means and standard deviations for the outcome variables assessed at pretreatment and 8 months following shelter departure are presented in Table 2. Figures 1 and 2 display in graphic form the initial outcome data for child conduct problems. Figure 1 displays data from mothers' reports on the Exter-

Table 2

Outcome Variables at Initial and 8-Month Assessments

Variable	Intervention condition				Comparison condition			
	Initial assessment		8-month assessment		Initial assessment		8-month assessment	
	M	SD	M	SD	M	SD	M	SD
Mothers' reports								
Child Externalizing Behavior (CBCL *T* Scores)	64	11	53	12	64	9	61	11
Mother psychological distress (SCL-90-R)	67	8	49	11	69	9	64	9
Observational codes								
Child antisocial behavior	62	16	48	8	64	38	55	13
Mother correct implementation of parenting skills	143	23	161	8	146	21	145	13
Mother warmth/involvement	158	17	168	10	158	6	155	19

Note. CBCL = Child Behavior Checklist; SCL-90-R = Symptom Checklist–90–Revised.

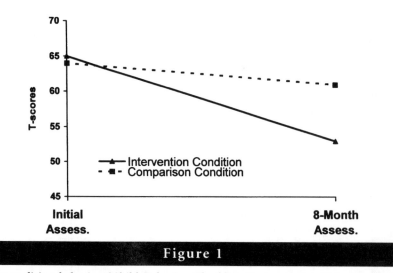

Figure 1

Externalizing behavior (Child Behavior Checklist *T* scores) at initial assessment (assess.) and 8 months later.

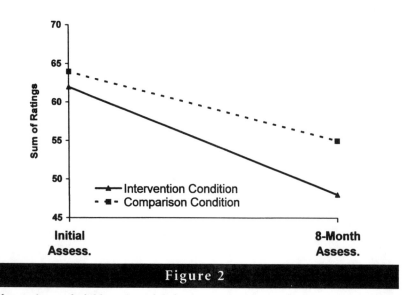

Figure 2

Observations of child antisocial behavior at initial assessment (assess.) and 8 months later.

nalizing Disorder (i.e., conduct problems) Scale of the CBCL; Figure 2 displays data from the home observation session. Both the mother report and observational data indicate that families receiving the intervention evidence reductions in child antisocial behavior. Such dramatic changes are not evident among families in the comparison condition. It should be noted further that each mother who received the intervention reported improvements in her child's behavior over the course of the intervention.

The positive benefits of our intervention were not limited to reductions in child conduct problems. Figures 3 and 4 present observational data for two dimensions of mothering (maternal warmth and involvement, and the appropriate use of parenting skills). Again, mothers in families receiving the intervention are observed to become more warm and involved with their children and to use parenting skills more effectively. Mothers in the comparison condition do not evidence such changes. Figure 5 presents data on mothers' reports of psychological distress (SCL-90-R). Mothers in families receiving the experimental in-

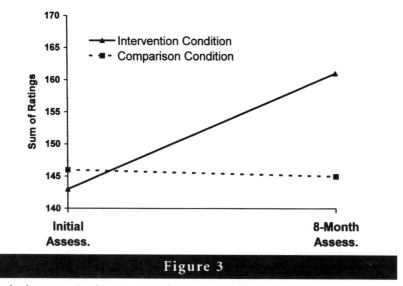

Figure 3

Mother's correct implementation of parenting skills at initial assessment (assess.) and 8 months later.

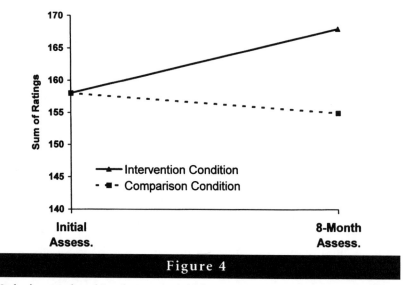

Figure 4

Mother's warmth and involvement at initial assessment (assess.) and 8 months later.

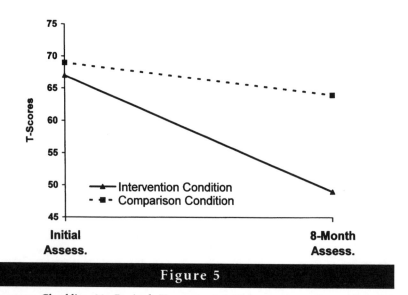

Figure 5

Symptom Checklist–90–Revised *T* scores at initial assessment (assess.) and 8 months later.

tervention report substantial reductions in psychological distress compared to mothers in the comparison condition.

Although the results displayed in Figures 1–5 are very preliminary, they provide initial evidence of our intervention's effectiveness. Mothers receiving our intervention have become less distressed and have improved their parenting, becoming both better managers of their children's behavior and increasing their display of warmth and involvement with their children. In response, children's behavior has improved remarkably. These results lead us to believe that our intervention is making a major contribution toward helping battered women and ameliorating the damaging effects of spousal violence on children.

Because many children who are exposed to domestic violence exhibit serious behavior problems, there is growing recognition that the children in such families could benefit from social and mental health services. In this chapter, we described our intervention efforts directed at a specific subset of these children: those who were exhibiting conduct problems, who were between the ages of 4 and 9 years, and who were departing from a battered women's shelter with their mothers to establish a residence independent of an abusive man. The preliminary results of the evaluation of our intervention are very encouraging. In the families who have received our intervention, the children's behavior has improved remarkably. The mothers in the families who have received our intervention have become less distressed and have improved their parenting. That is, these mothers have become more competent in managing their children's behavior and are warmer and more involved with their children. We believe our intervention helps reduce significantly the damaging effects of spousal violence on children.

We are continuing to evaluate the effects of our intervention with the initial sample of 34 families described in this chapter. We also are extending our intervention and evaluation efforts to a much larger sample of families in order to firmly establish the intervention's effectiveness and to begin to identify individual, family, and environmental factors that might increase our understanding of battering and its effects on children. Following further confirmation of our intervention's effectiveness, we intend to disseminate it to other shelters and to adapt it as indicated to meet the needs of other children of battered women.

REFERENCES

Achenbach, T. (1991). *Manual for the Child Behavior Checklist/4-18 and 1991 Profile*. Burlington: University of Vermont, Department of Psychiatry.

Bandura, A. (1973). *Aggression: A social learning analysis*. Englewood Cliffs, NJ: Prentice-Hall.

Bandura, A. (1986). *Social foundations of thought and action*. Englewood Cliffs, NJ: Prentice-Hall.

Baum, C. G., & Forehand, R. (1981). Long-term follow-up assessment of parent training by use of multiple outcome measures. *Behavior Therapy, 12,* 643–652.

Belsky, J. (1984). The determinants of parenting: A process model. *Child Development, 55,* 83–96.

Browne, A. (1987). *When battered women kill*. New York: Free Press.

Christopoulos, C., Cohn, D. A., Shaw, D. S., Joyce, S., Sullivan-Hanson, J., Kraft, S. P., & Emery, R. E. (1987). Children of abused women: I. Adjustment at time of shelter residence. *Journal of Marriage and the Family, 49,* 611–619.

Cicchetti, D., & Lynch, M. (1993). Toward an ecological/transactional model of community violence and child maltreatment. *Psychiatry, 56,* 96–118.

Cohen, S., & Wills, T. A. (1985). Stress, social support, and the buffering hypothesis. *Psychological Bulletin, 98,* 310–357.

Compas, B. E. (1987). Coping with stress during childhood and adolescence. *Psychological Bulletin, 101,* 393–403.

Conduct Problems Prevention Research Group. (1992). A developmental and clinical model for the prevention of conduct disorder: The FAST track program. *Development and Psychopathology, 4,* 509–527.

Dangel, R. F., & Polster, R. A. (1988). *Teaching child management skills*. New York: Pergamon Press.

Derogatis, L. (1977). *The SCL-90-R*. Baltimore: Clinical Psychometrics Research.

Dishion, T. J., & Patterson, G. R. (1992). Age effects in parent training outcome. *Behavior Therapy, 23,* 719–729.

D'Zurilla, T. J., & Goldfried, M. R. (1971). Problem solving and behavior modification. *Journal of Abnormal Psychology, 78,* 107–126.

Easterbrooks, M. A., & Emde, R. N. (1988). Marital and parent–child relationships: The role of affect in the family system. In R. A. Hinde & J. S. Hinde (Eds.), *Relationships within families: Mutual influences* (pp. 83–103). New York: Oxford University Press.

Emery, R. E. (1982). Interparental conflict and the children of discord and divorce. *Psychological Bulletin, 92,* 310–330.

Emery, R. E., Matthews, S., & Kitzmann, K. (1994). Child custody mediation and litigation: Parents' satisfaction and functioning a year after settlement. *Journal of Consulting and Clinical Psychology, 62,* 124–129.

Erel, O., & Burman, B. (1995). Interrelatedness of marital relations and parent–child relations: A meta-analytic review. *Psychological Bulletin, 118,* 108–132.

Eyberg, S. M. (1988). Parent–child interaction therapy: Integration of traditional and behavioral concerns. *Child and Family Behavior Therapy, 10,* 33–46.

Fantuzzo, J. W., DePaola, L. M., Lambert, L., Martino, T., Anderson, G., & Sutton, S. (1991). Effects of interparental violence on the psychological adjustment and competencies of young children. *Journal of Consulting and Clinical Psychology, 59,* 258–265.

Forehand, R. L., & Long, N. (1996). *Parenting the strong-willed child.* Chicago: Contemporary Books.

Forehand, R. L., & McMahon, R. J. (1981). *Helping the noncompliant child: A clinician's guide to parent training.* New York: Guilford Press.

Giles-Sims, J. (1985). A longitudinal study of battered children of battered wives. *Family Relations, 34,* 205–210.

Hembree-Kigin, T. L., & McNeil, C. B. (1995). *Parent–child interaction therapy.* New York: Plenum Press.

Hetherington, E. M., & Clingempeel, W. G. (1986). *Longitudinal study of adjustment to remarriage: Global coding manual.* Charlottesville: University of Virginia, Department of Psychology.

Hetherington, E. M., & Clingempeel, W. G. (1992). Coping with marital transitions: A family systems perspective. *Monographs of the Society for Research in Child Development, 57*(2–3, Serial No. 227).

Holden, G. W., & Ritchie, K. L. (1991). Linking extreme marital discord, child rearing, and child behavior problems: Evidence from battered women. *Child Development*, 62, 311–327.

Holden, G. W., Stein, J. D., Ritchie, K. L., Harris, S. D., & Jouriles, E. N. (1998). Parenting behaviors and beliefs of battered women. In G. W. Holden, R. A. Geffner, & E. N. Jouriles (Eds.), *Children exposed to marital violence: Theory, research, and applied issues* (pp. 289–334). Washington, DC: American Psychological Association.

Hotaling, G., & Sugarman, D. (1986). An analysis of risk markers in husband to wife violence: The current state of knowledge. *Violence and Victims*, 1(2), 101–124.

Hughes, H., & Luke, D. A. (1998). Heterogeneity in adjustment among children of battered women. In G. W. Holden, R. A. Geffner, & E. N. Jouriles (Eds.), *Children exposed to marital violence: Theory, research, and applied issues* (pp. 185–221). Washington, DC: American Psychological Association.

Jaffe, P. G., Sudermann, M., & Reitzel, D. (1992). Child witnesses of marital violence. In R. T. Ammerman & M. Hersen (Eds.), *Assessment of family violence: A clinical and legal sourcebook* (pp. 313–331). New York: Wiley.

Jaffe, P. G., Wilson, S., & Wolfe, D. (1986). Promoting changes in attitudes and understanding of conflict resolution among child witnesses of family violence. *Canadian Journal of Behavioural Science*, 18, 356–366.

Jaffe, P. G., Wolfe, D. A., & Wilson, S. K. (1990). *Children of battered women*. Newbury Park, CA: Sage.

Jouriles, E. N., Barling, J., & O'Leary, K. D. (1987). Predicting child behavior problems in maritally violent families. *Journal of Abnormal Child Psychology*, 15, 165–173.

Jouriles, E. N., & LeCompte, S. H. (1991). Husbands' aggression toward wives and mothers' and fathers' aggression toward children: Moderating effects of child gender. *Journal of Consulting and Clinical Psychology*, 59, 190–192.

Jouriles, E. N., Murphy, C. M., & O'Leary, K. D. (1989). Interspousal aggression, marital discord, and child problems. *Journal of Consulting and Clinical Psychology*, 57, 453–455.

Jouriles, E. N., & Norwood, W. D. (1995). Physical aggression toward boys and girls in families characterized by the battering of women. *Journal of Family Psychology, 9,* 69–78.

Kazdin, A. E. (1985). *Treatment of antisocial behavior in children and adolescents.* Homewood, IL: Dorsey.

Kazdin, A. E. (1987). Treatment of antisocial behavior in children: Current status and future directions. *Psychological Bulletin, 102,* 187–203.

Kolbo, J. R., Blakely, E. H., & Engleman, D. (1996). Children who witness domestic violence: A review of empirical literature. *Journal of Interpersonal Violence, 11,* 281–293.

Maccoby, E. E., & Mnookin, R. H. (1992). *Dividing the child.* Cambridge, MA: Harvard University Press.

Margolin, G. (1981). The reciprocal relationship between marital and child problems. In J. P. Vincent (Ed.), *Advances in family intervention, assessment, and theory* (pp. 131–182). Greenwich, CT: JAI Press.

Margolin, G., Sibner, L. G., & Gleberman, L. (1988). Wife battering. In V. B. Van Hasselt, R. L. Morrison, A. S. Bellack, & M. Hersen (Eds.), *Handbook of family violence* (pp. 89–117). New York: Plenum Press.

McCord, J. (1979). Some child rearing antecedents to criminal behavior in adult men. *Journal of Personality and Social Psychology, 37,* 1477–1486.

McDonald, R., & Jouriles, E. N. (1991). Marital aggression and child behavior problems: Research findings, mechanisms, and intervention strategies. *Behavior Therapist, 14,* 189–192.

Miller, G. E., & Prinz, R. J. (1990). Enhancement of social learning family interventions for childhood conduct disorder. *Psychological Bulletin, 108,* 291–307.

Moffitt, T. E. (1993). Adolescence-limited and life-course-persistent antisocial behavior: A developmental taxonomy. *Psychological Review, 100,* 674–701.

Nezu, A. M. (1986). Efficacy of a social problem-solving therapy approach for disorders in children. *Journal of Consulting and Clinical Psychology, 54,* 196–202.

O'Keefe, M. (1995). Predictors of child abuse in maritally violent families. *Journal of Interpersonal Violence, 10,* 3–25.

Patterson, G. R. (1982). *Coercive family process.* Eugene, OR: Castalia.

Patterson, G. R., DeBarsyshe, B. D., & Ramsey, E. (1989). A developmental perspective on antisocial behavior. *American Psychologist, 44,* 329–335.

Patterson, G. R., Reid, J. B., & Dishion, T. J. (1992). *Antisocial boys.* Eugene, OR: Castalia.

Peled, E., & Edleson, J. L. (1994). Advocacy for battered women: A national survey. *Journal of Family Violence, 9,* 285–296.

Pfiffner, L., Jouriles, E. N., Brown, M., Etscheidt, M., & Kelly, J. (1990). Effects of problem-solving therapy on outcomes of parent training for single-parent families. *Child and Family Behavior Therapy, 12,* 1–11.

Reid, J. B. (1993). Prevention of conduct disorder before and after school entry: Relating interventions to developmental findings. *Development and Psychopathology, 5,* 243–262.

Robinson, N. S., & Garber, J. (1995). Social support and psychopathology across the life span. In D. Cicchetti & D. J. Cohen (Eds.), *Developmental psychopathology: Vol. 2. Risk, disorder, and adaptation* (pp. 162–209). New York: Wiley.

Rossman, B. B., & Rosenberg, M. (1992). Family stress and functioning in children: The moderating effects of children's beliefs about their control over parental conflict. *Journal of Clinical Child Psychiatry, 33,* 699–715.

Rutter, M. (1983). Stress, coping, and development: Some issues and some questions. In N. Garmezy & M. Rutter (Eds.), *Stress, coping, and development in children* (pp. 1–41). New York: McGraw Hill.

Stokes, F. T., & Osnes, G. P. (1989). An operant pursuit of generalization. *Behavior Therapy, 20,* 337–355.

Straus, M. A. (1979). Measuring intrafamily conflict and violence: The Conflict Tactics Scale. *Journal of Marriage and the Family, 41,* 75–88.

Straus, M. A., & Gelles, R. J. (1988). How violent are American families? Estimates from the National Family Violence Resurvey and Other Studies. In M. A. Straus & R. J. Gelles (Eds.), *Physical violence in American families: Risk factors and adaptations to violence in 8,145 families* (pp. 95–112). New Brunswick, NJ: Transaction.

Straus, M. A., & Gelles, R. J. (1990). *Physical violence in American families: Risk factors and adaptations to violence in 8,145 families.* New Brunswick, NJ: Transaction.

Straus, M. A., Gelles, R. J., & Steinmetz, S. K. (1980). *Behind closed doors: Violence in the American family.* Garden City, NJ: Anchor Books.

Sullivan, C. M., Campbell, R., Angelique, H., Eby, K. K., & Davidson, W. S.

(1994). An advocacy intervention program for women with abusive partners: Six-month follow-up. *American Journal of Community Psychology, 22,* 101–122.

Sullivan, C. M., & Davidson, W. S. (1991). The provision of advocacy services to women leaving abusive partners: An examination of short-term effects. *American Journal of Community Psychology, 19,* 953–960.

Sullivan, C. M., Tan, C., Basta, J., Rumptz, M., & Davidson, W. S. (1992). An advocacy intervention program for women with abusive partners: Initial evaluation. *American Journal of Community Psychology, 20,* 309–332.

Tan, C., Basta, J., Sullivan, C. M., & Davidson, W. S. (1995). The role of social support in the lives of women exiting domestic violence shelters: An experimental study. *Journal of Interpersonal Violence, 10,* 437–451.

Texas Council on Family Violence. (1994). *Statistics on domestic violence.* (Available from Texas Council on Family Violence, 8701 N. MoPac Expressway St. 450, Austin, TX 78759)

U.S. Advisory Board on Child Abuse and Neglect. (1991). *Creating caring communities: Blueprint for an effective federal policy on child abuse and neglect.* Washington, DC: U.S. Government, Department of Health and Human Services.

U.S. General Accounting Office. (1992). *Child abuse prevention programs: Prevention programs need greater emphasis* (GAO/HRD-92-99). Washington, DC: Author.

Webster-Stratton, C., & Hammond, M. (1990). Predictors of treatment outcome in parent training for families with conduct problem children. *Behavior Therapy, 21,* 319–337.

Wolfe, D. A. (1991). *Preventing physical and emotional abuse of children.* New York: Guilford Press.

Wolfe, D. A., Jaffe, P., Wilson, S., & Zak, L. (1985). Children of battered women: The relation of child behavior to family violence and maternal stress. *Journal of Consulting and Clinical Psychology, 53,* 657–665.

Wolfe, D. A., Zak, L., Wilson, S., & Jaffe, P. (1986). Child witnesses to violence between parents: Critical issues in behavioral and social adjustment. *Journal of Abnormal Child Psychology, 14,* 95–104.

12

Child Custody Disputes and Domestic Violence: Critical Issues for Mental Health, Social Service, and Legal Professionals

Peter G. Jaffe and Robert Geffner

The criminal, civil, and family law proceedings involving the O. J. Simpson case have focused international attention on the issue of domestic violence. Almost forgotten in the media frenzy, however, have been the Simpson children, who typify millions of less publicized children. The Simpson children represent the silent victims of this violence, who fade into the background as if they were casual bystanders. These children victims are just beginning to be recognized in courts, clinics, and child protection agencies and to be the focus of research and intervention programs, as shown in the preceding chapters of this book. One of the many recent controversies within the justice system that was highlighted by the media in the Simpson case involves the custody of the children.

It may help to consider the desperate call that Nicole Brown Simpson made to the Los Angeles, California Police Department in 1989.

This chapter is based in part on material prepared by Peter Jaffe for the Family Violence Prevention Fund, San Francisco, California, judicial education curriculum entitled Domestic Violence and Children, and on presentations by both authors for the National and International Conferences on Children Exposed to Family Violence, June 1996 in Austin, Texas and June 1997 in London, Ontario.

Her fear and frustration in getting assistance were clear. Her children, ages 1 and 3 at that time, probably were awakened by the raised voices, screams, and noise from the assault and probably experienced significant trauma and terror. Were they frightened for their mother's life? Were they frightened for their own life? Were they frightened by their father's behavior? Were they confused about why their father would be behaving in such a manner? Did they understand the danger? Were they affected even if they did not understand what was happening? If an adult with more advanced cognitive and emotional understanding can experience these events in such a fearful manner, imagine the effect of these situations on a young child who does not have the ability to understand or cope. These are important issues, affecting approximately 10 million children who may be exposed to their mother being assaulted every year in the U.S. (Straus, 1991) and perhaps a proportional number in Canada and elsewhere.

Traditionally, society has shown less concern for the children exposed to marital violence. Awareness of child maltreatment has focused mainly on physical and sexual abuse. Only in recent years have social scientists recognized that children are adversely affected by being exposed to violence in their home (Jaffe, Wolfe, & Wilson, 1990). The scars are not always visible, but the short-term and potential long-term adjustment problems have been increasingly documented (see the preceding chapters in this book). Researchers, clinicians, and advocates for battered women across North America have tried to change these children's status from "forgotten" to "high risk" and in need of protection and specialized support services (Hughes & Marshall, 1995).

Although we have no personal knowledge of the court-ordered assessment and the detailed findings by the judge in the Simpson custody case, the decision by the judge to award Simpson managing custody forces distant observers to integrate the image of O. J. Simpson assaulting Nicole Brown (according to previous court findings and audiotapes) and the image of O. J. Simpson as a caring and loving father having the primary role of rearing these children. The decision in the Simpson custody case and in many others throughout North America stands in contrast to many recent court decisions and the Model Code of the

National Council of Juvenile & Family Court Judges (1994), which states:

> In every proceeding where there is at issue a dispute as to the custody of a child, a determination by the court that domestic or family violence has occurred raises a rebuttable presumption that it is detrimental to the child and not in the best interest of the child to be placed in sole custody, joint legal custody, or joint physical custody with the perpetrator of family violence. (Model Code 401)

Thus, this chapter addresses the fundamental issues regarding domestic violence and custody. We explore recent reports indicating that abusing a child's mother is in itself a form of profound psychological and emotional abuse that requires thoughtful consideration and significant weight in court decisions.

OVERVIEW OF THE IMPACT OF EXPOSURE TO DOMESTIC VIOLENCE

Studies on the incidence of violence in homes suggest a wide range of estimates depending on the research method and definition of violence. Two of the more recent comprehensive surveys estimate that at least 30% of all women suffer from some form of violence in an adult relationship during their life span. For 10% of the women, this violence is so severe that they worry for their personal safety and life (Canadian Panel on Violence Against Women, 1993; Rodgers, 1994). Their fears are well-founded when one considers that the majority of female homicide victims are killed by their partner, ex-partner, or boyfriend (Bachman & Saltzman, 1996).

Although the terms *family violence* and *domestic violence* are commonly used, the most accurate term is *maltreatment of women and children,* because women and children represent the vast majority of the victims. Men are also abused, but in most instances, men's violence against women creates greater injury, pain, and suffering, and a large proportion of women's violence toward men is in self-defense (Gelles & Straus, 1988; Pagelow, 1997).

Although many parents within violent families think that they have protected their children from the violence, between 80% and 90% of children indicate the opposite (Hilton, 1992; Jaffe et al., 1990). Most children not only are aware of what happened, but they can give detailed descriptions about the escalation of the violence. Children may be at their bedroom door or at the top of the stairs, or they may enter the kitchen shortly after a violent episode, but they know too well the reality of the violence and the emotional and physical consequences to their mother (Peled, 1993). At the extreme, when women are murdered by their husbands, children are present in approximately 25% of the cases (Crawford & Gartner, 1992).

The impact of exposure to violence has both short-term and long-term consequences that depend on the children's gender and stage of development. Preschool children who are exposed to this violence may suffer from nightmares or other sleep disturbances. The trauma in their lives causes great confusion and insecurity that may lead to regressive behavior, such as excessive clinging to adults or a fear of being left alone (see Graham-Bermann, 1998, and Hughes & Luke, 1998, this volume). Some children are polarized by constant fear and anxiety because the places and people who should afford them the greatest protection (home and parents) turn out to be the most dangerous (Gelles & Straus, 1988; Jaffe et al., 1990; Roy, 1988).

As the preceding chapters in this book have described, children exposed to their father's abuse of their mother may exhibit a range of internalizing and externalizing emotional and behavioral problems (see also Graham-Bermann & Levendosky, 1997; Hughes, 1997). These symptoms continue into adolescence, as one girl describes very clearly in *Children in the Crossfire* (Roy, 1988), which details interviews with 146 children from ages 11 to 17 years:

> I think that my nightmares after I left home helped me because when I awoke and realized that they were only dreams and that Dad wasn't there, I had nothing to be afraid of. I've got used to the idea that my dad is not present. The fact that he is not

nearby made the nightmares go away. That was a relief. I've really changed since I've been away from home. I used to be a nervous wreck living at home. When he'd be out, I'd be scared of what he'd do when he came home. I'd sit up and peek through the curtains to see if he'd be commin' in from a drunken binge. There was nothin' really to do at home besides doin' my homework and watchin' TV. It was hard waitin' for him to come home. Sometimes I'd feel like screamin'. (p. 128)

Aside from the more dramatic or visible symptoms of being exposed to violence, children may also exhibit more subtle signs of this trauma that are not apparent from traditional assessment and interview data. For example, children who are exposed to parental violence tend to hold beliefs that violence is an appropriate method in trying to resolve conflicts, especially in the context of an intimate relationship (Jaffe et al., 1990). Some children may see physical aggression as appropriate in gaining respect or control in a relationship and excusable if a perpetrator is drinking, or if a victim has supposedly done something to "provoke" him (i.e., they think the father's view of the violence was justified because the house was messy or dinner not ready on time). Moreover, some children may blame themselves over time for the violence, feeling that it is their duty to protect their mother or defuse their father's anger. They may feel that if they were perfect in their own home, their parents would not fight over them and cause more violence. This pronounced sense of personal responsibility begins at an early age and can continue into adulthood. Obviously these symptoms, as well as the previously mentioned ones, may impede children's development, affect their academic and community involvement, and affect their sense of personal competence (Hilton, 1992; Jaffe et al., 1990; Peled, 1993; Rossman & Rosenberg, in press).

Some children may feel so responsible for their mother's safety that they adjust their own lives to protect their mother. They may refuse to go to school and later receive the diagnosis of "school phobic" for this reason. Other children may go to school and present somatic concerns such as headaches and stomach pains so that they can return home to their mothers. In some circumstances, mothers do not discourage this behavior because of their own isolation, depression, and inability to set any limits for their children (Jaffe et al., 1990; Jaffe, Wolfe, Wilson & Zak, 1986).

Adolescents who have been exposed to violence develop their own coping strategies to deal with the trauma. At an adaptive level, with extended family or community supports, these young persons may try to separate and individuate from the family problem and seek more independent living and school or vocational pursuits. Unfortunately, many adolescents do not have adequate skills and social supports in place. These adolescents may attempt to cope through drug and alcohol abuse or by running away to potentially more dangerous environments (e.g., the streets). Often, they become involved in abusive dating relationships. Adolescent boys who have been exposed to violence are more likely to be abusive, and girls who have been exposed to violence are less likely to question dating violence (e.g., Carlson, 1990). Many of these adolescents do not even consider that this violent behavior is criminal in nature and could lead to sanctions by the court system (Mercer, 1987; Sudermann, Jaffe, & Hastings, 1995; Wolfe, Wekerle, Reitzel, & Gough, 1995). As can be seen in the recent research reported in the preceding chapters, though, growing up in such a family environment and being exposed to a father battering the mother tends to produce more anger, hostility, and aggression in boys and girls.

The long-term impact of being exposed to domestic violence is most apparent from retrospective studies of male perpetrators of violence and female survivors of violence in adult relationships. The majority of abusive husbands have grown up in families where they were exposed to their father's abuse of their mothers. The landmark studies in this field suggest that sons of severe batterers have wife abuse rates at 10 times the level of sons of nonviolent fathers. Women are less likely to seek assistance when they are abused if they have been exposed to violence in their family of origin (Gelles & Straus, 1988; Walker, 1989).

Several important issues and cautions need to be raised about the research on children who have been exposed to violence. Although being exposed to violence is an important factor, it rarely happens in isolation from other stressors in a child's life (e.g., repeated separations and disruptions, financial hardships, lack of adequate housing or shelter). In many circumstances, children may personally experience several forms of violence themselves aside from being exposed to their mother's victimization. The most conservative estimates suggest at least a minimum 30% overlap between wife assault and child abuse, and some studies and recent reviews have estimated an overlap of up to 70% (Barnett, Miller-Perrin, & Perrin, 1997; Bowker, Arbitell, & McFerron, 1988; Crowell & Burgess, 1996; Jaffe et al., 1990; Schechter & Edleson, 1994; Zorza, 1991).

It is also important to note that not all children are equally affected by being exposed to violence, and some children are quite resilient. In fact, some children from the same family sometimes develop in different ways, including boys who grow up to be nonviolent, nurturing fathers and husbands and girls who become confident and assertive. Researchers suggest several protective factors that need to be considered, including alternative adult role models, strong and positive attachments to mother, and extensive supports within the community (e.g., Kinnard, 1995). Clinical interventions (e.g., Peled, 1996; Silvern, Karyl, & Landis, 1995) and judicial interventions (e.g., Family Violence Project, 1990; Zorza, 1995) can promote safety and positive adjustment by recognizing these factors.

CHILDREN OF DOMESTIC VIOLENCE AND DIVORCE: THE FOCUS OF CUSTODY AND VISITATION DISPUTES

Children are a central focus in decisions battered women make about leaving the batterer or staying in the abusive relationship (Barnett & LaViolette, 1993; Hilton, 1992). Battered women often cite the children as a reason to remain with their spouse, in addition to other factors, such as fear, economic dependency, self-blame, and lack of community support (M. A. Dutton, 1996; Pagelow, 1997). They may rationalize their decision in terms of having greater economic security and at least the presence of a man (albeit a poor role model). They may also fear losing the children; many batterers threaten their partners with taking away the children and proving the partner to be an unfit mother. These fears are well-founded, because some research suggests that abusive husbands actually have a good chance of convincing judges that they should have custody (Enos, 1996; Zorza, 1995). Sometimes battered women are deprived economically to the point of being left homeless (Zorza, 1991). On the other hand, some battered women may decide to leave if they start to recognize the impact the violence has on their children. Most often, this decision happens after an incident of direct physical or sexual abuse (Henderson, 1990; Hilton, 1992) or when the women start to recognize the impact that exposure to the violence has on their children (M. A. Dutton, 1992).

The research on children of divorce and on children exposed to domestic violence has developed as two separate branches, which often leads to conflicting advice for battered women. The general literature on the impact of divorce stresses the negative influence of conflict on children and the positive influence of a co-parenting relationship where the children maintain an ongoing, supportive relationship with both parents. This is often true for nonviolent families (e.g., Wallerstein & Blakeslee, 1989). In reality, though, contested custody cases often represent a higher level of violence compared to the general population of divorcing adults (Johnston & Campbell, 1993). When domestic violence has been present, a co-parenting relationship and the impact of the conflict on the children often represents a negative influence on the children. Many battered women are placed in a situation where they are advised to promote a relationship and set aside their past conflicts with a spouse who may be a danger to themselves and their children. If they do not comply, they may be deemed "unfriendly or unfit parents," and they can lose custody to an abusive father (Enos, 1996; Zorza, 1992b).

One of the most important issues that often goes unrecognized by many legal and mental health professionals is that the violence does not end with separation. A large-scale study of children of battered women in shelters in California showed that separation tends to lead to an escalation of violence and a greater danger for the safety of their mother (Liss & Stahly, 1993; Stahly, 1990). In fact, many courts promote unsupervised visitation orders, and this may give abusive men an ongoing opportunity to expose children to violence or threats of violence (Geffner & Pagelow, 1990a; Pagelow, 1993, 1997).

Paradoxically, women may not be believed when violence is reported because they are seen as exaggerating incidents of violence as a way of manipulating the courts. In fact, many of the women who suffer posttraumatic stress disorder (e.g., M. A. Dutton, 1992) have been labeled as histrionic or worse. For example, a recent article discussed a "malicious mother syndrome" in divorce as an "explanation" for the animosity some women hold toward their former husbands, their attempt to blame the men for all the problems by accusing them of various behaviors, and their attempt to not allow them to see the children (Turkat, 1995). The American Psychological Association (APA) Presidential Task Force on Violence and the Family (1996) recently summarized the literature in this area and expressed concerns about the labeling and pathologizing of battered women in divorce and custody cases. When such labeling occurs, men's violence may be minimized as only an emotional reaction to the separation or completely ignored.

The conclusion that some critics of the court system have come to is that judges "consider father estrangement more traumatic to children than paternal abuse" (Taylor, 1992, p. 53). Even many mental health professionals, who should have benefited from several decades of research on domestic violence, still believe that as many as one in eight women are magnifying violence as a ploy in custody disputes (Johnston & Campbell, 1993). In addition, many professionals, judges, and others often believe that mothers are intentionally alienating their children from the fathers in divorce cases in order to gain an advantage in custody disputes. One author has even given a label to this supposed phenomenon: *parent alienation syndrome* (Gardner, 1992). This reason and label have been used in many cases to remove custody from a woman who has reported domestic violence. Thus, if children make allegations of abuse (physical or sexual) against their father during separation, divorce proceedings, or shortly thereafter, and the mother believes them, she may be "diagnosed" with parent alienation syndrome. This label becomes evidence of her mental instability and parental unfitness, so custody may then be awarded to the alleged abuser (Faller & DeVoe, 1995; Geffner, 1997). This circular argument has actually been used in many custody disputes to remove custody from one parent, usually the mother, on the basis of testimony from supposed mental health professionals who are called in as "expert witnesses," without any other evidence of inappropriate or poor parenting. In some of the cases we have reviewed, the mothers were not even allowed contact with their own children unless supervised by the father who had been accused by the children or the mother of one or more types of domestic violence.

The irony in the use of the term *alienation* is that many abusers seek custody as a way of punishing their partner, re-establishing control, and in fact demonstrating that the partner is a less valued and important person in the children's lives. Even Gardner (1996), who coined the term *parent alienation syndrome*, has raised concerns about the abuse of this diagnosis and the danger of professionals being premature in their assessment and custody plans. Irrespective of these problems, the literature on high-conflict divorce, domestic violence, and mild or moderate alienation suggests a common solution: offer sole custody to the mother who has been victimized; develop a safe and predictable schedule for visitation, possibly supervised; and abandon any short-term hope of cooperative parenting.

As many researchers and clinicians have pointed out, no research data support even the existence of such a syndrome or the claim that false allegations of abuse are prevalent in divorce cases (Faller, Olafson, & Corwin, 1993; Geffner, 1997; Pagelow, 1997). In fact, just the opposite seems to be true. There seems to be a relatively low percentage of allegations of child abuse in divorce cases (less than 10% of the cases), and when they do occur they are substantiated about as often as in the general population (e.g., Everson & Boat, 1989; Thoennes & Tjaden, 1990). Recent research has also indicated that many judges, police officers, social workers, and mental health professionals who do not have much specific training in the area of domestic violence and child maltreatment are more likely than those with such training to believe that many false allegations of sexual abuse are made in divorce cases (e.g., Everson, Boat, Bourg, & Robertson, 1996). The reality, as noted above, is that the overlap of battering and child maltreatment is significant, thereby increasing the likelihood that there may indeed be child maltreatment in these domestic violence cases. When the children feel safe or have been removed from the perpetrator, they may then disclose such allegations. It is clear that some parents attempt to alienate their children against the other parent, but no such syndrome or condition has been shown to exist. It is important to evaluate each case on its merits, without preconceived biases or unsubstantiated labels of pathology, and to be alert to the context and possible issues of domestic violence before conclusions or diagnoses are made.

A "no win" situation occurs for many battered women in court situations. If a mother has experienced battering and her children have been exposed to such violence and maltreatment, or if her children have disclosed allegations of physical or sexual abuse by their father, then the mother is supposed to protect them and report the allegations. If she does not do this, then she is subject to losing custody of her children because Child Protective Services may remove them as a result of her failure to protect. Some battered women have even been prosecuted when they have not protected their children from abuse by the father (APA Presidential Task Force, 1996; Pagelow, 1993). On the other hand, if they do believe their children, report the events and allegations, and take steps to stop contact with the alleged abuser, they are often accused of having the parent alienation syndrome. They then are subject to losing custody of their children in courts to the alleged abuser. This situation has been a tragic reality for many children exposed to marital violence or direct abuse.

In our professional experience in over 20 years of completing custody and visitation assessments, the nonidentification of domestic violence in divorce cases is the source of the real problems that occur. Many battered women underreport their own physical, sexual, or psychological maltreatment because of embarrassment, humiliation, or lack of trust in legal, social service, and mental health professionals. In addition, many professionals have neither the adequate expertise in the dynamics of domestic violence nor the adequate training for identifying these cases (APA Presidential Task Force, 1996; Davidson, 1994). Recently, many professional organizations and agencies have recommended better and mandated training for health care, mental health, social service, legal, and judicial professionals to improve their understanding and identification of domestic violence (American Medical Association [AMA], 1994; APA Presidential Task Force, 1996; Davidson, 1994; Hamberger, Burge, Graham, & Costa, in press).

In addition, many legal and mental health professionals do not sufficiently consider the potential dangerousness or lethality of domestic violence. Violent and life-threatening behavior is often minimized as a bad phase of a relationship or as caused by situational stress that will "settle down eventually." Most experts in the field emphasize the need for a thorough assessment of possible domestic violence, with a special focus on lethality that includes factors such as the presence of weapons, fantasies of homicide and suicide, stalking behaviors, and prior police involvement (Campbell, 1995b; Saunders, 1995). Excellent guidelines are available to help court services and community agencies develop a more comprehensive approach to this issue (e.g., APA Presidential Task Force, 1996; Campbell, 1995a; Hart, 1990a; Hilton, 1993). This screening for lethality should be conducted in all divorce cases, especially when children are involved. Research has indicated that separation or filing for divorce is potentially the most dangerous time for many battered women, as discussed below. Therefore, it is imperative that professionals involved in these cases have adequate expertise in evaluating the parties to determine the risk of danger and the likelihood of prior victimization (APA Ad Hoc Committee on Legal and Ethical Issues in the Treatment of Interpersonal Violence, 1996b; Campbell, 1995b; Saunders, 1995). Recently, the APA Ad Hoc Committee (1996b) has also warned of the potential dangers of not taking into account domestic violence when evaluating custody cases, working with alleged victims or offenders of interpersonal violence without expertise in domestic violence, and making custody recommendations without considering domestic violence or maltreatment.

As stated above, research clearly indicates that separation represents a significant risk period for escalating violence, and the batterer may become even more desperate in his attempt to control his partner (Mc-Mahon & Pence, 1993; Pagelow, 1993, 1997; Zorza, 1992b). Women in these circumstances may find themselves in a confusing maze of legal interventions related to criminal and civil proceedings (e.g., custody, child support, possession of the matrimonial home, visitation issues). Children who have been exposed to their mother's victimization may be even more vulnerable at this time (Jaffe et al., 1990). The community and court system need to recognize the plight of battered women and their children and to develop a coordinated approach involving legal, mental health, medical, and social service professionals (Enos, 1996; Family Violence Project, 1990; McMahon & Pence, 1993; Peled, Jaffe, & Edleson, 1995; Schechter & Edleson, 1994).

An example of such a program has been developed in Pennsylvania by the Women's Law Project (1996). Their handbook not only describes and explains the legal issues for battered women involved in divorce and custody issues, but it also presents a step-by-step process, with sample forms, for filing for divorce, custody, and protective orders; working with the court system; obtaining a lawyer; dealing with child maltreatment by the spouse; and going to court. Other programs have also been developed by the Family Violence Prevention Fund and the American Bar Association (ABA) Committee on Children and the Law. It is important for each jurisdiction to establish guidelines and to make this information easily available to battered women who file for divorce.

Members of various professional organizations have reviewed the literature and have recommended that exposure to marital violence be considered psychological maltreatment (AMA, 1994; APA Presidential Task Force, 1996; Davidson, 1994). Far too often in courts, spousal maltreatment has not been considered to be relevant for custody decisions because it is deemed to be separate from parenting abilities. Thus, if a father does not beat his child, then he is considered acceptable as joint or sole managing conservator of his children (Enos, 1996). However, research has shown that being exposed to such behaviors causes trauma to the children, which then suggests that this would indeed be a reflection of parenting ability. The various professional organizations listed above as well as numerous researchers and clinicians have now recommended that one parent abusing the other be a presumption of poor parenting, because battering a child's parent ignores the needs of the child, sets a poor example of conflict resolution, reflects negative attitudes toward women, and emphasizes the use of power to forcefully get one's own needs met at the expense of someone else (e.g., Geffner, 1997; Geffner & Pagelow, 1990a; Jaffe et al., 1990; Pagelow, 1993, 1997; Peled, 1996; Zorza, 1995). The recommendation from various interdisciplinary task forces is that battering of one parent would preclude the abusive parent from obtaining sole or joint custody of the children and that even visitation should be monitored until the batterer has successfully completed treatment for the abusive behavior and attitudes. This recommendation by the ABA, AMA, APA, and others has been incorporated into the statutes of various jurisdictions. The first state in the United States to do this was Louisiana, and several others have now followed suit. It is important for all those involved in custody decisions, whether mental health, social service, medical, legal, or judicial professionals, to understand these recommendations and the overall dynamics of domestic violence that make this necessary.

CRITICAL PERIODS FOR CHILDREN OF DIVORCING BATTERED WOMEN

In considering the plight of children exposed to violence in their family before, during, and after separation and divorce proceedings, several critical turning points may either promote safety or cause greater adjustment problems. The first critical point is women leaving safely, which obviously depends on community resources and support in finding safe shelter. Because the risk of a homicide is greatest during this initial period, the development of safety plans for women and children is essential (e.g., Browne, 1993; Geffner & Pagelow, 1990a, 1990b; Pagelow, 1993; Zorza, 1992b). Assessments of children of domestic violence suggest that they have limited skills in this area and require safety planning as a critical part of counseling and support services. The reality for many children is that their mothers do not find safety, housing,

or financial support, and so they return to the batterer. In some jurisdictions researchers have found that women leave five times before they
make the final break (i.e., before they are able to access sufficient support to consolidate their decision not to return). In this process the
children may be exposed to repeated violence and compounding disruptions in their lives (Canadian Panel, 1993).

If separation proceeds safely, then children may find themselves the
focus of a custody and visitation access dispute. The abusive parent
discovers that the most effective way at this point to hurt or attack their
spouse is through emotional and psychological abuse (Pagelow, 1993;
Taylor, 1992). The abuser denies the violence, and the mother's mental
health, alcohol or drug abuse, or fitness as a parent gets placed under
a legal microscope. Many of the symptoms that relate to coping with
violence caused by the batterer are held against the women or even
misinterpreted by traditional assessment techniques (e.g., APA Presidential Task Force, 1996; APA Ad Hoc Committee, 1996a; M. A. Dutton,
1992; Walker, 1989). The children find themselves the central pawns in
the struggle for power and control and are often confused about their
own feelings (Hughes, 1997). Their ambivalence is based in part on the
disruptions they experience. If they are in a safe place, they may miss
their old neighborhood, school, friends, and any positive aspects of their
paternal relationship (Peled, 1993). They may be angry at their mother
for disrupting their life, and in some circumstances, even promote ideas
of reconciliation (Jaffe et al., 1990). Early contact with their father can
easily encourage this "reconciliation," despite the violence ("If it wasn't
for your mother we could all be back together again"). These events
may leave the children extremely confused and ambivalent in their feelings about both parents (Johnston & Campbell, 1993; Peled, 1993).

In the next phase the children may find their mother, or themselves,
in more formal court proceedings where their perceptions and events
are questioned in the following manner:

1. Did violence actually occur in the relationship? Why did no one
   else know about it? Why are these issues being raised now in the
   context of a custody dispute (Taylor, 1992)?

2. Was the violence that bad or was it just the normal conflict that all parents experience? Isn't the problem over now that the couple has separated (Crawford & Gartner, 1992)?
3. Even if there was violence, isn't this only an issue for the parents and does it really affect the children? The children were not abused directly, so it cannot be a problem. Don't fathers have fundamental rights irrespective of their marital behavior (Jaffe et al, 1990)?
4. How much contact should the father have and what form should the contact take? Who should supervise contact and who decides when the father's behavior is inappropriate (McMahon & Pence, 1993)?

Many of these questions have now been addressed by research findings, as presented in this chapter and others in this book. The outcome of these questions depends on both parties' access to the legal system, the quality of skilled family lawyers for each parent, the availability of independent assessment facilities, the training-expertise in domestic violence by the evaluators, the education and awareness of the judge, and the access to community resources to manage supervised visitation (Jaffe & Austin, 1995). One could hypothesize that few jurisdictions have the resources and trained personnel to ease the burden on battered women and their children. Too often, children learn that their observations and experiences are not important, and whoever has the most physical, financial, and psychological power can persevere to win. Children in crisis, who openly disclose the violence and trauma, learn to be silent. They learn that disclosure of abuse only angers the person with the most power and others in authority roles and may have direct and indirect repercussions for themselves and their mother. In many of these cases, the children are accused of making up these allegations or of having been programmed to make the statements by their mother. For many children, their mother's silence during the relationship has set the model for them, and this pattern is difficult to change, especially if their safety is further jeopardized by any disclosure. However, some research is beginning to show that the use of victim advocates and the establishment of a coordinating agency or family violence council that

386

works with the battered woman and helps her in the legal system with protection orders and safety planning can change the attitudes of law enforcement, lead to more arrests, and result in completed court actions (e.g., Weisz, Tolman, & Bennett, 1995). In addition, judges who have been trained to understand the dynamics of family violence, and the fear and intimidation of the victims, tend to have a more supportive demeanor in the court; this then leads to more empowerment of the battered woman, and she is more likely to follow through with seeking and maintaining protection orders (Ptacek, 1995).

The final phase for many children is resignation, ignoring their own perceptions and feelings, and then withdrawal. In some circumstances, a never-ending war that continues in the court system and in the community begins. The children's adjustment may be compromised by ongoing threats and violence. Mothers may also end up with a level of resignation, depression, and a sense of helplessness that they may never be safe and free. They may seek to flee the jurisdiction and then face charges of abduction (Enos, 1996; Zorza, 1992a). They may be desperate and vulnerable, and they may get into another abusive relationship and then face child protection authorities who tell them that they are unfit mothers (Schechter & Edleson, 1994). Adolescents may turn against the mother in an attempt to win the approval, love, and affection of the father as they begin to identify with the power of the abuser. They may have seen that there were no negative consequences for the abusive use of power and control, and they may begin to model the aggressive behaviors in their own relationships with peers and their mother. This conversion during early adolescence of some children who had attempted to protect their mother from prior abuse has been noted by clinicians and advocates (Jaffe et al., 1990).

Thus, the outcome in these custody situations is based, in large measure, on the way services are coordinated and on the techniques and resources used. Table 1 provides an overview of the unique features of a visitation dispute, with and without allegations of violence, and the resulting demands on mental health, social service, medical, and legal professionals for a well-informed response.

Table 1

Special Issues in Visitation Disputes With Allegations of Domestic Violence

Issue	Normal visitation dispute	Visitation dispute with allegations of abuse
Central issue	Promoting children's relationship with visiting parent; co-parenting	Safety for mother and children
Focus of court hearing	Reducing hostilities; setting schedule	Assessing lethality risk and level of violence; protection
Assessment issues	Children's stage of development, needs, preferences	Impact of violence on mother and children; developmental needs
	Parenting abilities	Father's level of acceptance of responsibility
		Safety plan for mother and children
		Parenting abilities
Planning for future	Visitation schedule that meets needs of children	Consider suspended, supervised, or no visitation
Resources required	Mediation services	Specialized services and assessment with knowledge and training about domestic violence
	Divorce counseling for parents and children	Supervised visitation center
	Independent assessment/ evaluation	Coordination of court and community services

		Table 1 (*Continued*)	
			Visitation dispute
		Normal visitation	with allegations
Issue		dispute	of abuse
			Well-informed lawyers, judges, and mental health and social service professionals

Note. Developed by Peter G. Jaffe, PhD, C. Psych., for the Family Violence Prevention Fund.

POSSIBLE SOLUTIONS

Children who are exposed to marital violence represent a special challenge for the judicial system, especially when these children become the focal point of custody and visitation disputes. In meeting this challenge, the following are suggested as important aspects of an overall community response. Each of these approaches has been documented elsewhere, but few communities have had the commitment, resources, and legislative support fully to operationalize a comprehensive, coordinated response.

Media Campaigns

Information about the impact of violence should be available to the general public as part of broadly based media campaigns. This has been recommended by several task forces (e.g., AMA, 1994; APA Presidential Task Force, 1996). Because some battered women may seek safety for themselves and their children after they realize the impact of the violence (Hilton, 1992), it is important to publicize this information. As an example, there are self-help books and pamphlets that draw attention to women and their community supporters about this issue (e.g., Horley, 1988). Ultimately, the most effective strategies empower women to make the most appropriate decisions for themselves and for their children.

Education of Professionals and Others Working With Children

Of paramount importance is an increased awareness among legal, medical, education, social service, and mental health professionals that being exposed to violence is detrimental to children's development. Front-line professionals, such as counselors, teachers, social workers, police officers, nurses, and family physicians, need to recognize and respond to the early warning signs of domestic violence. For example, some school districts have increased training for their staff about domestic violence and have developed protocols, together with local shelters, on how to respond to children exposed to spouse abuse (e.g., Jaffe, Hastings, & Reitzel, 1992). Within the court system, several jurisdictions have increased judges' awareness about the extent of violence against women and children and how the court may inadvertently revictimize the most vulnerable persons (Canadian Judicial Council Seminar, 1993; Family Violence Project, 1990; Western Judicial Education Centre, 1993; Women's Law Project, 1996).

Assessment and Screening for Domestic Violence

Assessment of lethality and level of danger should be a central component of programs that have contact with battered women and their children (e.g., Campbell, 1995b; Geffner, 1996; Hart, 1990a). All agencies, clinical practices, emergency rooms, and courts should have some system established to screen for domestic violence. The initial screening may consist of only a few minutes of questioning or administering a self-report questionnaire to determine whether maltreatment may be occurring in the family. When there is an indication that this may be happening, a referral can be made immediately for a more in-depth assessment of psychological functioning, behaviors, attitudes, and risk of danger for the victim and her children.

Various instruments are available for such screening that may provide clinical information regarding the likelihood of domestic violence.

For example, Geffner and Pagelow (1990b) adapted a brief Spouse Abuse Identification Questionnaire (see the Appendix) that could be used in any setting to find out about the warning signs indicating the possibility of spouse abuse. It includes questions concerning family of origin issues of violence, abuse, and alcohol use; threats of abuse in the relationship; existence of controlling behaviors, isolation, possessiveness, jealousy, or intimidation; injuries as a result of being hit or abused in the relationship; injuries or threats concerning the children; threats or attempts at taking the children away from their mother; and expressions of anger, a bad temper, a "Jekyll and Hyde" personality, or fear of the partner losing control. An updated version of this questionnaire is shown in the Appendix.

Other questionnaires have also been devised to assess spouse abuse. Some examples include the Psychological Maltreatment of Women Inventory (Tolman, 1989, 1995), the Partner and Relationship Profile: A Package of Screening Instruments (Straus, Hamby, Boney-McCoy, & Sugarman, 1995), a modified version of the Conflict Tactics Scale called The Woman Abuse Scale (Saunders, 1995), and the Propensity for Abusiveness Scale (D. G. Dutton, 1995). In addition, one of the better instruments for assessing risk and lethality is the Danger Assessment Scale (Campbell, 1995b). Screening and assessing for domestic violence in divorce and custody disputes is an area in need of much more research, but these scales do provide clinical information that can be very important in identifying possible battered women so that safety planning and other steps can be recommended.

Unfortunately, not much research has been done on developing instruments for children in these violent families. It is important to assess the children in shelters and elsewhere to determine whether they might have been exposed to marital violence or have been a direct victim of child maltreatment as well (see Hughes, 1997, and the preceding chapters in this book). Psychological evaluations of these children are recommended to determine whether they have indeed suffered emotional trauma from the exposure to the marital violence. Once the assessments have been conducted, then appropriate treatment can be recommended for both the mother and her children.

Treating Children Exposed to Marital Violence

When children who have been exposed to marital violence are identified, they require specialized services and counseling programs to help them heal from their trauma. Some excellent group programs have been developed by organizations such as the Domestic Abuse Project in Minneapolis (e.g., Peled & Edleson, 1995). The need for individualized assessment and counseling programs has been well-documented (e.g., Silvern et al., 1995). Ten years ago these programs were only found in a few shelters through considerable advocacy work (Hughes & Marshall, 1995), but there is still a great need for such programs to be available on a communitywide basis in light of the extent of the problem. An evaluation of the effectiveness of these programs also is needed. A step in this direction was recently achieved by Wagar and Rodway (1995), who evaluated a group treatment approach for children exposed to wife abuse.

Programs that are sensitive to the diverse cultural backgrounds of women and children seeking refuge and counseling from abusive relationships are still in short supply (e.g., Dumont-Smith, 1995). There has been little research in this area and insufficient clinical programs that focus on ethnic and cultural issues in domestic violence intervention. Prevention programs are also needed for children. A good example of such a program that has been evaluated in the school system has recently been developed by Wolfe, Wekerle, Gough, Reitzel-Jaffe, and Grasley (1996).

Court-Related Assessment and Supervised Access Centers

In many cases, judges are only as effective as the quality of the information they have to consider in decision making and the community resources that are available to implement the court's recommendations. Two essential services that can assist the court in finding solutions for children who are dealing with the aftermath of domestic violence and a custody dispute are a court-related assessment service and a supervised visitation center. One community that has been able to develop these specialized and coordinated services is Duluth, Minnesota (Schechter, 1994). Other similar programs are beginning to be developed in numerous communities, but the number of centers for supervision of visitation are still insufficient. Supervised visitation between a batterer and his children has been recommended when domestic violence has occurred, as stated above, but monitoring this has been difficult in many jurisdictions. Despite the strong recommendations from several task forces that supervised access should be provided by a trained, neutral party, many judges appoint the parent(s) of the batterer or even a current spouse to supervise the visitation. This can lead to disastrous results and should be avoided.

Judges should also be cautious about conducting their own assessment of children's wishes through special interviews in their chambers or court. Although some judges have the necessary interviewing skills and knowledge of child development, the children's desires and needs should be examined in the context of a comprehensive evaluation and an assessment of children's best interests, especially in light of the dynamics of any domestic violence. This requires specialized skills in domestic violence training, child development, custody issues, diagnostic assessment, and interviewing. Comprehensive guidelines have been published for conducting custody evaluations in general (e.g., APA Committee on Professional Practices and Standards, 1994; Stahl, 1995), but special provisions and expertise are needed when domestic violence has occurred (APA Ad Hoc Committee, 1996b; Geffner & Pagelow, 1990a).

Mediation in Custody Disputes Involving Domestic Violence

Mediation and dispute resolution techniques have become quite popular in recent years, and many courts routinely order this in divorces and custody disputes. In general, mediation is a good idea that has become widely accepted. However, when domestic violence has occurred, then mediation is generally not appropriate (e.g., Geffner & Pagelow, 1990a; Pagelow, 1993, 1997). Mediation assumes that both parties have equivalent power and that they can negotiate, with the help of a trained mediator, to reach an agreement. The goal of mediation then is to reach an agreement. Many have argued that the basic tenets of dispute resolution are not met in domestic violence cases because battered women do not have equal power or bargaining ability and often are too intimidated and afraid to speak up or disagree with the batterer. Thus, they agree to terms of custody and visitation that often are not in the best interests of themselves or their children. In fact, the various task forces (ABA, AMA, and APA) have agreed with many advocates that mediation should never be ordered or forced on a battered woman. Geffner (1992) has suggested ways that mediation can be conducted in domestic violence situations providing that the parties independently desire this (as opposed to mandated), the mediator is trained in both dispute resolution and domestic violence, and the mediator ensures that any power differential is balanced so that a battered woman does not agree to anything that could be detrimental to herself or her children. Many argue that mediation should never be conducted in these cases regardless of the conditions (e.g., Hart, 1990b). This debate is likely to continue, and more research is needed in this area.

Coordinated Parenting Services

One of the most significant needs for abused women, abusive husbands, and children living in a violent environment is coordinated services. Services often represent a patchwork of strategies that do not address safety and counseling needs and in fact may be offering conflicting advice. This problem is most easily identified in the relationship between shelters and child protection services where advocates for women and those for children may take very different approaches to the same problem (Geffner, 1997; Schechter & Edleson, 1994). One of the more promising approaches (other than developing better guidelines on cooperative approaches) is the focus on parenting skills for women and men in violent families.

Women can be empowered to become more effective parents and deal with issues such as setting limits for children and keeping them free of involvement in adult issues (Bilinkoff, 1995). Family lawyers and service providers need to understand how violence affects women's ability to remain capable mothers. Battered women often require an interim adjustment period with their children to begin their own healing and recovery from abuse and isolation (e.g., Herman, 1992; Schlee &

O'Leary, 1995). Repeated exposure to long-term violence compounds these issues (Jaffe et al., 1990). In addition, family lawyers, in defending batterers, sometimes seem to promote additional minimization and denial on the part of their clients, which may pose more risk to battered women and their children (e.g., Ford, 1995). This can lead to even more victim blaming, which further hinders the parenting process.

Needed Legislation Concerning Custody in Domestic Violence Cases

Child custody legislation needs to reflect the reality of maltreatment in many American families experiencing a divorce. Generalized notions of joint custody and two equal parents cooperatively planning for their children's future is not likely for many couples. For battered women, this notion may prolong a nightmare of violence, abuse of power, and control in the family relationships. Zorza (1995) has pointed out that the most progressive legislation clearly makes the links between violence and children's adjustment problems and recognizes safety as the top priority. A recent report prepared for the ABA states this recommendation clearly:

> State legislatures should amend custody and visitation codes, creating custodial protections for abused parents and their children. These might include presumptions that custody not be awarded, in whole or in part, to a parent with a history of inflicting domestic violence, that visitation be awarded to such parent only if the safety and well-being of the abused parent and children can be protected, and that all awards of visitation incorporate explicit protections for the child and the abused parent. (Davidson, 1994, p. 15)

Similar recommendations have been made by other organizations as well, and they have added the strong recommendation that the perpetrator receive appropriate treatment and counseling (e.g., APA Presidential Task Force, 1996). There must also be an awareness in the legislation that many battered women are being prosecuted for situations that do not take into account their own victimization. These include failure to protect when a batterer has abused the children or forced her to participate (e.g., Enos, 1996), self-defense in homicide cases (e.g., Walker, 1993), and mandatory arrest when a battered women fights back (e.g., Hamberger, 1997).

Research Needs

Researchers need to collaborate on projects that allow for long-term prospective studies on children who are exposed to violence and experience prolonged divorce proceedings. As mentioned earlier, this research has been initiated through the work of Johnston and her colleagues (e.g., Johnston & Campbell, 1993) and others, but a more extensive effort is required to capture the complexity and cultural aspects of violence (e.g., Peled, 1993). Research involving children who are multiply victimized is also beginning (Rossman & Rosenberg, in press). In addition, research concerning many areas of domestic violence is also needed, as pointed out in recent reviews of the literature (APA Presidential Task Force, 1996; Crowell & Burgess, 1996; Geffner, 1997).

CONCLUSION

The possible approaches listed above require a new commitment to prioritize women and children's safety as an essential cornerstone of the justice system. Courts that have well-informed support staff and a range of community services (mental health and social service) can create a climate for judges and other professionals to make the most informed decisions for children in crisis. If the justice system cannot offer these children a vision of ending the violence, then the children's dream of a safe future is inconceivable. A recent report prepared for the ABA best summarized this challenge as follows:

> The time has now come for the entire legal profession to scrutinize and respond to this problem. The law must protect children who live in violent home environments. The law must work to save lives, to protect abused parents and their children by removing violent abusers, and to protect victim–parents from continued exposure to domestic violence without risking the loss of child custody to their batterers. (Davidson, 1994, p. 2)

APPENDIX

IDENTIFICATION OF VICTIMS OF
WIFE-PARTNER ABUSE

Bearing in mind that both victims and their abusers are likely to minimize or deny the occurrence of spouse abuse, professionals need to draw upon their training, experience, and their observation skills to make accurate assessments. The first clues may not be visible in the appearance or outward behavior of the clients. The initial interviews are very important in the process of identifying victims of spouse abuse. At least one interview with each spouse should be conducted in private. It is very important to determine the level of intimidation that may be occurring and how free the abused spouse may be to express feelings and opinions openly.

The interviewer can learn much by watching and listening during joint interviews. For example, pay attention to body language, and watch for eye contact, reactions indicating possible fear rather than ordinary nervousness, and avoidant posture. Listen for "permission" words between them. Does either party talk about men and women exclusively in terms of traditional stereotypes? Are these terms about the other gender negative? Be alert for indicators of jealousy pointing to possessiveness, immaturity, or low self-esteem.

Trained interviewers should be able to discover how important decisions are reached in the family, especially concerning financial matters. Yet they should be aware that the person who writes the checks does not necessarily have decision making powers; sometimes the controlling spouse merely delegates the check-writing and accounting duties to the other. The roles of each spouse should also be explored to determine domination and subservience. Details concerning how each spouse spends time at home, their chores, responsibilities, and decision making power provide indications of possible rigid role restrictions suggestive of potential abuse. The history of the individual or couple should include items about both their present relationship and their families of origin. Finally, if there are any children, the interviewer should seek information about them.

Physical abuse often is preceded by psychological abuse, and it usually is a gradual conditioning process. An abuser may begin by intimidation, such as verbal abuse, degrading the spouse, punching holes in walls with his first, or by destroying or disposing of possessions owned by, or at least valued by, the partner.

When clients come to a professional for intervention, legal help, medical services, individual, marriage or family counseling, it is relatively easy to include some of the questions presented below. It is important to identify any abuse in relationships since this information is rarely volunteered by the victims or offenders unless specific questions are asked.

Spouse Abuse Identification Questionnaire

_____ Were either you or your spouse physically abused in childhood? If so, in what way?

_____ Were either of you emotionally abused during childhood?

_____ Was there a history of violence in either of your families?

_____ If so, was the violence directed at the children, or was it directed at one parent by the other?

_____ Does either your spouse or his/her parents abuse alcohol? Do you? Do your parents?

_____ Does your spouse treat his/her parents roughly or disrespectfully?

_____ Has your spouse ever hit his/her parents, brothers, or sisters?

_____ Has your spouse ever threatened to harm you?

_____ Are your spouse's problems usually blamed on you or others?

_____ Have you been attacked or blamed when your spouse got angry?

_____ Are you afraid of your spouse's temper?

_____ When drinking, does your spouse get rough or violent?

_____ Has your spouse ever hurt you? When? What happened?

_____ Did your spouse ever hit a former spouse or lover?

_____ Has your spouse ever deliberately hurt or killed a pet?

_____ Does your spouse have a Dr. Jekyll and Mr. Hyde personality?

_____ Do you usually give in to settle arguments?

_____ Are your children afraid when your spouse is angry?

_____ Have you felt free to invite family or friends to visit you?

_____ Are you socially active or more socially isolated?

_____ Does your spouse listen in when you're talking on the phone?

_____ Does your spouse insist on going everywhere with you?

_____ Is your spouse suspicious of your every move?

_____ Is your spouse an extremely jealous person?

_____ Has your spouse ever forced or pressured you to have sex even though you did not want to?

_____ Have you ever called, or thought of calling, the police because an argument was getting out of control?

_____ Have your neighbors or friends ever called the police because of your situation?

_____ If the police were called, was your spouse arrested or given a citation?

_____ Does your spouse ever threaten to take the children where you could not find them?

_____ Did this ever occur?

_____ Do you feel safer when I talk with you alone?

Note. The ideas for the original version of this questionnaire originated in a subcommittee of the Domestic Violence/Family Court System Committee of the Los Angeles, California, Conciliation Court.
Adapted from "Victims of Spouse Abuse," by R. Geffner & M. D. Pagelow, 1990, in R. T. Ammerman & M. Hersen (Eds.), _Treatment of Family Violence: A Sourcebook_ (pp. 113–135), New York: Wiley. Copyright 1990 by R. Geffner. Adapted by permission of authors.

REFERENCES

American Medical Association. (1994). *National conference on family violence: Health and justice; Conference proceedings, Washington, DC.* Chicago: Author.

American Psychological Association, Ad Hoc Committee on Legal and Ethical Issues in the Treatment of Interpersonal Violence. (1996a). *Potential problems for psychologists working with the area of interpersonal violence.* Washington, DC: Author.

American Psychological Association, Ad Hoc Committee on Legal and Ethical Issues in the Treatment of Interpersonal Violence. (1996b). *Professional, ethical, and legal issues concerning interpersonal violence, maltreatment and related trauma.* Washington, DC: Author.

American Psychological Association, Committee on Professional Practice and Standards. (1994). Guidelines for the child custody evaluations in divorce proceedings. *American Psychologist, 49,* 677–680.

American Psychological Association Presidential Task Force on Violence and the Family. (1996). *Violence and the family: Report of the APA Presidential Task Force.* Washington, DC: Author.

Bachman, R., & Saltzman, L. E. (1996). *Violence against women: Estimates from the redesigned survey* (Bureau of Justice Statistics special report; NCJ No. 154348). Rockville, MD: U.S. Department of Justice.

Barnett, O. W., & LaViolette, A. D. (1993). *It could happen to anyone: Why battered women stay.* Newbury Park, CA: Sage.

Barnett, O. W., Miller-Perrin, C. L., & Perrin, R. D. (1997). *Violence across the life span: An introduction.* Thousand Oaks, CA: Sage.

Bilinkoff, J. (1995). Empowering battered women as mothers. In E. Peled, P. G. Jaffe, & J. L. Edleson (Eds.), *Ending the cycle of violence: Community responses to children of battered women* (pp. 97–195). Newbury Park, CA: Sage.

Bowker, L. H., Arbitell, M., & McFerron, J. R. (1988). On the relationship between wife beating and child abuse. In K. Yllo & M. Bograd (Eds.), *Feminist perspectives on wife abuse* (pp. 158–174). Newbury Park, CA: Sage.

Browne, A. (1993). Violence against women by male partners: Prevalence, incidence, and policy implications. *American Psychologist, 48,* 1077–1087.

Campbell, J. C. (Ed.). (1995a). *Assessing dangerousness: Violence by sexual of-fenders, batterers, and child abusers.* Thousand Oaks, CA: Sage.

Campbell, J. C. (1995b). Prediction of homicide of and by battered women. In J. C. Campbell (Ed.), *Assessing dangerousness: Violence by sexual of-fenders, batterers, and child abusers* (pp. 96–113). Thousand Oaks, CA: Sage.

Canadian Judicial Council Seminar. (1993). *Family violence and custody/access dispute proceedings: Current legal and clinical issues.* Conference Proceedings, Aylmer, PQ. Ottowa, Ontario: Author.

Canadian Panel on Violence Against Women. (1993). *Changing the landscape: Ending violence—achieving equality.* Ottawa, Ontario: Minister of Supply and Services, Canada.

Carlson, B. E. (1990). Adolescent observers of marital violence. *Journal of Family Violence, 5,* 285–299.

Crawford, M., & Gartner, R. (1992). *Woman killing, intimate femicide in Ontario: 1974–1990.* Toronto, Ontario, Canada: The Women We Honour Action Committee.

Crowell, N. A., & Burgess, A. W. (Eds.). (1996). *Understanding violence against women: Panel on research on violence against women, National Research Council.* Washington, DC: National Academy Press.

Davidson, H. (1994). *The impact of domestic violence on children: A report to the President of the American Bar Association* (2nd rev. ed.). Chicago: American Bar Association.

Dumont-Smith, C. (1995). Aboriginal Canadian children who witness and live with violence. In E. Peled, P. G. Jaffe, & J. L. Edleson (Eds.), *Ending the cycle of violence: Community responses to children of battered women* (pp. 275–283). Newbury Park, CA: Sage.

Dutton, D. G. (1995). A scale for measuring propensity for abusiveness. *Journal of Family Violence, 10,* 203–221.

Dutton, M. A. (1992). *Empowering and healing the battered woman: A model for assessment & intervention.* New York: Springer.

Dutton, M. A. (1996). Battered women's strategic response to violence: The role of context. In J. L. Edleson & Z. C. Eisikovits (Eds.), *Future interven-*

tions with battered women and their families (pp. 105–124). Thousand Oaks, CA: Sage.

Enos, V. P. (1996). Prosecuting battered mothers: State laws' failure to protect battered women and abused children. *Harvard Women's Law Journal, 19,* 229–268.

Everson, M. D., & Boat, B. (1989). False allegations of sexual abuse by children and adolescents. *American Academy of Child and Adolescent Psychiatry, 28,* 230–235.

Everson, M. D., Boat, B. W., Bourg, S., & Robertson, K. R. (1996). Beliefs among professionals about rates of false allegations of child sexual abuse. *Journal of Interpersonal Violence, 11,* 541–553.

Faller, K. C., & DeVoe, E. (1995). Allegations of sexual abuse in divorce. *Journal of Child Sexual Abuse, 4*(4), 1–25.

Faller, K. C., Olafson, E., & Corwin, D. (1993). Research on false allegations of sexual abuse in divorce. *The APSAC Advisor, 6*(3), 1, 7–10.

Family Violence Project. (1990). *Family violence: Improving court practices [Recommendations from the National Council of Juvenile and Family Court Judges' Family Violence Project].* Washington, DC: U.S. Department of Justice.

Ford, D. A. (1995, July). *Lawyers for the defense: Putting battered women at risk.* Paper presented at the 4th International Family Violence Research Conference, Durham, NH.

Gardner, R. (1992). *The parental alienation syndrome: A guide for mental health and legal professionals.* Cresskill, NJ: Creative Therapeutics.

Gardner, R. (1996). *Addendum to the parental alienation syndrome.* Cresskill, NJ: Creative Therapeutics.

Geffner, R. (1992). Guidelines for using mediation with abusive couples. *Psychotherapy in Private Practice, 10,* 77–92.

Geffner, R. (1996, August). Assessing abuse, harm, and potential lethality in interpersonal violence cases. In M. Vasquez (Chair), *Legal and ethical issues in the treatment of interpersonal violence.* Invited symposium presented at the 104th Annual Convention of the American Psychological Association, Toronto, Canada.

Geffner, R. (1997). Family violence: Current issues, interventions, and research. *Journal of Aggression, Maltreatment, & Trauma, 1,* 1–25.

Geffner, R., & Pagelow, M. D. (1990a). Mediation and child custody issues in abusive relationships. *Behavioral Sciences and the Law, 8,* 151–159.

Geffner, R., & Pagelow, M. D. (1990b). Victims of spouse abuse. In R. T. Ammerman & M. Hersen (Eds.), *Treatment of family violence: A sourcebook* (pp. 113–135). New York: Wiley.

Gelles, R. J., & Straus, M. A. (1988). *Intimate violence.* New York: Simon & Schuster.

Graham-Bermann, S., & Levendosky, A. (1997). The social functioning of pre-school-age children whose mothers are emotionally and physically abused. *Journal of Aggression, Maltreatment, & Trauma, 1,* 59–84.

Hamberger, L. K. (1997). Female offenders in domestic violence: A look at actions in their context. *Journal of Aggression, Maltreatment, & Trauma, 1,* 117–129.

Hamberger, L. K., Burge, S. K., Graham, A. V., & Costa, A. (Eds.). (in press). *Violence issues for health care educators and providers.* Binghamton, NY: Haworth Maltreatment & Trauma Press.

Hart, B. (1990a). *Assessing whether batterers will kill.* Reading: Pennsylvania Coalition Against Domestic Violence.

Hart, B. J. (1990b). Gentle jeopardy: The further endangerment of battered women and children in custody mediation. *Mediation Quarterly, 7,* 317–330.

Henderson, A. (1990). Children of abused wives: Their influence on the mothers' decisions. *Canada's Mental Health, 38,* 10–13.

Herman, J. L. (1992). *Trauma and recovery.* New York: Basic Books.

Hilton, N. Z. (1992). Battered women's concerns about their children witnessing wife assault. *Journal of Interpersonal Violence, 7,* 77–86.

Hilton, N. Z. (Ed.). (1993). *Legal responses to wife assault.* Newbury Park, CA: Sage.

Horley, S. (1988). *Love and pain: A survival handbook for women.* London: Bedford Square Press.

Hughes, H. M. (1997). Research concerning children of battered women: Clinical implications. In R. Geffner, S. B. Sorenson, & P. K. Lundberg-Love (Eds.), *Violence and sexual abuse at home: Current issues, interventions, and research in spousal battering and child maltreatment* (pp. 225–244). Binghamton, NY: Haworth Maltreatment & Trauma Press.

Hughes, H. M., & Marshall, M. (1995). Advocacy for children of battered women. In E. Peled, P. G. Jaffe, & J. L. Edleson (Eds.), *Ending the cycle of violence: Community responses to children of battered women* (pp. 121– 146). Newbury Park, CA: Sage.

Jaffe, P. G., & Austin, G. W. (1995, July). *The impact of witnessing violence on children in custody & visitation disputes: Current clinical and legal dilemmas.* Paper presented at the 4th International Family Violence Research Conference, Durham, NH.

Jaffe, P., Hastings, E., & Reitzel, D. (1992). Child witnesses of woman abuse: How can schools respond? *Response to Victimization of Women and Children, 14*(2), 12–15.

Jaffe, P. G., Wolfe, D., & Wilson, S. (1990). *Children of battered women.* Newbury Park, CA: Sage.

Jaffe, P. G., Wolfe, D., Wilson, S., & Zak, L. (1986). Emotional and physical health problems of battered women. *Canadian Journal of Psychiatry, 31,* 625–629.

Johnston, J. R., & Campbell, L. E. G. (1993). Parent-child relationships in domestic violence families disputing custody. *Family and Conciliation Courts Review, 31,* 282–298.

Kinnard, E. M. (1995, July). *Resilience in abused children.* Paper presented at the 4th International Family Violence Research Conference, Durham, NH.

Liss, M. B., & Stahly, G. B. (1993). Domestic violence and child custody. In M. Hansen & M. Harway (Eds.), *Battering and family therapy: A feminist perspective* (pp. 175–187). Newbury Park: Sage.

McMahon, M., & Pence, E. (1993). Doing more harm than good? Some cautions on visitation centers. In E. Peled, P. G. Jaffe, & J. L. Edleson (Eds.), *Ending the cycle of violence: Community responses to children of battered women* (pp. 186–208). Newbury Park, CA: Sage.

Mercer, S. L. (1987). *Not a pretty picture: An exploratory study of violence against women in high school dating relationships.* Toronto, Ontario, Canada: Education Wife Assault.

National Council of Juvenile & Family Court Judges. (1994). *Family violence: A model state code.* Reno, NV: Author.

Pagelow, M. D. (1993). Justice for victims of spouse abuse in divorce and child custody cases. *Violence and Victims, 8,* 69–83.

Pagelow, M. D. (1997). Battered women: A historical research review and some common myths. In R. Geffner, S. B. Sorenson, & P. K. Lundberg-Love (Eds.), *Violence and sexual abuse at home: Current issues, interventions, and research in spousal battering and child maltreatment* (pp. 97–116). Binghamton, NY: Haworth Maltreatment & Trauma Press.

Peled, E. (1993). *The experience of living with violence for preadolescent child witnesses of woman abuse.* Unpublished doctoral dissertation, University of Minnesota, Minneapolis.

Peled, E. (1996). "Secondary" victims no more: Refocusing intervention with children. In J. L. Edleson & Z. C. Eisikovits (Eds.), *Future interventions with battered women and their families* (pp. 125–153). Thousand Oaks, CA: Sage.

Peled, E., & Edleson, J. L. (1995). Process and outcome in small groups for children of battered women. In E. Peled, P. G. Jaffe, & J. L. Edleson (Eds.), *Ending the cycle of violence: Community responses to children of battered women* (pp. 77–96). Newbury Park, CA: Sage.

Peled, E., Jaffe, P. J., & Edleson, J. L. (Eds.). (1995). *Ending the cycle of violence: Community response to children of battered women.* Thousand Oaks, CA: Sage.

Ptacek, J. (1995, July). *Women's experience seeking restraining orders: The impact of judicial demeanor.* Paper presented at the 4th International Family Violence Research Conference, Durham, NH.

Rodgers, K. (1994). Wife assault: The findings of a national survey. *Juristat, 14,* 1–22. (Published by Statistics Canada and the Canadian Centre for Justice Statistics, Ottawa, Ontario)

Rossman, B. B. R., & Rosenberg, M. S. (1997). Psychological maltreatment: A needs analysis and applications for children in violent families. In R. Geffner, S. B. Sorenson, & P. K. Lundberg-Love (Eds.), *Violence and sexual abuse at home: Current issues, interventions, and research in spousal battering and child maltreatment* (pp. 245–262). Binghamton, NY: Haworth Maltreatment & Trauma Press.

Rossman, B. B. R., & Rosenberg, M. S. (in press). *Multiple victimization of children: Conceptual, developmental, research, and treatment issues.* Binghamton, NY: Haworth Maltreatment & Trauma Press.

Roy, M. (1988). *Children in the crossfire.* Deerfield Beach, FL: Health Communications.

Saunders, D. G. (1995). Prediction of wife assault. In J. C. Campbell (Ed.), *Assessing dangerousness: Violence by sexual offenders, batterers, and child abusers* (pp. 68–95). Thousand Oaks, CA: Sage.

Schechter, S. (1994, June). *Model initiatives linking domestic violence and child welfare*. Paper presented at the Domestic Violence and Child Welfare Conference, Racine, WI.

Schechter, S., & Edleson, J. L. (1994, June). *In the best interest of women and children: A call for collaboration between child welfare and domestic violence constituencies*. Paper presented at the Domestic Violence and Child Welfare Conference, Racine, WI.

Schlee, K. A., & O'Leary, K. D. (1995, July). *Treatment for abused women: Are there different effects for women with PTSD?*. Paper presented at the 4th International Family Violence Research Conference, Durham, NH.

Silvern, L., Karyl, J., & Landis, T. T. (1995). Individual psychotherapy for the traumatized children of abused women. In E. Peled, P. G. Jaffe, & J. L. Edleson (Eds.), *Ending the cycle of violence: Community responses to children of battered women* (pp. 43–76). Thousand Oaks, CA: Sage.

Stahl, P. M. (1995). *Conducting child custody evaluations: A comprehensive guide*. Thousand Oaks, CA: Sage.

Stahly, G. B. (1990, April). Battered women's problems with child custody. In G. B. Stahly (Chair), *New directions in domestic violence research*. Symposium conducted at the annual meeting of the Western Psychological Association, Los Angeles.

Straus, M. A. (1991, September). *Children as witness to marital violence: A risk factor for life-long problems among a nationally representative sample of American men and women*. Paper presented at the Ross Round Table on Children and Violence, Washington, DC.

Straus, M. A., Hamby, S. L., Boney-McCoy, S., & Sugarman, D. B. (1995, July). *The partner and relationship profile: A package of instruments for research and clinical screening*. Paper presented at the 4th International Family Violence Research Conference, Durham, NH.

Sudermann, M., Jaffe, P. G., & Hastings, E. (1995). Violence prevention programs in secondary schools. In E. Peled, P. G. Jaffe, & J. L. Edleson (Eds.), *Ending the cycle of violence: Community responses to children of battered women* (pp. 232–254). Thousand Oaks, CA: Sage.

Taylor, G. (1992). *In whose best interests? A working report on women's experience in custody and access disputes.* Vancouver, British Columbia: British Columbia Ministry for Women's Equality.

Thoennes, N., & Tjaden, P. (1990). The extent, nature, and validity of sexual abuse allegations in custody/visitation disputes. *Child Abuse & Neglect, 14,* 151–163.

Tolman, R. M. (1989). The development of a measure of psychological maltreatment of women by their male partners. *Violence & Victims, 4,* 159–178.

Tolman, R. M. (1995, July). *The validation of the Psychological Maltreatment of Women Inventory.* Paper presented at the 4th International Family Violence Research Conference, Durham, NH.

Turkat, I. D. (1995). Divorce related malicious mother syndrome. *Journal of Family Violence, 10,* 253–264.

Wagar, J. M., & Rodway, M. R. (1995). An evaluation of a group treatment approach for children who have witnessed wife abuse. *Journal of Family Violence, 10,* 295–306.

Walker, L. E. (1989). Psychology and violence against women. *American Psychologist, 44,* 695–702.

Walker, L. E. (1993). Battered women as defendants. In N. Z. Hilton (Ed.), *Legal responses to wife assault: Current trends and evaluation* (pp. 233–257). Newbury Park, CA: Sage.

Wallerstein, J. S., & Blakeslee, S. (1989). *Second chances: Men, women and children a decade after divorce.* New York: Tichnor & Fields.

Weisz, A., Tolman, R. M., & Bennett, L. (1995, July). *Effects of services to battered women on completed prosecutions and levels of police intervention.* Paper presented at the 4th International Family Violence Research Conference, Durham, NH.

Western Judicial Education Centre. (1993). *The role of the judge in the new Canadian reality* (Conference proceedings). Victoria, British Columbia, Canada: Author.

Wolfe, D. A., Wekerle, C., Gough, R., Reitzel-Jaffe, D., & Grasley, C. (1996). *The youth relationships manual: A group approach with adolescents for the prevention of woman abuse and the promotion of healthy relationships.* Thousand Oaks, CA: Sage.

Wolfe, D. A., Wekerle, C., Reitzel, D., & Gough, R. (1995). Strategies to address violence in the lives of high risk youth. In E. Peled, P. G. Jaffe, & J. L. Edleson (Eds.), *Ending the cycle of violence: Community responses to children of battered women* (pp. 255–274). Thousand Oaks, CA: Sage.

Women's Law Project. (1996). *Family violence & the child custody process: A legal guide for protecting children.* Philadelphia: Author.

Zorza, J. (1991). Woman battering: A major cause of homelessness. *Clearinghouse Review, 25,* 421–429.

Zorza, J. (1992a). *Defending a battered woman accused of parental abduction.* New York: National Center on Women and Family Law.

Zorza, J. (1992b). "Friendly parent" provisions in custody determinations. *Clearinghouse Review, 26,* 921–925.

Zorza, J. (1995). How abused women can use the law to help protect their children. In E. Peled, P. G. Jaffe, & J. L. Edleson (Eds.), *Ending the cycle of violence: Community responses to children of battered women* (pp. 147–169). Thousand Oaks, CA: Sage.

13

Appraisal and Outlook

George W. Holden, Robert Geffner,
and Ernest N. Jouriles

As a group, the 12 chapters in this volume represent an important advance in the understanding of children's response to exposure to marital violence. First, this volume provides an extended discussion of the theoretical and conceptual issues related to children from violent households. As this volume reveals, the domain of children's reactions to marital violence represents an important testing ground for the quality of our theories. Second, either directly or indirectly and in varying degrees of explicitness, almost all of the chapters in this volume address methodological issues associated with the topic. The third major contribution of the volume concerns the six empirical chapters that address different facets of the questions: "How do children react to marital violence?" and "What are the determinants of children's reactions to marital violence?" Finally, two chapters advance our understanding of how research findings can be used to address social problems by focusing on such topics as intervening with children who have been exposed to marital violence, law enforcement responses, and legal considerations in custody cases.

In addition to providing new and valuable empirical data about these children, this volume also presents work that is at the intersection of theory, research, and applications to an important social problem. Because this is such a new, evolving field, the state-of-the-science information presented in this volume should enhance our understanding and help stimulate further work in this area. Below we summarize and integrate the preceding chapters by focusing on theoretical and conceptual issues, methodological issues, variability in child outcome, and future research directions.

THEORETICAL AND CONCEPTUAL ISSUES

To some degree, all of the chapters in this volume address theoretical issues about how children are affected by living in maritally violent families. In fact, more than a dozen different psychological theories are used to explain the phenomena and issues involved; as the authors make clear, however, no single theory or even combination of theories can explain how children are affected by marital violence. The two chapters that deal most extensively with theoretical issues are those by Sandra Graham-Bermann and Mark Cummings. Graham-Bermann applies three key theories—social learning theory, trauma theory, and family relationships theory—to propose how children are affected in a variety of ways. At the same time, she recognizes the inherent developmental issues of the timing (i.e., age of child, chronicity of wife abuse) and child characteristics (protective factors) that interact in complex ways to contribute to child adjustment. She reminds us of the need for conducting theory-driven studies in this area and the necessity for better understanding the differing levels of context of the child, such as relationships both within and beyond the family (e.g., fathers, siblings, and peers).

Mark Cummings also makes a strong argument for the need to take a wider theoretical perspective in order to understand how children are affected. He points out that focusing on only father-to-mother violence as the key determinant of child adjustment is too limited. Overt marital physical combat represents only one element of the conflict situation and the marital relationship. There are many contextual elements of the conflict (e.g., resolutions) and parental exchanges (such as parental threats to leave the family) that may influence the child's physiological reactions and distress. Adopting a broader perspective also necessitates assessing other stressors the child may be exposed to and using a familywide perspective, whereby other parent variables such as warmth in the home are recognized.

A third chapter that addresses theoretical and conceptual issues is by Joy Osofsky. She calls for recognizing the broader context in which marital violence occurs: the dangerous and violent neighborhoods in which many of these families reside. Being exposed to the joint stressors of community and marital violence is likely to have a greater impact on child functioning than exposure to only one of these types of violence. Just what the effects may be most likely depend on the child's developmental level—whether the violence occurs in early childhood when a child is striving to develop a basic trust and sense of security in caregivers or during adolescence when the teenager is seeking to develop intimate relationships with peers. As Osofsky makes clear, children's outcomes are dependent on a complex interaction of child characteristics, exposure to violence, and quality of personal relationships.

METHODOLOGICAL ISSUES

Each of the six empirical studies provides one or more methodological innovations for better understanding children's responses to wife battering. As indicated in the introduction to this volume, previously published studies in this area have reported on the nature and extent of children's behavior problems, most often by using the Child Behavior Checklist (CBCL) by Achenbach. In fact, the CBCL was used as a key index of child functioning in all of the empirical chapters with only one exception. Similarly, all of the studies (with one exception) used Murray Straus's Conflict Tactics Scale (CTS) as an index (or partial index) of marital violence. Such instrument monopoly presents both advantages as well as limitations. The key advantages derived from using these instruments is that they are well known and the results are readily compared across studies. The problem, of course, is that by re-using the same instruments, new types of information cannot be learned.

Fortunately, the authors of the chapters in this volume have expanded on the types of measures used to provide new types of information about these families. For instance, this volume includes the first published reports concerning the relations between exposure to violence and cognitive functioning. In a pioneering study, Robbie Rossman takes a bold step by linking emotional effects of abuse with cognitive effects. She does this by assessing five types of cognitive variables (IQ test, digit span memory, theory of mind task, Piagetian accommodation task, and a leveling–sharpening task). Similarly, Timothy Moore and Debra Pepler look at cognitive outcomes by measuring reading, math achievement, and digit span memory.

The chapter authors have also used a variety of other instruments for collecting their data. Sternberg and her colleagues supplemented the CTS with the Family Interaction Questionnaire to get a fuller assessment of the levels of violence in the home. A number of different instruments were used to determine the quality of the mothers' functioning. Holden and his colleagues measured maternal stress, depression, and self-esteem to learn more about maternal functioning. Jouriles and his colleagues assessed maternal psychological distress, and Moore and Pepler collected information about the state of the mothers' health.

Several innovative or rarely used methods with this population deserve mention. Given the nature of the topic, it is particularly difficult to conduct factorial or experimental studies. An exemplary exception is found in the chapter by Mark Laumakis, Gayla Margolin, and Richard John. Through the clever experimental method of using carefully constructed tape-recorded conversations, the authors were able to study which aspects of marital conflict are particularly distressing to children. Laumakis and his colleagues developed audio recordings mimicking marital conversations (made by professional actors) as the stimuli for the children. After hearing each of six conversation vignettes, the children described their thoughts and feelings. Through this approach, they found that physical violence and threats to leave the relationship were particularly distressing to children.

Another unusual method was used by George Holden and his colleagues. Like the other studies, most of their data came from the reports of the mothers. However, some of that information was collected in response to context-specific vignettes presented on laptop computers in order to learn more about commonly occurring interactions and patterns of maternal behavior. A more common method but one that has rarely been used in studies with this population is actual behavioral observations. Two of the chapters (Holden et al. and Jouriles et al.) report observational data from mother–child interactions.

When trying to isolate the effects of exposure to physical marital violence, the use of comparison groups is essential. However, selecting which variables to make the comparison on is a difficult choice. Although marital violence occurs in all walks of life, typically the research is conducted on multiproblem families. One of the multiple problems these children face, as indicated in the introduction, is that they may also be victims themselves of physical maltreatment. Kathleen Sternberg and her colleagues use this unfortunate occurrence in their design by dividing their sample into four groups: children exposed to physical marital violence, children physically abused, children exposed who were also physically abused, and a comparison group. Only through such efforts can we isolate what effects are due to what experiences.

Another common problem experienced in many families characterized by marital violence is economic hardship. The study by Moore and Pepler is unique in its use of comparison groups that vary on economic resources and family structure. Their sample of children comes from four distinct groups: battered women in shelters, homeless families, single mother-headed families, and two-parent homes. As this study demonstrates, the use of such multiple comparison groups is essential for sharpening our understanding of the factors that make unique contributions to child adjustments.

As several authors point out in their chapters, it is critical that investigators conduct longitudinal, prospective studies. For example, when children at battered women's shelters are found to exhibit behavior problems, it is not known to what extent those problems persist over time. It could be that the children are reacting to the very real crisis that they are in but that they may act quite differently when they are in a stable living environment. Alternatively, the problems they have may reflect the accumulation of chronic exposure to marital violence. Only longitudinal studies can sort out the accuracy of those competing explanations. To varying degrees, three of the other chapters (Sternberg et al., Holden et al., and Jouriles et al.) report results from their longitudinal studies, thus providing some of the first such data on these children.

The chapter that makes the most substantial methodological contribution was by Kathleen Sternberg, Michael Lamb, and Samia Dawud-Noursi. Given that family violence almost always occurs in private, researchers must rely on reported data. How accurate are different family members when they report on violence? How well do each of the family members agree on whether the child has a behavior problem? Apparently, the answer is complex and depends on such factors as what the particular question is, how the information is collected, and who is the source. For example, one surprising finding was that children, in comparison with their mothers, tend to be underreporters of their behavior problems. At the same time, parents and their children can provide relatively similar information about whether the children have externalizing problems (which are readily observed) but not on internalizing problems. Evidently, no one source of data can be considered the gold standard. Rather, each source represents his or her own window on the violence, and that window may be slanted in several ways. As this chapter has highlighted, much more research is needed to better understand reasons for discrepancies in reports of violence and its impact.

In summary, the six studies reporting empirical data provide models of research in this area. By assessing new outcome variables, using multiple methods, collecting multiple sources of information, and using new methods, a much better understanding of these children and their environment has been gained. That is not to say that there is no room for improvement in these and similar studies. It is likely that no investigator is content with the current methods of assessing violence in the home. Similarly, most researchers may wish to include multiple comparison groups (e.g., Moore & Pepler and Sternberg et al.) but may be constrained by the high costs, time requirement, and ethical considerations. Future research in this area should continue to work toward developing increased sophistication of this particularly difficult but important area of research.

VARIABILITY IN CHILD OUTCOME

A central question addressed in this book is why there is such variability in children's reactions to marital violence. The six chapters in this volume report data coming from more than 1,200 children, the majority of whom were exposed to marital violence. The children studied in these chapters ranged in age from 2 to 13 years; 8- and 9-year-old children were found in every study.

In some ways, this book has only made that issue of variability in child outcome muddier by assessing a wider variety of effects (e.g., cognitive variables). However, the chapters also represent great strides in better answering that question. One of the first questions that people wonder about with regard to variability in responses to wife abuse is gender effects. Given that it is the mothers who are most often fleeing violent men, how does this relate to the child's gender? Timothy Moore and Debra Pepler carefully examine this issue with a large sample of children from different backgrounds. They found that girls in maritally violent homes were much more severely affected than boys: 53% of the girls had behavior problems at the clinical level, compared with only 12% of the boys. Similarly, Hughes and Luke found that twice as many boys were characterized as "doing well" than girls. These results conflict with some prior reports of gender and functioning (see chapter 1). More research that is focused on why girls may be affected differently than boys is needed.

One chapter that begins to address why one gender may be affected differently by family violence is by Mark Laumakis and his colleagues. They find some gender differences in the children's appraisals of the conflict vignettes: Boys from high-conflict homes evaluated the conversations more negatively than girls. The authors speculate that this sensitization may be due to physiological or socialization experiences. Boys from high-conflict homes were also more likely to report they would intervene in marital conflict than girls. This suggests that girls may react more passively to their mothers' abuse and internalize their distress. Many more studies into gender differences and their causes are needed to address this key question.

The chapter that most directly tackles the question of variability in child outcome is by Honore Hughes and Douglas Luke. Through a series of cluster analyses, they discover that children exposed to marital violence fall into five groups, ranging from those that are "hanging in there" or even "doing well" to those with high levels of behavior problems, high distress, or depression. That analysis represents an important and intriguing finding and must be followed up with investigations into the characteristics, experiences, or environment that appear to buffer some children from the effects that other children experience. However, before we can be too sanguine about some of the children exposed to marital violence, we must remember the cautionary point made by both Graham-Bermann and Cummings: Just because children may be functioning adequately or even well, that does not mean they are immune from future problems (a phenomenon known as "sleeper effects"). Sleeper effects may emerge at different points in their life, such as during adolescence when they begin dating. Nevertheless, the chapter by Hughes and Luke is a ground-breaking one in this area that calls for replication.

Robbie Rossman took a different approach to addressing the variability in children's outcome. In her effort to discover the impact of exposure to marital violence on children's cognitive and emotional functioning, she assessed a range of cognitive variables. As expected, exposure resulted in trauma symptoms and a variety of effects on the cognitive variables. Some of the cognitive outcomes did not attain the conventional level of statistical significance, but given the exploratory nature of this investigation, those findings should be taken as significant and important. Rossman concludes that those data lead to the implication that children may respond to marital violence in at least two different ways. Violence between parents is likely to result in trauma symptoms for the child, which lead to internalizing or externalizing problems. Second, exposure to violence may adversely affect how children process information which, in turn, can inhibit social competence and school functioning. Although these findings are preliminary, they give us new insight into why some children respond differently than others to marital violence.

Perhaps one of the most controversial topics addressed in this volume concerns the quality of mothering and its impact on the children. Many of the authors (e.g., Graham-Bermann, Osofsky, Moore & Pepler, Hughes & Luke) drew attention to the role mothers play. It is commonly assumed that one of the pathways by which violence toward women affects children is through its influence on mothering. In a series of three studies, George Holden and his colleagues question that assumption. They address two aspects of parenting: aggressive discipline and diminished affection and availability. Based on comparisons with a community sample, they conclude that there is evidence that mothers who are battered may use more aggressive parenting than nonbattered women of the same background, but they found little support for diminished parenting (e.g., affection, emotional availability). Furthermore, once the mothers were settled into a new environment and their level of stress was reduced, so too did their level of aggressive parenting. Interestingly, Jouriles and his colleagues report data that provide a caveat to these findings. In families with children displaying clinical levels of conduct problems, they found certain aspects of mothering (hostility, involvement) do not change much when families leave a battering relationship.

Each of the studies that directly or indirectly examines the issue of variability in child outcome should be regarded as preliminary. As a group, however, these studies represent an important advance in our understanding of the impact of exposure to marital violence. The next step is for research to replicate, sharpen, and extend the findings.

FUTURE RESEARCH

Almost all of the chapters in this volume included recommendations for future research. In fact, more than two dozen specific suggestions were made. Those suggestions can be organized around three themes. First, as was made clear in the theoretical–conceptual chapters, there is a pressing need to better understand the context in which the child is living. This means much more than just more thorough assessments of the extent of marital violence. A more comprehensive understanding of the environment means assessing the context external to the family, including whether the child is also exposed to community violence (see Osofsky) or experiences other stressors (poverty, racial discrimination). More attention to ethnic–racial group differences among these families is also needed (Graham-Bermann and Holden et al.). The internal family context warrants a more thorough understanding as well. For example, 2 key features of the family context that deserve more careful assessment in every study conducted in this area are the nature, frequency, and severity of the marital conflict and violence (Cummings and Laumakis et al.) and whether the child is also a victim of physical or psychological maltreatment (Jaffe & Geffner, Osofsky, and Sternberg et al.).

A second research theme is also a contextual one but focuses on the child's relationships. Investigations need to acquire a fuller understanding of the child's relationships with his or her mother. What is the quality of attachment? To what extent are the children victims of psychological maltreatment (an important predictor of adjustment according to Moore and Pepler)? As Holden et al. suggest, there is also a need to investigate the positive parenting qualities of battered women in order to document what such mothers do to prepare, protect, and deal with the aftermath of living in the violent environment. One other critical child relationship has largely been ignored by researchers: the child's relationship with the violent father. Other than assessments of physical and perhaps verbal maltreatment, there is a paucity of information about the batterers' child-rearing behavior. Much more research attention needs to be devoted to the fathers and the quality of their relationships with their children.

A third area for future research is more explicit examination of children's individual characteristics. For example, as the Laumakis et al. chapter made clear, children can have very different perceptions of the marital violence depending on their gender and prior history of marital conflict. Robbie Rossman makes the point of the need to investigate children's schemas and how those are constructed. For example, what role do mothers play in helping their children understand and cope with the violent environment?

Finally, as many of the chapter authors noted, it is essential to appreciate the child's developmental level. As Jaffe and Geffner suggest, there are likely to be sensitive, if not critical, periods of development at certain points in the lives of these children. This is important to consider when decisions concerning placement and child rearing are made.

APPLICATIONS

An important implicit message of this volume is the reminder of the close connection between theory, research, and application. As is made clear by the more than a dozen suggestions for social policy, a variety of social responses are needed to combat and prevent the victimization of these children. Some of the key applied issues are discussed in the chapter by Peter Jaffe and Robert Geffner and the earlier chapter by Joy Osofsky.

Given the nature of the crime of marital violence, researchers and the legal system must rely on reports from victims. There is a critical need to understand the nature of underreporting and overreporting marital violence. As Jaffe and Geffner point out, pseudosyndromes like "the malicious mother syndrome" and the "parent alienation syndrome" are finding their way into the legal system and our jargon as though they are real conditions. Consequently, judges and juries, not to mention researchers, need to understand the determinants of and influences on veridical reports—exactly what Sternberg and her colleagues investigated.

This volume has obvious implications concerning the issue of how to intervene with these children. The conclusion from Hughes and Luke's chapter is that these children need specialized, rather than generic, interventions. A single, narrowly focused intervention program for these children and their families probably will not work. As Ernest Jouriles and his colleagues suggest in their intervention model, a multicomponent intervention is essential for this population. Such interventions can then be adapted and tailored to meet the particular needs of the individuals involved.

A third issue for which good research is critically important concerns the question of child custody. How accurate are the fears that battered women do not provide adequate care for their children? The implication from the chapter by Holden et al. is that the critical need for the well-being of the child is not, in many cases, removal of the child from the mother but rather a reduction in stress levels for her. The research by Jouriles et al. also suggests that these mothers can profit by learning certain parenting skills. One related question that has not been addressed in this volume concerns the parenting abilities of batterers. Such information would directly speak to the issue of whether these fathers are competent to be awarded joint custody or even full custody.

These are just a few examples of how research and theory are directly tied into application. The present chapters provide some preliminary information, but many applications have not been addressed directly. These include prevention of intergenerational transmission, prevention of family violence in general, and treatment of problems. Many more studies are needed to provide comprehensive information to inform interventions and social policies.

CONCLUSION

The foremost goal of this book is to make the "invisible victims" (as Osofsky labels children exposed to marital violence) more visible. The more than 1,200 children studied for the research reported in this volume represent the millions of children in the U.S. and presumably hundreds of millions around the world who are exposed to marital violence. Sophisticated research designs, statistical analyses, and scholarly discussion are essential ingredients to help understand, treat, and ultimately prevent the negative effects of exposure to marital violence. Nevertheless, such data and academic discussion can distance the reader from the horrors and the trauma of the subject matter. Let us not forget the children's distress and terror aroused by violence between parents.

As has been made clear once again, those children's life stories represent tragedies, the violence is likely to produce permanent psychological scars, and it exemplifies a widespread failure of human relationships. However, despair about their condition must be tempered by hope. Through the resiliency of children, certain maternal behaviors, community responses, and foremost effective clinical and legal intervention, there is some optimism for the plight of children exposed to marital violence.

Name Index

Numbers in italics refer to listings in reference sections.

Aber, J. L., 24, *45*, 121, 122, *151*, 227, *251*
Abidin, R. R., 296, 299, 301, 306, 308, 322, *330*
Achenbach, T. M., 6, *15*, 31, *45*, 100, *112*, 127, 131, 134, 135, 139, 144, *152*, 164, 170, *180*, 186, 187, 190, *215*, 237, 238, *251*, 296, 300, 320, *330*, 358, *364*, 411
Adams, C. F., 55, *90*
Ahmed, K., 63, *92*
Ainslie, R., 78, *89*
Ainsworth, M. D. S., 229, *252*
Akiyama, H., 23, *45*
Aldenderfer, M. S., 195, *216*
Alexander, P. C., 188, *216*
Allen, J. P., 121, *151*, 227, *251*
Allen-Meares, P., 103, *113*
Allison, P. D., 160, *180*
Amato, P. R., 55, 59, *84*
Ammerman, R. T., *218, 220, 366, 403*
Anderson, G., *88*, 159, *181*, 339, *365*
Andres, J., 178, *180*
Angelelli, M. J., 10, *15*, 289, *330*
Angelique, H., 348, 352, *368*
Anthony, C., 291, 292, *330*
Antonucci, T. C., 23, *45*
Appel, A. E., 10, *15*, 289, *330*
Appelbone, P., 96, *112*
Arbitell, M., 377, *400*
Arbuckle, B., 128, *154*
Arias, L., 74, *85*
Arrindell, W. A., 210, *217*

Arroyo, W., 237, *255*
Ashton, R., 226, *252*
Auerbach, J. G., 151, *156*
Augustyn, M., 101, 103, *112, 117*
Austin, G. W., 386, *404*

Bachman, R., 373, *400*
Bahadur, M., 77, 78, *92*
Baldwin, D. V., 127, 128, *154*
Ballard, M. E., 55, 70, 72, 73, 77, *84, 85, 88*, 259, *285*
Balto, K., 261, *287*
Balton, C., 77, 78, *92*
Bandura, A., 98, *112*, 342, *364*
Banez, G. A., 282, *284*
Bank, L., 33, *51*
Banyard, V., 23, *47*
Barad, S. J., 128, *153*, 262, *287*
Baradaran, L. P. F., 128, *154*
Barard, S. J., 26, 27, *49*
Barling, J., 55, 56, *90*, 178, *182*, 293, 294, *332*, 346, *366*
Barnett, D. C., 40, *46*, 188, 195, 213, *216*
Barnett, O. W., 7, 9, *15*, 377, *400*
Barrett, K., *88*
Barth, J. M., 41, *50*
Basham, R. B., 306, *330*
Bassuk, E. L., 158, *180*
Basta, J., 348, 352, *369*
Bates, J. E., 149, *152*
Bauer, W. D., 128, *152*
Baum, A., 177, *180*
Baum, C. G., 347, *364*
Baumrind, D., *45*, 207, *216*
Beach, B., 61, 69, 73, *85*

Becerra, R., 22, *47*
Beck, A. T., 193, 200, 203, 208, *216, 320, 330*
Bedford, V. H., *45*
Bell, C. C., 99, 100, 104, 105, 107, *112, 114*
Bell, R., 128, 148, *153*
Bellack, A. S., *367*
Belsky, J., 343, *364*
Benjamin, A., 1, *15*
Bennett, L., 387, *407*
Bernzweig, J., 41, *46*
Berquier, A., 226, *252*
Bialik, R. J., 233, *252*
Bice Pitts, T., 264, *284*
Bilinkoff, J., 394, *400*
Bingham, R. D., 26, *52*, 237, *255*
Bird, H. R., 238, *252*
Black, D., 103, *112*
Blakely, E. H., 339, *367*
Blakeslee, S., 378, *407*
Blashfield, R. K., 188, 195, *216*
Blieszner, R., *45*
Block, J., 59, *85*
Block, J. H., 59, *85*
Blum, H. M., 163, *183*
Blumstein, A., 103, *113*
Boat, B. W., 381, *402*
Boggio, R., 60, *91*
Bograd, M., *400*
Boney-McCoy, S., 30, *53*, 391, *406*
BootsMiller, B., 188, *219*
Borgen, F. H., 188, 195, 213, *216*
Bornstein, M. H., *93, 113*
Bourg, S., 381, *402*
Bourg, W., 58, *90*
Bowker, L. H., 377, *400*
Bowlby, J., 40, *45*, 229, *252*
Boyle, M., 163, *183*
Brassard, M. R., 30, *48, 113*
Bretherton, I., 229, *252*
Breznitz, S., *52*
Brody, G. H., 74, *85*, 128, *152*, 177, *181*
Bronfenbrenner, U., 24, *45*

Brooks-Gunn, J., 111, *113*
Brown, M., 349, *368*
Browne, A., 45, *50*, 55, 60, *85*, 346, *364, 400*
Brunwald, K., 40, *46*
Buehler, C., 291, 292, *330*
Burge, S. K., 382, *403*
Burgess, A. W., 377, 396, *401*
Burman, B., 345, *365*
Burman, S., 103, *113*
Burns, G. L., 186, *216*
Butter, H. J., 233, *252*
Buzawa, C. G., 107, *113*
Buzawa, E. S., 107, *113*
Byles, J. A., 163, *183*
Byrne, C., 163, *183*

Cadman, D. I., 163, *183*
Campbell, J. C., 382, 390, 391, *401*
Campbell, L. E. G., 379, 385, 396, *404*
Campbell, R., 348, 352, *368*
Cantor, N., 42, *45*
Carlson, B. E., 2, *15*, 27, 35, *46*, 97, *113*, 160, *181*, 235, *252*, 262, *284*, 376, *401*
Carlson, V., 40, *46*, 121, *151, 184*, 227, *251, 252, 253*
Carnochan, J., 123, 151, *154*
Carrey, N. J., 233, *252*
Cascardi, M., 30, *46*
Case, R., 238, *252*
Cassidy, J., 229, *252*
Chalmers, D., 104, *116*
Charney, D. S., 226, *252*
Chase-Landsdale, P. L., 111, *113*
Cheskes, J., 74, *85*, 259, 260, *286*
Chew, C. M., 210, *216*, 313, *330*
Christensen, A., 78, *92*
Christianson, S., *254*
Christopoulos, C., 9, *15*, 160, 163, *181*, 186, *216*, 345, *364*
Cicchetti, D., 10, *17*, 23, 40, *46, 50, 52, 53*, 56, 63, 75, 78, *86, 89*, 105, *117*, 121, 122, 130, 137,

149, *151, 153, 155,* 160, 176, 177, *183, 184,* 186, 187, *221,* 227, 233, 248, *251, 252, 253, 255,* 259, 261, 262, *287, 288,* 343, *364, 368*

Clingempeel, W. G., 158, *182,* 358, *365*

Coatsworth, J. D., 23, *50*

Cohen, D. J., *46, 50, 52,* 98, 99, 103, 107, *114, 115,* 368

Cohen, G., 103, 105, *115*

Cohen, S., 349, *364*

Cohn, D. A., 9, *15,* 160, 163, *181,* 186, *216,* 345, *364*

Colbus, D., 128, 148, *153*

Coleman, S., 299, 313, 316, 319, 320, *331*

Compas, B. E., 211, *219,* 282, *284, 286,* 340, *364*

Conger, R. D., 70, 78, *89*

Cortes, R. M., 10, *17,* 23, *53,* 105, *117,* 130, 137, *155,* 160, 176, 177, *184,* 186, 187, *221,* 262, *288*

Cortex, R. M., 248, *255*

Corwin, D., 380, *402*

Costa, A., 382, *403*

Costanzo, P. R., 41, *51*

Coupet, S., 23, *47*

Courage, M. L., 225, *254*

Cowan, C. P., 41, *50,* 71, 74, *91*

Cowan, P. A., 41, *50,* 71, 74, *91*

Cox, M., *87,* 180, *182*

Cox, M. J., 73, *85*

Cox, R., 180, *182*

Coyne, J. C., 55, 59, *87,* 209, *216*

Crawford, J. W., 163, *183*

Crawford, M., 374, 386, *401*

Crick, N. R., 230, 231, *252,* 258, *284*

Crittenden, P. M., 40, *46,* 229, *252*

Crnic, K. A., 306, *330*

Crockenberg, S. B., 78, *85,* 258, 261, *285*

Crowell, N. A., 377, 396, *401*

Cummings, E. M., 12, 55–84, 56, 57, 58, 59, 60, 61, 62, 63, 64, 65, 66, 67, 70, 71, 72, 73, 74, 75, 76, 77, 78, 79, 81, 83, *84, 85, 86, 87, 88, 89, 92,* 103, *113,* 160, *181,* 185, *216,* 229, *252, 253,* 259, 260, 261, 262, 280, 281, 282, *285, 286, 287,* 291, 314, *330, 331,* 410, 416, 418

Cummings, J. S., 65, 66, 77, *86, 87,* 229, *252,* 259, 261, *285*

Cutler, S. E., 22, *47, 48*

Damasio, A. R., 224, 228, *253*

Dangel, R. F., 353, *364*

Davidson, H., 382, 383, 396, *401*

Davidson, L. M., 177, *180*

Davidson, W. S., 348, 352, *368, 369*

Davies, D., 37, 38, *46*

Davies, P. T., 55, 56, 57, 58, 59, 60, 61, 62, 64, 66, 67, 70, 71, 73, 74, 76, 78, 79, 81, 83, *86, 87,* 160, *181,* 185, *216, 252, 253,* 259, 262, 280, 281, *285*

Davis, D., 4, *17*

Davis, L. V., 27, 35, *46,* 160, *181*

Davis, M., 226, *252*

Davison, G. C., 264, 282, *285*

Dawud, S., 10, *17,* 23, *53,* 105, *117,* 130, 137, *155,* 160, 176, 177, *184,* 186, 187, *221,* 248, *255,* 262, *288*

Dawud-Noursi, S., 13, 121–151, 130, *155,* 177, *184,* 329, *334,* 414

DeBarsyshe, B. D., 342, *367*

Deni, R., 307, *330*

Dennig, M. D., 260, *288*

DePaola, L. M., *88,* 159, *181,* 339, *365*

Derogatis, L., 358, *364*

Descartes, R., 247, *253*

Deutch, A. Y., 226, *252*

DeVoe, E., 380, *402*

DeWolf, M., 41, *49*

Dishion, T. J., 33, *51*, 341, 342–347, 347, *364*, *368*

Dobash, R. E., 126, *152*

Dobash, R. P., 126, *152*

Dodge, K. A., 230, 231, *252*, 258, *284*

Dodge, K. E., 149, *152*

Donnerstein, E. I., *112*

Doumas, D., 262, *286*

Downey, G., 55, 59, 78, *87*, *88*, 209, *216*

Draft, S. P., 9, *15*

Drell, M., 102, 103, 105, *113*, *115*

Droegemueller, W., 3, *16*

Dubrow, N., 32, *47*

Dubrown, N. F., *46*

Dumont-Smith, C., 392, *401*

Dunn, L. M., 237, *253*

Dutton, D. G., 30, 38, *46*, 391, *401*

Dutton, M. A., 377, 378, 379, 385, *401*

Dyson, J. L., 1, *16*

Dziuba-Leatherman, J., 123, *153*

D'Zurilla, T. J., 352, *365*

Earls, F., 148, 150, *152*, *154*

Easterbrooks, M. A., 74, *87*, 291, *330*, 345, 346, *365*

Eby, K. K., 348, 352, *368*

Edelbrock, C. S., 6, *15*, 31, *45*, 100, *112*, 131, 134, 135, 139, *152*, 164, 170, *180*, 186, 190, *215*, 237, 238, *251*, 296, 300, 320, *330*

Edleson, J. L., 4, *17*, 212, *218*, *219*, 344, 348, *368*, 377, 383, 387, 392, 394, *400*, *402*, *404*, *405*, *406*, *407*, *408*

Edwards, G. L., 190, 200, *216*

Egeland, B., 98, *113*, 179, *183*, 233, *253*

Egler, L., 23, *47*

Egolf, B. P., 180, *181*

Eisenberg, N., 41, *46*

Eisikovits, Z. C., *402*, *405*

El-Sheikh, M., 55, 57, 59, 65, 70, 73, 74, 77, *85*, *86*, *87*, *88*, *92*, 259, 260, 261, 269, *285*, *286*, 314, *331*

Emde, R. N., 26, *52*, 74, *87*, 237, *255*, 291, *330*, 345, 346, *365*

Emery, R. E., 9, *15*, 55, 59, 61, 78, 83, 84, *88*, 157, 159, 160, 163, *181*, 185, 186, *216*, 281, *286*, 291, *331*, 345, 346, *364*, *365*

Emmelkamp, P. M., 210, *217*

Engleman, D., 339, *367*

Enos, V. P., 378, 383, 387, 396, *402*

Erber, S., 77, 78, *92*, 261, *287*

Erel, O., 5, *17*, 104, *115*, 124, 126, *154*, 345, *365*

Erickson, M. F., 98, *113*, 233, *253*

Erikson, E. H., 40, *47*, 98, *113*

Eron, L. D., 24, 33, 38, *47*, *49*

Esterson, A., 40, *50*

Eth, S., 237, *255*

Ethier, L. S., *155*

Etscheidt, M., 349, *368*

Everson, M. D., 380, 381, *402*

Eyberg, S. M., 190, *216*, 220, 354, *365*

Fabes, R. A., 41, *46*

Fairbanks, L., 237, *255*

Faller, K. C., 380, *402*

Fantuzzo, J. W., 4, 11, *16*, 27, 36, *47*, *88*, 111, *113*, 127, *152*, 159, *181*, 185, *217*, 305, *331*, 339, *365*

Farris, A. M., 58, 60, *90*

Feldman, R., 149, *155*

Feldman, S., 78, *88*

Fenichel, E., 95, 102, 106, *115*

Fick, A. C., 100, 102, *113*, *116*

Figueredo, A. J., 7, 10, *16*, 26, 28, 32, *51*, 111, *115*, 177, *183*, 187, *219*, 248, *254*, 294, 295, 313, 329, *333*

Finch, A. J., 190, 200, *216*

Fincham, F. D., 55, 58, 64, 65, 66, 67, 69, 70, 73, 74, 78, 81, 82, *85, 88, 89, 92,* 104, *114,* 157, *181,* 185, 207, 209, *216,* 230, *253,* 258, 259, 260, 261, 263, 280, 283, *286,* 292, *331*

Finkelhor, D., *53,* 55, 60, *85,* 123, *153*

Fish-Murry, C. C., 233, 238, *253*

Fitzgerald, L. F., *50*

Fleeson, J., 40, *52*

Fleiss, J. L., 270, *288*

Folkman, S., 64, *89, 91,* 258, 259, 260, *287*

Ford, D. A., 395, *402*

Forehand, R. L., 128, *152,* 158, 177, *181, 182,* 347, 353, *364, 365*

Forgays, D. K., 78, *85,* 258, 261, *285*

Forsythe, C. J., 282, *286*

Fox, N., *115*

Frederick, C., 237, *255*

Freud, S., 36, *47*

Friedman, S., *114*

Furstenberg, F. F., 160, *180*

Gaensbauer, T., 102, *113*

Gara, M. A., 188, *217*

Garbarino, J., 30, 32, *46, 47,* 99, *113*

Garber, J., 348, *368*

Garbin, M. G., 320, *330*

Gardner, R., 379, 380, *402*

Garmezy, N., 23, *47,* 110, *113,* 159, *181, 183,* 235, *253, 368*

Gartner, R., 374, 386, *401*

Gavelek, J. R., 35, *49*

Gee, C., 77, 78, *92,* 261, *287*

Geffner, R. A., 5, 15, *16, 91,* 182, *184, 217, 219,* 289, *331, 332, 333, 334, 366,* 371–400, 379, 380, 384, 391, 393, 394, 396, 397, *402, 403, 404, 405, 406,* 409–421, 418, 419

Gelles, R. J., 2, *16, 18,* 22, *53,* 107, *114,* 124, 125, 134, *155,* 178, *184,* 293, 294, 328, *334,* 346, *368,* 374, 376, *403*

Gentile, C., 237, *256*

Gerlsma, C., 210, *217*

Germain, R., 30, *48, 113*

Giles-Sims, J., 317, *331,* 346, *365*

Giovannoni, J., 22, *47*

Gjerde, P. J., 59, *85*

Gleberman, L., 344, *367*

Goetsch, V. L., *88,* 259, *286,* 314, *331*

Goldberg, D. P., 163, *181*

Goldberg, J., 238, *252*

Goldberger, L., *52*

Goldenberg, L., 188, *217*

Goldfried, M. R., 352, *365*

Goodman, L. A., *50*

Goodwin, J., 37, *47*

Gordis, E. B., 77, *89, 286*

Gorsuch, R. L., 193, *220*

Gottman, J. M., 55, 56, 60, 73, 78, *90, 91, 93,* 258, 263, 281, *286, 287*

Gough, R., 376, 392, *407*

Gould, M. S., 238, *252*

Graham, A. V., 382, *403*

Graham-Bermann, S. A., 12, 21–45, 22, 23, 26, 28, 30, 32, 33, 35, 37, 41, 42, 43, *47, 48, 49, 50,* 206, *218,* 249, *253,* 374, *403,* 410, 416, 417, 418

Grasley, C., 392, *407*

Gravetter, F. J., 273, *286*

Gray-Little, B., 33, *48*

Green, A. H., 37, *48*

Green, R. G., *112*

Green, S. M., 127, 148, 150, *154, 218*

Greenbaum, C., 10, *17,* 23, *53,* 105, *117,* 130, 137, *155,* 160, 176,

Greenbaum, C., (*continued*)
177, *184*, 186, 187, *221*, 248,
255, 262, *288*
Greenberg, M. T., *252*, 306, *330*
Greene, A., *86*, *89*
Groves, B. M., 98, 101, 103, 107,
112, *114*, *117*
Grusec, J. E., 30, *48*
Grych, J. H., 55, 58, 64, 65, 66, 67,
69, 73, 78, 81, 82, *89*, 104,
114, 157, *181*, 207, 209, *217*,
230, *253*, 258, 259, 260, 261,
263, 280, 283, *286*, 292, *331*
Guttmann, E., 30, *47*

Haldame, E. S., *253*
Hall, N. W., 157, *184*
Hamberger, L. K., 382, 396, *403*
Hamby, S. L., 30, 33, *48*, *53*, 391, *406*
Hamilton, E. E., 107, *116*
Hammer, M., 149, *155*
Hammond, M., 209, 212, *221*, 347,
369
Hanish, L., 41, *46*
Hann, D. M., 100, 111, *116*
Hansen, M., *405*
Hanson, K. L., 185, *220*, 233, *255*
Harold, G. T., 70, 78, *89*
Harris, S. D., 14, 106, *114*, 289–
330, 341, *366*, 412, 414, 417,
418, 420
Harrist, A., 78, *89*
Harrop, J. W., 178, *184*
Hart, B. J., 382, 390, 394, *403*
Hart, C. H., 30, 41, *48*, *49*
Hart, S. N., *48*, *113*
Hartup, W. W., *52*
Harway, M., *405*
Hastings, E., 376, 390, *404*, *406*
Hawkins, J. D., 110, *114*
Hayduk, L. A., 237, *254*
Heaton, M. K., 241, *255*
Hebb, D. O., 231, *254*
Heidt, E., 2, 7, *17*, 328, *334*
Helmers, L., 37, *52*

Hembree-Kigin, T. L., 354, *365*
Henderson, A., 378, *403*
Hennessy, K. D., 56, 63, 75, 78, *86*,
89, 259, 261, 262, *287*
Herbert, B., 96, *114*
Herman, J. L., 30, 37, 38, *49*, 394,
403
Herman, S. E., 188, *218*
Herrenkohl, E. C., 180, *181*
Herrenkohl, R. C., 180, *181*
Hersen, M., *218*, 220, 366, 367, *403*
Hershorn, M., 158, *182*, 295, *331*
Heston, J., 249, *254*
Hetherington, E. M., 158, 180, *182*,
358, *365*
Hill, H., 100, 111, *114*
Hillier, V. F., 163, *181*
Hilton, N. Z., 5, *16*, 293, 314, 315,
328, *331*, 374, 375, 378, 382,
389, *403*, *407*
Hinchey, F. S., 35, *49*
Hinde, J. S., *365*
Hinde, R. A., *330*, *365*
Hodges, W. F., 2, 7, *17*, 328, *334*
Holden, G. W., 1–15, 5, 7, 9, 10,
14, *15*, *16*, 28, *49*, 60, *90*, *91*,
106, *114*, *182*, *184*, 210, *217*,
219, 289–330, 294, 295, 296,
298, 299, 307, 313, 316, 319,
320, *330*, *331*, *332*, *333*, *334*,
341, 346, *366*, 409–421, 412,
414, 417, 418, 420
Holmbeck, G. N., 77, *92*
Holtzworth-Munroe, A., 329, *332*
Horley, S., 389, *403*
Horowitz, M. J., 225, *254*
Hotaling, G. T., 27, *53*, 341, *366*
Howe, M. L., 225, *254*
Howell, C. T., 127, 144, *152*, 187,
190, *215*
Howell, D. C., 211, *219*
Hubbard, R. M., 55, *90*
Huesmann, L. R., 24, 33, 38, *47*, *49*
Hughes, H. M., 10, 13, *16*, 27, 30,

49, 126, 128, *153*, 158, 160, 163, 173, 177, *182*, 185–215, 186, 187, 190, 192, 193, 206, 211, 212, 213, 214, *217, 218, 220*, 233, 248, *254, 255*, 262, *287, 332*, 339, *366*, 372, 374, 385, 392, *403*, 415, 416, 419

Hughes, S. O., 188, *218*
Humphreys, K., 188, *218*
Huston, A. C., 315, *332*

Iannotti, R., 77, *86*
Irwin, C., 38, *51*

Jacobs, C. A., 193, *220*
Jaffe, P. G., 4, 9, 15, *16, 17, 18*, 22, 26, 27, *49, 54*, 58, 63, *90, 93*, 102, 104, *114*, 121, 128, *153, 155, 156*, 157, 158, 159, 176, *182, 184*, 186, 212, *218, 221*, 242, 248, 249, 250, *254*, 262, 282, *287, 288*, 293, 296, 317, 325, *332, 334*, 339, 340, 341, 344, 345, *366, 369*, 371–400, 372, 374, 375, 376, 377, 383, 384, 385, 386, 387, 390, 395, *400, 402, 404, 405, 406, 407, 408*, 418, 419
James, C. B., 98, *115*
Janoff-Bulman, R., 40, *49*
Jastak, S., 164, *182*
Jayaratne, T. E., 32, *49*
Jenkins, E. J., 99, 100, 104, 105, 107, *112, 114*
Jenkins, J. M., 179, *182*
John, R. S., 5, 14, *17*, 56, 68, 72, 77, 78, *89, 91, 92*, 104, *115*, 124, 126, *154*, 257–284, 259, 260, 261, 262, 264, 269, 282, *286, 287, 288*, 290, *332*, 412, 415, 418
Johnson, M. K., 264, *285*
Johnson, O. G., *219*
Johnston, J. R., 59, *90*, 379, 385, 396, *404*

Jones, B., 123, 151, *153*
Jones, D., *287*
Jouriles, E. N., 7, 9, 14, *16*, 33, *49, 50*, 55, 56, 58, 60, 72, *90, 91*, 104, 106, *114, 115*, 125, 151, *153*, 178, *182, 184*, 209, 214, *218, 219*, 250, *254*, 281, *287*, 289–330, 290, 293, 294, 295, 314, *332, 333, 334*, 337–364, 339, 341, 346, 349, *366, 367, 368*, 409–421, 412, 413, 414, 417, 418, 419, 420
Joyce, S., 9, *15*, 159, 160, 163, *181*, 186, *216*, 345, *364*
Jung, K., 148, *152*

Kaniasty, K., 7, *17*
Kaplan, T., 103, *112*
Karbon, M., 41, *46*
Karraker, K., *86, 89*
Karyl, J., 2, 7, *17*, 328, *334*, 377, 392, *406*
Kaslow, N. J., 207, *218*
Katz, L. F., 55, 56, 60, 73, *90, 91*, 258, 263, 281, *286, 287*
Kaufman, J., 123, 149, 151, *153*
Kavanagh, K., 127, 128, *154*
Kazdin, A. E., 128, 148, *153*, 347, 367
Keita, G. P., *50*
Keith, B., 55, 59, *84*
Kelly, G. A., 42, *50*
Kelly, J., 349, *368*
Kempe, R. S., 3, *16*
Kerig, P. K., 41, *50*, 56, 70, 71, 74, 91
Kerns, K. A., 41, *50*
Kihlstrom, J., 42, *45*
Kinnard, E. M., 377, *404*
Kiser, L. J., 249, *254*
Kitzmann, K., 346, *365*
Klein, M., 40, *50*
Kluft, R. P., *52*
Klump, K., 188, *218*
Koby, E. V., 233, 238, *253*

Kolbo, J. R., 339, *367*

Koss, M. P., 7, 10, *16*, 26, 28, 32, *50*, *51*, 111, *115*, 177, *183*, 187, *219*, 248, *254*, 294, 295, 313, 329, *333*

Kostelny, K., 32, *47*

Kovacs, M., 190, 200, *218*

Kraft, S. P., 159, 160, 163, *181*, 186, *216*, 345, *364*

Kravic, J. N., 121, *153*

Krishnakumar, A., 291, 292, *330*

Krispin, O., 10, *17*, 23, *53*, 105, *117*, 130, 137, *155*, 160, 176, 177, *184*, 186, 187, *221*, 248, *255*, 262, *288*

Krueger, L., *92*, 259, 260, 261, 264, 269, *288*

Krystal, J. H., 226, *252*

Kurland, D. M., 238, *252*

Kurz, D., 5, *16*

Ladd, G. W., 41, *49*, *51*

Lahey, B. B., 127, 148, 150, *154*, *218*

Laing, R. D., 40, *50*

Lake, M., 70, *85*, 259, *285*

Lamb, M. E., 10, 13, *17*, 23, *53*, *86*, 105, *117*, 121–151, 128, 130, 137, 149, *153*, *154*, *155*, 160, 176, 177, *184*, 186, 187, *221*, 248, *255*, 262, *288*, 329, *334*, 414

Lambert, L., *88*, 159, *181*, 339, *365*

Lamphear, V. S., 122, *153*

Landis, T. T., 377, 392, *406*

Langhinrichsen-Rohling, J., 125, *154*

Lape, L., 73, *91*

Larkin, K., 72, 77, *85*

Larrance, D. T., 128, *154*

Laumakis, M. A., 14, 56, 68, 72, 77, *91*, 257–284, 290, *332*, 412, 415, 418

LaViolette, A. D., 377, *400*

Lazarus, R. S., 64, *91*, 258, 259, 260, *287*

Leavitt, L., *115*

LeCompte, S. H., 281, *287*, 294, 295, 314, *332*, 346, *366*

LeDeux, J. E., 231, *254*

Leekam, S. R., *255*

Lerner, Y., 151, *156*

Levendosky, A. A., 26, 28, 33, 35, 41, 42, 43, *48*, *50*, 249, 253, 315, *332*, 374, *403*

Levine, M. B., 3, *16*

Lewis, M. L., 102, *113*, 211, *220*

Lindahl, K., 60, 63, *91*

Lindquist, C. U., 4, 11, *16*, 27, 36, *47*, 111, *113*, 127, *152*, 305, *331*

Links, P., 163, *183*

Lintz, C., 241, *255*

Liss, M. B., 379, *404*

Litzenberger, B. W., 22, *47*

Loeber, R. M., 127, 148, 150, *154*, 187, 209, *218*

Loefkowitz, M. M., 24, *49*

Long, N., 158, *182*, 365

Lorey, F., 10, *17*, 23, *53*, 105, *117*, 130, 137, *155*, 160, 176, 177, *184*, 186, 187, *221*, 248, *255*, 262, *288*

Loseke, D. R., *16*

Luke, D. A., 13, 158, *182*, 185–215, 188, 196, 213, *219*, *332*, 339, *366*, 415, 416, 419

Lundberg-Love, P. K., *217*, *404*, *405*, *406*

Lushene, R., 193, *220*

Lynch, M., *46*, 343, *364*

Lynch, S., 42, *48*

Maccoby, E. E., 346, *367*

MacKinnon-Lewis, C., 128, *154*

Mahoney, A., 56, 60, 72, 73, *90*, *91*, 214, *218*, 290, *332*

Malcarne, V. L., 282, *284*

Malik, N., 60, 63, *91*, 241, *255*

Mallah, K., 248, *254*
Mannariono, A. P., 123, 151, *153*
Marans, S., 98, 99, 103, 107, *114,
    115*
Margolin, C., 133, *154*
Margolin, G., 5, 14, *17*, 56, 68, 72,
    77, 78, *89, 91, 92*, 102, 103,
    104, 105, *115*, 124, 126, *154*,
    257–284, 259, 260, 261, 262,
    264, 267, 269, 280, 282, *286,
    287, 288*, 290, *332*, 344, 345,
    367, 412, 415, 418
Marshall, L., 30, 33, *50*
Marshall, M., 212, *218*, 372, 392,
    404
Martinez, P., 100, *116*
Martini, D. R., 38, *50*
Martino, T., *88*, 159, *181*, 339, *365*
Masten, A. S., 23, *50, 52*, 132, *154*,
    157, 158, 177, *182*, 235, *253*
Mathews, M., *182*
Matthews, S., 346, *365*
Mattis, J., 23, *47*
McCloskey, L. A., 7, 10, *16*, 26, 28,
    32, *51*, 111, *115*, 177, *183*,
    187, *219*, 248, *254*, 294, 295,
    313, 329, *333*
McConaughy, S. H., 127, 144, *152*,
    187, 190, *215*
McCord, J., *183*, 341, *367*
McDaniel, E. D., 192, *219*
McDonald, R., 7, 14, *16*, 56, 72, *90*,
    209, 214, *218*, 290, *332, 333*,
    337–364, 339, *367*, 413, 414,
    417, 419, 420
McFarlane, A. C., 38, *51*
McFerron, J. R., 377, *400*
McGee, R. A., 22, 30, *51, 54*, 123,
    151, *154*
McLoyd, V. C., 24, *51*, 293, *333*
McMahon, M., 383, 386, *404*
McMahon, R. J., 353, *365*
McNeil, C. B., 354, *365*
Mercer, S. L., 376, *404*
Meyers, R. L., 73, *87*

Michaels, M., 128, 150, *155*
Miliotis, D. M., 23, *50*
Miller, D., 235, *254*
Miller, G. E., 347, *367*
Miller-Perrin, C. L., 7, 9, *15*, 377,
    400
Millsap, P. A., 249, *254*
Milner, J. S., 235, *254*
Min, K., 2, 7, *17*, 328, *334*
Minuchin, S., 21, *51*
Mnookin, R. H., 346, *367*
Moffitt, T. E., 341, *367*
Moore, J. G., 3, *17*
Moore, T. E., 13, 157–180, 178,
    180, 209, *219*, 232, *255*, 326,
    333, 412, 413, 415, 417, 418
Moos, R. H., 188, *219*
Morison, P., 132, *154*
Morris, N., *219*
Morrison, R. L., *367*
Moser, J., 128, 148, *153*
Mosk, M., 121, *156*
Moss, T. A., 241, *255*
Mowbray, C. T., 188, *219*
Murphy, C. M., 33, *49*, 56, *90*, 339,
    366
Murphy, L., 98, 107, *115*
Muth, S. M., 41, *49*
Myers, R. L., 76, *92*, 262, *285*

Nader, K., 100, 103, *116*, 237, *255*
Nakayama, D., 38, *50*
Navarre, S. G., 264, 282, *285*
Neeman, J., 23, *50*
Nelson, C. A., 45
Nezu, A. M., 349, *367*
Norris, F. H., 7, *17*
Norwicki, S., 164, *183*
Norwood, W. D., 7, 9, 14, *16*, 33,
    50, 56, 72, *90*, 214, *218*, 290,
    294, 295, 314, *332*, 337–364,
    346, *366*, 413, 414, 417, 419,
    420
Notarius, C. I., 77, *87*, 229, *252*,
    261, *285*

Nuechterlein, K., *52, 183*
Nunez, F., 237, *255*
Nussbaum, B. R., 186, *216*

O'Brien, M., 5, *17,* 77, 78, *92,* 104,
  115, 124, 126, *154,* 259, 260,
  261, 264, 269, 282, *287, 288*
Offord, D., 163, *183*
O'Keefe, M. K., 5, 9, *17,* 28, *51,*
  128, *154,* 177, *180,* 262, 281,
  288, 294, 295, 305, *333,* 346,
  367
Okun, A., 26, 28, *48,* 249, *253*
Olafson, E., 380, *402*
Oldham, J. M., *116*
O'Leary, K. D., 3, *17,* 30, 33, *46,*
  49, 55, 56, *90,* 125, 151, *153,*
  178, *182,* 293, 294, *332,* 339,
  346, *366,* 395, *406*
O'Leary, S. G., 104, *115,* 250, *254*
Ollendick, T. H., *89,* 220
O'Reilly, A., 60, 63, *86*
Orlofsky, J. L., 42, *51*
Ornitz, E., 37, *51*
Osborne, L. N., 58, 64, 70, 78, *88,*
  89, 92, 207, 209, *217*
Osnes, G. P., 351, *368*
Osofsky, J. D., 13, 95–112, 100,
  102, 103, 105, 106, 107, 111,
  113, 114, 115, 116, 290, *333,*
  411, 417, 418, 419, 420

Pagelow, M. D., 5, *16,* 101, *116,*
  374, 377, 379, 380, 381, 383,
  384, 385, 391, 393, 397, *403,*
  404
Paget, K., 192, *220*
Painter, S. L., 30, 38, *46*
Paley, B., 73, *85*
Parker, C. M., 186, *216*
Parker, R., 157, 158, 177, *183*
Parker, S., 101, 103, *112, 117*
Parkinson, D. L., 10, *16,* 126, *153,*
  160, 176, *182,* 186, 187, *218,*
  248, *254*

Pate, A. M., 107, *116*
Patterson, D. R., 186, *216*
Patterson, G. R., 33, *51,* 179, 180,
  183, 292, *333,* 341, 342–347,
  347, *364, 367, 368*
Payne, C. C., 73, *85*
Peebles, C., 111, *116*
Peled, E., 4, *17,* 212, *218, 219,* 344,
  348, *368,* 374, 375, 377, 383,
  384, 385, 392, 396, *400, 402,*
  404, 405, 406, 407, 408
Pellegrini, D. S., 77, *87,* 132, *154,*
  177, *183,* 229, *252,* 261, *285*
Pence, E., 383, 386, *404*
Pepler, D. J., 13, *47,* 157–180, 209,
  219, 232, *255,* 326, *333,* 412,
  413, 415, 417, 418
Perner, J., *255*
Perrin, R. D., 7, 9, *15,* 377, *400*
Persinger, M. A., 233, *252*
Pettit, G. S., 149, *152*
Pfiffner, L. J., 104, *115,* 250, *254,*
  349, *368*
Phares, V., 211, *219*
Piaget, J., 227, *255*
Pianta, R. C., 179, *183,* 233, *253*
Piers, E. V., 192, *219*
Pleck, E., 2, *17*
Poindexter, V. C., 33, *48*
Policansky, S. K., 38, *51*
Polster, R. A., 353, *364*
Porterfield, K., 26, 28, *48,* 249, *253*
Poulin, R., 41, *46*
Prince, R. H., 188, *219*
Prinz, R. J., 59, *93,* 347, *367*
Profilet, S. M., 41, *51*
Pruitt, D. B., 249, *254*
Ptacek, J., 387, *405*
Putallaz, M., 41, *51*
Putnam, F. W., 37, *52*
Pynoos, R. S., 37, *51, 52,* 98, 99,
  100, 102, 103, *115, 116,* 237,
  255

Query, L., 73, *91*

Rabideau, G. J., 56, 63, 75, 78, *86,*
89, 259, 261, 262, *287*
Radke-Yarrow, M., 72, 77, *87, 114,*
116, 181
Rae-Grant, N., 163, *183*
Ragozin, A. S., 306, *330*
Ramirez, M., 23, *50*
Ramsey, E., 342, *367*
Randolph, K. D., 260, *288*
Raphael, B., *116*
Rapkin, B. D., 188, 196, 213, *219*
Rappaport, J., 188, *219*
Rehm, L. P., 207, *218*
Reich, W., 148, 150, *152, 154*
Reid, J. B., 127, 128, *154,* 341,
342–347, 347, *368*
Reiss, D., 40, 42, *52, 113, 116, 181*
Reiter, S., 57, *88, 92*
Reitzel, D., 339, *366,* 376, 390, *404,*
407
Reitzel-Jaffe, D., 392, *407*
Rescorla, L., 157, 158, 177, *183*
Reynolds, C., 191, 192, *220*
Reynolds, W. M., 187, *220*
Riba, M. B., *116*
Richmond, B., 191, 192, *220*
Richters, J. E., *90,* 99, 100, *114,*
116, 128, *155,* 177, *181, 183*
Ridgeway, K., 229, *252*
Rieder, C., 233, 237, *255*
Ritchie, K. L., 5, 7, 9, 14, *16,* 28,
49, 60, *90,* 106, *114,* 210,
217, 289–330, 294, 295, 296,
298, 299, 316, 327, *331, 333,*
341, 346, *366,* 412, 414, 417,
418, 420
Rizley, R., 23, *46*
Roberts, A. R., *15, 113*
Robertson, K. R., 381, *402*
Robins, C., 264, *285*
Robinson, E. A., 190, *220*
Robinson, N. M., 306, *330*
Robinson, N. S., 348, *368*

Rodgers, K., 373, *405*
Rodway, M. R., 392, *407*
Rogers, M. J., 77, *92*
Rolf, J., *52, 183*
Romenofsky, M., 38, *50*
Romero, J., 241, *255*
Roosa, M. W., 2, 9, *17,* 28, *52,* 128,
150, *155,* 262, *288*
Rosario, M., 149, *155*
Roseby, V., 59, *90*
Rosenbaum, A., 3, *17,* 158, *182,*
295, *331*
Rosenbeck, R., 188, *218*
Rosenberg, M. S., 95, *116,* 207,
210, 212, *220, 255,* 282, *288,*
290, 320, 329, *333,* 339, *368,*
375, 396, *405*
Rosenberg, S., 188, *217*
Ross, A. W., 190, *216, 220*
Ross, G. R. T., *253*
Rossman, B. B. R., 14, 26, *52,* 185,
207, 210, 212, *220,* 223–251,
233, 237, 241, 248, *254, 255,*
282, *288,* 290, 329, *333,* 339,
368, 375, 396, *405,* 412, 416,
418
Rottman, B., *287*
Roy, M., 374, *405*
Rubin, K. H., *47*
Rubin, L., 158, *180*
Rubin, Z., *52*
Rumptz, M., 352, *369*
Russo, N. F., *50*
Rutter, M., 23, *52,* 65, *92,* 158, 160,
179, *183,* 340, *368*
Ryan, C., 38, *50*

Salzinger, S., 134, 149, *155*
Salzman, L. E., 373, *400*
Sameroff, A., 23, 25, *52*
Sameroff, A. J., *52*
Sandler, I. N., 2, 9, *17,* 28, *52,* 89,
262, *288*
Santostefano, S., 227, 232, 237, *255*
Saunders, D. G., 382, *406*

Saylor, C. F., 190, 200, *216*
Scarr, S., 21, *52*
Schaeffer, C. M., 188, *216*
Scharf, D., *114, 116, 181*
Schechter, S., 377, 383, 387, 392,
    394, *406*
Schellengach, C., *287*
Schlee, K. A., 394, *406*
Schmidt, K. L., 313, 319, 320, *331*
Schwartz, W. E., 22, *47*
Seeley, J. W., 30, *47*
Seid, M., 66, *89*, 104, *114, 286*
Seidman, E., 188, *219*
Seifer, R., 23, *52*
Shakoor, B., 104, *116*
Shaw, D. S., 9, *15*, 159, 160, 163,
    181, 186, *216*, 345, *364*
Shifflett-Simpson, K., 76, *92*
Shirk, S. R., 210, *220*
Shrout, P. E., 270, *288*
Sibner, L. G., 344, *367*
Siegel, A. W., 207, *218*
Siegel, C., 102, *113*
Silver, H. K., 3, *16*
Silverman, F. N., 3, *16*
Silverman, W. K., *89*
Silvern, L., 2, 7, *17*, 328, *334*, 377,
    392, *406*
Simpson, K. S., 66, 70, *86*, 259,
    260, 262, *285*
Sisson, L., *218*
Skinner, H. A., 195, *220*
Smith, D. A., *90*
Smith, E., 148, *152*
Smith, M. A., 179, *182*
Sorenson, S. B., 37, *52, 217, 404,*
    405, 406
Southwick, S. M., 226, *252*
Spaccarelli, S., 2, 9, *17*, 262, *288*
Spielberger, C. D., 193, *220*
Spiller, L. C., 14, 337–364, 413,
    414, 417, 419, 420
Spiracelli, S., 28, *52*
Sroufe, L. A., 40, 52, 65, 80, 92,
    179, *183*

Staghezza, B., 238, *252*
Stahl, P. M., 393, *406*
Stahly, G. B., 379, *404, 406*
Stall, M., 63, *92*
Stanger, C., 211, *220*
Starek, J., 2, 7, *17*, 328, *334*
Starr, R. H., Jr., *48*
Steele, B. F., 3, *16*
Steer, R. A., 193, 200, 203, 208,
    216, 320, *330*
Stein, J. D., 14, 106, *114*, 289–330,
    341, *366*, 412, 414, 417, 418,
    420
Steinberg, A., 37, *52*, 237, *255*
Steinman, M., 107, *117*
Steinmetz, S. K., 2, *18*, 22, *53*, 125,
    134, *155*, 293, 294, *334*, 346,
    368
Stephens, N., 14, 337–364, 413,
    414, 417, 419, 420
Sternberg, K. J., 10, 13, *17*, 23, *53*,
    105, *117*, 121–151, 124, 125,
    130, 137, 149, *155*, 160, 176,
    177, *184*, 186, 187, *221*, 248,
    255, 262, *288*, 329, *334*, 412,
    413, 414, 418, 419
Stevens, J. H., *182*
Stevenson, J. E., *47, 181*
Stevenson-Hinde, J., *330*
Stieglitz, E., 123, 151, *153*
Stocker, C., 63, *92*
Stokes, F. T., 351, *368*
Stolley, P., 157, 158, 177, *183*
Stone, G., 291, 292, *330*
Stouthamer-Loeber, M., 127, 148,
    150, *154*, 187, 209, *218*
Strachey, J., *47*
Straus, M. A., 2, 5, *17, 18*, 22, 30,
    53, 100, 111, *117*, 124, 125,
    134, *155*, 178, *184*, 192, 208,
    221, 235, 236, *256*, 268, *288*,
    293, 294, 295, 328, *334*, 338,
    346, *368*, 372, 374, 376, 391,
    403, 406, 411
Strickland, B. R., 164, *183*

Stuart, G. L., 329, *332*
Sudermann, M., 339, *366*, 376, *406*
Sugar, M., 37, *53*
Sugarman, D. B., 27, 30, *53*, 341, *366*, 391, *406*
Sullivan, C. M., 348, 352, *368*, *369*
Sullivan, H. S., 40, *53*
Sullivan-Hanson, J., 9, *15*, 160, 163, *181*, 186, *216*, 345, *364*
Sutton, S., *88*, 159, *181*, 339, *365*
Szatmari, P., 163, *183*
Szinovacz, M. E., 125, 151, *155*

Talovic, S., 133, *154*
Tan, C., 348, 352, *369*
Tarabulsy, G. M., *155*
Tasman, A., *116*
Taylor, G., 379, 385, *407*
Tein, J., 128, 150, *155*
Tellegen, A., 235, *253*
Terr, L. C., 37, 38, *53*
Tessier, R., *155*
Thoennes, N., 380, *407*
Thomas, H., 163, *183*
Thompson, B., 104, *114*
Tittsworth, S., 291, 292, *330*
Tjaden, P., 380, *407*
Tolman, R. M., 30, 33, *53*, 387, 391, *407*
Toney, N., *219*
Towle, C., 55, *92*
Trickett, P. K., 37, *52*, *287*
Turkat, I. D., 379, *407*
Turturo, K. A., 41, *53*
Twentyman, C. T., 128, *152*, *154*

Vagg, P. R., 193, *220*
van der Kolk, B. A., 226, 231, 233, 238, *253*, *256*
Van Hasselt, V. B., *367*
Vargo, M. C., 10, *16*, 126, *153*, *182*, 186, 187, *218*, 248, *254*
Vincent, J. P., 56, 72, *90*, 214, *218*, 290, *332*, *367*
Vissing, Y. M., 178, *184*

Vitulano, L., 123, 151, *153*
Vivian, D., 125, *154*
Vogel, D., 77, *86*, 259, 261, *285*
Vogel, R. S., 264, 282, *285*
Volling, B., 128, *154*

Waelde, L., 2, 7, *17*, 328, *334*
Wagar, J. M., 392, *407*
Walder, L. O., 24, *49*
Walker, L. E., 30, *53*, 293, 326, *334*, 376, 385, 396, *407*
Wallerstein, J. S., 378, *407*
Wallnau, L. B., 273, *286*
Walters, G. C., 30, *48*
Walters, R. H., 98, *112*
Ware, H. S., 14, 337–364, 413, 414, 417, 419, 420
Waters, E., 80, *90*, *92*
Webster-Stratton, C., 209, 212, *221*, 347, *369*
Wechsler, D., 164, *184*, 233, *256*, 265, *288*
Weinstein, C. D., 133, *154*
Weintraub, S., *52*, *183*
Weisz, A., 387, *407*
Weisz, J. R., 260, *288*
Wekerle, C., 376, 392, *407*
West, M. J., *332*
West, M. O., 59, *93*
Wewers, S., 100, *116*
Wieber, J., 73, *91*
Wilkinson, G. S., 164, *182*
Wills, T. A., 348, *364*
Wilson, A. G., 57, *86*, *87*, 259, 260, *285*
Wilson, B. J., 78, *93*
Wilson, J. P., *116*
Wilson, L., 24, *51*
Wilson, S. K., 4, 9, *16*, *18*, 22, 26, 27, *49*, *54*, 58, 63, *90*, *93*, 102, 104, *114*, 121, 123, 128, 151, *153*, *154*, *155*, *156*, 157, 158, 159, *182*, *184*, 186, 212, *218*, *221*, 242, 248, 249, 250, *254*, 262, 282, *287*, *288*, 293,

Wilson, S. K. (*continued*)
  296, 317, 325, *332, 334,* 339,
  340, 341, 344, 345, *366, 369,*
  372, 374, 375, 376, 377, 383,
  384, 385, 386, 387, 395, *404*
Wimberley, R. C., 235, *254*
Wimmer, J., *255*
Winnicott, D. W., 21, *53*
Wolchik, S. A., *89*
Wolfe, D. A., 4, 9, *16, 18,* 22, 26,
  27, 30, *48, 49, 51, 53, 54,* 58,
  63, *90, 93,* 102, 104, *114,*
  121, 123, 128, 151, *153, 154,*
  155, 156, 157, 158, 159, 176,
  182, 184, 186, 212, *218, 221,*
  237, 242, 248, 249, 250, *254,*
  256, 262, 282, *287, 288,* 293,
  296, 317, 325, *332, 334,* 339,
  340, 341, 344, 345, 353, 354,
  366, *366, 369,* 372, 374, 375,
  376, 377, 383, 384, 386, 387,
  392, 395, *404, 407*

Wolfe, V. V., 237, *256*
Woodward, C., 163, *183*
Worsham, N., 282, *284*

Yllo, K., *400*
Yuen, S. A., 123, 151, *154*

Zahn-Waxler, C., 72, 77, *86, 87,*
  103, *113*
Zak, L., 9, *18,* 26, *54,* 58, 63, *90,*
  93, 121, 128, *153, 155, 156,*
  158, 159, *184,* 186, *221,* 262,
  288, 296, 317, 325, *334,* 340,
  341, 345, *369,* 376, *404*
Zeanah, C., *116*
Zigler, E., 157, *184*
Zilber, N., 151, *156*
Zilli, A., 24, 33, 38, *47*
Zorza, J., 377, 378, 383, 384, 387,
  395, *408*
Zuckerman, B., 98, 101, 103, 107,
  112, 114, 117

Subject Index

Accommodation, 227, 238
ACQ. *See* Areas of Change Questionnaire
Adjustment problems, 6–7, 8. *See also* outcome variability
  for compared at-risk groups, 157–180
  critical turning points for children and, 384–389
  developmental psychopathology model and, 22–24, 69–70
  factors correlated with, 157–181
  family functioning disturbances and, 58–59
  multiple informants and, 187–188
  parenting quality and, 291–292
  relationships theory explanations and, 40–42
  sensitization and, 77–78
  studies linking battering with, 27–29
  trauma theory explanations and, 38–39
Adolescents, 374, 376
Advocacy services, 348–349
Age of child, 9, 31, 70–71, 410
  developmental impacts and, 102–109, 374, 376
  theoretical models and, 35–36, 43–44
Alienation, as term, 380
American Bar Association (ABA) Committee on Children and the Law, 383

Areas of Change Questionnaire (ACQ), 133
Articulated Thoughts During Simulated Situations (ATSS) paradigm, 264, 266–268
Assimilation, 227
ATS. *See* Attitudes Toward Spanking
Attachment theory, 227, 229–230. *See also* relationships theory
Attitudes Toward Spanking (ATS), 319–320
Attributional style
  of children in violent families, 230
  of parent, 61, 63, 73–74, 302–303, 328–329

Battered women's shelters, families from
  conduct problems and, 338–341
  developmental model and, 342–347
  evaluation of interventions with, 356–364
  intervention approaches and, 347, 350–356
  needs of women and, 347–349
Batterers. *See also* fathers
  child's relationship and, 71, 418
  custody considerations and, 15, 420
Beck Depression Inventory (BDI), 193

Behavioral problems, 6–7, 8. *See also* Child Behavior Checklist
cluster analysis and, 195
cognition–emotion interrelationships and, 245
families departing from shelters and, 338–341
mother's perceptions of, 303–304, 311–312, 323–324
multiple informants and, 137–144, 147
outcome of interventions and, 356–364
role of mother in interventions and, 353–356
social learning explanations and, 35

CBCL. *See* Child Behavior Checklist
CDI. *See* Children's Depression Inventory
Child abuse. *See also* child-directed maternal aggression
abused vs. exposed children and, 27–28, 63, 75, 105, 173
association between marital conflict and, 10, 60, 101, 289, 377
child maltreatment histories and, 122–124
child's relationship with batterer and, 418
cognition–emotion interrelationships and, 232–233
Child Behavior Checklist (CBCL), 6, 31–32, 134, 411
Child characteristics. *See also* age of child; coping responses; gender effects; outcome variability
child's understandings and, 24, 36–37, 38, 259–260
critical periods and, 384–389

outcome variability and, 7–9, 12, 206, 214, 290, 410
Child-directed maternal aggression. *See also* child abuse
changes in level of, 321–323
maternal stress and, 292–293, 295–296, 301–302, 313, 316, 322–323
physical, 173, 307–308, 312–317, 417
separation from batterer and, 346–347
verbal, 174–176
Child-rearing beliefs, 297–304, 310–311, 315, 375. *See also* child-directed maternal aggression; mothering, quality of; parenting, quality of
Children's Depression Inventory (CDI), 191
Children's Locus of Control Scale, 165, 171, 172
Child's conflict history, 75, 76–78, 83
social service agencies and, 122–123
two-phase reaction model and, 260, 261–262, 279, 280
Child's relationships. *See also* intrafamily relationships; social support
future research and, 418
Chronicity of violence, 10, 12, 206, 208, 410, 417
Cluster analysis, 13, 188, 416
groups of factors in, 194–195
patterns among clusters, 197–205
Cognition–emotion interrelationships
child abuse research and, 232–233
conceptual approaches to, 228–232
development and, 227–228

repetitive trauma and, 225–227
violence exposed children and,
235–250
Cognitive capacity measures, 237–
238
Cognitive–contextual model, 81
Cognitive control theory, 226–227,
231–232
Cognitive outcomes, 14, 227–228,
241, 412, 416–417. *See also*
school functioning; social
competence
changes in cognitive process
and, 230–232, 233
cognitive content distortion
and, 228–230, 233
by type of conflict, 269–270,
275–277
Community context. *See also*
neighborhood violence
ecological model and, 24
future research and, 417
Community violence, defined, 96,
97
Comparison group studies, 13, 413
Complex traumatic stress, 37–38
Computer-Presented Social Situations (CPSS), 299, 306
Conduct problems. *See* behavioral
problems
Conflict resolution, 410
ameliorated violence vs. constructive conflict and, 75–76
aspects of resolution, 76
emotional security hypothesis
and, 82–83
forms of marital discord and,
56–57, 263–284
modeling of conflict situations
and, 61, 63
positive outcomes and, 60
reduction of stress and, 74–76
Conflict Tactics Scale (CTS), 111,
411

Family Interaction Questionnaire and, 412
Contextual factors, 12, 13, 410–
411. *See also* emotional security hypothesis; intrafamily
relationships; neighborhood
violence; process-oriented
model
future research and, 213–214,
417–418
as mediating influences, 23,
206–207
stress and coping approach and,
64–65
theory and, 12, 410–411
Coping, defined, 64
Coping responses. *See also* child
characteristics; stress and
coping approach
cognition–emotion interrelationships and, 230
contextual perspective and, 64–
65
emotion-focused vs. problem-
focused strategies, 282
family systems theory and, 61
forms of coping, 260–261,
277–279
trauma theory explanations
and, 36–37
type of marital conflict and,
270–273, 277–279
Court-related assessment services,
392–393
CPSS. *See* Computer-Presented Social Situations
CTS. *See* Conflict Tactics Scale
Cultural variation. *See* ethnicity
Custody cases, 15, 420. *See also* divorce cases
children's experience in, 384–
389
court-related assessment services and, 392–393
determination of risk and, 382

Custody cases (*continued*)
  joint custody and, 59, 378
  legislation and, 395–396
  mother's risk of loss of custody,
    377–382
  societal concerns and, 371–373
  supervised visitation centers
    and, 392–393

Data sources, 412–413. *See also*
    comparison groups; reported
    data; simulation studies
  analogue vs. field procedures
    and, 71, 76, 103–104
  future research and, 32
  reporting accuracy and, 104
  use of multiple informants and,
    122–127
Depression. *See* depression, in
    child; maternal depression
Depression, in child, 7, 8, 199, 200,
    206
Developmental factors
  linkage between cognition and
    emotion and, 227–228
  theory and, 12, 68, 410
Developmental level, 418–419
Developmental psychopathology
    models, 12, 22–24, 67–69,
    98. *See also* family systems
    theory
  critical turning points and,
    384–389
  families departing from shelters
    and, 342–347
Digit span memory, 164–165, 238,
    412
Diminished parenting, 293–294,
    302–303, 308–311
Discipline, 14, 313–314, 342–347.
    See also parenting, quality of
Discrimination, as stressor, 417
Divorce cases. *See also* custody cases
  children as focus in, 377–384

critical periods for children in,
    384–389
  impacts of marital conflict and,
    59
  nonidentification of violence
    and, 382–383
  parent alienation syndrome
    and, 379–382
  screening for lethality and,
    382–383
Domestic Abuse Project (Minneap-
    olis), 392
Domestic violence (term), 5, 96–97
Double whammy effect, 10
Dual information pathways, 231,
    250

ECBI. *See* Eyberg Child Behavior
    Inventory
Ecological model, 12, 24
Economic hardship. *See* poverty
Emotion, linkage between cogni-
    tion and, 223–251
Emotional outcomes, 14, 102, 416–
    417
  by type of marital conflict, 269,
    273–274
Emotional security hypothesis, 12,
    67, 78–84, 160, 229–230,
    280
  component regulatory systems,
    81–82
  definition of emotional security,
    79–80
  supporting evidence for, 82–84
  theoretical tenets, 80–81
Emotion regulation, 82, 83, 84
Empirical issues, 415–417
Ethnicity, 10, 32, 213, 304–312,
    392
Exosystem, 24
Exposure, as term, 4–5, 22
Eyberg Child Behavior Inventory
    (ECBI), 190

Factorial studies, 412
Family Information Form (FIF),
163
Family Interaction Questionnaire,
412
Family members, role of, 354–355
Family relations theory, 12, 410.
See also family systems theory; intrafamily relationships; relationships theory
Family systems theory, 58–59
concept of triangulation, 292
conflict and adversity and, 58–
59, 65
conflict and system dysfunction
and, 59–61
cumulative impacts of family
stress, 61–63
positive outcomes and, 61–62
Family violence histories, and multiple informants, 135–137,
145–147
Family Violence Prevention Fund,
383
Fathers. See also batterers
child's relationship with, 71, 418
custody considerations and, 15,
377–378, 420
family role of, 43
quality of parenting by, 293,
294, 301
reported data from, 148–149
FIF. See Family Information Form
First National Family Survey data,
2
Future research recommendations,
29–32, 417–419
character of abuse and, 30–31
cluster analysis and, 213–214
community violence and, 109–
111
contextual factors and, 32, 417–
418
divorce process and, 396
economic status and, 213

emotional climate in home and,
30
ethnicity and, 32, 213
gender effects and, 31, 418–419
intrafamily relationships and,
417, 418
longitudinal studies and, 31
methodological issues and, 31–
32
process-oriented methods and,
63, 64–71
resilient children and, 31, 68–
69
social learning theory and, 33–
36
trauma theory and, 38–39

Gender effects, 9, 70–71, 160,
415–416
coping responses and, 262, 279,
280–282
developmental impacts, 374,
376
future research and, 31, 418–
419
maternal aggression and, 295
by type of at risk group, 168–
171, 176–177
General Health Questionnaire
(GHQ), 163–164
GHQ. See General Health Questionnaire

Harm, definitions of, 22
Health
of child, 7
maternal, 165, 176, 412
Home environment
future research and, 30
normal development and, 21
in violent marriages, 300–301
Homelessness, 158, 168–171
Homicide
incidence of, 95–96
witnessing of, 105–106, 374

Intergenerational cycle of violence, 104–105
Internalizing and externalizing problems, 7, 14, 27, 374–375, 416–417
cluster analysis variables and, 194
cognition-emotion interrelationships and, 239, 241–242, 247
in compared at-risk groups, 168–170
interventions and, 239, 241–242, 247, 360–361
Interventions, 14, 419–420. *See also* battered women's shelters, families from
cluster analysis and, 211–212
group treatment programs, 392
home-based, 350–352
instrumental support and, 352–353
multicomponent approach, 14, 340, 350–356, 419–420
parent training and, 353–356
protective factors and, 45
social support and, 352–353
specialized approach, 419
Intrafamily relationships, 12, 410. *See also* child's relationships
ecological model and, 24–25
future research and, 417, 418
internal representation of, 82, 84
trauma theory explanations and, 38
"Intraindividual" level, 25
"Intrusive reexperiencing," 39
IQ, 412
Israeli domestic violence study, 129–150

Joint custody, 59, 378
Joint stressors, 61–63, 411

Justice system. *See* custody cases; divorce cases

Legal considerations, 15, 420. *See also* custody cases; divorce cases; police officers, role of
Legislation, and custody cases, 395–396
Leveling–sharpening style, 227–228, 232, 237–238, 412
LISREL modeling, 237, 238, 242
Longitudinal studies, 13, 413–414
Israeli domestic violence study, 129–150
quality of parenting changes and, 317–325
sleeper effects and, 31
social networks and, 23
Long-term effects, 13, 31, 44, 68, 341, 376, 416

Macrosystem, 24
Maltreatment of women and children, as term, 373–374
Marital conflict
about child-related themes, 73
behaviors that increase distress, 72–74
behaviors that reduce distress, 74–76
children's conflict histories and, 75, 76–78, 83, 260, 261–262, 279
child responses to simulated dimensions of, 263–284
child's control of exposure to, 82
nature of, 56–57, 71–78, 262–263
positive marital relations and, 60, 63, 71–78
relation between family adversity and, 58–59, 65
relation between family systems and, 59–61

Marital violence, aspects of. *See also* chronicity of violence; physical conflict; psychological maltreatment; reporting of spousal violence; severity of violence
children's responses to differing aspects, 263–284
child's prior experience and, 418–419
cluster analysis variables and, 194
continuum of marital discord and, 56–57, 71–78
future research and, 412, 418–419
impacts of, 14, 412
separation and, 378–379, 382–383
violence type and, 34–35
Marital violence, as term, 5
Massachusetts Coalition of Battered Women Service Groups report, 105
Maternal depression
outcome variability and, 29–29, 59, 200
quality of parenting and, 208–209, 292
Maternal functioning measures, 165, 195, 323, 412. *See also* parenting, quality of
Math achievement, 164, 171–172, 412
McDaniel–Piers Young Children's Self-Concept Scale, 192
Media campaigns, 389–390
Mediation, in custody disputes, 393–394
Mental health issues, 7, 8–9, 28. *See also* depression; posttraumatic stress disorder
Methodological issues, 411–415. *See also* cognitive outcomes; comparison groups; data

sources; factorial studies; Israeli domestic violence study; longitudinal studies; relational measures; *entries for specific outcome measures*
analogue vs. field procedures and, 71, 76, 103–104
child maltreatment histories and, 122–124
generalizability and, 103–104
new outcome measures and, 412–415
reporting of spousal violence and, 124–127
spouse abuse assessment and, 390–391
traditional instruments and, 31–32, 411
use of multiple informants and, 127–129
Microsystem, 24–25. *See also* intrafamily relationships
Modeling of conflict situations, 61, 63
Moderating influences, 7, 9, 10, 23, 70–71. *See also* child characteristics; coping responses; protective factors
Mothering, quality of. *See also* child-directed maternal aggression; mothers
changes in level of aggression and, 321–323
diminished availability and, 14, 206–207, 293, 309, 417
maternal depression and, 208–209, 292
maternal stress and, 292–293, 295–296, 301–302, 313, 316, 322–323
physical aggression and, 173, 307–308, 312–317, 417
separation from batterer and, 346–347

Mothering (*continued*)
    verbal aggression and, 173–176,
      178–179
Mothers. *See also* child-directed
    maternal aggression; mother-
    ing, quality of
    attributional style of, 61, 63,
      73–74, 302–303, 328–329
    child-rearing beliefs of, 297–
      304, 310–311
    needs of, and interventions,
      347–349
    parenting skills training and,
      353–356
    risk of loss of custody, 377–382
Multiple informants, and discrep-
    ancies among reports, 5, 13,
      104, 127–129, 135–150, 177
    adjustment problems and, 187–
      188
    behavior problems and, 137–
      144, 147
    family violence histories and,
      135–137, 145–147

Name-calling, 267, 274, 276, 278.
    See also verbal aggression
Neighborhood violence, 13, 28, 32,
    96–97
    vs. domestic violence, 100–101
    rate of exposure to, 99–100
Nonverbal conflict, 73

Object relations theory. *See* rela-
    tionships theory
"Observers," children as, 4–5
Other stressors, 24, 289–290, 377,
    411, 417. *See also* contextual
    factors; divorce; homeless-
    ness; neighborhood violence;
    poverty
Outcome variability, 13, 185–215,
    290, 377, 415–417. *See also*
    age of child; cluster analysis;
    cognitive outcomes; emo-
    tional outcomes; gender ef-
    fects; mothering, quality of;
    parenting, quality of
    cluster patterns and, 197–199
    dimensions of conflict and,
      257–284
    quality of parenting and, 10, 14,
      206, 290, 291, 417
    resilient children and, 31, 68–
      69, 110–111, 186–187

Parent alienation syndrome,
    379–382
Parental Responses to Child Mis-
    behavior (PRCM), 319
Parenting, quality of, 291–330. *See*
    also child-directed maternal
    aggression; fathers; mother-
    ing, quality of
    batterers and, 15, 418, 420
    changes over time and, 317–
      325, 326–327
    child-directed aggression and,
      292–295
    cluster analysis and, 208–209
    coordinated parenting services
      and, 348, 394–395
    as custody consideration, 15,
      383–384, 420
    diminished parenting and, 293–
      294, 302–303, 308–311
    factors in, 342–347
    fathering and, 293, 294, 301
    future research and, 316, 418
    impact of marital violence on,
      106–107
    increased aggression and, 291–
      293
    outcome variability and, 10, 14,
      206, 290, 291, 417
    parent training and, 344, 349,
      353–356, 394–395
    positive attachment and, 38
    relationships theory explana-
      tions and, 41

trauma theory explanations and, 38

Partner and Relationship Profile, 391

Partner violence, as term, 5

Peabody Picture Vocabulary Test (PPVT), 237

Peers. *See* multiple informants

Personality characteristics of child, 10

Physical abuse of child. *See* child abuse; neighborhood violence

Physical conflict
  posttraumatic stress symptoms and, 39
  relative impact of, 72, 268, 274, 276, 278, 280, 412

Physiological effects, 226–227

Piagetian theory, 227

Piers–Harris Children's Self-Concept Scale, 192

Police officers, role of, 107–109

Posttraumatic stress disorder (PTSD)
  cognition–emotion interrelationships and, 223–251
  neighborhood violence and, 102–103
  physiological effects and, 226–227
  symptoms of exposed children and, 8, 37–39

Poverty, 24, 32, 417
  comparison group studies and, 13, 176

PPVT. *See* Peabody Picture Vocabulary Test

PRCM. *See* Parental Responses to Child Misbehavior

Preemptive processing, 231

Preschool children, 345, 374

Problem-solving skills, 352–353

Process-oriented model, 65–67. *See*

also developmental psychopathology models

Propensity for Abusiveness Scale, 391

Protective factors. *See also* child characteristics; contextual factors; moderating influences
  child's understandings and, 24, 36–37
  intervention and, 45

Psychological distress
  child's relationships with parents and, 418
  cluster analysis variables and, 194–195
  maternal, 412
  as response to violence, 55–56, 105

Psychological maltreatment. *See also* threats to leave
  exposure as, 412
  frequency of, 34–35
  impacts of, 39, 412
  legal relevance and, 383

Psychological Maltreatment of Women Inventory, 391

PTSD. *See* posttraumatic stress disorder

Public information, 389–390

Quality of parenting. *See* parenting, quality of

Racism, 24

RCMAS. *See* Revised Children's Manifest Anxiety Scale

Reading, 164, 171–172, 412

Relational measures, 412

Relationships theory, 12, 26–27, 40–42, 80

Reported data, 13, 412–413, 414. *See also* multiple informants
  accuracy of, 5, 104, 166, 168, 210–211, 414

Reported data (*continued*)
  battered women as informants,
    5, 128–129, 177, 414
  child reports, 104, 123, 128,
    148, 210, 374, 414
  discrepancies among reports, 5,
    13, 104, 127–129, 177, 187–
    188, 414
  perspective of informant and,
    211
  self-report biases and, 315–316
Reporting of spousal violence
  legal considerations and, 378–
    381, 420
  number of informants and,
    124–127
Research issues. *See also* empirical
    issues; future research; meth-
    odological issues; theoretical
    issues
  depth of research, 3–4
  limitations on research, 10–11
  recognition of problem, 2–4
Resignation, as child's response,
    387
Resilient children, 159–160, 186–
    187
  research recommendations and,
    31, 68–69, 110–111
Revictimization, 37–38
Revised Children's Manifest Anxi-
    ety Scale (RCMAS), 191–192
Risk and resilience model, 24. *See
    also* developmental psycho-
    pathology models

Schema construction, 26, 42,
    224–225, 418–419. *See also*
    relationships theory
School functioning, 7, 9, 14, 149,
    177–178, 232. *See also* Wide
    Range Achievement Test–
    Revised
  cognition–emotion interrela-
    tionships and, 246, 247

school avoidance and, 375–376
Screening for domestic violence,
    382, 390–391
Second National Family Violence
    Survey, 2
Self-esteem
  of child, 7, 8, 10, 194
  maternal, 323, 412
Sensitization, 76–78, 83, 261
Severity of violence, 10, 176, 178,
    417
Sexual abuse of child, 10, 22
Sharpening. *See* leveling–sharpen-
    ing style
Silence, as child's response, 385–
    387
Silent treatment, 73
Simpson, O. J. (case), 371–373
Simulation studies, 14, 413
  ATSS paradigm and, 264, 266–
    268
  CPSS program and, 299
SIP models. *See* social information
    processing models
Situational–contextual factors. *See*
    contextual factors
Sleeper effects, 13, 31, 44, 68, 376,
    416
Social competence, 7, 8, 14. *See
    also* behavioral problems
  adjustment variability and, 191
  cognition–emotion interrela-
    tionships and, 245, 246
  in compared at-risk groups,
    168–170
Social information processing
    (SIP) models, 230, 231
Social learning theory, 12, 26, 410
  explanations based on, 33–36,
    98–99, 292
  families departing from shelters
    and, 342–347
Social policy applications, 111–
    112, 419–420. *See also* cus-
    tody cases

Social service agencies, 122–123
Social support
    child adjustment problems and,
        28–29
    as intervention component,
        347–349, 352–353
    longitudinal studies and, 23
Somatic marker hypothesis, 228–
    229
Spill-over hypothesis, 291, 292,
    345–346
Spouse Abuse Identification Ques-
    tionnaire, 391, 397–399
State-Trait Anxiety Inventory
    (STAI), 193
Stress. See also complex traumatic
    stress; joint stressors; other
    stressors; posttraumatic
    stress disorder
    family, cumulative impacts of,
        61–63, 176, 292–293
    resiliency and, 68–69
Stress, defined, 64
Stress and coping approach, 64–67
Supervised visitation centers, 392–
    393
Systems approach, 97–98. See also
    family systems theory

"Task accomplishment," as protec-
    tive factor, 160
Teacher Report Form (TRF), 134,
    164
Terminological issues, 4–6, 22,
    373–374
Theoretical issues. See also family
    relations theory; social learn-
    ing theory; trauma theory
    contextual factors and, 12, 410–
        411
    developmental factors and, 12,
        410
    as research limitation, 11
    types of theories, 12, 410

Theory of Mind task, 238, 412
Threats to leave, 72, 274, 276, 278,
    280, 412
Timing of marital violence. See age
    of child; chronicity of vio-
    lence
Training
    parenting skills and, 344, 349,
        353–356, 394–395
    for professionals, 107–109, 382,
        390
Trauma symptoms. See internaliz-
    ing and externalizing prob-
    lems
Trauma theory, 12, 26, 36–39,
    230–231, 410
TRF. See Teacher Report Form
Triangulation, concept of, 292

Verbal aggression, marital, 268. See
    also conflict resolution
    as contextual factor, 55–57, 61,
        63, 68, 69, 290, 410–411
    correlates of child adjustment
        and, 158–159
    positive vs. negative tone of, 74,
        267, 273–274, 276
Verbal aggression, mother-to-child,
    173–176, 178–179
Violence exposure. See also neigh-
    borhood violence
    child's immediate responses to,
        55–56, 64, 258–259
    depth of research on, 3–4
    developmental outcomes and,
        22–24
    effects of, 6–11, 69–70,
        102–109
    extent of problem and, 1–2
    moderating influences and, 7, 9,
        10
    recognition of problem, 2–4
    reporting reliability and, 126
    two-phase reaction model and,
        258–261, 279–280

Visitation dispute, features of, 387, 388–389

Wechsler Intelligence Scale for Children–Revised (WISC-R), 164
Wide Range Achievement Test–Revised (WRAT-R), 164
Wife abuse (term), 5
Withdrawal, 73
"Witnesses," children as, 4–5

Woman Abuse Scale, 391
Women as aggressors, 5, 125–126. *See also* child-directed maternal aggression
Women's Law Project (Pennsylvania), 383
WRAT-R. *See* Wide Range Achievement Test–Revised

Youth Self Report (YSR), 134
YSR. *See* Youth Self Report

About the Editors

George W. Holden is associate professor in the Department of Psychology, University of Texas at Austin. He received his BA from Yale University and his MA and PhD from the University of North Carolina at Chapel Hill. Since earning his degree in developmental psychology with a minor in social psychology, he has been on the faculty at the University of Texas. From 1995 to 1997 he served as the director of the Institute of Human Development and Family Studies. Dr. Holden's research interests are in the area of social development, with a focus on parent–child relationships. He is especially interested in understanding the determinants of parental behavior, parental social cognition, and the causes and effects of family violence. His research has been supported by grants from the National Institute of Child Health and Human Development, the Guggenheim Foundation, and the Hogg Foundation for Mental Health. He is the author of numerous scientific articles and chapters and the book *Parents and the Dynamics of Child Rearing* (Westview Press, 1997). He is also the coeditor (along with J. Touliatos and B. Perlmutter) of the forthcoming second edition of *Family Measurement Techniques* (Sage Press).

Robert Geffner is the founder and president of the Family Violence and Sexual Assault Institute and a founding member of the East Texas Crisis Center and Shelter for Battered Women and their Children, both in Tyler, TX. A licensed psychologist and a licensed marriage, family, and child counselor who also holds a diplomate in clinical neuropsychology from the American Board of Professional Neuropsychology, Dr. Geffner was the clinical director of a large private practice mental health clinic in Tyler for more than 15 years. He has been a faculty member at the National Judicial College since 1990 and was a professor of psychology at the University of Texas at Tyler for 16 years. He has also served on several national and state committees dealing with various aspects of family psychology, family violence, child abuse, and family law, and he has been a consultant for the Department of Health and Human Services, National Center for Child Abuse and Neglect, the Department of Defense, and various branches of the military. He is the editor of several journals, including *Family Violence & Sexual Assault Bulletin; Journal of Child Sexual Abuse*; and *Journal of Aggression, Maltreatment, & Trauma;* co-editor of *The Journal of Emotional Abuse;* the co-author and co-editor of numerous books, including *A Psychoeducational Approach for Ending Wife/Partner Abuse: A Program Manual for Treating Individuals and Couples* (with C. Mantootch) and *Violence and Sexual Abuse at Home: Current Issues, Interventions and Research in Spousal Battering and Child Maltreatment* (with S. Sorenson and P. Lundberg-Love); and the author of numerous book chapters, articles, and research papers on family violence, sexual assault, child abuse, family and child psychology, custody issues, forensic psychology, neuropsychology, and diagnostic assessment.

Ernest N. Jouriles is associate professor of psychology at the University of Houston. He received his BA from Indiana University at Bloomington and his PhD from the State University of New York at Stony Brook. Since earning his degree in clinical psychology, he has been on the faculty at the University of Houston. Dr. Jouriles's interests are in understanding and ameliorating the negative effects of marital conflict and violence on children. He has published numerous scientific articles in the areas of marital conflict and child adjustment, domestic violence, and child maltreatment. His research has been supported by grants from the National Institute of Mental Health, the Interagency Consortium on Violence Against Women and Violence Within the Family Research, the Texas Higher Education Coordinating Board, the George Foundation, and the Hogg Foundation for Mental Health. Dr. Jouriles received an early career award from the Association for Advancement of Behavior Therapy for his research on marital and child problems.